Behavior Disorders: Perspectives and Trends

D1513087

THE LIPPINCOTT COLLEGE PSYCHOLOGY SERIES
Under the Editorship of
Dr. Carl P. Duncan, Northwestern University
and Dr. Julius Wishner, University of Pennsylvania

behavior
disorders

PERSPECTIVES and TRENDS

Second Edition

131941

Edited by
OHMER MILTON
ROBERT G. WAHLER

University of Tennessee
Knoxville

RC458
M52
1969

J. B. LIPPINCOTT COMPANY
NEW YORK PHILADELPHIA TORONTO

Fifth Printing

Copyright © 1969, 1965 by J. B. Lippincott Company
ISBN-0-397-47153-X
Library of Congress Catalog Card Number: 71-80064
Printed in the United States of America

All rights reserved. With the exception of brief
excerpts for review, no part of this book may be
reproduced in any form or by any means without written
permission from the publisher.

Preface

Two GENERAL THEMES permeate the articles in this volume: (1) the "disease" or "illness" view of certain of the disorders of thought and behavior has proven to be too restrictive and (2) newer and broader perspectives than the narrow one of "sickness" are being developed about many forms of aberrant behavior. The evidence against the "medical model" has continued to mount and the emerging views are of clearer prominence now than they were at the time of the first edition of this book. This revision is designed to make these developing positions more explicit than they often are in textbooks and to help clarify the thinking of students —whether they study these issues in a single course or extensively as in the pursuit of a career.

Of the thousands of articles that might have been included in this book, several factors determined the editors' final choices: first, we sought those which challenged the *status quo,* that is, provided meaningful evidence against the "medical model." Readability was our second requirement, as we wished to avoid highly technical jargon; and third, we looked for articles which reflected and clarified the new trend. At the same time, some of the selections which deal directly with procedures in care and treatment give a more detailed picture of those matters than is true in many textbooks. Finally, certain selections were chosen that represent several disciplines because one feature of the new trend is the demonstration that no one discipline has all the answers or a corner on truth.

There is a bewildering array of mental illness or mental disorder classifications; we have not attempted to cover all of them in this book. Rather than confounding the matter of labeling, grouping, or classifying, the selections are divided into two categories; those in Part I deal with various facets of the problems associated with understanding behavior disorders, and those in Part II deal with care or treatment.

We wish to acknowledge the courtesy of the publishers and authors who gave permission to include copyrighted material in this volume. We are grateful, also, to several authors for providing papers which have not been published elsewhere. Specific recognition is accorded on the first page of each contribution.

This revised edition reflects, too, suggestions for improvement made by several users of the first edition.

Very special thanks go to Mrs. Barbara Wickersham, Secretary in the Learning Research Center of The University of Tennessee, for her editorial and typing skills. Our appreciation is also extended to Miss Sally J. Byrnes, Editor, College Department, J. B. Lippincott Company, for the extraordinary care which she applied to our manuscript.

Finally, many graduate and undergraduate students during the past few years have afforded many stimulating hours of discussion and debate about the issues presented in this book.

Knoxville, Tennessee   OHMER MILTON
April, 1969   ROBERT G. WAHLER

Contents

Part 1: Issues

1   Perspectives and Trends   3
    Ohmer Milton and Robert G. Wahler

2   The Myth of Mental Illness   17
    Thomas Szasz

3   The Societal Reaction to Deviance: Ascriptive Elements
    in the Psychiatric Screening of Mental Patients in a
    Midwestern State Hospital   27
    Thomas J. Scheff

4   "Mental Illness" or Interpersonal Behavior?   44
    Henry Adams

5   Mental Disorders and Status Based on Race   56
    Robert J. Kleiner, Jacob Tuckman, and Martha Lavell

6   Two Descriptions of More or Less Identical Behavior   62
    August B. Hollingshead and Fredrick C. Redlich

7   Reaction Patterns to Severe, Chronic Stress in American
    Army Prisoners of War of the Chinese   63
    Edgar Schein

8   Individual and Social Origins of Neurosis   73
    Erich Fromm

9   The Quest for Identity   80
    Allen Wheelis

10 Love Me Diane: The Case History of a Criminal Psychopath   89
    John Bintz and Ronald Wilson

11   Family Dynamics and Origin of Schizophrenia   104
     Stephen Fleck

12   Schizophrenic Patients in the Psychiatric Interview: An
     Experimental Study of their Effectiveness at Manipulation   122
     Benjamin M. Braginsky and Dorothea D. Braginsky

Part 2: Alteration of Behavior

13   The Community and the Community Mental Health Center   133
     M. Brewster Smith and Nicholas Hobbs

14   Psychotherapy as a Learning Process   152
     Albert Bandura

15   Systematic Desensitization   175
     S. Rachman

16   Group Psychotherapy on Television: An Innovation with
     Hospitalized Patients   192
     Frederick H. Stoller

17   A Review of Psychiatric Developments in Family Diagnosis
     and Family Therapy   200
     Don D. Jackson and Virginia Satir

18   Justified and Unjustified Alarm Over Behavioral Control   220
     Israel Goldiamond

19   Personal Responsibility, Determinism, and the Burden of
     Understanding   245
     Edward Joseph Shoben, Jr.

20   Patient Role and Social Uncertainty: A Dilemma of the
     Mentally Ill   256
     Kai T. Erikson

21   The Hospital as a Therapeutic Instrument   273
     Robert A. Cohen

22   The Society of the Streets   282

23   Daytop Lodge—A New Treatment Approach for Drug Addicts   289
     Joseph A. Shelly and Alexander Bassin

24   Action for Mental Health   298

     Name Index   325

     Subject Index   331

PART 1

Issues

1. Perspectives and Trends

Ohmer Milton and Robert G. Wahler

The "disease" or "illness" view about all of the disorders of thought and behavior, prevalent for at least the past 25 years, has been demonstrated as being entirely too restrictive. The term "mental illness" has become a catch-all and in the thinking of many authorities is rather meaningless today. Broader perspectives than those of the "medical model" concerning both the determinants of and the methods for altering aberrant behavior are outlined here.

It was probably about 150 years ago that psychotic behavior—perhaps the only publicly or officially recognized form of deviancy at that time—was first thought of as a disease. In the ensuing years, what might be called the "disease" concept of psychosis has been extended to other forms of disorders of emotions, thought, and behavior, the zenith of this extension being reached in the early 1960's. Meanwhile, a trend has been developing *away* from the "disease" concept as one appropriate for all behavior deviations. This trend is being led by critical and creative thinkers in all of the disciplines most directly concerned with human behavior.

Whatever basic views are maintained have major implications for the nation's approach to the problems which are labeled, depending upon their professional sources, as mental illness, mental and emotional disorders, or disorders of thought and behavior. The manner in which these difficulties are conceptualized, including what the causative and maintaining factors are presumed to be, helps to determine what our society does about them. Furthermore, the manner in which the members of a group view these problems may determine, to a large degree, the way in which an individual who experiences these problems perceives them and seeks resolutions. The extensive publicity of the past few years about all forms of deviant behavior being "disease" or "illness" has probably created false expectations in many of those who need or seek help. For example, a mother who was educated in the "disease" view and whose adolescent son was quite disturbed emotionally, asked a psychologist: "What *attitudes* do you *prescribe* for me?"

THE DISEASE VIEW

Today many psychologists as well as researchers in other disciplines believe that the "disease" view has limited usefulness both for the understanding and the alteration of many of the emotional and mental disorders. When appearing before the Subcommittee on Labor and Public Welfare, 88th Congress, First Session, Nicholas Hobbs (1963) testified:

> Historically, a great step forward was made when mental disorders were declared to be an illness, and the sufferer to be in need of treatment rather than punishment. But the concept of mental disorder as the private illness of a person is no longer sufficient. . . . They grow out of, are exacerbated by, and contribute to family and community disorganization.

In a somewhat similar vein, the Board of Directors (1963) of the American Psychological Association in endorsing *Action for Mental Health* (Selection 24) observed:

> In accepting uncritically the traditional labels of health and illness contained in its charge from the Congress, the Joint Commission drew back from an opportunity for fundamental reformulation of the problems contained in society's concern with its ineffective and deviant members. Although the general tenor of the Commission's recommendations is courageous and imaginative, the conceptual farmework within which the problem of mental illness is defined in its Report is traditional, and does not take into account recent basic criticism of the medical model of health and illness in its application to disorders of thought and behavior.

Jerome D. Frank (1961) has commented in this fashion upon limited perspectives of the past for dealing with behavior disorders at the moment:

> Acceptance of the medical view of mental illness has led to neglect of group and community forces in production and relief of distress and maintenance of beneficial changes.

Marie Jahoda (1958), in seeking trends in thinking and points of agreement about these matters, concluded:

> No completely acceptable, all-inclusive concept exists for physical health or physical illness, and, likewise, none exists for mental health or mental illness. A national program against mental illness and for mental health does not depend on acceptance of a single definition and need not await it.

Whereas volumes would be needed to describe and explain the "medical model" and all of its ramifications, Hornstra (1962) has capsulated the essence of it in this succinct statement:

> The remarkable achievements of medicine had been based on the conception of disease as a state of affairs or a process which had a specific etiology, a predictable course, manifestations describable in signs and symptoms, and a predictable outcome modifiable by certain describable maneuvers. Mental illness became described according to the same basic notions. The discovery of knowledge of some etiological agents like the spirochete provided justifiable basis for the expectation that the problem about the etiology of mental illness could be solved along similar lines as in medicine. . . . In this framework psychopathology is viewed as an in-dwelling property of the patient, as something the patient has.

Many students may wish to see the particularly penetrating discussion of the "medical model" and a discerning analysis of its limitations in the "treatment" of psychological disorders as provided by Ullman and Krasner (1965).

At the time this model was first applied to psychotic behavior, it was useful because many institutionalized cases of that day *were*, in fact, *organic* in nature; their deviancies were the result of the syphilis spirochete, an "in-dwelling property." During the intervening years, though, that noxious agent has all but disappeared as a cause of "mental illness" or mental disorders, thanks to the twin utilization of detection and drugs. The fact must be borne in mind that not *all* psychotic behavior of that day was caused by the spirochete and we must remind ourselves that knowledge has advanced on many other fronts as well as on the biological one.

Currently there are few "medical model" proponents who believe that all forms of deviant behavior are due to organic malfunction. Nevertheless, like their physically oriented forerunners, they still tend to look "inside" the person for the determinants of aberrations. True, the causes are not thought to be physical, but they are considered organic by virtue of the fact that they are part of the *internal* state of the individual. To attribute a criminal's stealing, for example, to an inadequate superego is little different, in a sense, from attributing it to an overly active reticular system; both of these presumed causal variables are hypothetical and in both instances they are *internal*. Thus, while present-day advocates of the "medical model" tend to advance nonorganic causes for behavior deviations, the locus of their postulates is still the same—*inside* the person. This sort of emphasis seems to confuse students.

One way of clarifying the "medical model" position on causality is to distinguish between *past* or *developmental* antecedents of behavior on the one hand and *immediate* antecedents on the other; the internal factors referred to in this model are those which are immediate or current.

Past   Present

Historical ———————→ Disturbed ———————————→ Deviant Behavior

Experiences   Mental Apparatus

Figure 1. The "Medical Model" and Deviant Behavior

Figure 1 presents a schematic illustration of the "medical model": as a result of certain historical experiences (e.g., a demanding and critical mother during early childhood), an individual may develop disturbances in his mental apparatus (e.g., an inadequate self-concept); the mental apparatus then is a here-and-now or present-day cause of adult deviant behavior (e.g., consumption of excessive amounts of alcohol to the point of being unable to keep a job); the long-range, developmental, or historical antecedents were *outside* the person, that is, within his social environment at one time.

From the standpoint of altering the deviant behavior, the immediate, internal factors are those of prime importance—history is history and the past cannot be changed. Psychoanalysis (Freud, 1949) is an especially good example of a "medical model" theory and exemplifies, too, a method of modifying the internally disturbed mental apparatus. In this approach, the disturbed mental apparatus is thought to be primarily the result of early interactions with the environment; the psychoanalyst's goal is to produce significant changes in this apparatus.

How this is done is of interest since the method focuses almost exclusively on internal factors; the current environment or the here-and-now is rarely considered. Essentially the person is encouraged to describe his mental functioning, with particular emphasis upon the recall of early experiences. If the analysand is successful in uncovering those experiences which produced the disturbed mental apparatus, the road to change is near—or so goes the theory. By this time, it has been demonstrated clearly that the resulting insight is by no means always sufficient to bring about desired alterations in observable behavior. In fact, there is reason to believe that changes in deviant behavior can be produced without insight and that insight may be a product rather than a cause of such changes!

An example of the latter possibility is seen in a study by Wahler and Pollio (1968). These investigators utilized a learning theory approach (Selections 14 and 15) to modify the extremely dependent behavior of an eight-year-old boy. The therapeutic techniques essentially involved teaching the boy's mother and father to react differently to his dependent behavior. As such, no efforts were made to provide insight for the boy. In spite of this, as the youngster learned more independent behavior, his verbal awareness of his problems also changed. In a very real sense, he acquired insight concerning his dependency problems; in this instance, however, the insight came *after* and not *before* the behavioral changes.

The psychoanalytic position tends to ignore other factors which often contribute to the maintenance of deviant behavior—factors which are environmental or external. As we shall see later in discussing recent views in the field, the current environment can be a powerful source of control, a source which can either support deviant behavior or modify it.

Another major facet of the "medical model," stemming especially from conceptualizing "disease as a state of affairs or a process which had a specific etiology, a predictable course, manifestations describable in signs and symptoms, and a predictable outcome" (Hornstra, 1962), has been the creation of "diagnoses" or "labels." To oversimplify, a "diagnosis" becomes a word, or few words at most, which represent the underlying cause, symptoms, and treatment. In some instances, the label represents a specific entity such as diphtheria or "something the patient has."

In the realm of many physical ailments, of course, diagnoses have served their purposes admirably well. Such has not been the case for the "labels" or "diagnoses" for most forms of deviant behavior, although there have been strenuous efforts to create very specific and discrete categories. These labels suggest special entities or things—something one has—to many people (particularly beginning students), as when one hears reference to "*a* neurosis" or "*the* neurosis." In reality, most of the labels are shorthand descriptive expressions for a variety of behavioral characteristics; a person does not *have* a neurosis, he *behaves* in a manner which we call neurotic. It might be well to eliminate all the nouns in this area and use only the adjective "neurotic behavior." Indeed, Dr. Karl Menninger (1963), truly one of the pioneers and leaders in the field of mental and emotional disorders, has proposed that there has been entirely too much emphasis upon naming and labeling. He argues, in fact, that all of the names and labels which are so sacrosanct for many mental health workers be discarded.

Some sort of taxonomy is necessary, but a new or different one must avoid the overworked "disease" notion in which a single type of causation is implied; rather, allowances must be made for varied and divergent types of causation and attendant multiple approaches in "treatment." Recent efforts to devise a new classification scheme for behavior, currently referred to as "schizophrenia," the most prevalent of the major mental illnesses (Selection 24), are showing promise. Research is suggesting that there are two basic forms with differing antecedents, rather than the four or five classical "disease" types which were first described prior to 1900. In the "reactive" form, the deviant behavior seems to result primarily from environmental pressures or stresses. Response to appropriate care is good. The "process" or "evolutionary" form, on the other hand, continues to constitute a major puzzle as far as causation, development, and care are concerned.

The "disease" view appears to be prevalent and pervasive in the thinking of many individuals about most forms of deviant behavior. During the past fifteen or twenty years there has been repeated emphasis upon the terms "mental illness" and "disease" in many publications. By way of illustration:

> The most important thing for your patient's chances of recovery and for your own peace of mind is to realize that mental illnesses are illnesses like any others. (Stern, 1957)

> If everyone would just realize that mental illness is no different from any other prolonged disease and that a heart attack victim differs only from a mental victim in the localization of the affliction, the psychiatrist-therapist's job would be greatly simplified. (*Mind Over Matter*, 1962)

> While the signs of a neurosis frequently first appear in the late teens or in early adult life, the disease may have a background in events of early infancy. (*The Mind*, 1954)

> People with either mental or emotional illness need help from a medical specialist, just the same as people with pneumonia, or ptomaine. (*Some Things You Should Know About Mental and Emotional Illness*)

> At least 50% of all the millions of medical and surgical cases treated by private doctors and hospitals have a mental illness complication. (*Facts About Mental Illness*, 1963)

These direct and indirect references to "disease" for problems with such varied etiologies surely have promoted confusion and misunderstanding.

At the same time and almost without exception, the terminology which is used to describe and explain mental and emotional disorders and other deviant behavior continues to consist of terms and words which have long been associated with physical disabilities: "patient," "hospital," "cure," "therapy," "diagnosis," and "pathology." A favorite one is "psychopathology." Although none of these words necessarily has a narrow technical meaning or definition which restricts its use to the physical realm, it is highly probable that their frequent utilization for reference to disorders of thought and behavior does convey "disease" connotations to all people except perhaps highly trained or sophisticated ones. If that be true, misunderstanding has been and is being furthered.

In this connection, in our society, physical illness (or sickness or disease) has certain special significance for the sufferer. First, the victim or patient is not held *responsible* for his ailment—illness is something that happens to a person; for example, the body is invaded by some foreign agent or substance. True, the individual may be at least partially to blame for the

invasion—for instance, swimming in a stream he knows to be polluted—
but after he is declared to be "sick," he is absolved as far as care or treatment is concerned. Second, in order to become well, the victim is expected
—*and expects*—to be the more or less passive recipient of treatment, that is,
of *having things done to him*; for example, drugs are administered or surgery
is performed. In turn, there are the expectations that these interventions,
administered or imposed by others, will cure the ailment. Third, the sick
or ill person receives special considerations: if an employee, he is excused
from work, many times with pay; if a student, he is excused from classes
and other academic obligations for the duration of his ailment. It appears
likely that these attitudes about sickness or illness have been generalized
or extended to many forms of deviant behavior. Yet, such attitudes and
the actions which are based upon them are *not* appropriate or beneficial
for all the mental and emotional disorders (Selections 20, 22, and 23).

Still another line of evidence suggesting the prevalence of the "disease"
view has been the ever-expanding use of the term "mental illness." When
that term originated, it was probably applied only to those people who
were thought to be insane or psychotic or to those who in an earlier era
were called lunatic; but beginning early in this century, it began to lose
its original meaning. Currently and with increasing impetus since the late
1940's, it is used to designate not only those humans who are believed to
be psychotic but also those who exhibit any behavior which deviates to
any degree from some imagined norm. Such problems in behavior as
juvenile delinquency, marital strife, college and high school drop-outs,
racial prejudice, alienation, alcoholism, and many others are all labeled by
some authorities as "mental illness." A popular expression in our language
for the deviant or eccentric person is, "Sick! Sick! Sick!"; it is also fashion-
able to talk about our "sick" society.

Now if one is thinking of marital partners who fight—just a little or to
the extreme of a divorce—as being mentally ill, a fertile imagination is
required to conceive the "location of the affliction" anywhere within the
body of either combatant. If one happens to be thinking of racial prejudice
or of severe fright, it is extraordinarily difficult to view either one as being
similar in any way to "pneumonia or ptomaine." Indeed, all of the physical
analogies appear to be singularly incongruent for almost all of the "mental
illnesses."

The rapidly changing estimates of its prevalence also illustrate the
burgeoning of the "mental illness" category. Around 1940, the estimate
was one person in every sixteen, around 1950, it was one in thirteen, and
by 1960 or thereabouts, it was one in ten. The latter figure, of course,
amounts to 10 per cent of the population; one can easily conclude from
these estimates by decades that "mental illness" is increasing. In reality,
the criteria are changing and the term is becoming so broad as to approach

meaninglessness; there are some who believe it has already reached that state.

Since the 1960 estimate of one in ten is cited without any qualifications in many publications, some people have assumed that it is a well-established fact. Nothing could be further from the truth. Students, of course, should learn to be critical of such statistics and to question their origin and composition. It is difficult to tell where the one in ten figures originated, although the National Association for Mental Health (personal communication, 1964) attributed them to a study conducted by the Commission on Chronic Illness (1957) in Baltimore. That investigation epitomized, too, the great variety of behavior which is now labeled "mental illness." Moreover, a peculiar sampling approach was utilized and the examining and labeling procedures were highly suspect.

Actually, no studies of prevalence have met the criteria which the epidemiologists have specified, largely because some very formidable research problems are involved in meeting them. Morton Kramer (1957) has indicated that several basic issues must be resolved. The first requires some agreement as to what constitutes a specified type or form of behavior deviation today. (Some textbooks, to the contrary, indicate that there are no clear-cut, widely agreed-upon criteria.) The second necessitates the development of standardized methods for identifying cases in the general population. The third entails devising methods for measuring the duration of the "illness" or deviation, and the fourth requires the evaluation of the effects of "treatment." A fifth one must be mentioned: There needs to be some limiting of man's difficulties which are labeled as "disorders." Since none of these issues appears to be anywhere near resolution, all estimates of incidence and prevalence must be taken with the proverbial grain of salt.

In this regard, you may have encountered or will encounter such propaganda statements as these (they have appeared even in textbooks):

> The probability is one in twenty that any given individual will, at some time in his life, be a patient in a mental hospital. (Kimble and Garmezy, 1963)

> Estimates indicate that one out of every 10 babies born today will be hospitalized for mental illness at some time during his life. (Hilgard and Atkinson, 1967)

These two sets of figures illustrate remarkable carelessness with data. The one in twenty statistic is strikingly incompatible with well-documented data about mental hospital admissions; the number of persons admitted and readmitted each year has remained quite close to one-half of one per cent of the total population ever since 1930 (as far back as census data are available). The origin of the one in twenty prediction is unknown. The one in every ten baby statistic is a gross distortion of a carefully executed probability or actuarial investigation; it came from a study of babies born in New York state in 1940 (Goldhamer and Marshall, 1953). The expectation was one in ten that a baby would be admitted to a mental hospital by *age 75 provided* he lived to that age. The chances were predicted to be quite different for those living to other ages; for example, 30—one in 100; 45—one in 29; 90—one in five. The predictions one in ten *at* or *after* age 75 and one in five *at* or *after* age 90 are not surprising in view of what is well-known about the physical and mental ravages of old age.

All of these estimates and predictions have been called to your attention in some detail because they are cited frequently without the necessary qualifications and because they are reflections of the "disease" position.

THE CURRENT TREND

It is much easier to describe and criticize the "disease" view than it is to portray clearly the conceptual schemes which are gaining prominence. Basic to these schemes is a tendency to conceptualize the person and his current environment as interdependent systems; that is, the individual is not considered as an entity apart from the world in which he lives. For example, if one is to understand the neurotic's anxiety, one must know as much about his current situation as about him: What is his wife like? How about his children, his relatives, his boss? What is his economic position? What are his neighbors like? Certainly historical experiences play a role in the development of his present day behavior, but theorists now argue that current environmental factors support and maintain it.

Perhaps the term "psychosocial" best describes the current thinking about disordered behavior. That expression essentially implies an interaction between a person and his social environment—an interaction which may yield "normal" or deviant behavior. Just how these intereactions occur and how they produce their effects have been the subjects of prolific research. Investigators have differed widely in their specific approaches to the problem, but all have shared the "psychosocial model." As an example, Bernal, Duryee, Pruett, and Burns (1968) trained a mother to control her eight and one-half-year-old emotionally disturbed boy (there had been serious parental strife since the child's infancy) who at the same time was a severe disciplinary problem. He regulated all family activities and even dictated when his mother could sit in the living room. By utilizing learning principles and providing behavioral feedback to the mother via closed circuit television, her behavior was altered and in turn the boy's abusive behavior was reduced. She began also to feel and show affection for him as he did for her.

Past   Present
Historical ——————————→ Current ——————————→ Deviant Behavior
Experiences   Environment

Figure 2. The "Psychosocial Model"

Figure 2 presents a schematic illustration of the current trend; this one should be contrasted with the illustration of the "medical model" in Figure 1. In both instances, historical experiences are important as developmental causes of deviant behavior, as were certainly true with the eight and one-half-year-old; however, such experiences have their primary influence on the current environment, *not* on the mental apparatus. In other words, the nature of the *function* of the current environment is determined by the history. The present situation thus serves as an immediate cause of the deviant behavior; in a very real sense, the current environment may be seen as *maintaining* problems which were developed in the past. The critical difference between this view and that of the "medical model" is that of the locus of immediate causes; in the "medical model" the locus is *internal* while in the newer trend the locus is *external*.

To emphasize or focus upon outside causes of deviant behavior is not to deny that the individual has a mind; if the current environment is to influence behavior, it logically must do so through cognitive and emotional equipment. The intent of the newer approach is to produce a shift in our attention, a shift away from an exclusive concern with internal functioning and a shift toward examining those present variables which may elicit this functioning and thus produce or maintain deviant behavior.

Fortunately, the prestigious Joint Commission on Mental Illness and Health (Selection 24) has recommended:

> It should now be clear that one way around the impasse of public and professional attitudes that we appear to have erected would be to emphasize that persons with major mental illnesses are in certain ways *different* from the ordinary sick.

That body also emphasized that it is possible to treat the mentally ill (psychotics) as *human beings* and get good results. The Commission cites programs in which college students have worked and the great benefits which have accrued from their efforts.

As further indications of the "psychosocial" model, one author looks upon disorders of thought and behavior as "problems in living" (Selection 2); another one describes them as "interpersonal behavior" or inappropriate conduct (Selection 4).

Some support for these positions is found in the fact that patterns of disordered behavior tend to be different in the various social classes. Hollingshead and Redlich (1958) have demonstrated, in one of the most significant large-scale social studies in "mental illness" ever undertaken, that:

1) There is a relationship between the incidence of "mental illness" and social class—the incidence is higher in the lower class.

2) There is a relationship between the type of "mental illness" and social class—behavior labeled as neurotic tends to occur in the upper classes while behavior labeled as psychotic tends to occur in the lower classes.

3) There is a relationship between type of care or treatment received and social class—people in the upper classes receive care which is based upon our most up-to-date notions; those in the lower classes receive largely custodial care. The fact that these latter people lack money is *not* the sole determinant of this discrimination—some of it is due to misperceptions or distortions by the authorities or mental health experts. Similar or identical behavior by people in different social classes results in care that is drastically different (Selection 6).

Another noteworthy feature of this investigation was the fact that the original sample of patients was studied over a ten-year period. Myers and Bean (1968) found that the higher the social class of the patients, the less the likelihood of their still being hospitalized ten years later, that the lower-class patients were continuing to receive custodial care, and that if the lower-class patient returns to his community, there are serious employment and financial problems and a high degree of social isolation. These authors emphasize:

> In summary, social factors in the community, as well as in the treatment agency itself, operate to produce significant class differences in treatment outcome.

Other studies have tended to substantiate the results of these pioneering ones; lower class "mental patients" represent extremes in aggressive behavior and seem to experience or possess less frustration tolerance (Selection 5). George Albee (1968) has argued convincingly in this regard that our training centers for mental health workers, located predominantly in medical institutions, have been middle- and upper-class oriented and as a result there is little possibility of our understanding or dealing effectively with the myriad problems associated with the poor or disadvantaged. Such orientation means, too, an emphasis upon the *internal* state of the person and a disregard of the *external* situation.

Moreover, some abnormal behavior can be correlated with certain more or less specific external social stresses. To use extremes as illustrations, there was major disintegration in the behavior of men who were prisoners of the Nazis (Bettleheim, 1943) and radical changes in the value systems of some men who were subjected to Chinese Communist "brainwashing" (Selection 7). In the last mentioned selection, Edgar H. Schein states: ". . . it is my opinion that the process is primarily concerned with social forces, not with the strengths and weaknesses of individual minds." At the same time, several studies have shown that normal, well-adjusted people (often times college students) exhibit very abnormal behavior, including "hallucinations," when subjected to drastically reduced environmental stimulation (Solomon et al., 1961).

Still another integral element in the "psychosocial" position is that of *learning.* Continuing to use an extreme as an illustration, one of the current classifications of "mental illness" is "Dyssocial Reaction," one of the *Personality Disorders.* This label is applied to individuals who have *learned directly* to violate social codes; as a result of their violations, they are viewed as deviant in the eyes of society. That is, *some* individuals who steal have been taught deliberately to do so by their relatives and friends, in much the same sense that most of us have been taught not to steal. Such "dyssocial behavior" is clearly the result of *learning.*

Too, certain forms of abnormal behavior today involve principally the values, aspirations, and philosophies by which men live (Selection 9). Some of these intangible conflicts between "personal" and "social" are reflected to some extent in these words of John Steinbeck (1945):

> "It has always seemed strange to me," said Doc. "The things we admire in men, kindness, and generosity, openness, honesty, understanding, and feeling are the concomitants of failure in our system. And those traits we detest, sharpness, greed, acquisitiveness, meanness, egotism, and self-interest are the traits of success. And while men admire the quality of the first, they love the produce of the second."

Whatever these views are called, the important point is that the alleviation or resolution of a "psychosocial" conflict or problem requires procedures and processes entirely different from those required in the treatment of some invasion of the body, such as an infection. For one thing, while attempting to resolve conflicts or while engaging in learning different attitudes or beliefs, the individual cannot be a more or less passive recipient (Selections 22 and 23) as in the case of physical illness. Attitudes toward her son could *not* be *prescribed* for the mother who asked for them. Yet, in one large scale survey—*Americans View Their Mental Health* (Gurin et al., 1960)—it was reported of those who sought help for truly personal problems (not financial difficulties or other situational ones) that:

> Despite the fact that it takes an unusual degree of insight for an individual to admit that he needs help with a mental or emotional problem, only about one-fourth of those who sought assistance traced

their problems back to their own inadequacies . . . ; few were prepared to be told that they must accept at least a share of the responsibility for their problems and that they must change themselves accordingly.

Thus, the procedures which have been developed and which are being investigated and revised continually for dealing with certain of the "mental illnesses" reflect the role of "psychosocial" forces in the production and maintenance of these disorders. Psychotherapy, which is especially useful in many instances in the alleviation of anxiety and tension, is a *process* in which attitudes and feelings are altered as the result of the "patient" *learning with* and *from* another *person* (Selection 14). Increasing recognition of many of the limitations of psychotherapy has led to the development of Family Therapy; again the essential elements of *learning* or *relearning* are involved, but the mode of application is different (Selection 17). In some instances, technological advances such as television are being utilized (Selection 16).

The importance of psychosocial conflicts and learning is even receiving attention in mental hospitals, in that some of them are becoming less and less prison-like and hospital-like. For example, "open-door" hospitals have been operating in England, wherein the learning or acceptance of personal responsibility is more likely to occur (Selection 21). There have been recommendations that open-door hospitals be developed in the United States (Selection 24).

Of very special significance, at the moment, is the impact of this new trend upon the laws and commitment procedures governing the major mental illnesses (Functional Psychoses). Few textbooks inform students about the legal issues which play roles in these matters and the abuses which exist (Selection 3).

REFERENCES

Albee, George W. *Institutional and manpower training implications of the medical model for psychology*. Paper read at the Annual Meeting of the American Psychological Association, San Francisco, August 30, 1968.

American Psychological Association, Board of Directors. *Amer. Psychologist*, 18:307, No. 6, June, 1963.

Bernal, Martha E., *et al.* Behavior modification and the brat syndrome. *J. Consult. Clin. Psychol.*, 32:447-455, No. 4, August, 1968.

Bettelheim, Bruno. Individual and mass behavior in extreme situations. *J. abnorm. soc. Psychol.*, 38:417-452, 1943.

Commission on Chronic Illness. *Chronic illness in a large city*. Vol. IV of *Chronic illness in the United States*. Cambridge: Harvard University Press, 1957.

Frank, Jerome D. *Persuasion and healing*. Baltimore: Johns Hopkins Press, 1961, p. 221. By permission.

Freud, Sigmund. *An outline of psychoanalysis.* New York: W. W. Norton, 1949.

Goldhamer, Herbert, & Marshall, Andrew. *Psychosis and civilization.* Glencoe, Illinois: The Free Press, 1953.

Gurin, Gerald, .Veroff, Joseph, & Feld, Sheila. *Americans view their mental health.* New York: Basic Books, 1960, p. xxi. By permission.

Hilgard, Ernest R. & Atkinson, Richard C. *Introduction to psychology.* (4th ed.) New York: Harcourt, Brace & World, 1967, p. 570. By permission.

Hobbs, Nicholas. Statement on mental illness and retardation. *Amer. Psychologist,* 18:295-299, No. 6, June, 1963.

Hollingshead, August B. & Redlich, Frederick C. *Social class and mental illness.* New York: John Wiley & Sons, 1958.

Hornstra, Robjin. The psychiatric hospital and the community. Paper read at the Annual Workshop in Community Mental Health, Pisgah View Ranch, Candler, North Carolina, June 11-21, 1962.

Jahoda, Marie. *Current concepts of positive mental health.* New York: Basic Books, 1958, p. xi. By permission.

John Hancock Mutual Life Insurance Company. *The Mind.* Pamphlet, 1954, p. 15.

Kimble. Gregory A. & Garmezy, Norman. *Principles of general psychology.* (2nd ed.) New York: The Ronald Press, 1963, p. 523. By permission.

Kramer, Morton. A discussion of the concepts of incidence and prevalence as related to epidemiologic studies of mental disorder. *J. publ. Hlth,* 47:826-840, No. 7, July, 1957.

Menninger, Karl. *The vital balance.* New York: Viking Press, 1963.

Myers, Jermoe K. & Bean, Lee L. *A decade later.* New York: John Wiley & Sons, 1968, p. 211. By permission.

National Association for Mental Health, 10 Columbus Circle, New York, New York. Personal Communication to Ohmer Milton. January 10, 1964.

National Association for Mental Health. *Facts about mental illness, fact sheet.* 1963.

National Association for Mental Health. *Some things you should know about mental and emotional illness.* Leaflet (no date).

Solomon, Philip, *et al. Sensory deprivation.* Cambridge: Harvard University Press, 1961.

Steinbeck, John. *Cannery Row.* New York: Viking Press, 1945, p. 150. By permission.

Stern, Edith. *Mental illness: A guide for the family.* National Association for Mental Health, 1957, p. 1.

Tennessee Department of Mental Health. *Mind Over Matter,* Vol. 7, No. 4, 1962.

Ullman, Leonard P. & Krasner, Leonard. *Case studies in behavior modification.* New York: Holt, Rinehart and Winston, 1965.

Wahler, Robert G. & Pollio, Howard R. Behavior and insight: A case study in behavior therapy. *J. Exp. Res. Pers.,* 3:45-56, No. 1, June, 1968.

2. The Myth of Mental Illness

Thomas Szasz

In the opinion of Dr. Thomas Szasz, a psychiatrist, of the State University of New York, in Upstate Medical Center, Syracuse, N.Y., the view that mental illnesses are basically no different from all other diseases rests upon two fundamental errors: (1) assuming that a person's belief can be explained by a defect or disease of the nervous system and (2) making a symmetrical dualism between mental and physical (or bodily) symptoms. As for the first error, beliefs cannot be explained by defects or diseases of the nervous system. The second error is merely a habit of speech to which no known observations can be found to correspond.

Mental illnesses can be viewed more meaningfully as *problems in living*. The notion of mental illness has served mainly to obscure that fact. Sustained adherence to the myth of mental illness has allowed people to believe that mental health automatically insures the making of proper choices in everyday affairs of life. The facts, however, are to the contrary: "It is the making of good choices in life that others regard, retrospectively, as good mental health."

For a more thorough and extensive discussion of the "myth of mental illness" than is contained in his article, see Dr. Szasz's book under that title (Harper and Row).

My aim in this essay is to raise the question "Is there such a thing as mental illness?" and to argue that there is not. Since the notion of mental illness is extremely widely used nowadays, inquiry into the ways in which this term is employed would seem to be especially indicated. Mental illness, of course, is not literally a "thing"—or physical object—and hence it can "exist" only in the same sort of way in which other theoretical concepts exist. Yet, familiar theories are in the habit of posing, sooner or later—at least to those who come to believe in them—as "objective truths" (or "facts"). During certain historical periods, explanatory conceptions such as deities, witches, and microorganisms appeared not only as theories but as self-evident *causes* of a vast number of events. I submit that today mental illness is widely regarded in a somewhat similar fashion, that is, as the cause of innumerable diverse happenings. As an antidote to the complacent use of the notion of mental illness—whether as a self-

American Psychologist; 15: 113-118, #2, February, 1960. Reprinted by permission of the author and the American Psychological Association.

evident phenomenon, theory, or cause—let us ask this question: What is meant when it is asserted that someone is mentally ill?

In what follows I shall describe briefly the main uses to which the concept of mental illness has been put. I shall argue that this notion has outlived whatever usefulness it might have had and that it now functions merely as a convenient myth.

MENTAL ILLNESS AS A SIGN OF BRAIN DISEASE

The notion of mental illness derives its main support from such phenomena as syphilis of the brain or delirious conditions—intoxications, for instance—in which persons are known to manifest various peculiarities or disorders of thinking and behavior. Correctly speaking, however, these are diseases of the brain, not of the mind. According to one school of thought, *all* so-called mental illness is of this type. The assumption is made that some neurological defect, perhaps a very subtle one, will ultimately be found for all the disorders of thinking and behavior. Many contemporary psychiatrists, physicians, and other scientists hold this view. This position implies that people *cannot* have troubles—expressed in what are *now called* "mental illnesses"—because of differences in personal needs, opinions, social aspirations, values, and so on. *All problems in living* are attributed to physicochemical processes which in due time will be discovered by medical research.

"Mental illnesses" are thus regarded as basically no different than all other diseases (that is, of the body). The only difference, in this view, between mental and bodily diseases is that the former, affecting the brain, manifest themselves by means of mental symptoms; whereas the latter, affecting other organ systems (for example, the skin, liver, etc.), manifest themselves by means of symptoms referable to those parts of the body. This view rests on and expresses what are, in my opinion, two fundamental errors.

In the first place, what central nervous system symptoms would correspond to a skin eruption or a fracture? It would *not* be some emotion or complex bit of behavior. Rather, it would be blindness or a paralysis of some part of the body. The crux of the matter is that a disease of the brain, analogous to a disease of the skin or bone, is a neurological defect, and not a problem in living. For example, a *defect* in a person's visual field may be satisfactorily explained by correlating it with certain definite lesions in the nervous system. On the other hand, a person's *belief*—whether this be a belief in Christianity, in Communism, or in the idea that his internal organs are "rotting" and that his body is, in fact, already "dead"—cannot be explained by a defect or disease of the nervous system.

Explanations of this sort of occurrence—assuming that one is interested in the belief itself and does not regard it simply as a "symptom" or expression of something else that is *more interesting*—must be sought along different lines.

The second error in regarding complex psychosocial behavior, consisting of communications about ourselves and the world about us, as mere symptoms of neurological functioning is *epistemological*. In other words, it is an error pertaining not to any mistakes in observation or reasoning, as such, but rather to the way in which we organize and express our knowledge. In the present case, the error lies in making a symmetrical dualism between mental and physical (or bodily) symptoms, a dualism which is merely a habit of speech and to which no known observations can be found to correspond. Let us see if this is so. In medical practice, when we speak of physical disturbances, we mean either signs (for example, a fever) or symptoms (for example, pain). We speak of mental symptoms, on the other hand, when we refer to a patient's *communications about himself, others, and the world about him.* He might state that he is Napoleon or that he is being persecuted by the Communists. These would be considered mental symptoms *only* if the observer believed that the patient was *not* Napoleon or that he was *not* being persecuted by the Communists. This makes it apparent that the statement that "X is a mental symptom" involves rendering a judgment. The judgment entails, moreover, a covert comparison or matching of the patient's ideas, concepts, or beliefs with those of the observer and the society in which they live. The notion of mental symptom is therefore inextricably tied to the *social* (including *ethical*) *context* in which it is made in much the same way as the notion of bodily symptom is tied to an *anatomical* and *genetic context* (Szasz, 1957a, 1957b).

To sum up what has been said thus far: I have tried to show that for those who regard mental symptoms as signs of brain disease, the concept of mental illness is unnecessary and misleading. For what they mean is that people so labeled suffer from diseases of the brain; and, if that is what they mean, it would seem better for the sake of clarity to say that and not something else.

MENTAL ILLNESS AS A NAME FOR PROBLEMS IN LIVING

The term "mental illness" is widely used to describe something which is very different than a disease of the brain. Many people today take it for granted that living is an arduous process. Its hardship for modern man, moreover, derives not so much from a struggle for biological survival as from the stresses and strains inherent in the social intercourse of complex human personalities. In this context, the notion of mental illness is used to identify or describe some feature of an individual's so-called personality. Mental illness—as a deformity of the personality, so to speak —is then regarded as the *cause* of the human disharmony. It is implicit in this view that social intercourse between people is regarded as something *inherently harmonious*, its disturbance being due solely to the presence of "mental illness" in many people. This is obviously fallacious reasoning, for it makes the abstraction "mental illness" into a *cause*, even though this abstraction was created in the first place to serve only as a shorthand expression for certain types of human behavior. It now becomes necessary to ask: "What kinds of behavior are regarded as indicative of mental illness, and by whom?"

The concept of illness, whether bodily or mental, implies *deviation from some clearly defined norm*. In the case of physical illness, the norm is the structural and functional integrity of the human body. Thus, although the desirability of physical health, as such, is an ethical value, what health *is* can be stated in anatomical and physiological terms. What is the norm deviation from which is regarded as mental illness? This question cannot be easily answered. But whatever this norm might be, we can be certain of only one thing: namely, that it is a norm that must be stated in terms of *psychosocial, ethical,* and *legal* concepts. For example, notions such as "excessive repression" or "acting out an unconscious impulse" illustrate the use of psychological concepts for judging (so-called) mental health and illness. The idea that chronic hostility, vengefulness, or divorce are indicative of mental illness would be illustrations of the use of ethical norms (that is, the desirability of love, kindness, and a stable marriage relationship). Finally, the widespread psychiatric opinion that only a mentally ill person would commit homicide illustrates the use of a legal concept as a norm of mental health. The norm from which deviation is measured whenever one speaks of a mental illness is a *psychosocial and ethical one*. Yet, the remedy is sought in terms of *medical* measures which—it is hoped and assumed—are free from wide differences of ethical value. The definition of the disorder and the terms in which its remedy are sought are therefore at serious odds with one another. The practical significance of this covert conflict between the alleged nature of the defect and the remedy can hardly be exaggerated.

Having identified the norms used to measure deviations in cases of mental illness, we will now turn to the question: "Who defines the norms and hence the deviation?" Two basic answers may be offered: (*a*) It may be the person himself (that is, the patient) who decides that he deviates from a norm. For example, an artist may believe that he suffers from a work inhibition; and he may implement this conclusion by seeking help *for* himself from a psychotherapist. (*b*) It may be someone other than the patient who decides that the latter is deviant (for example, relatives, physicians, legal authorities, society generally, etc.). In such a case a psychiatrist may be hired by others to do something *to* the patient in order to correct the deviation.

These considerations underscore the importance of asking the question "Whose agent is the psychiatrist?" and of giving a candid answer to it (Szasz, 1956, 1958). The psychiatrist (psychologist or nonmedical psychotherapist), it now develops, may be the agent of the patient, of the relatives, of the school, of the military services, of a business organization, of a court of law, and so forth. In speaking of the psychiatrist as the agent of these persons or organizations, it is not implied that his values concerning norms, or his ideas and aims concerning the proper nature of remedial action, need to coincide exactly with those of his employer. For example, a patient in individual psychotherapy may believe that his salvation lies in a new marriage; his psychotherapist need not share this hypothesis. As the patient's agent, however, he must abstain from bringing social or legal force to bear on the patient which would prevent him from putting his beliefs into action. If his *contract* is with the patient, the psychiatrist (psychotherapist) may disagree with him or stop his treatment; but he cannot engage others to obstruct the patient's aspirations. Similarly, if a psychiatrist is engaged by a court to determine the sanity of a criminal, he need not fully share the legal authorities' values and intentions in regard to the criminal and the means available for dealing with him. But the psychiatrist is expressly barred from stating, for example, that it is not the criminal who is "insane" but the men who wrote the law on the basis of which the very actions that are being judged are regarded as "criminal." Such an opinion could be voiced, of course, but not in a courtroom, and not by a psychiatrist who makes it his practice to assist the court in performing its daily work.

To recapitulate: In actual contemporary social usage, the finding of a mental illness is made by establishing a deviance in behavior from certain psychosocial, ethical, or legal norms. The judgment may be made, as in medicine, by the patient, the physician (psychiatrist), or others. Remedial action, finally, tends to be sought in a therapeutic—or covertly medical—framework, thus creating a situation in which *psychosocial, ethical,* and/or *legal deviations* are claimed to be correctible by (so-called) *medical action.* Since medical action is designed to correct only medical deviations, it seems logically absurd to expect that it will help solve problems whose very existence had been defined and established on nonmedical grounds. I think that these considerations may be fruitfully applied to the present use of tranquilizers and, more generally, to what might be expected of drugs of whatever type in regard to the amelioration or solution of problems in human living.

THE ROLE OF ETHICS IN PSYCHIATRY

Anything that people *do*—in contrast to things that *happen* to them (Peters, 1958)—takes place in a context of value. In this broad sense, no human activity is devoid of ethical implications. When the values underlying certain activities are widely shared, those who participate in their pursuit may lose sight of them altogether. The discipline of medicine, both as a pure science (for example, research) and as a technology (for example, therapy), contains many ethical considerations and judgments. Unfortunately, these are often denied, minimized, or merely kept out of focus; for the ideal of the medical profession as well as of the people whom it serves seems to be having a system of medicine (allegedly) free of ethical value. This sentimental notion is expressed by such things as the doctor's willingness to treat and help patients irrespective of their religious or political beliefs, whether they are rich or poor, etc. While there may be some grounds for this belief—albeit it is a view that is not impressively true even in these regards—the fact remains that ethical considerations encompass a vast range of human affairs. By making the practice of medicine neutral in regard to some specific issues of value need not, and cannot, mean that it can be kept free from all such values. The practice of medicine is intimately tied to ethics; and the first thing that we must do, it seems to me, is to try to make this clear and explicit. I shall let this matter rest here, for it does not concern us specifically in this essay. Lest there be any vagueness, however, about how or where ethics and medicine meet, let me remind the reader of such issues as birth control, abortion, suicide, and euthanasia as only a few of the major areas of current ethicomedical controversy.

Psychiatry, I submit, is very much more intimately tied to problems of ethics than is medicine. I use the word "psychiatry" here to refer to that contemporary discipline which is concerned with *problems in living* (and not with diseases of the brain, which are problems for neurology). Problems in human relations can be analyzed, interpreted, and given meaning only within given social and ethical contexts. Accordingly, it *does* make a difference—arguments to the contrary notwithstanding—what the psychiatrist's socioethical orientations happen to be; for these will influence his ideas on what is wrong with the patient, what deserves comment or interpretation, in what possible directions change might be desirable, and so forth. Even in medicine proper, these factors play a role, as for instance, in the divergent orientations which physicians, depending on their religious affiliations, have toward such things as birth control and therapeutic abortion. Can anyone really believe that a psychotherapist's ideas concerning religious belief, slavery, or other similar issues play no role in his practical work? If they do make a difference, what are we to infer from it? Does it not seem reasonable that we ought to have different psychiatric therapies—each expressly recognized for the ethical positions which they embody—for, say, Catholics and Jews, religious persons and agnostics, democrats and communists, white supremacists and Negroes, and so on? Indeed, if we look at how psychiatry is actually practiced today (especially in the United States), we find that people do seek psychiatric help in accordance with their social status and ethical beliefs (Hollingshead & Redlich, 1958). This should really not surprise us more than being told that practicing Catholics rarely frequent birth control clinics.

The foregoing position which holds that contemporary psychotherapists deal with problems in living, rather than with mental illnesses and their cures, stands in opposition to a currently prevalent claim, according to which mental illness is just as "real" and "objective" as bodily illness. This is a confusing claim since it is never known exactly what is meant by such words as "real" and "objective." I suspect, however, that what is intended by the proponents of this view is to create the idea in the popular mind that mental illness is some sort of disease entity, like an infection or a malignancy. If this were true, one could *catch* or *get* a "mental illness," one might *have* or *harbor* it, one might *transmit* it to others, and finally one could get *rid* of it. In my opinion, there is not a shred of evidence to support this idea. To the contrary, all the evidence is the other way and supports the view that what people now call mental illnesses are for the most part *communications* expressing unacceptable ideas, often framed, moreover, in an unusual idiom. The scope of this essay allows me to do no more than mention this alternative theoretical approach to this problem (Szasz, 1957c).

This is not the place to consider in detail the similarities and differences between bodily and mental illnesses. It shall suffice for us here to emphasize only one important difference between them: namely, that whereas bodily disease refers to public, physicochemical occurrences, the notion of mental illness is used to codify relatively more private, sociopsychological happenings of which the observer (diagnostician) forms a part. In other words, the psychiatrist does not stand *apart* from what he observes, but is, in Harry Stack Sullivan's apt words, a "participant observer." This means that he is *committed* to some picture of what he considers reality—and to what he thinks society considers reality—and he observes and judges the patient's behavior in the light of these considerations. This touches on our earlier observation that the notion of mental symptom itself implies a comparison between observer and observed, psychiatrist and patient. This is so obvious that I may be charged with belaboring trivialities. Let me therefore say once more that my aim in presenting this argument was expressly to criticize and counter a prevailing contemporary tendency to deny the moral aspects of psychiatry (and psychotherapy) and to substitute for them allegedly value-free medical considerations. Psychotherapy, for example, is being widely practiced as though it entailed nothing other than restoring the patient from a state of mental sickness to one of mental health. While it is generally accepted that mental illness has something to do with man's social (or interpersonal) relations, it is paradoxically maintained that problems of values (that is, of ethics) do not arise in this process.[1] Yet, in one sense, much of psychotherapy may revolve around nothing other than the elucidation and weighing of goals and values—many of which may be mutually contradictory—and the means whereby they might best be harmonized, realized, or relinquished.

The diversity of human values and the methods by means of which they may be realized is so vast, and many of them remain so unacknowledged, that they cannot fail but lead to conflicts in human relations. Indeed, to say that human relations at all levels—from mother to child, through husband and wife, to nation and nation—are fraught with stress, strain, and disharmony is, once again, making the obvious explicit. Yet, what may be obvious may be also poorly understood. This I think is the case here. For it seems to me that—at least in our scientific theories of behavior—we have failed to *accept* the simple fact that human relations are inherently fraught with difficulties and that to make them even relatively harmonious requires much patience and hard work. I submit that the idea of mental illness is now being put to work to obscure certain difficulties which at present may be inherent—not that they need be unmodifiable—in the social intercourse of persons. If this is true, the concept functions as a disguise; for instead of calling attention to conflicting human needs, aspirations, and values, the notion of mental illness provides an amoral and impersonal "thing" (an "illness") as an explanation for *problems in living* (Szasz, 1959). We may recall in this connection that not so long ago it was devils and witches who were held responsible for men's problems in social living. The belief in mental illness, as something

[1] Freud went so far as to say that: "I consider ethics to be taken for granted. Actually I have never done a mean thing" (Jones, 1957, p. 247). This surely is a strange thing to say for someone who has studied man as a social being as closely as did Freud. I mention it here to show how the notion of "illness" (in the case of psychoanalysis, "psychopathology," or "mental illness") was used by Freud—and by most of his followers—as a means for classifying certain forms of human behavior as falling within the scope of medicine, and hence (by *fiat*) outside that of ethics!

other than man's trouble in getting along with his fellowman, is the proper heir to the belief in demonology and witchcraft. Mental illness exists or is "real" in exactly the same sense in which witches existed or were "real."

CHOICE, RESPONSIBILITY, AND PSYCHIATRY

While I have argued that mental illnesses do not exist, I obviously did not imply that the social and psychological occurrences to which this label is currently being attached also do not exist. Like the personal and social troubles which people had in the Middle Ages, they are real enough. It is the labels we give them that concerns us and, having labeled them, what we do about them. While I cannot go into the ramified implications of this problem here, it is worth noting that a demonologic conception of problems in living gave rise to therapy along theological lines. Today, a belief in mental illness implies—nay, requires—therapy along medical or psychotherapeutic lines.

What is implied in the line of thought set forth here is something quite different. I do not intend to offer a new conception of "psychiatric illness" nor a new form of "therapy." My aim is more modest and yet also more ambitious. It is to suggest that the phenomena now called mental illnesses be looked at afresh and more simply, that they be removed from the category of illnesses, and that they be regarded as the expressions of man's struggle with the problem of *how* he should live. The last mentioned problem is obviously a vast one, its enormity reflecting not only man's inability to cope with his environment, but even more his increasing self-reflectiveness.

By problems in living, then, I refer to that truly explosive chain reaction which began with man's fall from divine grace by partaking of the fruit of the tree of knowledge. Man's awareness of himself and of the world about him seems to be a steadily expanding one, bringing in its wake an ever larger *burden of understanding* (an expression borrowed from Susanne Langer, 1953). *This burden, then, is to be expected and must not be misinterpreted.* Our only *rational* means for lightening it is *more understanding*, and appropriate *action* based on such understanding. The main alternative lies in acting as though the burden were not what in fact we perceive it to be and taking refuge in an outmoded theological view of man. In the latter view, man does not fashion his life and much of his world about him, but merely lives out his fate in a world created by superior beings. This may logically lead to pleading non-responsibility in the face of seemingly unfathomable problems and difficulties. Yet, if man fails to take increasing responsibility for his actions, individually as well as collectively, it seems unlikely that some higher power or being would assume this task and carry this burden for him. Moreover, this seems hardly the proper time in human history for obscuring the issue of man's responsibility for his actions by hiding it behind the skirt of an all-explaining conception of mental illness.

CONCLUSIONS

I have tried to show that the notion of mental illness has outlived whatever usefulness it might have had and that it now functions merely as a convenient myth. As such, it is a true heir to religious myths in general, and to the belief in witchcraft in particular; the role of all these belief-systems was to act as *social tranquilizers*, thus encouraging the hope that mastery of certain specific problems may be achieved by means of substitutive (symbolic-magical) operations. The notion of mental illness thus serves mainly to obscure the everyday fact that life for most people is a continuous struggle, not for biological survival, but for a "place in the sun," "peace of mind," or some other human value. For man aware of himself and of the world about him, once the needs for preserving the body (and perhaps the race) are more or less satisfied, the problem arises as to what he should do with himself. Sustained adherence to the myth of mental illness allows people to avoid facing this problem, believing that mental health, conceived as the absence of mental illness, automatically insures the making of right and safe choices in one's conduct of life. But the facts are all the other way. It is the making of good choices in life that others regard, retrospectively, as good mental health!

The myth of mental illness encourages us, moreover, to believe in its logical corollary: that social intercourse would be harmonious, satisfying, and the secure basis of a "good life" were it not for the disrupting influences of mental illness or "psychopathology." The potentiality for universal human happiness, in this form at least, seems to me but another example of the I-wish-it-were-true type of fantasy. I do not believe that human happiness or well-being on a hitherto unimaginably large scale, and not just for a select few, is possible. This goal could be achieved, however, only at the cost of many men, and not just a few being willing and able to tackle their personal, social, and ethical conflicts. This means having the courage and integrity to forego waging battles on false fronts, finding solutions for substitute problems—for instance, fighting the battle of stomach acid and chronic fatigue instead of facing up to a marital conflict.

Our adversaries are not demons, witches, fate, or mental illness. We have no enemy whom we can fight, exorcise, or dispel by "cure." What we do have are *problems in living*—whether these be biologic, economic, political, or sociopsychological. In this essay I was concerned only with problems belonging in the last mentioned category, and within this group mainly with those pertaining to moral values. The field to which modern psychiatry addresses itself is vast, and I made no effort to encompass it all. My argument was limited to the proposition that mental illness is a myth, whose function it is to disguise and thus render more palatable the bitter pill of moral conflicts in human relations.

REFERENCES

Hollingshead, A. B., & Redlich, F. C. *Social class and mental illness.* New York: Wiley, 1958.

Jones, E. *The life and work of Sigmund Freud.* Vol. III. New York: Basic Books, 1957.

Langer, S. K. *Philosophy in a new key.* New York: Mentor Books, 1953.

Peters, R. S. *The concept of motivation.* London: Routledge & Kegan Paul, 1958.

Szasz, T. S. Malingering: "Diagnosis" or social condemnation? *AMA Arch Neurol. Psychiat.*, 1956, **76**, 432-443.

Szasz, T. S. *Pain and pleasure: A study of bodily feelings.* New York: Basic Books, 1957.   (a)

Szasz, T. S. The problem of psychiatric nosology: A contribution to a situational analysis of psychiatric operations. *Amer. J. Psychiat.*, 1957, **114**, 405-413.   (b)

Szasz, T. S. On the theory of psychoanalytic treatment. *Int. J. Psycho-Anal.*, 1957, **38**, 166-182.   (c)

Szasz, T. S. Psychiatry, ethics and the criminal law. *Columbia Law Rev.*, 1958, **58**, 183-198.

Szasz, T. S. Moral conflict and psychiatry. *Yale Rev.*, 1960, **49**, #4, 555-566.

3.   The Societal Reaction to Deviance: Ascriptive Elements in the Psychiatric Screening of Mental Patients in a Midwestern State Hospital

Thomas J. Scheff[*]

As Dr. Szasz (Selection 2) has mentioned, legal concepts are applied often in instances of major mental illness (few textbooks for

This report is part of a larger study, made possible by a grant from the Advisory Mental Health Committee of Midwestern State. By prior agreement, the state in which the study was conducted is not identified in publications. Published in *Social Problems*, 11, 401-413, Spring, 1964. Reprinted by permission of the author, the journal, *Social Problems*, and The Society for the Study of Social Problems.

* With the assistance of Daniel M. Culver.

beginning students make this point appropriately clear); sometimes the legalities play a determinative role in the fate of the "patient." One conclusion to draw from this paper by Scheff—of the University of California at Santa Barbara—is that the civil rights of people suspected of being psychotic are often denied because of the presumption of "illness." That pre-judgment also leads to decisions being made in a cavalier and untenable manner (confinement is confinement and a loss of freedom whether the place is called a prison or a mental hospital). As Hollingshead and Redlich (Selection 6) and Kleiner, Tuckman, and Lavell (Selection 5) have shown, it is poor people or those from the lower classes who are most likely to be the subjects of such victimization. Under these circumstances, "treatment" in the classical sense is of little moment.

Note carefully the assumptions which underlie these commitment practices—many of which stem from the "illness" notion. For a more thorough discussion than is contained in this paper see Dr. Scheff's book *Being Mentally Ill: A Sociological Theory* (Aldine).

Fortunately, a few states have begun to modify the laws and procedures which govern commitment. What are the laws governing commitment, and how are the procedures carried out in your state?

The case for making the societal reaction to deviance a major independent variable in studies of deviant behavior has been succinctly stated by Kitsuse:

> A sociological theory of deviance must focus specifically upon the interactions which not only define behaviors as deviant but also organize and activate the application of sanctions by individuals, groups, or agencies. For in modern society, the socially significant differentiation of deviants from the non-deviant population is increasingly contingent upon circumstances of situation, place, social and personal biography, and the bureaucratically organized activities of agencies of control.[1]

In the case of mental disorder, psychiatric diagnosis is one of the crucial steps which "organizes and activates" the societal reaction, since the state is legally empowered to segregate and isolate those persons whom psychiatrists find to be committable because of mental illness.

Recently, however, it has been argued that mental illness may be more usefully considered to be a social status than a disease, since the symptoms of mental illness are vaguely defined and widely distributed, and the definition of behavior as symptomatic of mental illness is usually dependent upon social rather than medical contingencies.[2] Furthermore, the

1 John I. Kitsuse, "Societal Reaction to Deviant Behavior: Problems of Theory and Method," *Social Problems*, 9 (Winter, 1962), pp. 247-257.

2 Edwin M. Lemert, *Social Pathology*, New York: McGraw-Hill, 1951; Erving Goffman, *Asylums*, Chicago: Aldine, 1962.

argument continues, the status of the mental patient is more often an ascribed status, with conditions for status entry external to the patient, than an achieved status with conditions for status entry dependent upon the patient's own behavior. According to this argument, the societal reaction is a fundamentally important variable in all stages of a deviant career.

The actual usefulness of a theory of mental disorder based on the societal reaction is largely an empirical question: to what extent is entry to the status of mental patient independent of the behavior or "condition" of the patient? The present paper will explore this question for one phase of the societal reaction: the legal screening of persons alleged to be mentally ill. This screening represents the official phase of the societal reaction, which occurs after the alleged deviance has been called to the attention of the community by a complainant. This report will make no reference to the initial deviance or other situation which resulted in the complaint, but will deal entirely with procedures used by the courts after the complaint has occurred.

The purpose of the description that follows is to determine the extent of uncertainty that exists concerning new patients' qualifications for involuntary confinement in a mental hospital, and the reactions of the courts to this type of uncertainty. The data presented here indicate that, in the face of uncertainty, there is a strong presumption of illness by the court and the court psychiatrists.[3] In the discussion that follows the presentation of findings, some of the causes, consequences and implications of the presumption of illness are suggested.

The data upon which this report is based were drawn from psychiatrists' ratings of a sample of patients newly admitted to the public mental hospitals in a Midwestern state, official court records, interviews with court officials and psychiatrists, and our observations of psychiatric examinations in four courts. The psychiatrists' ratings of new patients will be considered first.

In order to obtain a rough measure of the incoming patient's qualifications for involuntary confinement, a survey of newly admitted patients was conducted with the cooperation of the hospital psychiatrists. All psychiatrists who made admission examinations in the three large mental hospitals in the state filled out a questionnaire for the first ten consecutive patients they examined in the month of June, 1962. A total of 223 questionnaires were returned by the 25 admission psychiatrists. Although these returns do not constitute a probability sample of all new patients admitted

---

[3] For a more general discussion of the presumption of illness in medicine, and some of its possible causes and consequences, see the author's "Decision Rules, Types of Error and Their Consequences in Medical Diagnosis," *Behavioral Science*, 8 (April, 1963), pp. 97-107.

during the year, there were no obvious biases in the drawing of the sample. For this reason, this group of patients will be taken to be typical of the newly admitted patients in Midwestern State.

The two principal legal grounds for involuntary confinement in the United States are the police power of the state (the State's right to protect itself from dangerous persons) and *parens patriae* (the State's right to assist those persons who, because of their own incapacity, may not be able to assist themselves).[4] As a measure of the first ground, the potential dangerousness of the patient, the questionnaire contained this item: "In your opinion, if this patient were released at the present time, is it likely he would harm himself or others?" The psychiatrists were given six options, ranging from Very Likely to Very Unlikely. Their responses were: Very Likely, 5%; Likely, 4%; Somewhat Likely, 14%; Somewhat Unlikely, 20%; Unlikely, 37%; Very Unlikely, 18%. Three patients, or 1%, were not rated.

As a measure of the second ground, *parens patriae*, the questionnaire contained the item: "Based on your observations of the patient's behavior, his present degree of mental impairment is: None ———; Minimal ———; Mild ———; Moderate ———; Severe ———. The psychiatrists' responses were: None, 2%; Minimal, 12%; Mild, 25%; Moderate, 42%; Severe, 17%. Three patients, or 1%, were not rated.

To be clearly qualified for involuntary confinement, a patient should be rated as likely to harm self or others (Very Likely, Likely, or Somewhat Likely) and/or as Severely Mentally Impaired. However, voluntary patients should be excluded from this analysis, since the court is not required to assess their qualifications for confinement. Excluding the 59 voluntary admissions (26% of the sample), leaves a sample of 164 involuntary confined patients. Of these patients, 10 were rated as meeting both qualifications for involuntary confinement, 21 were rated as being severely mentally impaired, but not dangerous, 28 were rated as dangerous but not severely mentally impaired, and *102 were rated as not dangerous nor as severely mentally impaired*. [Italics added by Editors.] Three patients were not rated.

According to these ratings, there is considerable uncertainty connected with the screening of newly admitted involuntary patients in the state, since *a substantial majority (63%) of the patients did not clearly meet the statutory requirements for involuntary confinement*. [Italics added by Editors.] How does the agency responsible for assessing the qualifications for confinement, the court, react in the large numbers of cases involving uncertainty?

On the one hand, the legal rulings on this point by higher courts are

4 Hugh Allen Ross, "Commitment of the Mentally Ill: Problems of Law and Policy," *Michigan Law Review*, 57 (May, 1959), pp. 945-1018.

quite clear. They have repeatedly held that there should be a presumption
of sanity. The burden of proof of insanity is to be on the petitioners, there
must be a preponderance of evidence, and the evidence should be of a
"clear and unexceptionable" nature.[5]

On the other hand, existing studies suggest that there is a presumption
of illness by mental health officials. In a discussion of the "discrediting" of
patients by the hospital staff, based on observations at St. Elizabeth's
Hospital, Washington, D. C., Goffman states:

> [The patient's case record] is apparently not regularly used to record
> occasions when the patient showed capacity to cope honorably and
> effectively with difficult life situations. Nor is the case record typically
> used to provide a rough average or sampling of his past conduct.
> [Rather, it extracts] from his whole life course a list of those incidents
> that have or might have had "symptomatic" significance. . . . I think
> that most of the information gathered in case records is quite true,
> although it might seem also to be true that almost anyone's life course
> could yield up enough denigrating facts to provide grounds for the
> record's justification of commitment.[6]

Mechanic makes a similar statement in his discussion of two large
mental hospitals located in an urban area in California:

> In the crowded state or county hospitals, which is the most typical
> situation, the psychiatrist does not have sufficient time to make a very
> complete psychiatric diagnosis, nor do his psychiatric tools provide
> him with the equipment for an expeditious screening of the patient . . . .

> In the two mental hospitals studied over a period of three months, the
> investigator never observed a case where the psychiatrist advised the
> patient that he did not need treatment. Rather, all persons who ap-
> peared at the hospital were absorbed into the patient population re-
> gardless of their ability to function adequately outside the hospital.[7]

A comment by Brown suggests that it is a fairly general understanding
among mental health workers that state mental hospitals in the U. S.
accept all comers.[8]

Kutner, describing commitment procedures in Chicago in 1962, also
reports a strong presumption of illness by the staff of the Cook County
Mental Health Clinic:

[5] This is the typical phrasing in cases in the *Dicennial Legal Digest,* found under the
heading "Mental Illness."

[6] Goffman, *op. cit.,* pp. 155, 159.

[7] David Mechanic, "Some Factors in Identifying and Defining Mental Illness,"
Mental Hygiene, 46 (January, 1962), pp. 66-75.

[8] Esther Lucile Brown, *Newer Dimensions of Patient Care,* Part I, New York:
Russell Sage, 1961, p. 60, fn.

Certificates are signed as a matter of course by staff physicians after little or no examination . . . . The so-called examinations are made on and assembly-line basis, often being completed in two or three minutes, and never taking more than ten minutes. Although psychiatrists agree that it is practically impossible to determine a person's sanity on the basis of such a short and hurried interview, the doctors recommend confinement in 77% of the cases. It appears in practice that the alleged-mentally-ill is presumed to be insane and bears the burden of proving his sanity in the few minutes allotted to him. . . .[9]

These citations suggest that mental health officials handle uncertainty by presuming illness. To ascertain if the presumption of illness occurred in Midwestern State, intensive observations of screening procedures were conducted in the four courts with the largest volume of mental cases in the state. These courts were located in the two most populous cities in the state. Before giving the results of these observations, it is necessary to describe the steps in the legal procedures for hospitalization and commitment.

Steps in the Screening of Persons Alleged to be Mentally Ill

The process of screening can be visualized as containing five steps in Midwestern State:

1. The application for judicial inquiry, made by three citizens. This application is heard by deputy clerks in two of the courts (C and D), by a court reporter in the third court, and by a court commissioner in the fourth court.

2. The intake examination, conducted by a hospital psychiatrist.

3. The psychiatric examination, conducted by two psychiatrists appointed by the court.

4. The interview of the patient by the guardian *ad litem*, a lawyer appointed in three of the courts to represent the patient. (Court A did not use guardians *ad litem*.)

5. The judicial hearing, conducted by a judge.

These five steps take place roughly in the order listed, although in many cases (those cases designated as emergencies) step No. 2, the intake examination, may occur before step No. 1. Steps No. 1 and No. 2 usually take place on the same day or the day after hospitalization. Steps No. 3, No. 4, and No. 5 usually take place within a week of hospitalization. (In courts C and D, however, the judicial hearing is held only once a month.)

9 Luis Kutner, "The Illusion of Due Process in Commitment Proceedings," *Northwestern University Law Review,* 57 (Sept., 1962), pp. 383-399.

This series of steps would seem to provide ample opportunity for the presumption of health, and a thorough assessment, therefore, of the patient's qualifications for involuntary confinement, since there are five separate points at which discharge could occur. According to our findings, however, these procedures usually do not serve the function of screening out persons who do not meet statutory requirements. At most of these decision points, in most of the courts, retention of the patient in the hospital was virtually automatic. A notable exception to this pattern was found in one of the three state hospitals; this hospital attempted to use step No. 2, the intake examination, as a screening point to discharge patients that the superintendent described as "illegitimate," i.e., patients who do not qualify for involuntary confinement.[10] In the other two hospitals, however, this examination was perfunctory and virtually never resulted in a finding of health and a recommendation of discharge. In a similar manner, the other steps were largely ceremonial in character. For example, in court B, we observed twenty-two judicial hearings, all of which were conducted perfunctorily and with lightning rapidity. (The mean time of these hearings was 1.6 minutes.) The judge asked each patient two or three routine questions. Whatever the patient answered, however, the judge always ended the hearings and retained the patient in the hospital.

What appeared to be the key role in justifying these procedures was played by step No. 3, the examination by the court-appointed psychiatrists. In our informal discussions of screening with the judges and other court officials, these officials made it clear that although the statutes give the court the responsibility for the decision to confine or release persons alleged to be mentally ill, they would rarely if ever take the responsibility for releasing a mental patient without a medical recommendation to that effect. The question which is crucial, therefore, for the entire screening process is whether or not the court-appointed psychiatric examiners presume illness. The remainder of the paper will consider this question.

Our observations of 116 judicial hearings raised the question of the adequacy of the psychiatric examination. Eighty-six of the hearings failed to establish that the patients were "mentally ill" (according to the criteria stated by the judges in interviews).[11] Indeed, the behavior and responses

[10] Other exceptions occurred as follows: the deputy clerks in courts C and D appeared to exercise some discretion in turning away applications they considered improper or incomplete, at step No. 1; the judge in Court D appeared also to perform some screening at step No. 5. For further description of these exceptions see the author's "Social Conditions for Rationality: How Urban and Rural Courts Deal with the Mentally Ill," *American Behavioral Scientist*, 7 (March, 1964), pp. 21-24.

[11] In interviews with the judges, the following criteria were named: Appropriateness of behavior and speech, understanding of the situation, and orientation.

of 48 of the patients at the hearings seemed completely unexceptionable. Yet the psychiatric examiners had not recommended the release of a single one of these patients. Examining the court records of 80 additional cases, there was still not a single recommendation for release.

Although the recommendation for treatment of 196 out of 196 consecutive cases strongly suggests that the psychiatric examiners were presuming illness, particularly when we observed 48 of these patients to be responding appropriately, it is conceivable that this is not the case. The observer for this study was not a psychiatrist (he was a first year graduate student in social work) and it is possible that he could have missed evidence of disorder which a psychiatrist might have seen. It was therefore arranged for the observer to be present at a series of psychiatric examinations, in order to determine whether the examinations appeared to be merely formalities or whether, on the other hand, through careful examination and interrogation, the psychiatrists were able to establish illness even in patients whose appearance and responses were not obviously disordered. The observer was instructed to note the examiner's procedures, the criteria they appeared to use in arriving at their decision, and their reaction to uncertainty.

Each of the courts discussed here employs the services of a panel of physicians as medical examiners. The physicians are paid a flat fee of ten dollars per examination, and are usually assigned from three to five patients for each trip to the hospital. In court A, most of the examinations are performed by two psychiatrists, who went to the hospital once a week, seeing from five to ten patients a trip. In court B, C, and D, a panel of local physicians was used. These courts seek to arrange the examinations so that one of the examiners is a psychiatrist, the other a general practitioner. Court B has a list of four such pairs, and appoints each pair for a month at a time. Courts C and D have a similar list, apparently with some of the same names as court B.

To obtain physicians who were representative of the panel used in these courts, we arranged to observe the examinations of the two psychiatrists employed by court A, and one of the four pairs of physicians used in court B, one a psychiatrist, the other a general practitioner. We observed 13 examinations in court A and 13 examinations in court B. The judges in courts C and D refused to give us the names of the physicians on their panels, and we were unable to observe examinations in these courts. (The judge in court D stated that he did not want these physicians harassed in their work, since it was difficult to obtain their services even under the best of circumstances.) In addition to observing the examinations by four psychiatrists, three other psychiatrists used by these courts were interviewed.

The medical examiners followed two lines of questioning. One line was to inquire about the circumstances which led to the patient's hospitalization, the other was to ask standard questions to test the patient's orientation and his capacity for abstract thinking by asking him the date, the President, Governor, proverbs, and problems requiring arithmetic calculation. These questions were often asked very rapidly, and the patient was usually allowed only a very brief time to answer.

It should be noted that the psychiatrists in these courts had access to the patient's record (which usually contained the Application for Judicial Inquiry and the hospital chart notes on the patient's behavior), and that several of the psychiatrists stated that they almost always familiarized themselves with this record before making the examination. To the extent that they were familiar with the patient's circumstances from such outside information, it is possible that the psychiatrists were basing their diagnoses of illness less on the rapid and peremptory examination than on this other information. Although this was true to some extent, the importance of the record can easily be exaggerated, both because of the deficiencies in the typical record, and because the way it is usually utilized by the examiners.

The deficiencies of the typical record were easily discerned in the approximately one hundred applications and hospital charts which the author read. Both the applications and charts were extremely brief and sometimes garbled. Moreover, in some of the cases where the author and interviewer were familiar with the circumstances involved in the hospitalization, it was not clear that the complainant's testimony was any more accurate than the version presented by the patient. Often the original complaint was so paraphrased and condensed that the application seemed to have little meaning.

The attitude of the examiners toward the record was such that even in those cases where the record was ample, it often did not figure prominently in their decision. Disparaging remarks about the quality and usefulness of the record were made by several of the psychiatrists. One of the examiners was apologetic about his use of the record, giving us the impression that he thought that a good psychiatrist would not need to resort to any information outside his own personal examination of the patient. A casual attitude toward the record was openly displayed in 6 of the 26 examinations we observed. In these 6 examinations, the psychiatrist could not (or in 3 cases, did not bother to) locate the record and conducted the examination without it, with one psychiatrist making it a point of pride that he could easily diagnose most cases "blind."

In his observations of the examinations, the interviewer was instructed to rate how well the patient responded by noting his behavior during the interview, whether he answered the orientation and concept questions correctly, and whether he denied and explained the allegations which resulted in his hospitalization. If the patient's behavior during the interview obviously departed from conventional social standards (e.g., in one case the patient refused to speak), if he answered the orientation questions incorrectly, or if he did not deny and explain the petitioners' allegations, the case was rated as meeting the stautory requirements for hospitalization. Of the 26 examinations observed, eight were rated as Criteria Met.

If, on the other hand, the patient's behavior was appropriate, his answers correct, and he denied and explained the petitioners' allegations, the interviewer rated the case as not meeting the statutory criteria. Of the 26 cases, seven were rated as Criteria Not Met. Finally, if the examination was inconclusive, but the interviewer felt that more extensive investigation might have established that the criteria were met, he rated the cases as Criteria Possibly Met. Of the 26 examined, 11 were rated in this way. The interviewer's instructions were that whenever he was in doubt he should avoid using the rating Criteria Not Met.

Even giving the examiners the benefit of the doubt, the interviewer's ratings were that in a substantial majority of the cases he observed, the examination failed to establish that the statutory criteria were met. The relationship between the examiners' recommendations and the interviewer's ratings are shown in the following table.

TABLE 1   OBSERVER'S RATINGS AND EXAMINERS' RECOMMENDATIONS

Observer's Ratings		Criteria Met	Criteria Possibly Met	Criteria Not Met	Total
Examiners'	Commitment	7	9	2	18
Recommendations	30-day Observation	1	2	3	6
	Release	0	0	2	2
	Total	8	11	7	26

The interviewer's ratings suggest that the examinations established that the statutory criteria were met in only eight cases, but the examiners recommended that the patient be retained in the hospital in 24 cases, leaving 16 cases which the interviewer rated as uncertain, and in which retention was recommended by the examiners. The observer also rated the patient's expressed desires regarding staying in the hospital, and the time taken by the examination. The ratings of the patient's desire concerning staying or leaving the hospital were: Leave, 14 cases; Indifferent, 1 case; Stay, 9 cases; and Not Ascertained, 2 cases. In only one of the 14 cases in which the patient wished to leave was the interviewer's rating Criteria Met.

The interviews ranged in length from five minutes to 17 minutes, with the mean time being 10.2 minutes. Most of the interviews were hurried, with the questions of the examiners coming so rapidly that the examiner often interrupted the patient, or one examiner interrupted the other. All of the examiners seemed quite hurried. One psychiatrist, after stating in an interview (before we observed his examinations) that he usually took about thirty minutes, stated:

> It's not remunerative. I'm taking a hell of a cut. I can't spend 45 minutes with a patient. I don't have the time, it doesn't pay.

In the examinations that we observed, this physician actually spent 8, 10, 5, 8, 8, 7, 17, and 11 minutes with the patients, or an average of 9.2 minutes.

In these short time periods, it is virtually impossible for the examiner to extend his investigation beyond the standard orientation questions, and a short discussion of the circumstances which brought the patient to the hospital. In those cases where the patient answered the orientation questions correctly, behaved appropriately, and explained his presence at the hospital satisfactorily, the examiners did not attempt to assess the reliability of the petitioner's complaints, or to probe further into the patient's answers. Given the fact that in most of these instances the examiners were faced with borderline cases, that they took little time in the examinations, and that they usually recommended commitment, we can only conclude that their decisions were based largely on a presumption of illness. Supplementary observations reported by the interviewer support this conclusion.

After each examination, the observer asked the examiner to explain the criteria he used in arriving at his decision. The observer also had access to the examiner's official report, so that he could compare what the examiner said about the case with the record of what actually occurred during the interview. This supplementary information supports the conclusion that the examiner's decisions are based on the presumption of illness, and sheds light on the manner in which these decisions are reached:

1. The "evidence" upon which the examiners based their decision to retain often seemed arbitary.

2. In some cases, the decision to retain was made even when no evidence could be found.

3. Some of the psychiatrists' remarks suggest prejudgment of the cases.

4. Many of the examinations were characterized by carelessness and haste.

The first question, concerning the arbitrariness of the psychiatric evidence, will now be considered.

In the weighing of the patient's responses during the interview, the physician appeared not to give the patient credit for the large number of correct answers he gave. In the typical interview, the examiner might ask the patient fifteen or twenty questions: the date, time, place, who is President, Governor, etc., what is 11 x 10, 11 x 11, etc., explain "Don't put all your eggs in one basket," "A rolling stone gathers no moss," etc. The examiners appeared to feel that a wrong answer established lack of orientation, even when it was preceded by a series of correct answers. In other words, the examiners do not establish any standard score on the orientation questions, which would give an objective picture of the degree to which the patient answered the questions correctly, but seem at times to search until they find an incorrect answer.

For those questions which were answered incorrectly, it was not always clear whether the incorrect answers were due to the patient's "mental illness," or to the time pressure in the interview, the patient's lack of education, or other causes. Some of the questions used to establish orientation were sufficiently difficult that persons not mentally ill might have difficulty with them. Thus one of the examiners always asked, in a rapid-fire manner: What year is it? What year was it seven years ago? Seventeen years before that?" etc. Only two of the five patients who were asked this series of questions were able to answer it correctly. However, it is a moot question whether a higher percentage of persons in a household survey would be able to do any better. To my knowledge, none of the orientation questions that are used have been checked in a normal population.

Finally, the interpretations of some of the evidence as showing mental illness seemed capricious. Thus one of the patients, when asked, "In what way are a banana, an orange, and an apple alike?" answered, "They are all something to eat." This answer was used by the examiner in explaining his recommendation to commit. The observer had noted that the patient's behavior and responses seemed appropriate and asked why the recommendation to commit had been made. The doctor stated that her behavior had been bizarre (possibly referring to her alleged promiscuity), her affect inappropriate ("When she talked about being pregnant, it was without feeling,") and with regard to the question above:

> She wasn't able to say a banana and an orange were fruit. She couldn't take it one step further, she had to say it was something to eat.

In other words, this psychiatrist was suggesting that the patient manifested concreteness in her thinking, which is held to be a symptom of mental illness. Yet in her other answers to classification questions, and to proverb interpretations, concreteness was not apparent, suggesting that the examiner's application of this test was arbitrary. In another case, the physician stated that he thought the patient was suspicious and distrustful, because he had asked about the possibility of being represented by counsel at the judicial hearing. The observer felt that these and other similar interpretations might possibly be correct, but that further investigation of the supposedly incorrect responses would be needed to establish that they were manifestations of disorientation.

In several cases where even this type of evidence was not available, the examiners still recommended retention in the hospital. Thus, one examiner, employed by court A, stated that he had recommended 30-day observation for a patient whom he had thought *not* to be mentally ill, on the grounds that the patient, a young man, could not get along with his parents, and "might get into trouble." This examiner went on to say:

> We always take the conservative side. [Commitment or observation] Suppose a patient should commit suicide. We always make the conservative decision. I had rather play it safe. There's no harm in doing it that way.

It appeared to the observer that "playing safe" meant that even in those cases where the examination established nothing, the psychiatrists did not consider recommending release. Thus in one case the examination had established that the patient had a very good memory, was oriented and spoke quietly and seriously. The observer recorded his discussion with the physician after the examination as follows:

> When the doctor told me he was recommending commitment for this patient too (he had also recommended commitment in the two examinations held earlier that day) he laughed because he could see what my next question was going to be. He said, "I already recommended the release of two patients this month." This sounded like it was the maximum amount the way he said it.

Apparently this examiner felt that he had a very limited quota on the number of patients he could recommend for release (less than two percent of those examined).

The language used by these physicians tends to intimate that mental illness was found, even when reporting the opposite. Thus in one case the recommendation stated: "No gross evidence of delusions or hallucinations." This statement is misleading, since not only was there no gross evidence, there was not any evidence, not even the slightest suggestion of delusions or hallucinations, brought out by the interview.

These remarks suggest that the examiners prejudge the cases they examine. Several further comments indicate prejudgment. One physician stated that he thought that most crimes of violence were committed by patients released too early from mental hospitals. (This is an erroneous belief.)[12] He went on to say that he thought that all mental patients should be kept in the hospital at least three months, indicating prejudgment concerning his examinations. Another physician, after a very short interview (8 minutes), told the observer:

> On the schizophrenics, I don't bother asking them more questions when I can see they're schizophrenic because *I know what they are going to say*. You could talk to them another half hour and not learn any more.

Another physician, finally, contrasted cases in which the patient's family or others initiated hospitalization ("petition cases," the great majority of cases) with those cases intiated by the court:

> The petition cases are pretty *automatic*. If the patient's own family wants to get rid of him you know there is something wrong.

The lack of care which characterized the examinations is evident in the forms on which the examiners make their recommendations. On most of these forms, whole sections have been left unanswered. Others are answered in a peremptory and uninformative way. For example, in the section entitled Physical Examination, the question is asked: "Have you made a physical examination of the patient? State fully what is the present physical condition."; a typical answer is "Yes. Fair. ," or, "Is apparently in good health." Since in none of the examinations we observed was the patient actually physically examined, these answers appear to be mere guesses. One of the examiners used regularly in court B, to the question "On what subject or in what way is derangement now manifested?" always wrote in "Is mentally ill." The omissions, and the almost flippant brevity of these forms, together with the arbitrariness, lack of evidence, and prejudicial character of the examinations, discussed above, all support the observer's conclusion that, except in very unusual cases, the psychiatric examiner's recommendation to retain the patient is virtually automatic.

Lest it be thought that these results are unique to a particularly backward Midwestern State, it should be pointed out that this state is noted for its progressive psychiatric practices. It will be recalled that a number of the psychiatrists employed by the court as examiners had finished

---

[12] The rate of crimes of violence, or any crime, appears to be less among ex-mental patients than in the general population. Henry Brill and Benjamin Maltzberg, "Statistical Report Based on the Arrest Record of 5354 Ex-patients Released from New York State Mental Hospitals During the Period 1946-48." Mimeo available from the authors; Louis H. Cohen and Henry Freeman, "How Dangerous to the Community Are State Hospital Patients?," *Connecticut State Medical Journal*, 9 (Sept., 1945), pp. 697-700; Donald W. Hastings, "Follow-up Results in Psychiatric Illness," *Amer. Journal of Psychiatry*, 118 (June, 1962), pp. 1078-1086.

their psychiatric residencies, which is not always the case in many other states. A still common practice in other states is to employ, as members of the "Lunacy Panel," partially retired physicians with no psychiatric training whatever. This was the case in Stockton, California, in 1959, where the author observed hundreds of hearings at which these physicians were present. It may be indicative of some of the larger issues underlying the question of civil commitment that, in these hearings, the physicians played very little part; the judge controlled the questioning of the relatives and patients, and the hearings were often a model of impartial and thorough investigation.

Discussion

Ratings of the qualifications for involuntary confinement of patients newly admitted to the public mental hospitals in a Midwestern State, together with observations of judicial hearings and psychiatric examinations by the observer connected with the present study, both suggest that the decision as to the mental condition of a majority of the patients is an uncertain one. The fact that the courts seldom release patients, and the perfunctory manner in which the legal and medical procedures are carried out, suggest that the judicial decision to retain patients in the hospital for treatment is routine and largely based on the presumption of illness. Three reasons for this presumption will be discussed: financial, ideological, and political.

Our discussions with the examiners indicated that one reason that they perform biased "examinations" is that their rate of pay is determined by the length of time spent with the patient. In recommending retention, the examiners are refraining from interrupting the hospitalization and commitment procedures already in progress, and thereby allowing someone else, usually the hospital, to make the effective decision to release or commit. In order to recommend release, however, they would have to build a case showing why these procedures should be interrupted. Building such a case would take much more time than is presently expended by the examiners, thereby reducing their rate of pay.

A more fundamental reason for the presumption of illness by the examiners, and perhaps the reason why this practice is allowed by the courts, is the interpretation of current psychiatric doctrine by the examiners and court officials. These officials make a number of assumptions, which are now thought to be of doubtful validity:

1. The condition of mentally ill persons deteriorates rapidly without psychiatric assistance.
2. Effective psychiatric treatments exist for most mental illnesses.

3. Unlike surgery, there are no risks involved in involuntary psychiatric treatment; it either helps or is neutral, it can't hurt.

4. Exposing a prospective mental patient to questioning, cross-examination, and other screening procedures exposes him to the unnecessary stigma of trial-like procedures, and may do further damage to his mental condition.

5. There is an element of danger to self or others in most mental illness. It is better to risk unnecessary hospitalization than the harm the patient might do himself or others.

Many psychiatrists and others now argue that none of these assumptions are necessarily correct.

1. The assumption that psychiatric disorders usually get worse without treatment rests on very little other than evidence of an anecdotal character. There is just as much evidence that most acute psychological and emotional upsets are self-terminating.[13]

2. It is still not clear, according to systematic studies evaluating psychotherapy, drugs, etc., that most psychiatric interventions are any more effective, on the average, than no treatment at all.[14]

3. There is very good evidence that involuntary hospitalization and social isolation may affect the patient's life: his job, his family affairs, etc. There is some evidence that too hasty exposure to psychiatric treatment may convince the patient that he is "sick," prolonging what might have been an otherwise transitory episode.[15]

4. This assumption is correct, as far as it goes. But it is misleading because it fails to consider what occurs when the patient who does not wish to be hospitalized is forcibly treated. Such patients often become extremely indignant and angry, particularly in the case, as often happens, when they are deceived into coming to the hospital on some pretext.

5. The element of danger is usually exaggerated both in amount and

---

[13] For a review of epidemiological studies of mental disorder see Richard J. Plunkett and John E. Gordon, *Epidemiology and Mental Illness*. New York: Basic Books, 1960. Most of these studies suggest that at any given point in time, psychiatrists find a substantial proportion of persons in normal populations to be "mentally ill." One interpretation of this finding is that much of the deviance detected in these studies is self-limiting.

[14] For an assessment of the evidence regarding the effectiveness of electroshock, drugs, psychotherapy, and other psychiatric treatments, see H. J. Eysenck, *Handbook of Abnormal Psychology*, New York: Basic Books, 1961, Part III.

[15] For examples from military psychiatry, see Albert J. Glass, "Psychotherapy in the Combat Zone," in *Symposium on Stress*, Washington, D. C., Army Medical Service Graduate School, 1953, and B. L. Bushard, "The U. S. Army's Mental Hygiene Consultation Service," in *Symposium on Preventive and Social Psychiatry*, 15-17 (April, 1957), Washington, D. C.: Walter Reed Army Institute of Research, pp. 431-43. For a discussion of esesntially the same problem in the context of a civilian mental hospital, cf. Kai T. Erikson, "Patient Role and Social Uncertainty—A Dilemma of the Mentally Ill," *Psychiatry*, 20 (August, 1957), pp. 263-275. (See Selection 20)

degree. In the psychiatric survey of new patients in state mental hospitals, danger to self or others was mentioned in about a fourth of the cases. Furthermore, in those cases where danger is mentioned, it is not always clear that the risks involved are greater than those encountered in ordinary social life. This issue has been discussed by Ross, an attorney:

> A truck driver with a mild neurosis who is "accident prone" is probably a greater danger to society than most psychotics; yet, he will not be committed for treatment, even if he would be benefited. The community expects a certain amount of dangerous activity. I suspect that as a class, drinking drivers are a greater danger than the mentally ill, and yet the drivers are tolerated or punished with small fines rather than indeterminate imprisonment.[16]

From our observations of the medical examinations and other commitment procedures, we formed a very strong impression that the doctrines of danger to self or others, early treatment, and the avoidance of stigma were invoked partly because the officials believed them to be true, and partly because they provided convenient justification for a pre-existing policy of summary action, minimal investigation, avoidance of responsibility and, after the patient is in the hospital, indecisiveness and delay.

The policy of presuming illness is probably both cause and effect of political pressure on the court from the community. The judge, an elected official, runs the risk of being more heavily penalized for erroneously releasing than for erroneously retaining patients. Since the judge personally appoints the panel of psychiatrists to serve as examiners, he can easily transmit the community pressure to them, by failing to reappoint a psychiatrist whose examinations were inconveniently thorough.

Some of the implications of these findings for the sociology of deviant behavior will be briefly summarized. The discussion above, of the reasons that the psychiatrists tend to presume illness, suggests that the motivations of the key decision-makers in the screening process may be significant in determining the extent and direction of the societal reaction. In the case of psychiatric screening of persons alleged to be mentally ill, the social differentiation of the deviant from the non-deviant population appears to be materially affected by the financial, ideological, and political position of the psychiatrists, who are in this instance the key agents of social control.

Under these circumstances, the character of the societal reaction appears to undergo a marked change from the pattern of denial which occurs in the community. The official societal reaction appears to reverse the presumption of normality reported by the Cummings as a characteristic of informal societal reaction, and instead exaggerates both the amount and

[16] Ross, *op. cit.*, p. 962.

degree of deviance.[17] Thus, one extremely important contingency influencing the severity of the societal reaction may be whether or not the original deviance comes to official notice. This paper suggests that in the area of mental disorder, perhaps in contrast to other areas of deviant behavior, if the official societal reaction is invoked, for whatever reason, social differention of the deviant from the non-deviant population will usually occur.

CONCLUSION

This paper has described the screening of patients who were admitted to public mental hospitals in early June, 1962, in a Midwestern State. The data presented here suggest that the screening is usually perfunctory, and that in the crucial screening examination by the court-appointed psychiatrists, there is a presumption of illness. Since most court decisions appear to hinge on the recommendation of these psychiatrists, there appears to be a large element of status ascription in the official societal reaction to persons alleged to be mentally ill, as exemplified by the court's actions. This finding points to the importance of lay definitions of mental illness in the community, since the "diagnosis" of mental illness by laymen in the community initiates the official societal reaction, and to the necessity of analyzing social processes connected with the recognition and reaction to the deviant behavior that is called mental illness in our society.

[17] Elaine Cumming and John Cumming, *Closed Ranks,* Cambridge, Mass.: Harvard University Press, 1957, p. 102; for further discussion of the bipolarization of the societal reaction into denial and labeling, see the author's "The Role of the Mentally Ill and the Dynamics of Mental Disorder: A Research Framework," *Sociometry,* 26 (December, 1963), pp. 436-453.

4.   "Mental Illness" or Interpersonal Behavior?

Henry Adams

Dr. Adams, who is Chief Psychologist of the Alcoholism and Drug Addiction Division of the Area Community Mental Health Center in Washington, D.C., asserts that the label "mental illness" is applied to patterns of maladaptive or inappropriate *conduct* rather than to any altered body state. In turn, the inappropriate conduct is the result of faulty or inadequate *social learning experiences.*

American Psychologist; 19:191-197, #3, March, 1964. Reprinted by permission of the author and the American Psychological Association. This is a revised version of a paper presented at the Seventieth Annual Convention of the American Psychological Association on a symposium entitled: " 'Mental Illness': Is There Any Such Thing?" St. Louis, Missouri, August 30, 1962.

The past 100 years or so have been characterized by an *impersonal* approach to personality; this approach to "mental illness" has served to obscure rather than to communicate. The survey of "moral therapy" of 175 years ago is especially interesting and cogent.

Dr. Adams' position is that "mental illness" results from two types of antecedent conditions: 1) inadequate opportunities for the learning of necessary social skills, and 2) the appearance of difficult or problematic social situations for which the individual lacks effective solutions, skills or previously learned techniques. Treatment, of course, must provide opportunities for the acquisition of new social skills.

There is no such thing as a "mental illness" in any significantly meaningful sense. In medicine the term "illness" is used in a literal, nonfigurative way to denote an undesirable alteration or change away from optimal levels of organic bodily functioning. But the term "mental illness" is applied to various patterns of behavior considered maladaptive or inappropriate by implicit psychological and social standards (Szasz, 1960, 1961).

The concept of a functional mental illness is a *verbal analogy*. While it is appropriate to speak of neurological disorders as true organic illnesses of the nervous system, comparable to organic illnesses involving the circulatory or digestive system, it seems questionable to apply the term "illness" to arbitrarily defined patterns of behavior, particularly when there may be no evidence of any physiological malfunctioning. The plain fact is that the term "mental illness" is applied in an indiscriminate way to a motley collection of interpersonal behavior patterns. Often there is no positive evidence whatever of any physiological or organic malfunctioning, as in the so-called "functional disorders." Actually, organic physical illnesses and the functional types of mental illnesses are defined by *different kinds of criteria,* and they are modified or ameliorated ("treated" or "cured") by *fundamentally different procedures.*

Failure to clarify these distinctions has had unfortunate consequences. Efforts toward understanding and effective alleviation have long been hampered by the semantic confusion which results when the word "illness" is used to denote both physical disease entities and maladaptive patterns of interpersonal behavior. This ambiguous usage has perpetuated the glib fallacy that mental and physical illnesses are the same thing. It has interfered with the understanding of fundamental psychological phenomena and made for an ineffectual and often harmful approach to some of the most serious recurring problems in human relationships.

This semantic confusion is an important fact in the history of psychiatry since 1800. A number of studies have been published in recent years on the "moral therapy" of the early nineteenth century (Bockoven, 1956, 1957; Brown, 1960; Joint Commission on Mental Illness and Health,

1961; Rees, 1957). These studies all agree that the results of moral therapy (at a time when physical medicine was in a relatively primitive stage of development) compare favorably with the very best mental-hospital programs of today. "Moral therapy" was essentially a program of planned psychological retraining within a positive, sympathetic social milieu.

Moral therapy had its inception near the end of the eighteenth century under the leadership of Pinel, Tuke, Chiarugi, and others. The word "moral" was used at that time in a sense comparable to the contemporary usage of the words "psychological" or "interpersonal." During that era more attention began to be given to

> social and environmental factors in the causation of mental illness, and it was found that organic changes in the brain were rather rare at post mortem examinations. The insane came to be regarded as normal people who had lost their reason as a result of having been exposed to severe psychological and social stresses. These stresses were called the moral causes of insanity, and moral treatment aimed at relieving the patient by friendly association, discussion of his difficulties, and the daily pursuit of purposeful activity; in other words, social therapy, individual therapy, and occupational therapy. Moral treatment reached its zenith in the years between 1820 and 1860. The results of treatment during that period were outstandingly good and bear comparison with some of the figures obtainable today. For example, in all patients admitted to the York Retreat [in England] within three months of the onset of illness—between the years 1796 and 1861 the discharge rate was 71%. . . . These are truly remarkable figures, especially when one takes into consideration that a substantial portion of the patients must have been general paralytics, for which there was at that time no effective treatment [Rees, 1957, pp. 306-307].

Cope and Packard (1841) reported on the results of moral treatment in state institutions in the United States. They mentioned institutions in nine states and observed that with moral treatment "ninety per cent of the recent cases can be restored so as to be able to maintain themselves and family." Bockoven (1956) found comparable figures from private institutions utilizing moral treatment. Beginning in the 1820's, the Hartford Retreat reported recoveries in over 90% of all patients admitted with mental illnesses of less than a year's duration. Bockoven also supplied statistics extending from 1833 to 1950 on discharges from the Worcester State Hospital in Massachusetts. During the 1833-1852 period, when moral therapy was being practiced, 71% of all patients ill less than 1 year when admitted were discharged as recovered or improved. Patients discharged during the years 1833-1846 were later followed up until 1893, and it was found that half suffered no recurrences.

Despite ample evidence of its effectiveness, moral therapy was quietly abandoned in American and British mental institutions after 1860 and later almost completely forgotten. The consequences are illustrated by Bockoven's (1956) data from the Worcester State Hospital, showing that recovery rates declined over 90% after 1860, reaching their lowest point between 1923 and 1950 (pp. 292-293). Certainly, one may raise legitimate questions about these old statistics and the validity of conclusions drawn from them. Nevertheless, every recent study on the subject of moral therapy agreed that the results have not been surpassed during the contemporary period, despite all the advances made by physical medicine since 1860.

One important reason for its abandonment was that moral therapy was supposed to be a form of treatment for mental illnesses. But as physical medicine developed during the late nineteenth century, it was thought that the types of procedures found effective with physical illnesses could be carried over unaltered into the treatment of mental illnesses. Since both kinds of phenomena were defined as illnesses this notion sounded reasonable, so long as no one inquired seriously into the possibility that there might be an error in semantics.

An additional factor in the abandonment of moral therapy was that it was regarded as "unscientific" according to the scientific and medical doctrines which developed in the intellectual climate of the last half of the nineteenth century. These doctrines held that true science is impersonal and concerned solely with material things, that feeling, beauty, and moral values are mere illusions in a world of fact, that the human will is powerless against the laws of nature and society, and that every observable phenomenon is reducible to the motions of material particles.[1] Since psychiatric patients were regarded as suffering from a medical condition defined as mental illness, it was held that treatment procedures had to rest on a scientific physical basis, as conceptualized by a mechanistic, materialistic view which held that things rather than persons were the only reality. In keeping with this tough-minded impersonal dogma, the psychological sensitivity and insight which were major factors in the success of moral therapy were dismissed from serious consideration as mystical, sentimental, and unscientific. The treatment of hospitalized psychiatric patients became cold, distant, and unfeeling, consistent with a Zeitgeist of impersonal scientism. Discharge and recovery rates, which had been high wherever moral therapy programs were in effect, declined steadily after 1860. In time, falling discharge rates led to the piling up of

---

[1] The doctrines of nineteenth-century impersonal scientism have been more fully described elsewhere by Barzun (1958). He analyzes the modes of thought inherited from that era and shows how strongly they still influence contemporary thinking. Bockoven (1956) notes that the widespread acceptance of these doctrines in both popular and scientific circles contributed to the abandonment of moral therapy after 1860.

chronic patients in hospitals, attitudes of hopelessness, and a growing belief in the "incurability" of insanity. This pessimistic belief had become widespread by 1900, despite the fact that 70% to 90% recovery rates had been commonplace in 1840 during the moral therapy era.

As recovery rates fell and the treatment of hospitalized patients became more detached and impersonal, leaders in psychiatry turned to the laboratory hoping to find a scientific cure for mental illness. They were persuaded that the answers lay in the discovery and identification of physical disease entities. Physicalistic and mechanistic concepts of mental illness were adopted by analogy with physical medicine, while efforts to understand psychiatric patients as individual persons were largely discontinued (Zilboorg, 1941). Patients were no longer thought of as human beings with problems in human relationships, but as "cases." This impersonal approach led one of the leading American psychiatrists of the 1880's to state in all sincerity that the insane do not suffer unhappiness, and that depressed patients go through the motions of acting sad in a machinelike fashion without feeling genuine sadness (Bockoven, 1956). As Brown's (1960) data indicate, changing attitudes of the medical profession at different historical periods have played a great part in changing rates of discharge and chronicity among hospitalized patients.

The great irony is that after 100 years these laboratory-centered physically oriented research efforts have failed to produce techniques for the "treatment" and "cure" of functional personality disorders significantly more effective than the best techniques of 1840. Actually, the most progressive contemporary mental-hospital programs are those which have revived practices much like those generally prevalent during the moral-therapy era (Greenblatt, York, & Brown, 1955; Rees, 1957).

THE IMPERSONAL APPROACH TO PERSONALITY

The theoretical concepts most widely used in the mental-health professions today consist largely of misleading analogies, metaphors, and figures of speech. These sonorous but inappropriate terms have made for confusion, trained incapacities, and intellectual stagnation. The Joint Commission on Mental Illness and Health (1961) has commented on this stagnation with the observation that "twentieth-century psychiatry can add little" to Pinel's principles for the moral treatment of psychotics, which were first published in 1801,

> except to convert them into modern terminological dress, contribute more systematic thought to the significance of various symptoms, intensify the doctor-patient relationship through scientific knowledge of

psychological mechanisms, treat the patient as a member of a social group which expects him to behave in accepted ways, and specify that moral treatment has been subject to an incredible amount of distortion and misinterpretation . . . [pp. 29-30].

Similarly, psychotherapy in essentially its present-day form was described by Reil in a book published in the year 1803 (Harms, 1957c). Almost every important issue in contemporary clinical psychology was discussed at length by leaders of the moral-therapy movement between 1790 and 1860 (Harms, 1957a, 1957b, 1957c; Roback, 1961).

Much of the terminology now used in contemporary psychology developed in an intellectual climate of impersonal scientism quite different in its basic outlook from the humanitarianism of the moral-therapy era. Psychology first arose as a separate independent science during the 1870's and 1880's. Reflecting the predominant spirit of their times, the early founders of experimental psychology were not concerned with the systematic understanding of human problems and personal relationships. Instead, they imitated the outward appearances and procedures of the physical and biological sciences, hoping that they too might thus be regarded as true scientists. They felt that in order to be scientifically respectable they had to study man impersonally, using techniques, assumptions, and conceptual approaches much like those of the physical and biological sciences. For example, the doctrine of determinism was carried over from the physical sciences without any empirical evidence to show that it was appropriate in explaining human conduct.

The impersonal approach adopted in the late nineteenth century is reflected in the conceptual language of psychology today. These concepts center around words borrowed from nonpsychological fields such as medicine, physics, mechanical engineering, biology, and electronics. This point is best illustrated by listing some verbal analogies commonly used in psychology. All the examples listed below appeared in psychological or psychiatric journals, or in books written for professional readers:

1. *Pseudomedical analogies:* mental illness, mental health, mental hygiene, prophylaxis, diagnosis, pathology, prognosis, etiology, therapy, treatment, cure, trauma, nosology, catharsis, syndrome, neurosis, psychosis, psychopathy, sick

2. *Pseudophysical and pseudoengineering analogies:* motor apparatus, dynamics, reaction potential, valences, field forces, psychic energy, power system, energy transformation, tension, stress, drive, mechanism, dynamogenesis, adjustment, reinforcing machine

3. *Pseudobiological analogies:* organism, homeostasis, phenotypic, genotypic, polymorphous, ontogenetic

4. *Pseudoelectronic analogies:* input, output, amplitude, radar, circuit, feedback, scanning, encoding, signals, charge, discharge, servomechanism

5. *Pseudogenitourinary and pseudogastrointestinal (i.e., psychoanalytic) analogies:* urethral character, phallic character, castration, oral optimism, anal submission, vaginal libido organization, anal-expulsive expression

Such analogies implicitly suggest that human behavior is *just like* the events observed in the nonpsychological sciences from which these words were borrowed. In using such terminology a false assumption is unwittingly made (but rarely recognized) that the *psychological phenomena* to which these terms are applied are therefore just like the *nonpsychological phenomena* where the terms originated. It is taken as *having already been decided* that these words are suitable for labeling and describing human behavior. The actions of living persons are thus conceptualized in the language of impersonal things and processes. Having accepted this glib semantic juggling, it is then quite easy to coin confusing, misleading slogans such as "mental illness is just like any other illness."

What is "Mental Illness"?

What is the phenomenon to which the label "mental illness" is applied? It is applied to arbitrarily designated types of maladaptive interpersonal behavior, often accompanied by reports of subjective discomfort, unsatisfying human relationships, and social rejection.

Explicit distinctions must be made between these behavioral phenomena and illnesses of the body. Physical illnesses (including neurological disorders) are not in themselves patterns of interaction with other persons. They are disturbances in the organic functions of the body. So far as immediate experience is concerned, a bodily illness such as a cold, fever, or pneumonia is an abnormal, usually unpleasant, subjective condition which *happens to* the individual person. It is not a direct overt manifestation of his characteristic patterns of interacting with others.

But, in cases where the term "mental illness" is used and no organic pathology is in evidence, the term refers to some arbitrarily defined pattern of conduct, with "symptoms" of a psychosocial rather than a medical nature. Any effective program directed toward "cure" must consequently provide opportunities for learning new, more adaptive patterns. It should be remembered that the learning process is a normal function of the nervous system, regardless of the nature of the material being learned, be it the subject of medicine, playing a musical instrument, or new social skills.

A COMPREHENSIVE APPROACH TO INTERPERSONAL BEHAVIOR

Mental illness is a phenomenon involving interpersonal behavior, not a health or medical problem. Programs of alleviation and prevention must therefore rest upon a systematic understanding of interpersonal conduct. A considerable body of recent research in this area suggests that the basic dimensions are surprisingly simple. The supposed complexity of personality and interaction between persons has been shown to be a purely semantic, verbal complexity, rather than a real complexity in actual fact.

These empirical studies have three distinguishing features: (*a*) The basic observations involve interpersonal actions. To be more explicit, the observations are focused on the acts of *persons* interacting with other *persons*, rather than organisms, psychobiological units, dynamic systems, or other impersonal abstractions. (*b*) The observers are concerned not with superficial stylistic features, but with the *content* of the interpersonal acts themselves. Content variables are to be contrasted with formalistic or stylistic variables, such as percentage of adjectives, manner of speaking, speed of tapping, etc. "Content" refers to *what* the individual person is doing or communicating to others by word and deed. (*c*) The investigators aim for *comprehensiveness*, classifying every act systematically in relation to every other.

Most of these studies have dispensed with terminology not meaningfully related to observable conduct. If behavior can be systematically described in *behavioral* terms, there is no need for the confusing nonpsychological analogies and metaphors which have long plagued the mental-health professions. It becomes unnecessary to borrow words from medicine, engineering, or electronics to describe human relationships. This approach makes it possible to clarify fundamental principles which have long been concealed by inappropriate, misleading jargon.

The results of these studies indicate that all interpersonal behavior, both adaptive ("healthy" or "normal") and maladaptive ("sick" or "abnormal"), can be meaningfully categorized within one systematic frame of reference. In a review of these studies, Foa (1961) was impressed by the "strong convergence" of thinking and results obtained in research on interpersonal interaction, since the investigators "proceeded from different research traditions, studied different types of groups . . . and, apparently, followed independent lines of design and analysis. The convergence is toward a simple ordered structure for the organization of interpersonal behavior." Foa suggested that the observations can be ordered into a simple comprehensive framework "that accounts for the empirical interrelations in a parsimonious and meaningful manner." The findings "suggest a circumplex structure around the two orthogonal axes of Dominance-Submission and Affection-Hostility."

Let us examine these two axes or dimensions in more detail. One pole of the Dominance-Submission axis is defined by acts of self-confident, assertive leadership and achievement in the face of obstacles. At the opposite pole are acts of passivity, submissiveness, and acquiescence. This dimension is of course a continuum, with most acts falling midway between extremes. The Affection-Hostility dimension reflects variations in the degree of positive or negative effect manifested toward others. The positive extreme describes warm, friendly, kind, affiliative acts, while the negative extreme describes hostile, critical, angry, disaffiliative acts.

Foa suggests that "an interpersonal act is an attempt to establish the emotional relationship of the actor toward himself and toward the other person," and that "the same act states the position of the actor toward the self and toward the other. . . ." Each type of behavior is thus meaningful toward the self and the other person. The Dominance-Submission axis defines the degree of acceptance or rejection of self, while the Affection-Hostility axis defines the degree of acceptance or rejection of the other. An interpersonal act may be regarded as the Cartesian product of these two sets of values.

The basic framework systematized by this two-dimensional structure has been described repeatedly ever since the time of Hippocrates. If there are only two dimensions of variation in the content of interpersonal acts, and the individual's personality is identified by the relative frequency, intensity, and nature of his acts, we have a simple but comprehensive basis for categorizing all personality types. Classification above and below the mean of these two axes would give four categories which correspond roughly to the traditional four temperaments, as they have been delineated by Hippocrates, Galen, Kant, Wundt, Höffding, Herbart, Külpe, Ebbinghaus, Klages, and Pavlov (Allport, 1961). Thus, persons with the "sanguine" temperament would show behavior which falls above the mean on both dimensions. Such persons typically show active leadership, optimism, and assertiveness, coupled with friendly acceptance of others. Likewise, the other three groups correspond to the traditional choleric, melancholic, and phlegmatic temperaments.

Freud has alluded to these dimensions in his writings (Leary, 1957, pp. 71-72). He has delineated a love-hate, sex-aggression, libido-mortido, or Eros-Thanatos polarity, which is comparable to the Affection-Hostility dimension. He also refers to power or domination in social interaction, analogous to Foa's Dominance-Submission dimension. This two-dimensional structure has appeared in the theories of Parsons, Merton, and Stagner (Leary, 1957, pp. 73-74). It has been used with impressive results in the coaction-compass analysis of the Rorschach (Gottlieb & Parsons, 1960; Lodge & Gibson, 1953) and in scoring and interpreting the TAT (Leary, 1956, 1957).

These dimensions recur in factor-analytic studies of the MMPI. Welsh (1956) reviewed the results of 11 analyses of the MMPI and found consistent agreement as to the first two factors but little agreement as to any additional factors. He developed two special scales, A and R, as measures of these factors. For example, subjects scoring high on A tend to agree with items expressing obsessional thinking, negative emotional tone, pessimism, personal sensitivity, and malignant mentation. Such items express attitudes typical of the "melancholic temperament" as depicted for many centuries. High A scorers would fall below the mean on both dimensions. In their overt behavior they show passivity and negative effect toward themselves and others (Dahlstrom & Welsh, 1960).

Jackson and Messick (1961) investigated response style on the MMPI and found that most of the variance was due to two response-set factors. One was an acquiescence factor like Foa's Dominance-Submission dimension. The other was a factor of social desirability, which is essentially the same as the Affection-Hostility dimension, a similarity which may not be recognized immediately. But it has been found that individuals who respond to personality questionnaires in socially desirable directions typically behave in bland, friendly, conventional ways, while those responding in the opposite fashion tend to be blunt, outspoken, critical of conventional standards, and uninhibited in the presence of others. Jackson and Messick noted that the test vectors emerging from their analysis of the MMPI tended toward a circular arrangement, like the circumplex structure described by Foa.

If the response to each item on the MMPI is viewed as a separate interpersonal communication, the convergences between MMPI studies and direct behavioral observations are not surprising. These convergences are all the more significant since the MMPI was developed to facilitate psychiatric diagnosis. The clinical scales of the MMPI were initially validated against Kraepelinian disease-entity diagnostic criteria. The results of these MMPI factor-analytic studies imply that the Kraepelinian labels presently employed in psychiatric diagnosis are nonexistent verbal abstractions.

A factor analysis of rating scales and questionnaires by Goldman-Eisler (1953) tested certain hypotheses drawn from psychoanalytic theory. Two orthogonal factors emerged, the first being a factor of "oral" optimism versus "oral" pessimism. Oral optimists show the same traits of active, friendly, assertiveness as the sanguine temperament, while oral pessimists show the contrasting patterns of the melancholic temperament. The second factor was interpreted as Impatience-Aggression-Autonomy versus Deliberation-Conservatism-Dependence. The traits of impatience, aggression, and autonomy are analogous to the hostile dominance of the choleric temperament, while deliberation, conservatism, and dependence describe the affectionate submissiveness ascribed to the phlegmatic temperament. The factor loadings emerging from this analysis were interrelated in a circular order, much like the circumplex structure of interpersonal behavior described by Foa and the circular array of MMPI test vectors suggested by Jackson and Messick. Although Goldman-Eisler considered her findings as a confirmation of psychoanalytic theory, her results are much like those of other investigators whose theoretical orientation was quite different. The convergences between her results and other studies imply that the elaborate verbal complexities of psychoanalytic theory are needlessly involved. The empirical data can be much more parsimoniously explained.

It is clear that the same fundamental patterns have been repeatedly observed by many contemporary and historical writers, even though the words used may seem very different. These similarities and convergences would not have been so consistently noted unless there were certain universal features in all human conduct. Apparently these universal features were perceived, understood, and implicitly acted upon during the moral therapy era, overlooked by later generations enamoured of impersonal scientism, and spelled out once again in recent empirical investigations. It seems obvious that a sound understanding of human behavior must begin with these universal features rather than the vague jargon that has dominated psychological and psychiatric theorizing to date.

How do these universal features relate to mental health and mental illness? Within the two-dimensional circular structure outlined above an elaborate system has been developed for classifying the interpersonal behavior of both psychiatric patients and "normals" (Leary, 1956, 1957). The major differences between mental illness and mental health are to be found in the characteristic frequency, intensity, and nature of interpersonal acts.

For example, schizophrenics manifest intense degrees of passivity and hostility by unconventional, bizarre, negativistic, and distrustful acts. In contrast, hysterics prefer bland, pleasant, friendly, conventional types of interaction. Hostile, rebellious, and distrustful acts are infrequent and extremely mild in intensity among hysterics. These two contrasting types of interpersonal behavior have long been considered mental illnesses. Both are differentiated from normality, adjustment, or mental health, i.e., versatile, appropriate, effective, adaptive behavior patterns. In this semantic usage the words "illness" and "health" are applied to observable patterns of conduct, not to states of the mind or body. The most effective programs of "therapy," "treatment," or "cure" for these illnesses are those which succeed best in altering the characteristic nature, frequency, and intensity of maladaptive acts in the direction of greater moderation, versatility, appropriateness, and effectiveness.

The more we question the terminology of the mental-health professions today, the more obvious its inadequacies become. It is doubtful that any major advances can be expected so long as understanding is obscured by unsuitable, misleading terms. Every concept in our professional vocabulary needs to be carefully and critically reassessed by asking the question: "*Is it appropriate?*" Many fundamental problems need to be completely restated in words that communicate rather than obfuscate. Suitable *psychological* terminology is badly needed to clarify numerous vaguely worded, inappropriately phrased, and poorly understood questions in psychology today. Only in this way can psychologists create a basis for genuine understanding of human behavior.

REFERENCES

Allport, G. W. *Pattern and growth in personality.* New York: Holt, Rinehart & Winston, 1961.

Barzun, J. *Darwin, Marx, Wagner: Critique of a heritage.* (2nd ed.) Garden City, N. Y.: Doubleday Anchor, 1958.

Bockoven, J. S. Moral treatment in American psychiatry. *J. nerv. ment. Dis.,* 1956, 124, 167-194, 292-321. (Reprinted in book form: New York: Springer, 1963.)

Bockoven, J. S. Some relationships between cultural attitudes toward individuality and care of the mentally ill: An historical study. In M. Greenblatt, D. J. Levinson, & R. H. Williams (Eds.), *The patient and the mental hospital.* Glencoe, Ill.: Free Press, 1957. Pp. 517-526.

Brown, G. W. Length of hospital stay and schizophrenia: A review of statistical studies. *Acta psychiat. neurol. Scand., Copenhagen,* 1960, 35, 414-430.

Cope, T. P., & Packard, F. A. *A second appeal to the people of Pennsylvania on the subject of an asylum for the insane poor of the commonwealth.* Philadelphia: Waldie, 1841.

Dahlstrom, W. G., & Welsh, G. S. *An MMPI handbook: A guide to use in clinical practice and research.* Minneapolis: Univer. Minnesota Press, 1960.

Foa, U. G. Convergences in the analysis of the structure of interpersonal behavior. *Psychol. Rev.,* 1961, 68, 341-353.

Goldman-Eisler, Frieda. Breastfeeding and character formation. In C. Kluckhohn & H. A. Murray (Eds.), *Personality in nature, society, and culture.* (2nd ed.) New York: Knopf, 1953. Pp. 146-184.

Gottlieb, Ann L., & Parsons, O. A. A coaction compass evaluation of Rorschach determinants in brain damaged individuals. *J. consult. Psychol.,* 1960, 24, 54-60.

Greenblatt, M., York, R. H., & Brown, Esther L. *From custodial to therapeutic care in mental hospitals.* New York: Russell Sage Foundation, 1955.

Harms, E. The early historians of psychiatry. *Amer. J. Psychiat.*, 1957, 113, 749-752. (a)

Harms, E. Historical considerations in the science of psychiatry. *Dis. nerv. Sys.*, 1957, 18, 397-400. (b)

Harms, E. Modern psychotherapy—150 years ago. *J. ment. Sci.*, 1957, 103, 804-809. (c)

Jackson, D. N., & Messick, S. Acquiescence and desirability as response determinants on the MMPI. *Educ. psychol. Measmt.*, 1961, 21, 771-790.

Joint Commission on Mental Illness and Health. *Action for mental health.* New York: Basic Books, 1961.

Leary, T. *Multilevel measurement of interpersonal behavior.* Berkeley, Calif.: Psychological Consultation Service, 1956.

Leary, T. *Impersonal diagnosis of personality.* New York: Ronald Press, 1957.

Lodge, G. T., & Gibson, R. L. A coaction map of the personalities described by H. Rorschach and S. J. Beck. *J. proj. Tech.*, 1953, 17, 482-488.

Rees, T. P. Back to moral treatment and community care. *J. ment. Sci.*, 1957, 103, 303-313.

Roback, A. A. *History of psychology and psychiatry.* New York: Citadel Press, 1961.

Szasz, T. S. The myth of mental illness. *Amer. Psychologist*, 1960, 15, 113-118.

Szasz, T. S. *The myth of mental illness.* New York: Hoeber-Harper, 1961.

Welsh, G. S. Factor dimensions A and R. In G. S. Welsh & W. G. Dahlstrom (Eds.), *Basic readings on the MMPI in psychology and medicine.* Minneapolis: Univer. Minnesota Press, 1956. Pp. 264-281.

Zilboorg, G. *A history of medical psychology.* New York: Norton, 1941.

5. Mental Disorders and Status Based on Race

Robert J. Kleiner, Jacob Tuckman, and Martha Lavell

This paper is the report of a study similar to that of Hollingshead and Redlich (Selection 1, page 13); it was, however, conducted on a much smaller scale and in a different community—Philadelphia.

The findings of this study parallel those of the Hollingshead and Redlich study in many respects. Whereas on the surface, at any rate, these authors adhere to the "disease" conception of "mental illness,"

Psychiatry; 23:271-274, 1960. Reprinted by permission of the author and by special permission of the William Alanson White Psychiatric Foundation, Inc. Copyright 1960 by the William Alanson White Psychiatric Foundation, Inc. *Robert J. Kleiner.* B.S. C.C.N.Y. 48; M.S. Western Reserve Univ. 50; Ph.D. Univ. of Pa. 57. Director of Research and Statistics, Commonwealth Mental Health Center, Pa. Dept. of Public Welfare, Philadelphia 56-. *Jacob Tuckman.* Ph.D. Columbia Univ. 34. Chief, Section of Psychological Services, Education and Standards, Division of Mental Health, Dept. of Public Health, Philadelphia 55-. *Martha Lavell,* M.S.S. Smith College School for Social Work 31. Editorial Asst., *Amer. J. Psychiatry* 47-53; Statistician, Division of Mental Health, Dept. of Public Health, Philadelphia 56-59.

their conclusions are within a social context: "In prevention, efforts must be directed to removing social barriers to goals consistent with the person's potential and needs."

The relationship between mental disorder and personal and social characteristics, such as sex, race, age, marital status, nativity, occupation, and so on, has been demonstrated.[1] The findings of these descriptive studies would appear to suggest the following general hypothesis: Differences in social experience inherent in the range of personal and social characteristics will result in differential breakdown patterns. The purpose of the present study is to examine the mental breakdown pattern of two groups differing widely in social experience because of differences in their status in the society. One is a high-status group, whites; the other a low-status group, nonwhites. All live in Philadelphia. Two groups were selected for study because data with respect to mental breakdown were readily accessible.

It is hardly necessary to present evidence showing a difference in status between whites and nonwhites. Such evidence is available not only by observation, but also in data from more objective sources. The 1950 census of population in Philadelphia shows important differences between the two groups. Nonwhites have less schooling, a lower occupational status, and lower income than whites. Life expectancy is lower for nonwhites, owing to higher morbidity and death rates. Obviously the factors of schooling, occupation, income, and life expectancy are interrelated, and it seems reasonable to say that they are a function of status.

In any low-status group, the frustration imposed by a controlling or hostile social environment will presumably lead to psychological responses of tension, anxiety, and hostility and be reflected in behavioral symptoms of extreme aggression or extreme withdrawal. Moreover, such responses to frustration, which are constantly reinforced in day-to-day living, will presumably also result in increased vulnerability to mental disorder, showing itself in a higher rate of mental illness—already demonstrated for nonwhites by Malzberg[2]—as well as in the onset of illness at an earlier age.

Two hypotheses will be tested in this paper: First, the pattern of

[1] Robert M. Frumkin, "Occupation and Major Mental Disorders," pp. 136-160; in *Mental Health and Mental Disorder*, edited by Arnold M. Rose; New York, Norton, 1955. August B. Hollingshead and Fredrick C. Redlich, "Social Stratification and Psychiatric Disorders," *Amer. Sociological Rev.* (1953) 18:163-169. B. Malzberg, *Social and Biological Aspects of Mental Disease*; Utica, N.Y., State Hosp. Press, 1940.

[2] See footnote 1.

mental disorder will show a greater prevalence of extreme aggressive behavior (paranoid schizophrenic reactions) or extreme withdrawal behavior (other schizophrenic reactions) for the low-status than for the high-status group. Second, the low-status group will show an earlier onset of mental illness than will the high-status group.

THE DATA

The data for this study were obtained from the records of all first admissions from the city of Philadelphia to any state mental hospital in the Commonwealth of Pennsylvania for the five-year period from May, 1951, to May, 1956. This constituted a population of 3,004 men and women. The available information on this group included race, sex, diagnosis (according to the nomenclature of the American Psychiatric Association), occupation, marital status, and age. Since the number of cases in many diagnostic categories was too small to allow for statistical analysis, closely related categories were combined, thereby giving twelve groupings for study.

Table 1 shows the occupational distribution of male first admissions for the high-status, or white, group, and for the low-status, or nonwhite, group. It is evident that the low-status group is significantly lower in occupational status than is the high-status group. This difference parallels that found between whites and nonwhites in the general population.[3]

The data in Table 2 show clearly that the pattern of mental disorder of the low-status group differs significantly from that of the high-status group, for both men and women. The low-status group shows a greater concentration in paranoid and in other schizophrenic reactions, represent-

TABLE 1   OCCUPATION OF MALE FIRST ADMISSIONS BY RACE*

Occupational Category	White (N=1000)	Nonwhite (N=504)
Professional and managerial	7%	4%
Clerical and sales	6	2
Skilled	20	10
Semiskilled	9	7
Unskilled	21	42
Service	8	14
Not stated	29	22

* $x^2 = 105.06$, $df = 5$, $p < .001$. Unskilled and service categories were combined in the analysis.

[3] Both white and nonwhite male first admissions are significantly lower in occupational level than are their respective groups in the general population.

ing extreme aggression or extreme withdrawal, respectively. By contrast, the high-status group shows a greater concentration in chronic brain syndrome with cerebral arteriosclerosis; this suggests not only a longer period free from breakdown but also the relatively greater importance of organic factors. The greater concentration of this syndrome in the high-status group cannot be explained by the group's greater longevity; even though women live longer than men, there is little or no difference between men and women in the high- or low-status groups. In this sample, women are older than men in both groups. The lower incidence of paranoid and other schizophrenic reactions in the high-status group cannot be attributed to their greater age or to their greater utilization of private facilities for the care of the mentally ill. Even if all first admissions diagnosed as chronic brain syndrome with cerebral arteriosclerosis were excluded from the sample, the high-status group would still show less schizophrenia (52 percent) than the low (66 percent). A study of first admissions to private mental hospitals in the Philadelphia area showed only 9 percent with a diagnosis of schizophrenia.[4] Assuming that the high-status group contributed 100 percent of the first admissions to private hospitals, combined public and private first admissions would serve only to accentuate the differences between high- and low-status groups. Thus the data in Table 2 tend to support the first hypothesis.

TABLE 2   PSYCHIATRIC DIAGNOSIS BY RACE AND SEX

| | Male* | | Female† | |
Diagnosis	White (N=1,000)	Nonwhite (N=504)	White (N=1,059)	Nonwhite (N=397)
Chronic brain syndrome with arteriosclerosis	30%	16%	34%	16%
Chronic brain syndrome with convulsive disorder	1	2	1	1
Chronic brain syndrome, other	9	14	5	6
Mental deficiency	6	4	3	2
Involutional psychosis	3	‡	5	2
Affective psychosis	3	1	4	3
Paranoid schizophrenia	21	32	21	34
Schizophrenia	12	18	15	26
Paranoia	1	2	‡	1
Other psychosis	4	4	7	8
Psychoneurosis	1	‡	2	0
Personality disorder	9	6	2	1

* White and nonwhite: $\chi^2 = 85.02$, $df = 11$, $p < .001$.
† White and nonwhite: $\chi^2 = 89.19$, $df = 11$, $p < .001$.
‡ Less than 0.5%.

[4] Kleiner, "A Comparative Study of State and Private Hospitals," unpublished report, Pa. Dept. of Public Welfare, Bureau of Mental Health, 1958.

The differences between the low- and high-status groups with respect to the pattern of mental disorder cannot be attributed to differences in occupational distribution. For those in professional and managerial occupations, the percentage showing paranoid and other schizophrenic reactions is 39 for the low-status group and 33 for the high-status group; for sales and clerical, the respective percentages are 55 and 36; for skilled, 51 and 33; for semiskilled, 55 and 47; for unskilled, 57 and 47; and for personal service, 57 and 27. By contrast, the percentage with chronic brain syndrome with arteriosclerosis in the professional and managerial occupations is 33 for the low-status group and 37 for the high; in sales and clerical, the respective percentages are 11 and 26; in skilled, 22 and 32; in semiskilled, 15 and 25; in unskilled, 12 and 22; and in personal service, 24 and 36.

These findings suggest that occupation in itself is insufficient to explain the differences between the low- and high-status groups. They suggest, instead, that other status dimensions such as social distance, opportunities for advancement, job satisfaction, and so on, operate within any particular occupational category.

Marital separation and divorce can, it is assumed, be used as one index of interpersonal tensions, and thus reflect extreme aggressive and withdrawal behavior. Table 3 shows a higher incidence of separation and divorce in the low-status group than in the high-status group. The difference between these groups parallels that found between white and nonwhite in the general population.[5]

TABLE 3   MARITAL STATUS BY RACE AND SEX

| | Male* | | Female† | |
Marital Status	White (N=1,000)	Nonwhite (N=504)	White (N=1,059)	Nonwhite (N=397)
Single	43%	44%	33%	24%
Married	29	26	27	29
Separated or divorced	10	18	11	20
Widowed	11	5	26	22
Not stated	7	7	3	5

* White and nonwhite: $\chi^2 = 36.37$, $df = 4$, $p < .001$.
† White and nonwhite: $\chi^2 = 29.31$, $df = 4$, $p < .001$.

Table 4 shows the median age to be lower for the low-status group than for the high within each diagnostic category. This applies to both men and women. Although the number of cases is small in some categories, there is no deviation from the pattern. When the Sign Test is

[5] Both white and nonwhite first admissions (male and female) show significantly more separation and divorce than their respective groups in the general population.

TABLE 4   MEDIAN AGE BY PSYCHIATRIC DIAGNOSIS,* RACE, AND SEX†

	Male				Female			
	White		Nonwhite		White		Nonwhite	
Diagnosis	N	Median Age	N	Median Age	N	Median Age	N	Median Age
Chronic brain syndrome with arteriosclerosis	303	72.5	83	65.7	358	76.5	62	70.9
Chronic brain syndrome, other ...	93	53.1	70	51.6	50	53.3	25	46.5
Mental deficiency ..	59	29.3	22	15.9	35	28.5	9	27.5
Involutional psychosis	31	59.7	2	55.0	56	53.3	9	51.3
Affective psychosis .	28	50.0	5	32.5	38	47.9	11	42.5
Paranoid schizophrenia	210	34.7	160	32.0	226	39.5	133	35.6
Schizophrenia	119	30.8	93	28.5	164	34.4	104	29.2
Other psychosis ...	40	55.8	18	46.7	71	51.3	33	46.3
Personality disorder	85	26.4	31	23.0	19	...	5	...

* Data not computed for diagnostic categories where both groups had less than 25 cases or where one group had less than two cases.
† Sign test: $p < .001$.

used, the pattern is highly significant. This therefore confirms the second hypothesis.

CONCLUSIONS

The concentration of the low-status group in paranoid and other schizophrenic reactions does not appear to be chance occurrence. These mental disorders, representing extremes in aggressive or withdrawal behavior, are reactions triggered by a frustrating environment. The greater vulnerability of the low-status group to mental breakdown suggests that its "frustration tolerance" is impaired earlier and more frequently in the face of the greater pressures and restrictions of the social environment.

In this study, status has been defined in terms of racial membership. Using other indices of status, such as occupational level or social class, other studies have shown a relationship between status and vulnerability to mental breakdown. Frumkin found that occupations low in the occupational scale have the highest rates of first admissions with major mental disorders.[6] Hollingshead and Redlich found a greater prevalence of psychotic disorders in the low than in the high social classes.[7] These findings

[6] See footnote 1.
[7] See footnote 1.

may be interpreted as additional evidence that low-status groups are more susceptible to mental breakdown.

The implications for diagnosis and treatment are clear. Greater attention needs to be given to the patient's experiences resulting from his group membership, in conjunction with attention to his personality dynamics. In prevention, efforts must be directed to removing social barriers to goals consistent with the person's potential and needs.

6.   Two Descriptions of More or Less Identical Behavior

August B. Hollingshead and Fredrick C. Redlich

> In these two very brief descriptions of the more or less identical behavior of two young women, note that the resultant care which they received was drastically different. The "treatment" for each of these two cases stemmed largely *not* from any objective evaluation or diagnosis as is the case in physical disease but rather from highly subjective opinions of many people including the subjective ones of *two* mental health specialists.
>
> As you may recognize, these two descriptions of behavior illustrate one of Dr. Szasz's (Selection 2) main points: "In actual contemporary social usage, the finding of a mental illness is made by establishing a deviance in behavior from certain psychosocial, ethical, or legal norms."

The case histories of two compulsively promiscuous adolescent females will be drawn upon to illustrate the differential impact of class status on the way in which lay persons and psychiatrists perceive and appraise similar behavior. Both girls came to the attention of the police at about the same time but under very different circumstances. One came from a core group class I family, the other from a class V family broken by the desertion of the father. The class I girl, after one of her frequent drinking and sexual escapades on a weekend away from an exclusive boarding school, became involved in an automobile accident while drunk. Her family immediately arranged for bail through the influence of a member of an outstanding law firm; a powerful friend telephoned a newspaper contact, and the report of the accident was not published. Within twenty-four hours, the girl was returned to school. In a few weeks the school authorities realized that the girl was pregnant and notified her parents. A psychiatrist was called in for consultation by the parents with the expec-

From the book *Social Class and Mental Illness;* by August B. Hollingshead and Fredrick C. Redlich; John Wiley and Sons, New York, pp. 175-176, copyright, 1958. Reprinted by permission of the publisher.

tation, expressed frankly, that he was to recommend a therapeutic interruption of the pregnancy. He did not see fit to do this and, instead, recommended hospitalization in a psychiatric institution to initiate psychotherapy. The parents, though disappointed that the girl would not have a "therapeutic" abortion, finally consented to hospitalization. In due course, the girl delivered a healthy baby who was placed for adoption. Throughout her stay in the hospital she received intensive psychotherapy and after being discharged continued in treatment with a highly regarded psychoanalyst.

The class V girl was arrested by the police after she was observed having intercourse with four or five sailors from a nearby naval base. At the end of a brief and perfunctory trial, the girl was sentenced to a reform school. After two years there she was paroled as an unpaid domestic. While on parole, she became involved in promiscuous activity, was caught by the police, and sent to the state reformatory for women. She accepted her sentence as deserved "punishment" but created enough disturbance in the reformatory to attract the attention of a guidance officer. This official recommended that a psychiatrist be consulted. The psychiatrist who saw her was impressed by her crudeness and inability to communicate with him on most subjects. He was alienated by the fact that she thought masturbation was "bad," whereas intercourse with many men whom she hardly knew was "O.K." The psychiatrist's recommendation was to return the girl to her regular routine because she was not "able to profit from psychotherapy."

7. Reaction Patterns to Severe, Chronic Stress in American Army Prisoners of War of the Chinese

Edgar Schein

Seldom in the everyday course of affairs, in attempting to understand deviant behavior, do we have the opportunity to observe either *very extreme* situations or the behavior which occurs therein. During the Korean conflict our enemies utilized drastic and severe approaches and techniques for the purpose of *changing the behavior* of their captives.

Journal of Social Issues; 13:21-30, 1957. Reprinted by permission of the author and the Society for the Psychological Study of Social Issues. This work was completed while the author was a captain, U. S. Army Medical Service Corps, assigned to the Walter Reed Army Institute of Research. I would like to acknowledge the invaluable help and guidance of Dr. David McK. Rioch and Capt. Harold Williams as well as the staff of the Neuropsychiatric Division of the Walter Reed Army Institute of Research. Portions of this paper were read at the meetings of the Group for the Advancement of Psychiatry, Asbury Park, New Jersey, November, 1956.

This paper by Dr. Schein is perhaps a more realistic and accurate description of the techniques of "brainwashing" than any others you may have encountered. The Chinese Communists utilized, in the main, psychological-social influences which were designed to change attitudes, values, and beliefs. As you will see, those procedures, referred to as "brainwashing," were effective in many instances in destroying or altering the "sense of identity" or "sense of self."

Dr. Schein asserts that the Chinese Communists do not appear to be interested in obtaining transient submission; instead they seem to be interested in producing changes in man's behavior which will be lasting and self-sustaining.

In this paper I will outline some of the constellations of stress which prisoners of war faced during the Korean conflict, and describe some of the reaction patterns to these stresses. Rather than presenting a complete catalogue of their experiences (3), I have selected those aspects which seem to me to throw some light on the problem of collaboration with the enemy. I will give particular emphasis to the *social* psychological factors, because the Chinese approach to treatment of prisoners seemed to emphasize control over groups, rather than individuals.

My material is based on a variety of sources. I was in Korea during the repatriation, and had the opportunity to interview extensively 20 unselected repatriates. This basic material was supplemented by the information gathered by three psychiatrists, Drs. Harvey Strassman, Patrick Israel, and Clinton Tempereau, who together had seen some 300 men. On board ship returning to the United States, I also had the opportunity to sit in on bull sessions among repatriates in which many of the prison experiences were discussed. Additional details were obtained from the Army dossiers on the men.

The typical experience of the prisoner of war must be divided into two broad phases. The first phase lasted anywhere from one to six months beginning with capture, followed by exhausting marches to the north of Korea and severe privation in inadequately equipped temporary camps, terminating in assignment to a permanent prisoner of war camp.

The second phase, lasting two or more years, was marked by chronic pressures to collaborate and to give up existing group loyalties in favor of new ones. Thus, while physical stresses had been outstanding in the first six months, psychological stresses were outstanding in this second period.

The reactions of the men toward capture were influenced by their overall attitude toward the Korean situation. Many of them felt inadequately prepared, both physically and psychologically. The physical training, equipment, and rotation system all came in for retrospective criticism, though this response might have been merely a rationalization for being captured. When the Chinese entered the war they penetrated into rear areas, where they captured many men who were taken completely by surprise. The men felt that when positions were over-run, their leadership was often less than adequate. Thus, many men were disposed to blame the UN command for the unfortunate event of being captured.

On the psychological side, the men were not clearly aware of what they were fighting for or what kind of enemy they were opposing. In addition, the reports of the atrocities committed by the North Koreans led most men to expect death, torture, or non-repatriation if captured.

It was in such a context that the soldier found his Chinese captor extending his hand in a friendly gesture and saying "Welcome" or "Congratulations, you've been *liberated*." This Chinese tactic was part of their "lenient policy" which was explained to groups of prisoners shortly after capture in these terms: because the UN had entered the war illegally and was an aggressor, all UN military personnel were in fact war criminals, and *could* be shot summarily. But the average soldier was, after all, only carrying out orders for his leaders who were the real criminals. Therefore, the Chinese soldier would consider the POW a "student," and would teach him the "truth" about the war. Anyone who did not cooperate by going to school and by learning voluntarily could be reverted to his "war criminal" status and shot, particularly if a confession of "criminal" deeds could be obtained from him.

In the weeks following capture, the men were collected in large groups and marched north. From a physical point of view, the stresses during these marches were very severe: there was no medicine for the wounded, the food was unpalatable and insufficient, especially by our standards, clothing was scarce in the face of severe winter weather, and shelter was inadequate and overcrowded. The Chinese set a severe pace and showed little consideration for weariness that was the product of wounds, diarrhea, and frostbite. Men who were not able to keep up were abandoned unless they were helped by their fellows. The men marched only at night, and were kept under cover during the day, ostensibly as protection against strafing by our own planes.

From a psychological point of view this situation is best described as a recurring cycle of fear, relief, and new fear. The men were afraid that they might die, that they might never be repatriated, that they might never again have a chance to communicate with the outside, and that no one even knew they were alive. The Chinese, on the other hand, were reassuring and promised that the men would be repatriated soon, that conditions would improve, and that they would soon be permitted to communicate with the outside.

One of the chief problems for the men was the disorganization within the group itself. It was difficult to maintain close group ties if one was competing with others for the essentials of life, and if one spent one's resting time in overcrowded huts among others who had severe diarrhea and were occasionally incontinent. Lines of authority often broken down, and with this, group cohesion and morale suffered. A few men attempted to escape, but they were usually recaptured in a short time and returned to the group. The Chinese also fostered low morale and the feeling of being abandoned by systematically reporting false news about United Nations defeats and losses.

In this situation goals became increasingly short-run. As long as the men were marching, they had something to do and could look forward to relief from the harsh conditions of the march. However, arrival at a temporary camp was usually a severe disappointment. Not only were physical conditions as bad as ever, but the sedentary life in overcrowded quarters produced more disease and still lower morale.

What happened to the men under these conditions? During the one- to two-week marches they became increasingly apathetic.[1] They developed a slow, plodding gait, called by one man a "prisoners' shuffle." Uppermost in their minds were fantasies of food: men remembered all the good meals they had ever had, or planned detailed menus for years into the future. To a lesser extent they thought of loved ones at home, and about cars which seemed to them to symbolize freedom and the return home.

In the temporary camps disease and exposure took a heavy toll in lives. But it was the feeling of many men, including some of the doctors who survived the experience, that some of these deaths were not warranted by a man's physical condition. Instead, what appeared to happen was that some men became so apathetic that they ceased to care about their bodily needs. They retreated further into themselves, refused to eat even what little food was available, refused to get any exercise, and eventually lay down as if waiting to die. The reports were emphatic concerning the lucidity and sanity of these men. They seemed willing to accept the prospect of death rather than to continue fighting a severely frustrating and depriving environment.

Two things seemed to save a man who was close to such "apathy" death: getting him on his feet and doing something, no matter how trivial, or getting him angry or concerned about some present or future problem. Usually it was the effort of a friend who maternally and insistently motivated the individual toward realistic goals which snapped him out of such a state of resignation. In one case such "therapy" consisted of kicking the man until he was mad enough to get up and fight.

Throughout this time, the Chinese played the role of the benevolent but handicapped captor. Prisoners were always reminded that it was their *own* Air Force bombing which was responsible for the inadequate

---

[1] A more detailed discussion of the apathy reaction may be found in Strassman, Thaler, and Schein (4).

supplies. Furthermore, they were reminded that they were getting treatment which was just as good as that which the average Chinese was getting. One important effect of this was that a man could never give *full* vent to his hostility toward the Chinese, even in fantasy. In their *manner* and *words* they were usually solicitous and sympathetic. The Chinese also implied that conditions could be better for a prisoner if he would take a more "cooperative" attitude, if he would support their propaganda for peace. Thus a man was made to feel that he was himself responsible for his traumatic circumstances.

Arrival at a permanent camp usually brought relief from many of these physical hardships. Food, shelter, and medicine, while not plentiful, appeared to be sufficient for the maintenance of life and some degree of health. However, the Chinese now increased sharply their efforts to involve prisoners in their own propaganda program, and to undermine loyalties to their country. This marks the beginning of the second phase of the imprisonment experience.

The Chinese program of subversion and indoctrination was thoroughly integrated into the entire camp routine and involved the manipulation of the entire social milieu of the prison camp. Its aims appeared to be to manage a large group of prisoners with a minimum staff of guards, to indoctrinate them with the Communist political ideology, to interrogate them to obtain intelligence information and confessions for propaganda purposes, and to develop a corps of collaborators within the prisoner group. What success the Chinese had stemmed from their *total* control of the environment, not from the application of any one technique.

The most significant feature of Chinese prisoner camp control was the systematic destruction of the prisoners' formal and informal group structure. Soon after arrival at a camp, the men were segregated by race, nationality, and rank. The Chinese put their own men in charge of the platoons and companies, and made arbitrary selections of POW squad leaders to remind the prisoners that their old rank system no longer had any validity. In addition, the Chinese attempted to undermine *informal* group structure by prohibiting any kind of group meeting, and by systematically fomenting mutual distrust by playing men off against one another. The most effective device to this end was the practice of obtaining from informers or Chinese spies detailed information about someone's activities, no matter how trivial, then calling him in to interrogate him about it. Such detailed surveillance of the men's activities made them feel that their own ranks were so infiltrated by spies and informers that it was not safe to trust anyone.

A similar device was used to obtain information during interrogation. After a man had resisted giving information for hours or days, he would be shown a signed statement by one of his fellow prisoners giving that same information. Still another device was to make prisoners who had not collaborated look like collaborators, by bestowing special favors upon them.

A particularly successful Chinese technique was their use of testimonials from other prisoners, such as the false germ-warfare confessions, and appeals based on familiar contexts, such as peace appeals. Confessions by prisoners or propaganda lectures given by collaborators had a particularly demoralizing effect, because only if resistance had been *unanimous* could a man solidly believe that his values were correct, even if he could not defend them logically.

If the men, in spite of their state of social disorganization, did manage to organize any kind of group activity, the Chinese would quickly break up the group by removing its leaders or key members and assigning them to another camp.

Loyalties to home and country were undermined by the systematic manipulation of mail. Usually only mail which carried bad news was delivered. If a man received no mail at all, the Chinese suggested that his loved ones had abandoned him.

Feelings of social isolation were increased by the complete information control maintained in the camps. Only the Communist press, radio, magazines, and movies were allowed.

The weakening of the prisoner group's social structure is particularly significant because we depend to such an extent on consensual validation in judging ourselves and others. The prisoners lost their most important sources of information and support concerning standards of behavior and beliefs. Often men who attempted to resist the Chinese by means other than *outright* obstruction or aggression failed to obtain the active support of others, often earning their suspicion instead.

At the same time, the Chinese did create a situation in which meaningful social relationships could be had through common political activity, such as the "peace" committees which served as propaganda organs. The Chinese interrogators or instructors sometimes lived with prisoners for long periods of time in order to establish close personal relationships with them.

The Communist doctrines were presented through compulsory lectures followed by compulsory group discussions, for the purpose of justifying the conclusions given at the end of the lectures. On the whole, this phase of indoctrination was ineffective because of the crudeness of the propaganda material used in the lectures. However, its constant repetition seemed eventually to influence those men who did not have well formed political opinions to start with, particularly because no counter-arguments could be heard. The group discussions were effective only if their monitor was someone who could keep control over the group and keep it on the topic of discussion. Attempts by the Chinese to use "progressive" POWs in the role of monitors were seldom successful because they aroused too much hostility in the men.

The Chinese also attempted to get prisoners to use mutual criticism and self-criticism in the fashion in which it is used within China.[2] Whenever a POW was caught breaking one of the innumerable camp rules, he was required to give an elaborate confession and self-criticism, no matter how trivial the offense. In general, the POWs were able to use this opportunity to ridicule the Chinese by taking advantage of their lack of understanding of slang and American idiom. They would emphasize the wrong parts of sentences or insert words and phrases which made it apparent to other prisoners that the joke was on the Chinese. Often men were required to make these confessions in front of large groups of other prisoners. If the man could successfully communicate by a linguistic device his lack of sincerity, this ritual could backfire on the Chinese by giving the men an opportunity to express their solidarity (by sharing a communication which could not be understood by the Chinese). However, in other instances, prisoners who viewed such public confessions felt contempt for the confessor and felt their own group was being undermined still further by such public humiliation.

Various tales of how prisoners resisted the pressures put on them have been widely circulated in the press. For example, a number of prisoners ridiculed the Chinese by playing baseball with a basketball, yet telling the Chinese this was the correct way to play the game. Such stories suggest that morale and group solidarity was actually quite high in the camps. Our interviews with the men suggest that morale climbed sharply during the *last six to nine months* of imprisonment when the armistice talks were underway, when the compulsory indoctrination program had been put on a voluntary basis, and when the Chinese were improving camp conditions in anticipation of the repatriation. However, we heard practically no stories of successful group resistance or high morale from the first year or so in the camps when the indoctrination program was seriously pursued by the Chinese. (At that time the men had neither the time nor the opportunity to play any kind of games, because all their time was spent on indoctrination activities or exhausting labor.)

Throughout, the Chinese created an environment in which rewards such as extra food, medicine, special privileges, and status were given for cooperation and collaboration, while threats of death, non-repatriation, reprisal against family, torture, decreases in food and medicine, and imprisonment served to keep men from offering much resistance. Only imprisonment was consistently used as an actual punishment. *Chronic* resistance was usually handled by transferring the prisoner to a so-called "reactionary" camp.

Whatever behavior the Chinese attempted to elicit, they always *paced* their demands very carefully, they always required some level of *participation* from the prisoner, no matter how trivial, and they *repeated* endlessly.

[2] See paper by Robert J. Lifton in *Journal of Social Issues*, Vol. 13, 1957.

To what extent did these pressures produce either changes in beliefs and attitudes, or collaboration? Close observation of the repatriates and the reports of the men themselves suggest that the Chinese did not have much success in changing beliefs and attitudes. Doubt and confusion were created in many prisoners as a result of having to examine so closely their own way of thinking, but very few changes, if any, occurred that resembled actual *conversion* to Communism. The type of prisoner who was most likely to become *sympathetic* toward Communism was the one who had chronically occupied a low status position in this society, and for whom the democratic principles were not very salient or meaningful.

In producing collaboration, however, the Chinese were far more effective. By collaboration I mean such activities as giving lectures for the Communists, writing and broadcasting propaganda, giving false confessions, writing and signing petitions, informing on fellow POWs, and so on; none of these activities required a personal change of belief. Some 10 to 15 per cent of the men chronically collaborated, but the dynamics of this response are very complex. By far the greatest determinant was the amount of pressure the Chinese put on a particular prisoner. Beyond this, the reports of the men permit one to isolate several sets of motives that operated, though it is impossible to tell how many cases of each type there may have been.

1) Some men collaborated for outright opportunistic reasons; these men lacked any kind of stable group identification, and exploited the situation for its material benefits without any regard for the consequences to themselves, their fellow prisoners, or their country.

2) Some men collaborated because their egos were too weak to withstand the physical and psychological rigors; these men were primarily motivated by fear, though they often rationalized their behavior; they were unable to resist any kind of authority figure, and could be blackmailed by the Chinese once they had begun to collaborate.

3) Some men collaborated with the firm conviction that they were infiltrating the Chinese ranks and obtaining intelligence information which would be useful to the UN forces. This was a convenient rationalization for anyone who could not withstand the pressures. Many of these men were initially tricked into collaboration or were motivated by a desire to communicate with the outside world. None of these men became ideologically confused; what Communist beliefs they might have professed were for the benefit of the Chinese only.

4) The prisoner who was vulnerable to the ideological appeal because of his low status in this society often collaborated with the conviction that he was doing the right thing in supporting the Communist peace movement. This group included the younger and less intelligent men from backward or rural areas, the malcontents, and members of various

minority groups. These men often viewed themselves as failures in our society, and felt that society had never given them a chance. They were positively attracted by the immediate status and privileges which went with being a "progressive," and by the promise of important roles which they could presumably play in the peace movement of the future.

Perhaps the most important thing to note about collaboration is the manner in which the social disorganization contributed to it. A man might make a slanted radio broadcast in order to communicate with the outside, he might start reading Communist literature out of sheer boredom, he might give information which he knew the Chinese already had, and so on. Once this happened, however, the Chinese rewarded him, increased pressure on him to collaborate, and blackmailed him by threatening exposure. At the same time, in most cases, his fellow prisoners forced him into further collaboration by mistrusting him and ostracising him. Thus a man had to stand entirely on his own judgment and strength, and both of these often failed. One of the most common failures was a man's lack of awareness concerning the effects of his own actions on the other prisoners, and the value of these actions for the Chinese propaganda effort. The man who confessed to germ warfare, thinking he could repudiate such a confession later, did not realize its immediate propaganda value to the Communists.

A certain percentage of men, though the exact number is difficult to estimate, exhibited chronic resistance and obstructionism toward Chinese indoctrination efforts. Many of these men were well integrated with secure, stable group identifications who could withstand the social isolation and still exercise good judgment. Others were chronic obstructionists whose histories showed recurring resistance to any form of authority. Still others were idealists or martyrs to religious and ethical principles, and still others were anxious, guilt-ridden individuals who could only cope with their own strong impulses to collaborate by denying them and overreacting in the other direction.

By far the largest group of prisoners, however, established a complex compromise between the demands of the Chinese and their own value system. This adjustment, called by the men "playing it cool," consisted primarily of a physical and emotional withdrawal from the whole environment. These men learned to suspend their feelings and to adopt an attitude of watching and waiting, rather than hoping and planning. This reaction, though passive, was not as severe as the apathy described earlier. It was a difficult adjustment to maintain because some concessions had to be made to the Chinese in the form of trivial or well-timed collaborative acts, and in the form of a feigned interest in the indoctrination program. At the same time, each man had to be prepared to deal with the hostility of his buddies if he made an error in judgment.

Discussion

This paper has placed particular emphasis on the social psychological factors involved in "brainwashing" because it is my opinion that the process is primarily concerned with social forces, not with the strengths and weaknesses of individual minds. It has often been asserted that drugs, hypnotic techniques, refined "mental tortures" and, more recently, implanted electrodes can make the task of the "brainwasher" much easier by rendering the human mind submissive with a minimum of effort.[3] There is little question that such techniques can be used to elicit confessions or signatures on documents prepared by the captor; but so can withdrawal of food, water, or air produce the same results. The point is that the Chinese Communists do not appear to be interested in obtaining merely a confession or *transient* submission. Instead, they appear to be interested in producing changes in men which will be lasting and self-sustaining. A germ-warfare confession alone was not enough—the POW had to "testify" before an international commission explaining in detail how the bombs had been dropped, and had to tell his story in other prison camps to his fellow POWs.

There is little evidence that drugs, post-hypnotic suggestion, or implanted electrodes can now or ever will be able to produce the kind of behavior exhibited by many prisonrs who collaborated and made false confessions. On the other hand, there is increasing evidence (1, 2) that Russian and Chinese interrogation and indoctrination techniques involve the destruction of the person's social ties and identifications, and the partial destruction of his ego. If this is successfully accomplished, the person is offered a new identity for himself and given the opportunity to identify with new groups. What physical torture and deprivation are involved in this process may be either a calculated attempt to degrade and humiliate a man to destroy his image of himself as a dignified human being, or the product of fortuitous circumstances, i.e., failure of supply lines to the prison, loss of temper on the part of the interrogator, an attempt to inspire fear in other prisoners by torturing one of them, and so on. We do not have sufficient evidence to determine which of these alternatives represents Communist intentions; possibly all of them are involved in the actual prison situation.

Ultimately that which sustains humans is their personality integration born out of secure and stable group identifications. One may be able to produce temporary submission by direct intervention in cortical proc-

[3] For example, see paper by James G. Miller in *Journal of Social Issues*, Vol. 13, 1957.

esses, but only by destroying a man's self-image and his group supports can one produce any lasting changes in his beliefs and attitudes. By concerning ourselves with the problem of artificially creating submission in man, we run the real risk of overlooking the fact that we are in a genuine struggle of ideas with other portions of the world and that man often submits himself directly to ideas and principles.

To understand and combat "brainwashing" we must look at those social conditions which make people ready to accept new ideas from anyone who states them clearly and forcefully, and those social conditions which give people the sense of integrity which will sustain them when their immediate social and emotional supports are stripped away.

REFERENCES

(1) Hinkle, Lawrence E. and Wolff, Harold C. Communist Interrogation and Indoctrination of "Enemies of the State." *Archives of Neurology and Psychiatry,* 1956, *76,* 115-174.
(2) Lifton, Robert L. "Thought Reform" of Western Civilians in Chinese Communist Prisons. *Psychiatry,* 1956, *19,* 173-198.
(3) Schein, Edgar H. The Chinese Indoctrination Program for Prisoners of War. *Psychiatry,* 1956, *19,* 149-172.
(4) Strassman, Harvey D., Thaler, Margaret, and Schein, Edgar H. A Prisoner of War Syndrome: Apathy as a Reaction to Severe Stress. *American Journal of Psychiatry,* 1956, *112,* 998-1003.

8. Individual and Social Origins of Neurosis

Erich Fromm

Dr. Erich Fromm has been associated for many years with modifications and expansions of many psychoanalytic ideas and principles. In this article he offers a reinterpretation of the classic "Oedipus Complex"—considered by many for a long time to be the basis of neurotic behavior. According to Dr. Fromm, the feelings which the small child has for his parents are related to the type of authority which they exercise—*rational* or *irrational.*

Since the time this paper was published, Dr. Fromm has added a third type of authority—*anonymous* (discussed in his book *The Sane Society*). At the moment, he believes that many of us are guided both as children and adults, not so much by any direct means, but rather by "subtle persuasion" and "hidden forms of coercion"; much advertising, for example, influences us indirectly. The result of anonymous

American Sociological Review; 9: 380-384, 1944. Reprinted by permission of the author and the American Sociological Association. Presented to the annual meeting of the Eastern Sociological Society, Columbia University, April 22-23, 1944.

authority is people who have no convictions of their own, who exhibit no individuality, and who have little sense of self.

Dr. Fromm does not deny the importance of childhood experiences in the formation of neurotic behavior; he seems to attribute greater significance to the group within which an individual lives as an adult.

The history of science is a history of erroneous statements. Yet these erroneous statements which mark the progress of thought have a particular quality: they are productive. And they are not just *errors* either; they are statements, the truth of which is veiled by misconceptions, is clothed in erroneous and inadequate concepts. They are rational visions which contain the seed of truth, which matures and blossoms in the continuous effort of mankind to arrive at objectively valid knowledge about man and nature. Many profound insights about man and society have first found expression in myths and fairy tales, others in metaphysical speculations, others in scientific assumptions which have proven to be incorrect after one or two generations.

It is not difficult to see why the evolution of human thought proceeds in this way. The aim of any thinking human being is to arrive at the *whole* truth, to understand the *totality* of phenomena which puzzle him. He has only *one* short life and must want to have a vision of the truth about the world in this short span of time. But he could only understand this totality if his life span were identical with that of the human race. It is only in the process of historical evolution that man develops techniques of observation, gains greater objectivity as an observer, collects new data which are necessary to know if one is to understand the *whole*. There is a gap, then, between what even the greatest genius can visualize as the truth, and the limitations of knowledge which depend on the accident of the historical phase he happens to live in. Since we cannot live in suspense, we try to fill out this gap with the material of knowledge at hand, even if this material is lacking in the validity which the essence of the vision may have.

Every discovery which has been made and will be made has a long history in which the truth contained in it finds a less and less veiled and distorted expression and approaches more and more adequate formulations. The development of scientific thought is not one in which old statements are discarded as false and replaced by new and correct ones; it is rather a process of continuous *reinterpretation* of older statements, by which their true kernel is freed from distorting elements. The great pioneers of thought, of whom Freud is one, express ideas which determine the progress of scientific thinking for centuries. Often the workers in the field orient themselves in one of two ways: they fail to differentiate between the essential and the accidental, and defend rigidly the whole system of the master, thus blocking the process of reinterpretation and clarification; or they make the same mistake of failing to differentiate between the essential and the accidental, and equally rigidly fight against the old theories and try to replace them by new ones of their own. In both the orthodox and the rebellious rigidity, the constructive evolution of the vision of the master is blocked. The real task, however, is to reinterpret, to sift out, to recognize that certain insights had to be phrased and understood in erroneous concepts because of the limitations of thought peculiar to the historical phase in which they were first formulated. We may feel then that we sometimes understand the author better than he understood himself, but that we are only capable of doing so by the guiding light of his original vision.

This general principle, that the way of scientific progress is *constructive reinterpretation of basic visions* rather than repeating or discarding them, certainly holds true of Freud's theoretical formulations. There is scarcely a discovery of Freud which does not contain fundamental truths and yet which does not lend itself to an organic development beyond the concepts in which it has been clothed.

A case in point is Freud's theory on the origin of neurosis. I think we still know little of what constitutes a neurosis and less what its origins are. Many physiological, anthropological and sociological data will have to be collected before we can hope to arrive at any conclusive answer. What I shall do is to use Freud's view on the origin of neurosis as an illustration of the general principle which I have discussed, that reinterpretation is the constructive method of scientific progress.

Freud states that the *Oedipus complex* is justifiably regarded as the kernel of neurosis. I believe that this statement is the most fundamental one which can be made about the origin of neurosis, but I think it needs to be qualified and reinterpreted in a frame of reference different from the one Freud had in mind. What Freud meant in his statement was this: because of the sexual desire the little boy, let us say, has for his mother, he becomes the rival of his father, and the neurotic development consists in the failure to cope with the anxiety rooted in this rivalry in a satisfactory way. I believe that Freud touched upon the most elementary root of neurosis in pointing to the conflict between the child and parental authority and the failure of the child to solve this conflict satisfactorily. But I do not think that this conflict is brought about essentially by the sexual rivalry, but that it results from the child's reaction to the pressure of parental authority, the child's fear of it and submission to it. Before I go on elaborating this point, I should like to differentiate between two kinds of authority. One is *objective*, based on the competency of the person in authority to function properly with respect to the task of guidance he has to perform. This kind of authority may be called *rational* authority. In contrast to it is what may be called *irrational* authority, which is based on the power which the authority has over those subjected to it and on the fear and awe with which the latter reciprocate.

It happens that in most cultures human relationships are greatly determined by irrational authority. People function in our society as in most societies, on the record of history, by becoming adjusted to their social role at the price of giving up part of their own will, their originality and spontaneity. While every human being represents the whole of mankind with all its potentialities, any functioning society is and has to be primarily interested in its self-preservation. The particular ways in which a society functions are determined by a number of *objective* economic and political factors, which are given at any point of historical development. Societies have to operate within the possibilities and limitations of their particular historical situation. In order that any society may function well, its members must acquire the kind of character which makes them *want* to act in the way they *have* to act as members of the society or of a special class within it. They have to *desire* what objectively is *necessary* for them to do. *Outer force* is to be replaced by *inner compulsion*, and by the particular kind of human energy which is channeled into character traits. As long as mankind has not attained a state of organization in which the interest of the individual and that of society are identical, the aims of society have to be attained at a greater or lesser expense of the freedom and spontaneity of the individual. This aim is performed by the process of child training and education. While education aims at the development of a child's potentialities, it has also the function of reducing his independence and freedom to the level necessary for the existence of that particular society. Although societies differ with regard to the extent to which the child must be impressed by irrational authority, it is always part of the function of child training to have this happen.

The child does not meet society directly at first; it meets it through the medium of his parents, who in their character structure and methods of education represent the social structure, who are the psychological agency of society, as it were. What, then, happens to the child in relationship to his parents? It meets through them the kind of authority which is prevailing in the particular society in which it lives, and this kind of authority tends to break his will, his spontaneity, his independence. But man is not born to be broken, so the child fights against the authority represented by his parents; he fights for his freedom not only *from* pressure but also for his freedom to be himself, a full-fledged human being, not an automaton. Some children are more successful than others; most of them are defeated to some extent in their fight for freedom. The ways in which this defeat is brought about are manifold, but whatever they are, the scars left from this defeat in the child's fight against irrational authority are to be found at the bottom of every neurosis. This scar is represented in a syndrome the most important features of which are: the weakening or paralysis of the person's originality and spontaneity; the weakening of the self and the substitution of a pseudo-self, in which the feeling of "I am" is dulled and replaced by the experience of self as the sum total of expectations others have about me; the substitution of autonomy by heteronomy; the fogginess, or, to use Dr. Sullivan's term, the parataxic quality of all interpersonal experiences.

My suggestion that the Oedipus complex be interpreted not as a result of the child's sexual rivalry with the parent of the same sex but as the child's fight with irrational authority represented by the parents does not imply, however, that the sexual factor does not play a significant role, but the emphasis is not on the incestuous wishes of the child and their necessarily tragic outcome, its original sin, but on the parents' prohibitive influence on the normal sexual activity of the child. The child's physical functions—first those of defecation, then his sexual desires and activities—are weighed down by moral considerations. The child is made to feel guilty with regard to these functions, and since the sexual urge is present in every person from childhood on, it becomes a constant source of the feeling of guilt. What is the function of this feeling of guilt? It serves to break the child's will and to drive it into submission. The parents use it, although unintentionally, as a means to make the child submit. There is nothing more effective in breaking any person than to give him the conviction of wickedness. The more guilty one feels, the more easily one submits because the authority has proven its own power by its right to accuse. What appears as a feeling of guilt, then, is actually the fear of displeasing those of whom one is afraid. This feeling of guilt is the only one which most people experience as a moral problem, while the genuine moral problem, that of realizing one's potentialities, is lost from sight. Guilt is reduced to disobedience and is not felt as that which it is in a genuine moral sense, self-mutilation.

To sum up this point, it may be said that it is the defeat in the fight against authority which constitutes the kernel of the neurosis, and that not the incestuous wish of the child but the stigma connected with sex is one among the factors in breaking down his will. Freud painted a picture of the necessarily *tragic* outcome of a child's most fundamental wishes: his incestuous wishes are bound to fail and force the child into some sort of submission. Have we not reason to assume that this hypothesis expresses in a veiled way Freud's profound pessimism with regard to any basic improvement in man's fate and his belief in the indispensable nature of irrational authority? Yet this attitude is only one part of Freud. He is at the same time the man who said that "from the time of puberty onward the human individual must devote himself to the great task of freeing himself from the parents"; he is the man who devised a thera- peutic method the aim of which is the independence and freedom of the individual.

However, defeat in the fight for freedom does not always lead to neu- rosis. As a matter of fact, if this were the case, we would have to consider the vast majority of people as neurotics. What then are the specific con- ditions which make for the neurotic outcome of this defeat? There are some conditions which I can only mention: for example, one child may be broken more thoroughly than others, and the conflict between his anxiety and his basic human desires may, therefore, be sharper and more unbearable; or the child may have developed a sense of freedom and originality which is greater than that of the average person, and the de- feat may thus be more unacceptable. But instead of enumerating other conditions which make for neurosis, I prefer to reverse the question and ask what the conditions are which are responsible for the fact that so many people do *not* become neurotic in spite of the failure in their per- sonal fight for freedom. It seems to be useful at this point to differentiate between two concepts: that of defect and that of neurosis. If a person fails to attain freedom, spontaneity, a genuine experience of self, he may be considered to have a severe defect, provided we assume that freedom and spontaneity are the objective goals to be attained by every human being. If such a goal is not attained by the majority of members of any given society, we deal with the phenomenon of *socially patterned defect*. The individual shares it with many others; he is not aware of it as a defect, and his security is not threatened by the experience of being dif- ferent, of being an outcast, as it were. What he may have lost in richness and in a genuine feeling of happiness is made up by the security of fitting in with the rest of mankind—*as he knows them*. As a matter of fact, his very defect may have been raised to a virtue by his culture and thus give him an enhanced feeling of achievement. An illustration is the feeling of guilt and anxiety which Calvin's doctrines aroused in men. It may be said that the person who is overwhelmed by a feeling of his own powerless- ness and unworthiness, by the unceasing doubt of whether he is saved or condemned to eternal punishment, who is hardly capable of any genuine joy and has made himself into the cog of a machine which he has to serve, has a severe defect. Yet this very defect was culturally patterned; it was looked upon as particularly valuable, and the individual was thus protected from the neurosis which he would have acquired in a culture where the defect would give him a feeling of profound inadequacy and isolation.

Spinoza has formulated the problem of the socially patterned defect very clearly. He says: "Many people are seized by one and the same effect with great consistency. All his senses are so strongly affected by one object that he believes this object to be present even if it is not. If this happens while the person is awake, the person is believed to be insane. . . . But if the *greedy* person thinks only of money and possessions, the *ambitious* one only of fame, one does not think of them as being insane, but only as annoying; generally one has contempt for them. But *factually* greediness, ambition, and so forth are forms of insanity, although usually one does not think of them as 'illness.' " These words were written a few hundred years ago; they still hold true, although the defect has been culturally patterned to *such* an extent now that it is not generally thought any more to be annoying or contemptuous. Today we come across a person and find that he acts and feels like an automaton; that he never experiences anything which is really his; that he experiences himself entirely as the person he thinks he is supposed to be; that smiles have replaced laughter, meaningless chatter replaced communicative speech; dulled despair has taken the place of genuine pain. Two statements can be made about this person. One is that he suffers from a defect of spontaneity and individuality which may seem incurable. At the same time it may be said that he does not differ essentially from thousands of others who are in the same position. With *most* of them the cultural pattern provided for the defect saves them from the outbreak of neurosis. With *some* the cultural pattern does not function, and the defect appears as a severe neurosis. The fact that in these cases the cultural pattern does not suffice to prevent the outbreak of a manifest neurosis is in most cases to be explained by the particular severity and structure of the individual conflicts. I shall not go into this any further. The point I want to stress is the necessity to proceed from the problem of the *origins of neurosis* to the problem of the *origins of the culturally patterned* defect; to the problem of the *pathology of normalcy*.

This aim implies that the psychoanalyst is not only concerned with the readjustment of the neurotic individual to his given society. His task must be also to recognize that the individual's ideal of normalcy may contradict the aim of the full realization of himself as a human being. It is the belief of the progressive forces in society that such a realization is possible, that the interest of society and of the individual need not be antagonistic forever. Psychoanalysis, if it does not lose sight of the human problem, has an important contribution to make in this direction. This contribution by which it transcends the field of a medical specialty was part of the vision which Freud had.

9.   The Quest for Identity

Allen Wheelis

Since the relationships which children have with their parents have changed during the past fifty years or so (in the form of altered child-rearing practices) the nature of *neuroses* has also changed during that time; that is, neurotic behavior of today has quite different characteristics than did neurotic behavior around the turn of the century. Formerly, neurotic behavior appeared mainly as a rather specific symptom such as a phobia, an obsession, or a compulsion; today what we are likely to label as *neurosis* in a person is vague and amorphous complaints; for example, "I'm just not happy" and "I can't seem to get along well with others."

Dr. Wheelis extends the neurotic concept to include many of us; the uncertainty persists of "Who Am I?" and "What is the meaning of life?" In other words, in mid-century America *neurosis* is little "sense of identity." This may partially explain "alienation" or "dropping out."

THE EVOLUTION OF SOCIAL CHARACTER

THE OLD AND THE NEW

With increasing frequency in recent years a change in the character of the American people has been reported and described.[1] The change is within the lifetime of most persons of middle or advanced years, and the process of change is still underway. The social character[2] of ourselves

W. W. Norton and Company, New York; Chapter 1, The Evolution of Social Character, pages 17-25 and 38-44; 1958. Reprinted from *The Quest For Identity* by Allen Wheelis by permission of W. W. Norton & Company, Inc. Copyright © 1958 by W. W. Norton & Company, Inc. Also permission for British Commonwealth and Empire, except Canada from Laurence Pollinger, Ltd. Dr. Wheelis is a psychiatrist staff member of the Mt. Zion Psychiatric Clinic and an instructor in the San Francisco Psychoanalytic Institute.

[1] David Riesman, Nathan Glazer, and Revel Denny, *The Lonely Crowd* (New Haven: Yale University Press, 1950); Henry Steele Commager, *The American Mind* (New Haven: Yale University Press, 1950); Erik Erikson, *Childhood and Society* (New York: W. W. Norton & Company, 1950); Margaret Meade, *Male and Female* (New York: William Morrow & Company, 1949); Walter Lippman, *The Public Philosophy* (Boston: Little Brown & Company, 1955).

[2] The concept of social character refers not to the character of society, but, somewhat paradoxically, to the character of individuals. It is that nucleus of individual character which is shared by a significantly large social group. Since it is what we have in common with others, we take it for granted and most of the time are unaware of its existence.

and our children is unmistakably different from what we remember of the character of our grandparents.

Our grandparents had less trouble than we do in finding themselves. There were lost souls, to be sure, but no lost generation. More commonly then than now a young man followed his father, in character as in vocation, and often so naturally as to be unaware of having made a choice. Though the frontier was gone, there was still, for those who needed it, the open west. Sooner rather than later one found his calling; and, having found it, failure did not readily cause one to reconsider, but often was a goad to greater effort. The goal was achievement, not adjustment; the young were taught to work, not to socialize. Popularity was not important, but strength of character was essential. Nobody worried about rigidity of character; it was supposed to be rigid. If it were flexible you couldn't count on it. Change of character was desirable only for the wicked.

Many of us still remember the bearded old men: the country doctor, the circuit rider, the blacksmith, the farmer. They were old when we were young, and they are dead now. We remember the high shoes, the heavy watch chain, the chewing tobacco, the shiny black suit on Sunday. The costume and make-up may still be seen, as they turn up in plays now and then. The character that went with them is disappearing, and soon even its memory will be lost.

Nowadays the sense of self is deficient. The questions of adolescence—"Who am I?" "Where am I going?" "What is the meaning of life?"—receive no final answers. Nor can they be laid aside. The uncertainty persists. The period of being uncommitted is longer, the choices with which it terminates more tentative. Personal identity does not become fixed, does not, therefore, provide an unchanging vantage point from which to view experience. Man is still the measure of all things, but it is no longer the inner man that measures; it is the other man. Specifically, it is the plurality of men, the group. And what the group provides is shifting patterns, what it measures is conformity. It does not provide the hard inner core by which the value of patterns and conformity is determined. The hard inner core has in our time become diffuse, elusive, often fluid. More than ever before one is aware of the identity he appears to have, and more than ever before is dissatisfied with it. It doesn't fit, it seems alien, as though the unique course of one's life had been determined by untoward accident. Commitments of all kinds—social, vocational, marital, moral—are made more tentatively. Long-term goals seem to become progressively less feasible.

Identity[3] is a coherent sense of self. It depends upon the awareness that one's endeavors and one's life make sense, that they are meaningful in the context in which life is lived. It depends also upon stable values, and upon the conviction that one's actions and values are harmoniously related. It is a sense of wholeness, of integration, of knowing what is right and what is wrong and of being able to choose.

During the past fifty years there has been a change in the experienced quality of life, with the result that identity is now harder to achieve and harder to maintain. The formerly dedicated Marxist who now is unsure of everything; the Christian who loses his faith; the workman who comes to feel that his work is piecemeal and meaningless; the scientist who decides that science is futile, that the fate of the world will be determined by power politics—such persons are of our time, and they suffer the loss or impairment of identity.

Identity can survive major conflict provided the supporting framework of life is stable, but not when that framework is lost. One cannot exert leverage except from a fixed point. Putting one's shoulder to the wheel presupposes a patch of solid ground to stand on. Many persons these days find no firm footing; and if everything is open to question, no question can be answered. The past half century has encompassed enormous gains in understanding and in mastery; but many of the old fixed points of reference have been lost, and have not been replaced.

The change in social character is often described as a decline of individualism; but individualism means many things, and not all of them have declined. Individualism means self-reliance, productive self-sufficiency, following one's chosen course despite social criticism, and bearing personally the risks of one's undertakings; and all of these are on the wane. Ours is an age of reliance on experts, of specialized production, of deference to public opinion, and of collective security. But individualism means, also, the awareness of individuality, and this has increased. For accompanying the other changes there has occurred an extension of awareness.

Modern man has become more perceptive of covert motivations, in both himself and others. Areas of experience formerly dissociated from consciousness have become commonplace knowledge. Passivity, anxiety, disguised hostility, masochism, latent homosexuality—these are not new

---

[3] "Identity" is used throughout this work in its ordinary lay meaning. In psychoanalytic literature it bears a larger and more precise meaning, indicating a psychic organization which develops in successive phases throughout life, and which is partly unconscious. *Cf.* Erik Erikson, "The Problem of Ego Identity," *Journal of the American Psychoanalytc Association*, vol. 4, no. 1 (January, 1956), pp. 56-121.

with the present generation; what is new is the greater awareness of them. We deride the affectations which this heightened awareness so facilely serves—the "parlor psychiatry," the "curbstone interpretation"—but overlook the emergent fact of extended awareness of which the affectation is symptomatic. As man has lost his sense of identity he has, paradoxically, discovered more of those elements of his nature out of which identity may be formed, the raw materials with which to build. In losing the whole he has found some of the previously lost parts.

This extended awareness is both cause and effect of the loss of identity. It is a cause for the reason that identity is harder to achieve if renegade motivations have free access to consciousness. If one is able to deny with finality those lurking tendencies that run counter to the dominant trends of personality, then it is easier to know who one is and where one stands. This is of relevance in comparing the unsure man of today with his very sure grandfather. His sense of identity is less firm, but the elements he is called upon to integrate are more numerous and less homogeneous. The identity of his grandfather was like the log cabin of the frontier; it was small and dark, but it was put up with dispatch and was sturdy and snug. The grandson is fumbling as a builder, and keeps hankering to turn the whole job over to a professional architect; but it is to be noted that his job is harder. The materials with which he must work are more variegated. Their proper integration would achieve not a log cabin, but a more complicated and interesting structure, admitting more light and air and providing more room for living.

The extended awareness is also an effect of the loss of identity for the reason that, being unsure of who one is and where one stands, it behooves one to be more alert and perceptive. A firm sense of identity provides both a compass to determine one's course in life and ballast to keep one steady. So equipped and provisioned, one can safely ignore much of the buffeting. Without such protection more vigilance is needed; each vicissitude, inner and outer, must be defined and watched.

A change has occurred, also, in the dimensions of our existence. During this century, it is said, our lives have been both lengthened and narrowed. This makes reference to our longer life expectancy and to the increasing industrialization that is thought to diminish the meaning of life by the kind of work it imposes. The increased life span is indisputable, and doubtless much clerical and assembly line work is monotonous. Yet in a somewhat different sense the dimensional change is just the opposite of that proposed: our lives have been enriched crosssectionally and diminished longitudinally.

In our time the range and variety of experience has been enormously extended. It is less integrated and less stable, but it is far wider. in scope. Fifty years ago the great orchestras could be heard in only a few cities; now they are heard, by radio and recording, in every village across the continent. Comparable changes have occurred in the availability of all the arts. Better means of communication enable us to experience meanings that occur at great distances, better methods of travel to experience persons and areas heretofore inaccessible. Though these experiences are more easily had by the rich, they are to a notable degree available, also, to the assembly-line worker whose life is thought to be so impoverished. A war in Korea, a play on Broadway, a new philosophy in France—all are experienced more quickly and more widely than ever before.

Nor has the depth or meaningfulness of this experience been diminished. When radios became common it was sometimes predicted that the musical taste of the nation would be depraved by the constant din of jazz. In fact, the relatively small amount of serious music that was broadcast along with the jazz developed the musical appreciation of millions. Serious music is now understood and valued by a far higher proportion of the people than would have been possible without the advent of radio. "Twenty years ago you couldn't sell Beethoven out of New York," reports a record salesman. "Today we sell Palestrina, Monteverdi, Gabrielli, and renaissance and baroque music in large quantities."[4] Parallel developments could be cited for countless other areas of experience. The gain in breadth of experience has generally been accompanied by a gain, also, in depth. Not only is the man of today constantly informed of a larger number of world events than was his grandfather; he understands them better. And within his own home he understands his children better. In all of these ways our lives have been cross-sectionally enriched.

But as our span of years has increased, our span of significant time has diminished. In some measure we have lost the sense of continuity with past and future. More and more quickly the past becomes outdated, and if we look back two or three generations the character and values of our forebears become as strange to us as their beards and high collars. Family portraits no longer hang in homes; there is no place for them in modern houses. And as we have lost touch with the past, so we have lost touch with the future. We know that we are in motion but do not know where we are going, and hence cannot predict the values of our children. Our grandfathers are likely to have dreamt of leaving as legacy a tract of land which would stay in the family and be maintained by their descendants; of building a house that would endure and be lived in after they were gone; of a profession that would become a tradition and be

4 Quoted by Daniel Bell, "The Theory of Mass Society," *Commentary*, vol. 22, no. 1 (July, 1956), pp. 75-83.

carried on by sons; of a name that would be wrought in iron over the carriage gate, the prestige of which would be shared and furthered by all who bore it. Seeing how these dreams have come to naught in us, we no longer try to direct or even to foresee the values of our descendants. We cannot now, with loving foresight, further their ends; for we do not know what ends they will pursue, nor where. We feel lucky if we can give our children an education. The founders of this country had a lively sense of the future, knew that posterity would vindicate their revolution, their moving west, their capitalism, their competition, their church. We—who have no idea of what posterity will honor—live more largely in the present.

Becker has pointed out that this is an age in which we cannot feel that we understand anything until we know its history.[5] As we become more aware of how things change, it becomes more important to know how they developed, how they got to be the way they are. But this does not mean that we feel more related to the past and future. It is rather the other way round: our feeling of estrangement in time and of the transience of the present prompts the historical approach. The historical approach is a symptom of our trouble. We are trying to recapture the sense of continuity, to find again the durable patterns of life—hoping we shall not lose altogether our connections with those who have lived before and those who will live after.

THE CHANGE IN NEUROTIC PATTERNS

Doctor Thurston was a kind man and often was sympathetic with emotional disorders. He would prescribe tonics, advise work, and would give generously of encouragement and reassurance. When these measures did not help, however—as often they did not—and when the patient became more demanding, his patience would be short. Of a neurotic woman he would say, "She's not sick, she's got hysterics." If her complaints were only in her mind then obviously they were not real. "She just *thinks* she's sick." If he had made his call under difficult conditions, he would be cross, would feel that his time was being wasted. If she should prove hard to handle, his sense of moral indignation would be indicated by his readiness to shift the diagnosis from hysteria to malingering. This was the attitude, also, of the patient's family and of society. She would re-

[5] "Historical-mindedness is so much a preconception of modern thought that we can identify a particular thing only by pointing to the various things it successively was before it became that particular thing that it will presently cease to be." Carl L. Becker, *The Heavenly City of the Eighteenth-Century Philosophers* (New Haven: Yale University Press, 1932), p. 19.

ceive little indulgence, but would be regarded with humor or derision. It was a disgrace, and if she did not snap out of it the disgrace would deepen.

This intolerance amounted to a pressure against the emergence or admission of neurosis, and it had varying effects. It forced the suppression of symptoms or the ability to live with them and despite them and to keep going. It forced, also, some curable neurotics into suicide, and it locked up and made custodial cases of some who, in a different setting, might have recovered.

This pressure has, in large measure, been replaced by tolerance. Now there is no difference in degree of reality between mental and physical illness; one is as genuine as the other. They differ in origin, development, and recovery, but are alike in that in neither case is one expected simply to "snap out of it." By this change in attitude neurosis has been admitted into the realm of medicine, becoming entitled thereby to the designation of illness, with all the rights and privileges pertaining thereunto. Among these are the right to professional attention and the privilege of delivering responsibility for the care and cure of one's illness into the hands of a physician. From the untoward consequences of this latter development psychiatrists are still trying, somewhat awkwardly, to extricate themselves.

The new orientation is regarded as a great social gain. Not only does it banish the old bigotry; it will also—we are assured—diminish the prevalence and severity of neurosis. For with the elimination of the stigma, the need for secrecy is gone. Since our culture does not enforce the suppression of neurosis, one is more free to acknowledge the difficulty and to seek help. And since psychiatric treatment is regarded as the royal— and, usually, the only—road to recovery, it is assumed that more people will get well.

Such optimism overreaches itself. Get well from what? Most often nowadays it is from loneliness, insecurity, doubt, boredom, restlessness, and marital discord. The hysteria of the last century has mysteriously disappeared—as completely as the intolerance with which it was viewed. The tolerant psychoanalyst of today deals rather with vague conditions of maladjustment and discontent. For it has come about that, as the social attitude toward neurosis has changed, the patterns of neuroses have themselves undergone a change of equal magnitude.[6] This is within the personal experience of older psychoanalysts. Younger analysts become

[6] ". . . the patient of today suffers most under the problem of what he should believe in and who he should—or, indeed, might—be or become; while the patient of early psychoanalysis suffered most under inhibitions which prevented him from being what and who he thought he knew he was." Erik Erikson, *Childhood and Society* (New York: W. W. Norton & Company, 1950), p. 239.

aware of it from the discrepancy between the older descriptions of neuroses and the problems presented by the patients who come daily to their offices. The change is from symptom neuroses to character disorders.

A symptom neurosis was understood as a breakthrough in distorted form of a previously repressed impulse. The neurosis appeared as a phobia, an obsession, a compulsion, or as a physical symptom without a physical cause; was characterized by a definite, and often sudden, onset; and occurred in the setting of a relatively well-integrated and adequately functioning personality. It had the quality of a syndrome or illness. Diagnosis was relatively easy. It was the classical indication for psychoanalysis, and with such conditions analysis has had its greatest success. Insight was often quickly effective. Analyses were short, a matter of months rather than years. Such a case has always been considered ideal for teaching purposes, and its current rarity can be attested by almost any analyst in training.

In contrast, the more frequently encountered character disorder of today cannot be adequately understood as the eruption of a previously repressed impulse; for the defensive warping of character is apt to loom larger and prove more troublesome than the erupting impulse. The conflict is less likely to manifest itself in the form of specific symptoms or to have the quality of a syndrome, but is vague and amorphous, pervading the entire personality. Complaints of a general nature become more common, such as, "difficulties in relations with people," "I'm just not very happy, feel I ought to be getting more out of life," or "I'm too rigid." Normality has largely replaced morality as a standard of operational adequacy.[7] The significance of inner conflict to all manner of difficulties in living has been so incontrovertibly established that, for many people, any condition of unhappiness is *prima facie* evidence of neurosis and hence reason enough to consult a psychoanalyst. Diagnosis becomes increasingly difficult; no one term covers the many things that are wrong; and case reports conclude with formulations of remarkable length and complexity—for example, "reactive depression in a decompensating narcissistic-compulsive character with paranoid, hysterical, and some psychopathic tendencies." With such conditions psychoanalysis is less successful, insight less curative. The analyst speaks less often of "cure" and more frequently of "progress." Analyses become longer, three years and more being quite common; and the time is long past when a second analysis was claim to distinction. The goals of analysis are not fully achieved; both patient and therapist must settle for less than had been hoped for.

[7] Norman Reider, "The Concept of Normality," *Psychoanalytic Quarterly*, vol. 19 (1950), pp. 43-51.

THE DECLINE OF WILL

Toward the end of the long analyses that now have become so common, the therapist may find himself wishing that the patient were capable of more push, more determination, a greater willingness to make the best of it. Often this wish eventuates in remarks to the patient: "People must help themselves"; "Nothing worthwhile is achieved without effort"; "You have to try." Such interventions are seldom included in case reports, for it is assumed that they possess neither the dignity nor effectiveness of interpretation. Often an analyst feels uncomfortable about such appeals to volition, as though he were using something he didn't believe in, and as though this would have been unnecessary had only he analyzed more skillfully. The deficiency of will in the patient is mirrored by the loss, in the analyst, of a belief in the efficacy of will. The same culture produces both patient and analyst, and it is a culture in which the strength of individuals is no longer thought to be located in the strength of will.

When human affairs appear to be inexorably determined by forces over which man has no control, the concept of will has little significance. When human affairs are characterized by a sense of freedom, when society concerns itself with the rights and dignity of the individual, the concept of will is of great significance. Since the Renaissance, man's sense of freedom has increased to a point probably unequalled in any prior civilization, achieving such expressions as "I am the master of my fate; I am the captain of my soul." At the same time the material universe was more and more being found to be rigorously determined, more precisely and measurably conforming to natural law. Newtonian mechanics captured the physical sciences for determinism. But, paradoxically, the technological advantages of viewing the universe as "determined" enhanced man's sense of being "free." One cannot build an aeroplane, for example, without allegiance to determinism; yet the creation of an aeroplane tends to support man's sense of standing outside the causal network, of being the master and manipulator of determined events. And so for centuries the inner life of man, the realm of free will, lay outside causality. Even after Darwin captured the biological sciences for determinism there still seemed to be a place for will in human affairs, and as late as 1892 William James maintained that a sense of integrity depends primarily on the ability to will effectively.[8]

More recently the concept of will has passed into partial eclipse. It is

---

[8] ". . . we measure ourselves by many standards. Our strength and our intelligence, our wealth and even our good luck, are things which warm our heart and make us feel ourselves a match for life. But deeper than all such things, and able to suffice unto itself without them, is the sense of the amount of effort which we can put

still central to those popular books on self-improvement which crowd the best-seller lists; but in psychology it has lost its position as a primary mental function and has become an epiphenomenon. Among the sophisticated the use of the term "will power" has become perhaps the most unambiguous badge of naïveté. It has become unfashionable to try, by one's unaided efforts, to force one's way out of a condition of neurotic misery; for the stronger the will the more likely it is to be labeled a "counterphobic maneuver." The unconscious is heir to the prestige of will. As one's fate formerly was determined by will, now it is determined by the repressed in mental life. Knowledgeable moderns put their backs to the couch, and in so doing they fail occasionally to put their shoulders to the wheel. As will has been devalued, so has courage; for courage can exist only in the service of will, and can hardly be valued higher than that which it serves. In our understanding of human nature we have gained determinism and lost determination—though these two things are neither coordinate nor incompatible.

10.   Love Me Diane: The Case History of a Criminal Psychopath

John Bintz and Ronald Wilson

This case history is a unique one in that the senior author grew up in the same town as did the subject and attended school with him. Several years later he worked as a reporter in the town and became the friend of many of those who figured in the case—police and court officials, several school officials, and social workers.

Whereas many case studies of adults depend by necessity upon the truthfulness of the subject, this one is based primarily upon first-hand observations.

Individuals placed in this category exhibit, in the main, overt maladaptive behavior—"acting out"—rather than mental or emotional symptoms. They manifest a marked lack of ethical or moral development and an inability to follow socially approved codes of behavior. Procedures and techniques for changing the behavior of these people have been mostly in vain. Experimentation during recent years, however, is beginning to suggest promising and appropriate approaches. (Selections 22 and 23)

The data for this case study were collected by the senior author under the direction of the junior author while both were members of the Department of Psychology at the State University of Iowa, Iowa City. Dr. Bintz is now at the University of California at Davis while Dr. Wilson is at the University of Louisville School of Medicine. All names in the case study are fictitious. Used by permission.

forth. . . . He who can make none is but a shadow; he who can make much is a hero." William James, *Psychology* (New York: Henry Holt & Company, 1892), p. 458.

The term "psychopath" (some prefer "sociopath") is a sub-category of *character disorders* or *conduct disorders* or *personality disorders*.

James William Ranson (Jim) is an articulate, handsome, intelligent young man. He is also a psychopath. Born in 1935, he collected twenty-seven entries on his police record as a teen-ager and served a year in a training school for boys. During the next ten years he was convicted of major crimes on four occasions, and he has spent more of his adult life in jail than out.

Jim can be classified as psychopathic on the basis of several criteria: psychiatric diagnosis, psychological test score, and the presence of defining behavioral characteristics. At age seventeen he was diagnosed as psychopathic by the staff at the state training school, and a personality test (MMPI) given later showed him to be 3.5 standard deviations above the mean on the psychopathic deviant scale. The behavioral definition by which Jim will be evaluated is one given by McCord and McCord (1956): "The psychopath is an asocial, aggressive, highly impulsive person, who feels little or no guilt and is unable to form lasting bonds of affection with other human beings."

The purpose of this case study is to provide illustrative material from the subject's life history that qualifies him for inclusion in this category. The material also touches on family relationships and social factors that may have contributed to his development as a psychopath. The data are drawn from institutional and police records, from newspaper reports, from interviews with the subject and other principal figures in this study, and from the personal experience of the senior author, who was acquainted with the subject during the years these events took place.

FAMILY BACKGROUND

Jim Ranson was fourth born in a family of five children. Two elder sisters and a brother were born during the depression; he was followed five years later by another sister and a brother who died shortly after birth.

His father was born in 1890, the son of a Missouri farmer. He left home during early adolescence and for the next forty years was frequently on the move, especially during the depression when he was forced to relocate the family periodically in pursuit of available jobs. In 1929 he met and married his second wife, who was twenty years his junior, and from this union came the five children of the Ranson family.

At the outbreak of World War II he settled permanently in a low-rent district of River City and worked in a nearby tractor plant until his retirement.

Mr. Ranson was a hard and frequent drinker, a fact that led to many family arguments and other unpleasant situations during the early life of the Ranson children. Jim describes his father's drinking and related problems as follows:

> I can remember many hours spent waiting in the car with my mother, brother, and sisters while he was drinking. When drunk, he and my mother argued a great deal. This was always painful to listen to and difficult to avoid. I remember one occasion when he was extremely drunk, I was fifteen or sixteen, he was berating my mother with which to my firmest convictions were totally false charges of infidelity. I grabbed him and dragged him down the stairs and held him until he calmed down. My mother called the police who threw him in jail overnight. As far as I know, this was his first and only arrest in his life.

While his drinking posed a crucial problem for the family, Mr. Ranson had some positive characteristics as well. In 1955, when his wife was diagnosed as having terminal cancer, he gave up drinking entirely to make her final years more comfortable. After her death, Mr. Ranson maintained the home for his youngest daughter and eventually helped finance her training for a nursing career. In retrospect, Jim gives this evaluation of his father.

> He is and always has been an extremely honest and hard-working man. I have the deepest respect for him on these two points but this is just about where my respect ends. I begrudge him for his lack of foresight in siring five living children on his economic potential in the midst of a depression; I begrudge him for his drinking, but yet, I must remember he is a simple man with little formal education. I respect him greatly for his final treatment of my mother and little sister.

Mrs. Ranson, as opposed to her husband, was rigidly against drinking, smoking, and swearing. She was a simple woman from a large and indigent family, and among her own children she seemed particularly disposed to Jim.

> I feel that I was the favored son and Mother was fairly submissive toward me, always giving me almost everything I wanted. This increased over the years as she felt she had let me down in some way and was trying to make it up.
>
> I feel that I did not respect either one of my parents because of their intelligence, and I feel this has had a lot to do with my make-up.

Homestead

Jim's home town is divided by a river that functions as a convenient geographical index of social status. Middle-class families have houses on one side of the river; upper-class families have houses on the same side and summer cabins on the other side. Behind these cabins live the lower-class families—the further back from the river, the lower the class.

The Ransons lived a mile from the river on a road that originally led to the town dump and consequently is called the "dump road" by the townspeople. Inhabitants of this area were referred to as river rats since the river regularly flooded the area in the spring and forced the families to move temporarily until the water subsided. The Ranson home was located on a small knoll and thus escaped flooding, but the children had to wade through knee-deep water to catch the school bus each morning. While this served as an amusement in the early years, by the time they reached high school the children regarded the experience as a humiliating one, particularly when a crowd of onlookers gathered from town to witness the passage.

On the other hand, the river formed a bayou behind the Ranson house which was suitable for swimming in the summer and ice skating in the winter. These recreational facilities made the Ransons early favorites among their peers.

The house itself was a small, two-bedroom affair. One of the bedrooms was occupied by Jim and his brother in one bed, his parents in another bed, and his youngest sister in the third. Sanitary facilities were quite primitive and for a number of years there was no running water. The family owned an acre of land, but aside from sporadic efforts to raise a few chickens and pigs no serious attempt was made to cultivate the land.

EARLY DEVELOPMENT

The member of the family who made the deepest impression on Jim was his older brother Lloyd. As a model for identification, he had some serious defects. Jim describes him as follows:

> My brother is good looking, but I believe him to be about 80 or 90 IQ. He quit school during the ninth grade to go to work in a factory.
>
> He was always a bully, promiscuous, and adventurous. He was always involved with some local girl, before I was even old enough to realize what was going on. He started drinking early, and had several scrapes with the law. He had rough companions, whom I later inherited, who helped me on my way.

He married a tramp, ended up in a stolen car, and was given the choice of jail or the army, as this was the Korean wartime. I cannot directly link him to my life of crime, although he introduced me to those who later helped me along. Also he condoned some of my early petty thievery.

A sample of Lloyd's influence may be gathered from the following event. When Jim was eleven years old his brother arranged a group participation session with a compliant neighborhood girl. Jim resisted at first but after much urging he finally consummated his first sexual experience in front of a gallery of cheering spectators.

At about the same time an episode of minor thievery occurred that shaped his behavior in many later situations. He stole some change from his mother's pocketbook. His father's reaction was immediate and definite, whipping both brothers until Jim confessed. However once the guilt was established there was no more punishment. This became such a predictable pattern with his father that Jim learned to avoid punishment by confessing as soon as accused, regardless of whether he was guilty or not. In consequence, physical punishment was a rare occurrence for him.

A pattern of petty thievery was laid down during this period when Jim and a friend enjoyed remarkable success in stealing hunting and fishing equipment from a neighbor's house and were never apprehended. When their scope finally broadened to a hardware store, they were caught, but neither the parents nor the police were notified; the owner simply banished the boys from the store for life. The relative ease with which these thefts were accomplished and the minimal consequences of being caught seem to set the stage for more ambitious programs of stealing that appeared later in Jim's career.

School work came easily for Jim and was a source of satisfaction for him. He progressed through the fifth grade in a one-room country school, then transferred for one year to a larger but much less-disciplined school attended solely by lower-class children. Aside from coming to resent his home and his socio-economic status, he quickly discovered that his intellectual brightness had no coin among these students; only athletic prowess and fighting skill counted for social status. On one occasion, he recalled being ordered to stand in front of a basketball hoop for several minutes and shoot until he made a basket. The entire class jeered his failures. Out of these experiences he developed a strong interest in becoming a proficient athlete, and during the high school years he became a competent, if not prominent, performer in football, basketball, and wrestling.

During this year he made two friends who became his inseparable companions and who later collaborated in some of his criminal activities. His first entries in the records of the Juvenile Bureau were recorded at this time, one for being truant from school and the other for throwing snowballs at an older woman.

The significance of social status became even more apparent to Jim the following year when he transferred to a city-wide junior high school. All children from the community attend this school, but there is a rigid stratification of class sections on the basis of intelligence. Although it is not the purpose in theory, this stratification tends to parallel the social-class structure of the community, so that the children in the "brighter" section are drawn largely from professional and upper-class families.

Jim was one of the few who crossed class lines; he was placed in an upper division and consequently left most of his previous friends and classmates. While this assignment was to his advantage in several respects, it exerted fresh social pressure for better grades and better clothes. Grades proved to be no problem; but satisfactory clothing called for additional finances, and he resorted to a series of thefts. His favorite target during the summer months was the dressing room at the local swimming pool, and it was two years before he was finally caught. The thefts had become so frequent that a trap was set with a planted billfold, but when he was apprehended he confessed only to the thefts of the preceding year, not the current year. The record notes that he seemed rather "smart-aleck" about the whole affair, and Jim's one painful recollection about his arrest was the injury to his social standing caused by the scene it created among the crowd at the swimming pool. The punishment consisted of revoking his season pass to the pool for the rest of the summer.

The next two years, his sophomore and junior years in high school, were relatively uneventful. Although Jim was sensitive about a shortage of money and clothes, he nevertheless was integrated into the most popular clique in high school without these tangible assets. He posted a creditable record in the classroom and became a successful member of the wrestling team. He also managed to get himself elected as president of his Sunday school class, although this was possibly done as a farce. But the biggest boost to his social standing came from a period of steady dating with the daughter of one of the wealthiest families in town. The girl was attractive, highly popular, and an honor student. She was also virtuous, and Jim remembers her as one of the very few girls whom he respected. The limitations posed by infrequent petting sessions, however, led him to seek other outlets, and these were readily available.

Jim worked at a roller-skating rink during the same period he dated this girl, and he collected a succession of compliant girls who frequented the rink. He was also an active member of the YMCA at the time, and it was through one of his contacts there that he was exposed to his first homosexual experience. A young bachelor teacher, one of the leaders at the YMCA, invited Jim to spend the week-end at the family farm nearby, and Jim accepted the invitation without apparent knowledge of the man's motives. While the week-end seduction was being consummated Jim feigned sleep, and no mention of the episode was ever made. Subsequently the man purchased clothing for Jim; this was accepted, but further week-end invitations were declined.

Jim's first serious scrape with the law—one that led ultimately to a term in the state training school—occurred with a girl whom he had picked up at the skating rink. He was formally charged with rape, although his memory of the event is that, "I may have frightened her, but I did not force her." The police records compiled at the time quote him as saying that he petted with her for several hours in the back seat of a car driven by two other boys. He then suggested intercourse, intimating that if she did not comply she would have to submit to all three boys and then walk home. The girl engaged in intercourse with Jim, and when she was taken home it was agreed that nothing would be said about the affair.

Later that night the girl's father phoned the Ranson's home. Jim intercepted the call, and suspecting the nature of the call, he impersonated his father. After much discussion with the girl's father, the matter was seemingly resolved by an agreement that Jim would never be allowed to see the girl again and that he would receive a beating when he came home.

Despite the agreement, Jim was summoned to municipal court a few days later on a charge of rape and sentenced to five years at the state training school. He received a bench parole immediately, but on condition that the sentence would be activated if any parole violation occurred.

The entire incident had little effect on Jim's social status. Many of the parents objected strongly to him, but within the peer group there was no basic change in attitude; in fact, the general feeling was one of sympathy that he got caught. He continued to date the socially prominent girl who was his steady companion during this period and later arranged several dates with the girl whom he was accused of raping.

Over the next two years the skating rink gradually lost its popularity as a focal point for student activity, particularly for the middle- and upper-class youth. Jim continued to work at the rink, and he split his allegiance between the tougher group who still frequented the rink and the more socialized group that had pushed on to other activities. His behavior was in large part conditioned by the crowd he associated with at any given time. He spent the summer prior to his senior year almost entirely with the rink crowd, during which he committed a series of minor offenses that caused his parole to be revoked. Within a two-week period he was caught sleeping with a girl, charged with a series of traffic violations, and arrested for stealing a tire and a case of soft drinks. After the theft he was sentenced to one year at the state training school for boys, which of course eliminated his senior year in high school.

At the training school Jim completed his work for a high school diploma and also learned to operate a linotype machine, a skill that he has never since used. He also studied the Bible and religion, but with limited results.

> I became quite interested in religion and I read the Bible faithfully. I gave up my plans for living a pure life the first night I was out and met up with a old, blond, sexy friend of mine. As I reflect upon this religious experience, I can easily see that I had no actual concept of God at that time.
>
> Anyway the school was nothing except a waste of my senior year, and it gave me a chance to meet up with more experienced thieves than I. I do not feel that the law was justified in sending me there. I had done very little, and what I had done was quite petty.

Jim's adjustment to the school was hectic. In the first two months he was charged with eleven different incidents. The initial diagnosis of psychopath was made at this time. Jim's counselor described him in the following terms:

> This boy is a severe maladjustment case. He has a lot of characteristics of an adolescent psychopath. He is very impulsive, cannot profit from experience, daydreams too much. He has a strong desire to enter into social situations and to be a leader, yet is unsuccessful. He is very sensitive, hostile, belligerent, and uncooperative. None of these traits make him a socially acceptable person.
>
> He looks upon himself as better and smarter than most people. I don't know if he honestly feels this way or if he is merely covering up his inadequacies and feelings of inferiority.
>
> He thinks the training school is no good; the laws are no good. He cannot see where he will learn anything here. He is fearful that he will not stay out of trouble.
>
> He may adjust quickly, or he may turn into a trouble maker. If he adjusts okay, his vocational plans for college should be encouraged. He is bright enough. However, he may lack the personality integration for such a long-sustained work period.

When Jim returned to River City a year later, his class had graduated, and many of his friends had left. Those who remained had taken jobs in the local factories. And the year in training school had drastically revised Jim's social standing. He was no longer considered an abused victim of adult mores but rather as a young hoodlum who had been in trouble most of his life and was undoubtedly headed for more. Jim did little to convince people otherwise.

When I got out, I got a job running a drill press in a factory, bought a convertible, and was dating every night that I could get hold of a girl. My main ambition in life was sex. I had yet to go on my first drunk. I refused to drink, I think perhaps because I witnessed too many of my father's performances.

Soon after my release, I developed an acute taste for cunnilingus.

THE CRIMINAL YEARS

Disillusioned upon his return to River City, Jim rapidly drifted back to his old ways. He volunteered for the draft that summer because he felt "I could make good in the army, and make a new start in life." He received a letter of recommendation from the Juvenile Bureau but was then classified 4-F because of poor vision. Afterwards—and in the company of his two inseparable companions from the grade-school years, Harry Patten and Bill Neff—he went to New Orleans. The three boys hitch-hiked and committed break-ins whenever they needed money. In New Orleans they were arrested for vagrancy when they couldn't find work, and they returned to River City.

Upon their return one of Jim's companions found that his mother had moved and closed down the home, leaving him without money or a base of operations. Jim says, "I do not know if I felt sympathy for him or restlessness in myself, but I agreed to steal with him." One night they broke into a tavern and removed the safe, which was found to contain $1700. Despite the impulsiveness of the theft and lack of planning, the two were never apprehended. Jim said that his share of the money was "blown on clothes, girls, and my car."

This was the first major theft committed by Jim, and it was by far the most successful one. It was planned and executed in an impulsive moment, without any real need for money, and these characteristics apply to all of his later thefts as well.

Encouraged by their success, Jim and Harry committed a second theft soon afterwards. They chose a lumber yard located at a well-lighted intersection of two major highways. After entering through a boarded-up window, they rifled several desk drawers and hammered at the safe but only succeeded in knocking the handle off. They were arrested the following day, and Jim still had the burglary tools in his car. He served ninety days in the county jail for this attempted burglary.

Some three months after his release, a fourteen-year-old girl was arrested on charges of sexual misconduct, and on questioning it was discovered that she had been involved with several score young men. Because of the large number involved, the police decided to press charges only against the girl and the boys they considered to be constant troublemakers. Jim and his companions fell into this category. Jim considers this incident one of the major turning points in his life.

> I was dating a couple of pretty nice girls and felt things were going smoothly before this young tramp got arrested, a tramp whom I had gang-banged at least a month before. I was arrested and charged with statutory rape and sat in jail for over two months and finally copped out to a lesser charge of indecent exposure, for which I received six months in jail. As you can see, I was getting started. This was, I believe, a point in life where I felt if things would have gone the other way, I would still be a free man. I had been trying to lead a fairly honest life.
>
> My family, of course, stuck by me once again. I sometimes felt that they had let me down somewhere along the line, and were trying to make it up to me or to take the blame themselves.

While Jim was in jail, his mother developed cancer and twice attempted to commit suicide. During the final two months of his sentence, Jim was permitted to leave jail with his sister and visit his mother at night in the hospital. She died one week after his release.

As mentioned earlier, Jim's father had become more responsible and dependable during his wife's final illness, and he arranged a job for Jim after his release. The only requirement was a satisfactory physical exam, but here again Jim failed to pass the eye test.

> This is another point where I felt I was cheated by life. I wanted this job quite badly. I wanted to stay out of jail. I had Rebecca, a very pretty, young girl who had waited for me, and I wanted to marry her. But this failure was very disheartening.
>
> I had been out of jail two weeks, my mother dead one week, when Bill and I drank some beer, by now I was drinking some, and took some codeine, and decided to rob a certain bootlegger that we knew.

Jim and Bill reasoned that the bootlegger would be a relatively safe target, since if he reported the robbery it would lead to an investigation of his own activities. The plan called first for stealing a pair of guns from a junk dealer. Later that night, masked and equipped with pistols, they entered the trailer home of the bootlegger and told him to "give us everything you have here." The bootlegger thought the guns were cap pistols, and he wrestled with the two boys while calling to his neighbor for help. Jim and Bill escaped as the neighbor called the police.

They were arrested the next day. The evidence against them included tracks in the fresh snow leading directly to Jim's house, a positive matching of the tracks with the shoes worn by the two boys, and a piece of fur from Jim's coat found on a barbed-wire fence adjacent to the trailer. The junk dealer also reported seeing the boys drive back and forth past his lot earlier in the day, and a positive identification was made of footprints leading to the shed where his guns were stored.

Both boys were nineteen years old when they entered the state penitentiary for five year terms on conviction of assault with intent to rob. Jim was told by the parole board that he would serve the full five years since, in view of his past record, he should have received a stiffer sentence. In fact, however, he served less than three years and during that period received no disciplinary reports. He made an excellent adjustment from the viewpoint of the prison officials, although it was less satisfactory from a personal standpoint.

The chief problem for Jim was lack of opportunity for heterosexual contacts. This was partially relieved at first by masturbation and later with homosexuals. He also acquired the technique of mainlining benzedrine. His job at the prison was that of head bookkeeper for kitchen stores; it was regarded as a politician's job by the inmates, and Jim was quite satisfied with it. The social climate of the prison did not suit him, however, and he resented having to associate with men of inferior quality.

> I resented being put into a situation where I had to mix freely and reciprocally with a conglomeration of morons, loud mouths, and just plain nuts. I felt and knew that I was mentally superior and basically better mannered and more sensitive than those around me.

Jim was twenty-two at the date of discharge. His first night out he purchased a syringe and some benzedrine and later became drunk enough to pass out and miss his bus home. The following night he met an ex-convict with whom he had worked in prison. The two of them broke into a number of places before dawn.

A former girl friend, Rebecca, contacted Jim soon after his release. During his stay in prison she had married a man from a wealthy, old-line family who was just completing his college career. Over the next five months the relationship between Jim and Rebecca progressed to the point where her husband left her, and she planned to marry Jim as soon as the divorce was final.

Jim said, "I pictured myself as hopelessly in love with this beautiful girl, who had thrown everything away for me." Nevertheless he was persuaded to strike out for California by his friend from prison, and he told Rebecca he would send for her after securing a job.

Whatever his initial intentions, a job was never located, and Jim lived off the proceeds of rolling drunks and a number of small thefts. He was arrested once, but the evidence was circumstantial and he served only ninety days in the county jail. When he returned to River City, he found that Rebecca had rejoined her husband, and they had moved to Phoenix.

Soon after his return, Jim reapplied for a job at the factory where he had previously failed the eye test. This time a friend in the office obtained a copy of the eye chart for him prior to the physical exam.

> Through this subterfuge, for the first time I had a good paying, steady job. One where I did not have to worry when I would get my check. I made a vow not to steal. For the first time in my life I felt secure and independent. I did not have any bills, and I was able to start building up my wardrobe and get things I had always wanted.

After working at the plant for three months, he volunteered for the night shift so that he might attend college. The college in River City hesitated to admit him in view of his past record, but after a personal interview the Registrar was sufficiently impressed to admit him on a trial basis the following semester.

MARRIAGE

By this time, Jim had moved from his father's home and shared an apartment in a nearby town with his friend Harry. The two enjoyed a succession of willing but unattractive girls, and among them was the girl whom Jim later married.

> Diane was a tramp, I could tell from the start. She forced the introduction and the first date. I had sexual relationships with her on the first date, she was my third sexual partner on that particular day. She was neat, but not really attractive. For the next four and a half months we were intimate almost every night. She wanted to marry, I did not. I could not see myself married to this plain-looking tramp. In fact, toward the last, I was trying to think of a scheme to get rid of her without hurting her.

Diane was eighteen, some five years younger than Jim, when the two met while she was attending a beautician's school. She was not beautiful, she lacked the range of intelligence and interests that Jim had, and she seemed almost amoral. But she was genuinely attached to Jim and resisted her parents' efforts to break up the relationship, even though they threatened to disown her.

Jim looks back on this period as the happiest in his life. He had a steady, well-paying job and money for things that were essential to him; clothing, his car, a girl, and such incidentals as a tennis racket and transistor radio. And by entering college he hoped to prepare himself for a better job and cancel out his previous record as an irresponsible troublemaker. But the idyll lasted only five months and then collapsed.

I started getting deeper and deeper in debt because I wanted a better and better car. Only one finance company would handle me because I was an ex-con. They hi-jacked me, but I did not mind, I was making good money. Then I burned the motor out of the car on which I still owed $400. I thought I might once again try stealing to pay off this car and get another, better one. The $1700 theft when I was seventeen is a dream that has kept me going. I have often thought that if I had never stolen that $1700, I would have given up long ago.

The opportunity for theft presented itself when he once more met his acquaintance from prison who was unemployed and also in debt. The two planned and attempted a break-in despite the pleadings of Diane, who offered to work as a prostitute to obtain money.

The break-in was spectacularly unsuccessful. When the police spotted Jim's car in front of the distributing company and noticed burglary tools in the back seat, they became suspicious and called for reinforcements. Soon the building was surrounded by a score of policemen and deputies. Through a quirk of fate the two men escaped through the cordon and spent a month as fugitives before finally being captured.

We spent the next twenty-nine days engaged in breaking and entering and two armed robberies which I enjoyed very much. During these twenty-nine days of running I did a lot of thinking, a lot of penitent, wishful thinking; wishing that I had told my friend to go to hell, wishing I had married my old faithful dog of a girl friend. I knew beyond the shadow of a doubt that I was headed for the penitentiary.

Following his capture, Jim was brought back to River City to face charges of breaking and entering. He spent three and a half months attempting to confess to a lesser charge, but the State Attorney was convinced he could win a conviction without compromising the original charge. Finally Jim pleaded guilty and was sentenced to ten years in the state penitentiary.

He was often visited by Diane at the country jail during the months before the trial, and he finally married her before going to prison. They could not afford wedding rings, so as a substitute Jim had the words "Love me, Diane" tattooed on his penis.

I had decided that if the faithful, old tramp of a girl friend still wanted me, I would marry her, probably because I wanted mail, visits, and money while in prison. While in jail, she was ever so good to me. I actually felt something akin to what I had always read that love was like.

When we were married, her parents threatened to disown her, but she did not seem to mind. Finally her mother came over to our side, and she has been a wonderful friend ever since. Her father now seems passive, although he has since offered me a job upon my release.

About a month and a half after we were married, my wife shacked up with another guy for about a week. She begged me to forgive her and take her back, which I did. Both she and her mother about had a nervous breakdown.

This was not Diane's first illicit lover nor her last. About six months later she told Jim that she was pregnant by another man and she subsequently gave birth to a baby boy.

At first, I blew my top, and told her that I did not want to see her ever again. Then, as she started crying and all that jazz, I told her that I would be happy to retain her as my wife and to support the child. First, I offered her her freedom, but she did not want a divorce.

Of course, her constant infidelity has weighed heavily upon me. At times I have been quite depressed, but I feel that I have stood up rather well.

For some reason when the baby was born, I seemed to be as happy as she was. I guess I was happy for her sake, because I realized how desperately she wanted a child. She begged me to give her one and I would not, maybe because of the responsibility. I have realized how lonely she is, and I hoped that this child will take the place of her lovers.

Then again, sometimes I feel I am punishing myself. Maybe by taking this load on myself, a tramp for a wife and an illegitimate child, I am making restitution to society. This seems to explain why I married a known tramp, when all my life I vowed that when I did marry, it would be a virgin.

I once read that, 'to be able to love when you can't have love, is a real test for love.' I have applied this criterion to our marriage, and in spite of my wife's actions, I still want her.

But the decision was no longer in Jim's hands. His wife became pregnant once again, and this time she wanted to marry the man. After the divorce, Diane and her new husband moved from River City back to her home town. The marriage had little effect upon her promiscuity, and she availed herself of a variety of partners over the next few years. When Jim was eventually paroled from prison he drove over a hundred miles twice a month to visit his former wife and spend the day with her. The relationship was quite satisfactory on this basis and continued for six months, until they tired of seeing each other.

During previous confinements Jim had been a model prisoner and had received no disciplinary reports in over four years of prison time. This time, whether because of frustrations in his marital life or for some other reason, he was even more aggressive than other convicts and started fights on seven occasions.

> On these occasions, I was so blinded by rage that I forgot all possible consequences. Luckily the first six times, no one was around, but on the seventh, I was put in solitary confinement.

Possibly because of these acting-out problems, he was given LSD-25 as part of an experiment by the prison psychiatrist. There is no record indicating whether the treatment was effective or not.

THE PRESENT SITUATION

Jim was paroled after serving a portion of his sentence for breaking and entering. He has been out for two years, his longest period of freedom since his conviction for rape at age sixteen. Although he has violated his parole in a number of minor ways (drinking, driving, leaving town), Jim has committed no crimes since his release. He is twenty-eight years old now and is again employed at the factory where he rigged the eye test. The pay is the highest in town, but the workers must be prepared for periodic lay-offs. Jim considers the job a strictly temporary one until something better comes along.

He has the drawbacks of many psychopaths. He is intellectually capable of a much better job than his past record and education qualify him for. And he is not emotionally adapted for the tedium and monotony of the jobs available to him. The taste for excitement and for the better life is deeply ingrained, and there is a curious quality of haughtiness and social opportunism in his attitudes that belies any genuine appreciation of other people.

> I feel that I am a sensitive person and do not share the run-of-the-mill convict's dream of the eternal whiskey bottle and the sexy broad. I do now and always have disdained the company of the ignorant, loud-mouthed, haughty people, such as is found in the factories, prisons, and honky-tonks.
>
> I have always preferred and felt more at ease with a higher type of associates, yet I am seemingly incapable or lacking the initiative to rise up to their standards.

Superficially, ten years of crime and punishment seem to have given him a perspective on his life, a more definite commitment to sidestep the impulsive ventures of the past. At least he articulates the right words about restraint and social responsibility.

I do not at the present moment feel useless or wasted; I have the capabilities, potential, and dreams; and I believe that I now possess the initiative.

Ever since that night I realized I was caught once again, I regretted my actions and have felt that, if given another chance, I could and would become a decent citizen.

I fully believe that I am entirely burned out with crime and doing time. To be completely honest though, I have experienced similar thoughts and convictions before and have failed. Perhaps I am just fooling myself but I tell myself this time I will use my head; when temptation arises I will stop and think a few minutes. I will weigh the consequences pro and con. I will evaluate my assets and then make my decision. If I could do this, I know I will never heist another safe or break into another place.

But the crucial issue is whether these statements reflect a deep-rooted internalized set of standards that can stand the press of temptation, or whether they compose an evanescent catechism that only touches the surface. Jim's family and friends have heard these comments before, to their relief, and later seen them broken on impulse. Has he now achieved a degree of personality integration and stability that did not exist before? General experience with psychopaths would encourage only the most guarded optimism. But Jim now has two years behind him without an actionable crime. Perhaps he has turned the corner.

REFERENCES

McCord, W., & McCord, J. *Psychopathy and delinquency.* New York: Grune & Stratton, 1956.

11.   Family Dynamics and Origin of Schizophrenia

Stephen Fleck

This paper is a report of a long-term study of the families of young upper-class schizophrenia patients—chosen for investigation because families from this socio-economic level are more likely to remain intact than families of lower-class status and thus be available for lengthy observation and study. It is easy to see how some of the

Psychosomatic Medicine; 22: 333-343, 1960. Reprinted by permission of the author, a member of the Department of Psychiatry, Yale University School of Medicine, New Haven, Conn. and by permission of Hoeber Medical Division, Harper and Row. The research reported here has been supported by grants from the National Institute of Mental Health and from the Social Research Foundation. Presented in part at the program honoring Dr. John C. Whitehorn during the Meeting of the Johns Hopkins Medical and Surgical Association, Feb. 27, 1959, Baltimore, Md.

characteristics of these upper-class families might exist in even more exaggerated form in lower-class families where the incidence of schizophrenia is highest. Schizophrenia is the most prevalent of all the *psychotic disorders* or *functional psychoses*. As you will notice in the final paper in Part II—*Action for Mental Health*—schizophrenia is considered to be one of the major mental illnesses.

This paper by Dr. Fleck has been included because many mental health workers are of the strong opinion that schizophrenia, too, is the result of personal and social forces rather than organic or constitutional one. As you recall, Dr. Adams (Selection 4) maintained that "mental illness" is the result of faulty or inadequate social learning experiences. This paper reflects some of those which occur within the family setting.

This article will provide some background for the material about hospital care in Part II (Selections 20 and 21).

An intensive study of the families of young upper-class schizophrenic patients, initiated by Dr. Theodore Lidz in 1952, is now in its seventh year (not counting the first year's pilot study by Drs. Lidz and Beulah Parker.)* The team whose research is reported here consisted of two and occasionally more psychiatrists, a social worker, a psychologist, and research assistants. We selected families in which at least the mother and one sibling were available for the study. In most of our families both parents have been available because the bias in our sample has been intentionally directed toward better organized families than would be provided by a random sample of the families of schizophrenics.[31, 52]† By dealing mostly with structurally intact families unencumbered by serious economic problems, we hoped to eliminate some of the more extraneous disorganizing factors that beset so many lower-class families.[24]

Contact with some of the families has been maintained through most of the research period and with all at least over many months. Interviews, held weekly in many cases, most commonly have involved the social worker and a family member.[9] Several parents, however, have been seen by one of the psychiatrists for long periods, although usually not at weekly intervals. Also, we often sought out and interviewed other relatives, especially grandparents, friends, and sometimes former servants. Home visits by the social worker have been made at least once in almost every instance. In addition, all available members of each nuclear family have been given a battery of psychological tests.[47] We have found it more useful not to record interviews verbatim but to dictate them as promptly as possible after a session. Even this condensed raw material

* Other collaborators: Alice Cornelison, M.S.S., Dorothy Terry, Ph.D., Daniel X. Freedman, M.D., Eleanor Kay, M.A., and Sarah Schafer, M.A.

† In this article the reference numbers refer to the bibliography at the end of the article.

on some families extends to several volumes of typed material. When satisfied that we had learned as much as we were likely to about a family, or when the patient had been discharged, we summarized the material in 50-100 typewritten pages. We feel that the data for 16 families are at this time reasonably complete.

On one level, the findings can be stated quite simply. No family that functioned or had ever functioned in a way that could be characterized as wholesome or normal or as falling within the usual range of family life has been found. All were severely disturbed, distorted by conflict, and beset by role uncertainties of family members other than the patient. I recognize that such a statement is methodologically not very satisfactory, but the team has been more concerned with describing and delineating the difficulties and disturbances that characterize these families than with an attempt to establish some sort of controlled study. I shall, however, attempt to spell out some of these differences between the study families and other families later on. We have been encouraged in the pursuit of our approach by the concordant findings of other groups who have studied families of schizophrenics in recent years, such as the National Institute of Mental Health,[5, 53] the group under Drs. Don Jackson and Gregory Bateson in Palo Alto,[3, 22, 26] and in particular, by similar findings abroad.[2, 10] Notably, Alanen of Finland has made a statement almost identical with the above: All but 16 of 100 mothers of schizophrenic patients he studied suffered from a clear neurosis or more serious psychopathologic disturbance, but each of these 100 families had to be considered severely disturbed.[2]

It is not easy, however, to list and delineate the abnormalities in family function that we have discerned manifest in disturbed family interaction and in the personalities of its members. In part, such a list encompasses the titles of previous publications, each only a fragment of the total reconstruction of family histories and the histories of the persons in it. This presentation also can deal only with some segments of the unexpectedly rich and complicated material that we have accumulated so far. Despite a multifaceted approach, we are by no means certain that we have as yet grasped the total picture of all the essentials of interaction in these families that have been studied from months to many years, or for that matter, of family dynamics in general. Our task is further complicated by the absence of a set of concepts (or a communication model for group interaction) that would simultaneously convey both a cross section of transactions at a given time and a longitudinal historical dimension.

The family is a unique type of group and operates under more complicated dynamics than do the synthetic groups usually studied in detail by sociologists or psychologists. Our traditional psychodynamic concepts alone are not suited to the description and analysis of the family-group process over a period of time. We have borrowed from social anthropologists and sociologists,[6] especially from Parsons,[42, 43] Kluckhohn,[28] and group psychologists[44] in an effort to place some of our work in a suitable frame of reference.[7, 16, 21, 48, 49] Without their work and that of many others in allied disciplines, we would have no suitable models to answer our needs at least in part.[12, 20] As I seek to describe some of our findings, it must be emphasized that different methods of abstraction as well as different conceptual approaches have been employed in describing different phases of the disturbed family milieu.

Certain facets of the disturbed family interaction we have observed have been separated out rather artificially, but the respective areas of interaction blend and, in actuality, of course, occur together. For the psychiatrist it is naturally easier to describe individual personal characteristics. In this work, however, impressive as the abnormalities of each family member often are, not to mention those of the patient, we have found that family interaction and the interlocking roles and role shifts appear to have more bearing upon the development of schizophrenia in one member than the characteristics of individual parents or siblings.

PARENTAL PERSONALITIES

At the start it became obvious to us, as it has to others, that many mothers of schizophrenic patients appear severely disturbed, often bordering on the psychotic.[1, 2, 23, 34, 40, 45, 46] Many such personal characteristics of these mothers have been described by others, notably by Dr. Trudi Tietze.[51] We are not yet prepared, however, to amplify these earlier descriptions or to render them more inclusive but should note that none of them applies to all the mothers we have studied. We have found a wider range of disturbances, and no one personality type has emerged. At least half the mothers of our patients were psychotically disturbed. We are in the process of examining the characteristics of mothers in various ways, including the use of a sorting technique employing several hundred items, a modification of a similar study undertaken by Don Jackson and his colleagues.[26] Some of the disturbed interaction patterns and irrational rearing techniques of these mothers will become evident in later sections; here, I note our conclusion that in any analysis of material personalities and in searching for common characteristics, the mothers of schizophrenic sons and of schizophrenic daughters must be considered separately.[38]

We realized soon that the intrapsychic disturbances of the mothers were not nearly as relevant to what happened to one or more children in the family (especially to the child who became schizophrenic) as was the fact that these women were paired with husbands who would either acquiesce to their many irrational and bizarre notions of how the family should be run or who would constantly battle with and undermine an already anxious and insecure mother.[34, 35] Furthermore, half the families were dominated by an equally irrational, often paranoid father paired with a submissive, acquiescing spouse, or at least by a disturbed husband who clashed with a constantly nagging and depreciating wife. Our first communication therefore concerned the characteristics of some of these fathers.[33] We have noted that while no characteristic type of disturbed father occurred in our series, many were so caught up in their personal problems—very often conscious and unconscious concerns about their masculinity—that they could not function in a parental fashion. Some used the child to gratify their narcissistic needs for admiration or completion of their selves quite as much as has been observed in the mother-child relationships of schizophrenic patients.[23, 32] Still others abdicated parental roles in the face of hostile, chronically nagging, and domineering spouses but might possibly have fulfilled parental functions more adequately if they had married supportive, less disturbed women. The reverse can also be said of some mothers, as Lidz and Lidz noted many years ago.[31] As far as the development of schizophrenia in an offspring is concerned, we now believe that more typical profiles for either parent may emerge if we group them according to the patient's sex.[38, 40]

PARENTAL INTERACTION

We have discerned and attempted to describe the disturbed interaction as certain patterns seemed to become understandable. These patterns, we believe, have a significant impact upon our patients' development and seem pertinent to symptomatology, if not to the basic illness. We have documented these intrafamilial disturbances with detailed examples in a number of papers and in this paper summarize them only briefly.

Schismatic Families

Schismatic families are beset by chronic strife and controversy, primarily between the parents. The friction may focus on specific issues such as religion or the family's social status, and these topics are constantly dragged into family discussion and interaction. Usually, however, such specific contents are only the outward symptom of a basic distrust and often hatred of one spouse for the other.[35]

The Readings were such a family. A paranoid, grandiose, and autocratic father dominated it. After 20 years of marriage he had remained emotionally closer to his mother than to his wife. He was very intelligent and productive, but he resisted his wife's burning ambition to rise in the social scale—a source of constant open controversy between them. However, any issue was apt to produce a fight, and when the older of their two daughters became schizophrenic at 21, the illness, the hospitalization, and the treatment all offered more opportunities for mutual nagging, for undermining the other's plans and hopes, and for holding each other responsible for this disaster. The patient spent most of her time in catatonic muteness, possibly the only way open to her to remove herself from the family battlefield.

The topic of her illness and its relation to the family dynamics will receive further comment in a following section.

The schismatic families in which the parents undermine each other's worth, despising each other as man or woman, depriving each other of much needed support (often a narcissistic need in at least one of the parents), can create insurmountable identity problems for their offspring. To be like one parent incurs the wrath or disparagement of the other, and neither parent may be very self assured about his gender to begin with. We can trace in this way some of the identity problems of schizophrenics and also can appreciate that young people raised in such families break down just at a time when a sense of identity essential to a more independent social role outside the home is expected of them in early adulthood.[37, 39]

Skewed Families

Another form of distorted family milieu has been designated as skew. Such families differ from schismatic ones in that the marriage itself may be peaceful and mutually satisfactory because the spouses have overtly or covertly reached a compromise concerning a serious personality defect in one or the other. Usually one partner had given in to the more disturbed and domineering one, but peace between them may be maintained at the expense of the children because the parental alliance also preempts their emotional resources, and then truly parental obligations suffer.[35]

Mr. Lamb, for instance, was a very successful business man but a most inadequate parent. As a young adult he had been an outstanding athlete but had to leave his school for disciplinary reasons. Soon after marriage he began to drink heavily, and by the time his wife became pregnant for the first time, he was an alcoholic. From the time of the son's conception on, he made every possible effort to retain all of his wife's attention and affection, and to keep her away from his son, who later was our patient. Mr. Lamb was much less competitive with a subsequent daughter. His wife largely acceded to his demands and wishes although she was aware of her son's unfulfilled needs. Instead of standing up to the father and objecting to his behavior, she tended to look at times to the son for emotional support that the husband could not give her. Moreover, she encouraged the talented son to fulfill her own artistic tendencies. These were entirely lost on her husband, who openly criticized the son as effeminate, weak, and unathletic, after having thwarted the son's earlier efforts to be physically active by sneering at the child's performance in games or sports.

At 20 the son indeed showed all these characteristics. But he had absorbed more from the parental interaction. The father drank, and yet both spouses maintained that he was not an alcoholic. He was unfaithful, and this also remained masked except for one occasion on which it became a community-wide scandal. Cheating and lying caused the patient's removal from school prior to his hospitalization, and prevarication remained a serious handicap in his therapeutic relationship for a long time. During the first year of his hospitalization he also lorded it over the staff, as well as his mother, treating everybody like an underling, as his father had often done at home.

The father had been a sham from the son's point of view. Instead of a father he was a competitor; the lack of integrity in his personal life could not be concealed, despite the parental conspiracy to deny the obvious. The concealment and deceit were reflected in the patient's symptoms and behavior in schizophrenic form.

Knowing the family history thoroughly and from many different vantage points, one is at a loss to find a position at any time to which this youngster could have regressed in order to re-experience some degree of security or satisfaction. Only autistic withdrawal seemed open to him. To live up to his father's "expectations" he had to be weak and passive in one sense, and an athlete in another; to please his mother he had to be artistic; but to assume a male role in any area carried the threat of incestuous closeness to his mother and indeed constituted a threat to his father's shaky masculinity. Thus, in this type of family also we can observe that the patient in his personality development is confronted with irreconcilable identity prototypes.

As far as these identity problems in young schizophrenics are concerned, we find that equivalent phenomena have been pointed out in a more general way by Erickson in his writings on identity crisis.[11, 37] We shall return to this topic later in connection with sexual problems.

The skew in the family can exist in another form: The dominant emotional dyad may be one parent and one offspring.[39] In these latter families the assignment to either group becomes somewhat arbitrary. Not only may a parental schism lead to hostile pairings or camps in the family, but one of these couplings may pre-empt the family's emotional resources just as importantly as the parental coalition illustrated above.

THE IRRATIONALITY OF THE FAMILY MILIEU AND SYMPTOM FORMATION

Another skewed family may illustrate this important process observed in many of our families—the transmission of irrationality or, one might almost say, the learning of symptoms.[8, 14, 36]

Young Dollfuss came to us from another hospital, to which he had been admitted following a serious suicide attempt. Although relatively compliant and cooperative at first, he soon became increasingly resistant to hospital routines, spoke less and less with anybody, neglected his appearance, grew a beard, and would not allow his hair to be cut, so that long locks soon framed his shoulders. Being unusually tall, he not only looked like the Messiah but was indeed preoccupied with strange mystical religions—seemingly of his own invention. As if this appearance were not bizarre enough in the setting of an unbelievably messy room in which he hoarded food, a typical daily scene showed him almost naked, sitting on his toilet, studying stock quotations in the *Wall Street Journal*. It may be noted in passing that he showed a typically schizophrenic phenomenon, exhibiting severe psychotic and delusional behavior, unable to have any comfortable human contact, while still able to select a stock portfolio for his therapist that he predicted correctly would increase 40 per cent on the market in a year's time—a coexistence of abnormal and normal high-order mentation never encountered in any known organic brain disorder.

As we began to learn about the family background, it became clear that the patient conducted his hospital life in the same autocratic, pompous, and captious manner in which the father had governed the parental household. Mr. Dollfuss was an ingenious and successful foreign-born manufacturer, but at home he ruled his roost like an Eastern potentate, a role for which he also claimed divine sanction and inspiration via a special mystical cult that he shared only with a very few select friends. The patient would permit only a chosen few of the staff into his sanctum, just as the father had secluded himself in his bedroom during most of the time that he spent at home, with only his wife and the children's governess permitted to enter and attend to his needs. Mr. Dollfuss, successful inventor and merchant, would sit there in his underclothes reading religious books by the hour. The entire household participated in the religious rites, the mother sharing his beliefs completely and continuing to do so even after his death, which according to the cult meant continuing life in a different form; the widow did not dare to disavow his teachings, because she believed he would know of it.

More than imitation and caricaturization of the father's behavior were involved. Both the patient and his only sister were emotionally deprived children who were isolated from the parents *and* from the surrounding community because the family milieu was so aberrant. Thus, when not mute, the patient often consented to communicate only in foreign languages, as if to emphasize his and the family's estrangement from the surroundings. He "communicated" his sense of deprivation by hoarding food, and during one stage of his illness by devising a complicated airline system designed exclusively for transporting and distributing food supplies in such a way that his needs would be gratified from all over the world.

This case provides a striking example of the irrationality of the parental relationship that came to pervade the entire household and of the aberrant patterns that the child had to cope with and ultimately learn himself, in order to live within the family. To question the bizarre family milieu, as he became aware that people outside did live and perceive the world differently, might have endangered his place as a child, leading to further distance from the parents or others in the household, all of whom shared or seemed to share the abnormal mode of life. To live outside this family the child had to learn other ways of living, if he could—and our patient could not.

Violation of Generation Boundaries

We were further impressed that in both skewed and schismatic families, one child might perceive that in reality he was more important to one or the other parent than was the spouse. In schismatic families, loyalty to one parent, often seductively engendered by that parent, might invite hostility and derogation from the other, just as the spouse to whom the child was close was despised by the partner. In addition to the obvious difficulties this created for the child who sought or needed to identify with one parent, such disregard of the familial generation boundaries had important bearing on the sexual confusions and panics from which practically all schizophrenics suffer.[15] Finally, by being all-important to one parent, or to both as a pawn of battle, the patient became predisposed to symptoms of grandiosity.

The skew in some families, as already described, might consist of a close, erotically colored continuing relationship between one parent and a child. Typically this kind of bond was highly charged with anxiety, since the two individuals never could find a comfortable distance or closeness in their interaction.[53] Therefore, the catatonic issue, "If I make one move, something terrible is going to happen—somebody will be harmed if I initiate a move," was a reality chronically confronting patients who grew up in such families.

We have discovered—especially in connnection with the issue of institutionalization itself—that some parents were truly incapable of living without the child and could not tolerate the separation imposed by hospitalization;[13] this conclusion confirms earlier reports by the Lidzes,[32] Hill,[23] and others,[5, 19] based on findings in individual therapy that the so-called symbiotic tie between patient and parent may be more essential to the parent's existence than to that of the patient. When a mother a thousand miles away awakens every morning at 6 A.M. because this is 7 A.M. Eastern time and the moment when her schizophrenic son receives his insulin injection and continues to experience the insulin injection vicariously through the morning over all this distance, day after day, we can appreciate that she cannot leave her son long in the hands of his therapists. We can also understand why the son is right in claiming that every move he makes is of world-shaking consequence because, indeed, it is so to his mother, whose anxiety he in turn heightened by letting her know in detail "how the insulin softened his brain."

We have described in another communication a skewed family containing twins, one of whom became our patient.[39] The birth of these twins was the mother's longed-for triumph over her own nonidentical twin sister, and the twins became the center of her life as well as the masters of the family's existence. Shortly after their birth the father was evicted from his wife's bed and bath rooms and, together with the older son, was relegated literally to inferior roles in the house, being permitted, for example, to use only the basement lavatory. One day when the mother, who was given to temper tantrums, received a spanking from one of the twins, the father tried to intercede, but the mother forbade him to interfere. Most of the violations of the generation boundaries we have noted are somewhat less bizarre and drastic, but not necessarily less damaging to a child's need to find a child's role and position in the family, on the basis of which further personality development and socially adaptive growth can proceed.[15, 37, 42, 43]

SEXUAL PROBLEMS

In connection with the Lamb case we have referred to the serious impediments such a family situation can represent to the development in a child of a sense of identity, and also how difficult it may be for an offspring to find in two warring parents suitable prototypes for identification. Whether fighting with each other or supporting each other at the expense of adequate reality presentation to their offspring, most of our parents were usually also very insecure about their own sexuality.

During visiting hours one of our patients, Dora Nussbaum, suddenly ran from her room in greater panic than observed ever before during several months of hospitalization. On investigation it was learned that she suddenly panicked while sitting on her bed with her father. We knew already that the patient had often fallen asleep in her father's arms. The mother had told us of her disgust over these intimacies between father and daughter, which bothered Mrs. Nussbaum all the more because of the absence of any physical intimacies between herself and her husband. This was a schismatic family in which the parents had become irreconcilably estranged because of a feud between their respective primary families, to whom both spouses were still very much attached. Dora's older brother and the mother had a workable if not close relationship, but Dora was disliked by the mother and preferred by the father, a condition that resulted in a rather incestuous bond between them. In adolescence, Dora began to object to his habit of frequently sleeping on her bed, out of fear that she would become pregnant (we have no evidence of actual incestuous behavior). However, frequent close physical contact was resumed during Dora's psychosis at times when the father tried to calm her. One of Dora's early psychotic manifestations was fear that she would be raped while at the same time she behaved promiscuously with strangers. The father claimed to be impotent but tried to make his wife and daughter believe that he had a mistress. Whether true or not, it bespeaks his insecure masculinity, also expressed in other effeminate, narcissistic tendencies.

Thus one can discern the roots of a schizophrenic patient's sexual and incestuous problems and their close relationship to panic states, symptoms which become understandable through scrutiny of the family background and dynamics.[15, 37]

Another father, who never achieved satisfactory sexual relations with his wife, promoted both homosexual and incestuous tendencies in his schizophrenic son. He often spoke to him about arranging dates for him, specifically mentioning an actress who, he pointed out, resembled his mother very strongly. The father also arranged for a friend whom he knew to be homosexual to share the boy's bedroom, besides taking showers himself with the son, comparing the size of their genitals or rubbing each other's backs. During therapy it was learned that one of the patient's tenacious symptoms—a magical need to repeat certain figures—was specifically related to conscious efforts to keep incestuous ideas in abeyance.

In the Reading family, which was split into two camps (page 108), the patient was also aware of the incestuous potential. Her suspicious, cantankerous father, who preferred her over the sister—not to mention his wife, whom he blamed for the illness—also was highly critical of the hospital, as well as suspicious that we were giving him "a run for his money." Realistically, she made no progress, possibly at least in part because of the father's disapproval of our efforts, a parallel to his undermining the mother's social and educational ambitions for her daughters. There were many threats to remove the patient from the hospital, and this he finally did. Once he proposed the following therapeutic solution: the family should split up, the mother and the patient's sister, who formed one faction, would live together, and he would live with and look after the patient himself. When the patient learned of this plan, she made one of her few excursions into reality from her state of catatonic muteness and stated, "I'll do anything for my father, but he can't have me that way."

We have spelled out in more detail in two other communications the nature of the many areas of family dysfunction that we have observed and their possible specific implications for the development of conscious incestuous and homosexual conflicts on the part of patients.[15, 39] The entire family interaction may promote such conscious preoccupations rather than further repression in offspring and parents alike. The continuation of incestuous impulses may be an index of family disorganization, a view supported by Parson's psychosocial formulations.[42, 43] We found that Parson's essential prerequisites of family life, which must exist if a child is to de-eroticize his parental attachments, acquire a sexual identity, and prepare for sociocultural adaptation, are often absent in the families we have studied.[11, 16, 43] Among the prerequisites that most, if not all, of our parents failed to observe were the maintenance of generation boundaries, a personal sense of security in each as to sexual, parental, and social roles, a certain degree of marital harmony, the ability to share or compromise on cultural values, and a capacity for role reciprocity.[37, 49]

SOCIOCULTURAL ISOLATION

We have illustrated how some of our families do not maintain differential roles in the sense of parents who nurture and lead as against children who are dependent and learn; that sexuality in these families is not limited to parental activity; that the parents, although often competent in their jobs or professions, are rigid, inflexible, and uncompromising in their intrafamilial behavior, and that many provide a home life quite deviant from the surrounding culture. The social life of these families often appears very limited, except that some families are still anchored in the patient's grandparental families or in one of the parent's collateral sibling families. There is failure to form a nuclear family of their own. This we found in six of our schismatic families; in a sense, this failure also constitutes another form of violating generation boundaries—at least in modern America.

Individual parental pathologic traits and role deficiences aside, it is therefore the irrational and idiosyncratic environment that these families create which seems most important and which has led us to speak of "*folie à famille*" in situations like that of the Dollfusses.[14] Furthermore, not only does the transmission of aberrant percepts seem specifically related to the later development of schizophrenic manifestations, but the feedback between the children and parents creates a self-perpetuating, irrational, and ambivalence-laden atmosphere. The interaction circuit may be one of axe-grinding between parents, or of a parent and child alternating between avoiding anxiety-arousing closeness—incestuous closeness—and efforts to overcome icy distance, but whichever it is, all family members must adapt to it in different roles.

Even if these family environments were not as deviant from the surrounding culture as many are, one gets the impression that intrafamilial life of the kinds described may absorb so much energy that but little emotional investment seems possible for learning and socializing tasks outside the home. Moreover, in many of these families the tools, especially the communication tools essential to the establishment of meaningful relationships outside the family, are simply not furnished.[14, 38] Thus, a vicious cycle exists because the aberrant family environment is self perpetuating unless corrected from the outside. But the isolating nature of the pathological forces within the family deprives its members of meaningful contacts with the outside world, and, therewith, of the potential corrective impact of intimate interaction with people outside the family circle. For instance, the incest issue may arouse enough guilt feelings in one or the other member to render difficult any other friendships; but in the absence of cathected relationships outside the family, those within become all the more intense and conflictful. The child caught in the special bind with a parent is most crucially affected. Seeking friends outside the bond endangers the very essential tie to the parent, and the absence of other ties renders the bond to that parent more intense and more ambivalent.

GENERAL COMMENT

Although the evidence is impressive, even from the fraction of our material presented, that the families discussed are unusually disturbed, we cannot state with certainty the extent to which the families are distinctive in structure and *modi operandi.* The nature of the abnormalities and the distortions of family life that we have observed fall into behavioral categories such as personal, interpersonal, group dynamics, and psychology, and their specific relevance to the development of schizophrenia remains to be documented in detail by further search and study.

We do not intend to promulgate an environmental interpersonal approach as against a genetic or biochemical path to the etiology of schizophrenia. Our material is not suited to settle questions of causation, as we are not searching for a particular cause but have been exploring essentially uncharted territory. This material, pertinent to schizophrenia, may also help us to understand better the mode of transmission from generation to generation of the highest cerebral functions, in particular all those specifically human functions concerned with interpersonal communication through complicated, abstract, verbal and nonverbal symbols, whether normal or schizophrenic. Thus, the study of schizophrenia leads us to the problems of personality development in the human and to the broad question of how meaning and logic and a sense of identity are acquired.

We have previously stated that schizophrenia can be viewed as one possible outcome of personality development, or as Sullivan phrased it, a "way of life."[50] This view does not exclude organic determinants, as genetic and nongenetic physiochemical influences obviously underlie and impinge upon the learning processes through which every individual must pass to acquire an identity and to develop his intellectual and sociocultural adaptive capacities. The physiological aspects of learning processes are only partially understood, but the development and the integration of symbolic processes and behavior occur after birth, whereas only simple reflexlike response patterns can be acquired prenatally.[25, 30] It seems fruitful, therefore, to scrutinze postnatal interactional phenomena, and such studies indeed render a great deal of this learning or transmission of behavior and attitudes, whether schizophrenic or not, more understandable, even if done retrospectively. This was expressed by Adolf Meyer 50 years ago: "We are, I believe, justified in directing our attention to the factors which we see at work in the life history of so-called dementia praecox. We are justified in emphasizing the process of crowding-out of normal reactions, of a substitution of inferior reactions some of which determine a cleavage along distinctly psychological lines incompatible with reintegration."[41] I am not citing these words because they may be truer or more appealing than other statements, but rather because if one rereads Bleuler,[4] Kraepelin,[29] Jung,[27] Meyer,[41] Freud,[18] and others who worked in this field half a century or more ago, recent studies of others and our own data seem to bear out Meyer's admonition above all others.

To explain bizarre behavior such as that of our Christ-like patient who sat in his bathroom with the *Wall Street Journal*, we neither have to fall back on or search for obscure pathological tissue processes on the one hand, nor do we have to speculate about all the possible symbolic meanings of such an activity, which is not to say that either consideration is irrelevant. Nor must we inject some psychotomimetic drug or postulate some sudden regressive break in the personality make-up to find explicable some of the other symptoms we described. To understand how items of behavior developed, however, is not necessarily to understand causality—certainly not the causality of as complicated a condition or process, whichever it may be, as schizophrenia. As long as there is no physical or chemical indicator for schizophrenia, we are left essentially with a conglomerate of clinical manifestations in making a diagnosis and are no better off today in this respect than was Bleuler half a century ago,[4] when he stressed that diagnosis rests on the psychological manifestations. In our day we prefer a still less limited area of diagnostic criteria by considering the patient's interpersonal behavior.

How can we be certain that the family interactions we have observed are pathological? Can we or anybody undertake "control studies?" If so, what variables should be controlled? We have designedly put this problem aside. It has taken months and years to arrive at reasonably plausible and congruous reconstructions of fewer than 20 families in terms of the personalities involved and their interaction patterns. Our data in themselves and even for the same family differ in reliability in that we have direct evidence about some phenomena from several sources and only plausible conjectures concerning other observations. Obviously, to duplicate such a study in detail would be an enormous task and open to question from the beginning if done by a different team because of the different personalities involved. We have undertaken recently to study also families of upper-class delinquents—not to compare variables, but to see how, if at all, these families differ, in the hope that we can sharpen our conceptualizations.[38]

Another question is: How are the phenomena described related to schizophrenia? Obviously we have not explained or made understandable all possible schizophrenic manifestations, nor is it likely that all of them are rooted in family interaction. Our data indicate, however, that the study of these families sheds much light on many schizophrenic manifestations, and that aspects of the parental personalities and of intrafamilial behavior of all members determine much of what we consider characteristic or pathognomonic of schizophrenia when we, as diagnosticians, approach a patient.

Another question that seemed formidable at first concerned the presence of "normal" and schizophrenic siblings in the same family. We have been working on this problem recently and have found it to be much less difficult. The patients' siblings are not unaffected by the abnormal environment. But when the entire family situation is known and the respective roles are understood, the development of the siblings' personalities, whether more nearly schizophrenic or more nearly normal, also fits into the total family pattern.[2a, 38]

Summary

In summary, some of the characteristic forms of family dysfunction related to schizophrenic manifestations that we observed are: (1) failure to form a nuclear family in that one or both parents remain primarily attached to one of his or her parents or siblings; (2) family schisms due to parental strife and lack of role reciprocity; (3) family skews when one dyadic relationship within it dominates family life at the expense of the needs of other members; (4) blurring of generation lines in the family, e.g., (a) when one parent competes with children in skewed families, (b) when one parent establishes a special bond with a child giving substance to the schizophrenic's claim that he or she is more important to a parent than the spouse, and (c) when continued erotization of a parent-child relationship occurs; (5) pervasion of the entire family atmosphere with irrational, usually paranoid, ideation; (6) persistence of conscious incestuous preoccupation and behavior within the group; (7) sociocultural isolation of the family as a concomitant of the six preceding conditions; (8) failure to educate toward and facilitate emancipation of the offspring from the family, a further consequence of points 1-5; (9) handicapping of a child in achieving sexual identity and maturity by the parents' uncertainty over their own sex roles; and (10) presentation to a child of prototypes for identification that are irreconcilable in the necessary process of consolidating his own personality.

Intensive work with these families has therapeutic implications which transcend our research plans as such and therewith the scope of this presentation. Other investigators of family dynamics have focused more on this aspect of the schizophrenia problem. The further development of rational psychotherapy, whether with the patient alone or with the family group, will depend upon better understanding and clarification of the complex interrelatedness of family dynamics, ego development, and identity formation. Thus, the study of schizophrenia and the quest for its origins leads us to the question of human development, and better understanding of the latter may illuminate the nature of schizophrenia as well as facilitate the treatment of schizophrenic patients.

REFERENCES

1. Abrahams, J., and Varon, E. J. *Maternal Dependency and Schizophrenia: Mother and Daughter in a Therapeutic Group.* New York, Internat. Univ. Press, 1953.
2. Alanen, Y. O. The mothers of schizophrenic patients. *Acta psychiat.· et neurol. scandinav.* Suppl. 124, 1958.
2a. Alanen, Y. O. Work in progress.
3. Bateson, G., Jackson, D. D., Haley, J., and Weakland, J. Towards the theory of schizophrenia. *Behavioral Sc. 1:* 251, 1956.
4. Bleuler, E. Dementia Praecox oder Grupper der Schizophrenien. In Aschaffenburg, G., Ed. *Handbuch der Psychiatrie.* Leipzig & Wien, 1911.
5. Bowen, M. Family relationships in schizophrenia. Presented at Hawaiian Divisional Meeting of American Psychiatric Association, May, 1958.
6. Bott, E. *Family and Social Network.* London, Tavistock Publications, 1957.
7. Buell, B., *et al. Classification of Disorganized Families for Use in Family Oriented Diagnosis and Treatment.* New York, New York, Community Research Associates, Inc., 1953.
8. Cameron, N. The paranoid pseudo-community revisited. *Am. J. Sociology 65:* 52, 1959.
9. Cornelison, A. Casework interviewing as a research technique in a study of families of schizophrenic patients. *Ment. Hyg., 44:* 551-559, 1960.
10. Delay, J., Deniker, P., and Green, A. Le milieu familial des schizophrenics. *Encéphale 46:* 189, 1957.
11. Erikson, E. The problem of ego identity. *J. Am. Psychoanalyt. A. 4:* 56, 1956.
12. Fisher, S., and Mendell, D. The communication of neurotic patterns over two and three generations. *Psychiatry 19:* 41, 1956.
13. Fleck, S., *et al.* The intrafamilial environment of the schizophrenic patient. III. Interaction between hospital staff and families. *Psychiatry 20:* 343, 1957.
14. Fleck, S., *et al.* The intrafamilial environment of the schizophrenic patient. V. The understanding of symptomatology through the study of family interaction. Presented at meeting of the American Psychiatric Association, May 15, 1957.
15. Fleck, S., *et al.* The intrafamilial environment of the schizophrenic patient. Incestuous and homosexual problems. In Masserman, J. H., Ed. *Science and Psychoanalysis: Inidvidual and Familial Dynamics.* New York, Grune, 1959, vol. II.
16. Flugel, J. C. *Man, Morals and Society: A Psychoanalytic Study.* New York, Internat. Univ. Press, 1955.
17. Frazee, H. E. Children who later become schizophrenics. *Smith Coll. Studies in Social Work 23:* 125, 1953.
18. Freud, S. Neurose and Psychose (1924). In *Gesammte Werke.* London, Imago, 1940, vol. XIII.
19. Fromm-Reichmann, F. Notes on the mother role in the family group. *Bull. Menninger Clin. 4:* 132, 1940.
20. Gerard, D. L., and Siegel, J. The family background of schizophrenia. *Psychiat. Quart. 24:* 47, 1950.

21. Goldberg, E. M. Experiences with families of young men with duodenal ulcer and "normal" control families: Some problems of approach and method. *Brit. J. M. Psychol. 26:* 204, 1953.

22. Haley, J. The family of the schizophrenic: A model system. *J. Nerv. & Ment. Dis.,* in press.

23. Hill, L. *Psychotherapeutic Interaction in Schizophrenics.* Chicago, Univ. Chicago Press, 1955.

24. Hollingshead, A. B., and Redlich, F. *Social Class and Mental Illness.* New York, Wiley, 1958.

25. Hooker, D. Unpublished address to medical sociology seminar, Yale University, 1958.

26. Jackson, D. D. The question of family homeostasis. *Psychiat. Quart.* Suppl. *31:* 79, 1957.

27. Jung G. *The Psychology of Dementia Praecox.* New York, Nerv. & Ment. Dis. Publ. Co., 1936.

28. Kluckhohn, F. *Variants in Value Orientations.* Evanston, Ill., Row Peterson, 1957.

29. Kraepelin, E. Zur Diagnose und Prognose der Dementia Praecox. *Allg. Ztschr. Psychiatrie. 56:* 254, 1899.

30. Langworthy, O. R. *Development of Behavior Patterns and Myelinization of the Nervous System in the Human Fetus. Contributions to Embryology No. 124.* Washington, D. C., Carnegie Institute, 1933.

31. Lidz, R. W., and Lidz, T. The family environment of schizophrenic patients. *Am. J. Psychiat. 106:* 332, 1949.

32. Lidz, R. W., and Lidz, T. Therapeutic considerations arising from the intense symbiotic needs of schizophrenic patients. In Brady, G., and Redlich, F., Eds., *Psychotherapy with Schizophrenics.* New York, Internat. Univ. Press, 1952.

33. Lidz, T., *et al.* The intrafamilial environment of the schizophrenic patient. I. The father. *Psychiatry 20:* 329, 1957.

34. Lidz, T., *et al.* The intrafamilial environment of the schizophrenic patient. IV. Parental personalities and family interaction. *Am. J. Orthopsychiat. 28:* 764, 1958.

35. Lidz, T., *et al.* The intrafamilial environment of schizophrenic patients. II. Marital schism and marital skew. *Am. J. Psychiat. 114:* 241, 1957.

36. Lidz, T., *et al.* The intrafamilial environment of the schizophrenic patient. VI. The transmission of irrationality. *A.M.A. Arch. Neurol. & Psychiat. 79:* 305, 1958.

37. Lidz, T., and Fleck, S. Schizophrenia, human integration and the role of the family. In *The Etiology of Schizophrenia,* New York. Basic Books, p. 323, 1960.

38. Lidz, T., and Fleck, S. Studies in progress.

39. Lidz, T., *et al.* The intrafamilial environment of the schizophrenic patient: VII. The differentiation of personalities and symptoms in identical twins. Unpublished.

40. Mark, J. D. The attitudes of mothers of male schizophrenics towards child behavior. *J. Abnorm. & Social Psychol. 48:* 185, 1953.

41. Meyer, A. The dynamic interpretation of dementia praecox. *Am. J. Psychol. 21:* 385, 1910.

42. Parson, T. The incest taboo in relation to social structure and the socialization of the child. *Brit. J. Sociology 5:* 101, 1954.

43. Parsons, T. Social Structure and the Development of Personality. *Psychiatry 21:* 321, 1958.
44. Parsons, T., et al. *Family, Socialization and Interaction.* Glencoe, Ill., Free Press, 1955.
45. Prout, C. T., and White, M. A. A controlled study of personality relationships in mothers of schizophrenic male patients. *Am. J. Psychiat. 107:* 251, 1951.
46. Reichard, S., and Tillman, C. Patterns of parent-child relationships in schizophrenia. *Psychiatry 13:* 247, 1950.
47. Sohler, D. T., et al. The prediction of family interaction from a battery of projective tests. *J. Proj. Tech. 21:* 199, 1957.
48. Spiegel, J. P. The resolution of role conflict with the family. *Psychiatry 20:* 1, 1957.
49. Spiegel, J., et al. *Integration and Conflict in Family Behavior. Report 27.* Topeka, Kan., Group for the Advancement of Psychiatry, 1954.
50. Sullivan, H. S. *The Interpersonal Theory of Psychiatry (Part III).* Edited by Perz, H. S., and Gavel, M. L. New York, Norton, 1953.
51. Tietze, T. A study of mothers of schizophrenic patients. *Psychiatry 12:* 55, 1949.
52. Wahl, C. W. Antecedent factors in family histories of 392 schizophrenics. *Am. J. Psychiat. 110:* 668, 1954.
53. Wynne, L. C., et al. Pseudo-mutuality in the family relations of schizophrenics. *Psychiatry 21:* 205, 1958.

12. Schizophrenic Patients in the Psychiatric Interview: An Experimental Study of Their Effectiveness at Manipulation

Benjamin M. Braginsky and Dorothea D. Braginsky[1]

The "sickness" notion has been partially responsible for schizophrenic (one of the *major* mental illnesses, Selection 24) patients being viewed as helpless, inert, and ineffective people who are at the complete mercy of their environment. These views, in turn, may have accounted to some degree for their legal rights being ignored, as indicated in Selection 3. Several recent studies have indicated that those people, labeled "schizophrenic," are not passive pawns. The present study, as one example, suggests that these people do indeed exert control over their surroundings. Moreover, it raises questions about the validity of the "psychiatric interview" as did Selection 3. The ideas of these authors about the inadequacies of the "medical model" are elaborated in their book *Methods of Madness,* published by Holt, Rinehart and Winston.

Journal of Consulting Psychology, 31:543-547, #6, 1967. Reprinted by permission of the authors and the American Psychological Association.
[1] The authors would like to express their appreciation to Doris Seiler and Dennis Ridley for assisting with the data collection.

The senior author is now at Wesleyan University (Connecticut), while the junior author is at Fairfield University.

The present investigation is concerned with the manipulative behavior of hospitalized schizophrenics in evaluative interview situations. More specifically, the study attempts to answer the question: Can schizophrenic patients effectively control the impressions (impression management, Goffman, 1959) they make on the professional hospital staff?

Typically, the mental patient has been viewed as an extremely ineffectual and helpless individual (e.g., Arieti, 1959; Becker, 1964; Bellak, 1958; Joint Commission on Mental Illness and Health, 1961; Redlich & Freedman, 1966; Schooler & Parkel, 1966; Searles, 1965). For example, Redlich and Freedman (1966) described the mental patient and his pathological status in the following manner: "There is a concomitant loss of focus and coherence and a profound shift in the meaning and value of social relationships and goal directed behavior. This is evident in the inability realistically to implement future goals and present satisfactions; they are achieved magically or through fantasy and delusion. . . [p. 463]." Schooler and Parkel (1966) similarly underline the mental patients' ineffectual status in this description: "the chronic schizophrenic is not Seneca's 'reasoning animal,' or Spinoza's 'social animal,' or even a reasonably efficient version of Cassirer's 'symbol using animal'. . . . Since he violates so many functional definitions of man, there is heuristic value in studying him with an approach like that which would be used to study an alien creature [p. 67]."

Thus, the most commonly held assumptions concerning the nature of the schizophrenic patient stress their effectuality and impotency. In this context one would expect schizophrenics to perform less than adequately in interpersonal situations, to be unable to initiate manipulative tactics, and, certainly, to be incapable of successful manipulation of other people.[2]

In contrast to the above view of the schizophrenic, a less popular orientation has been expressed by Artiss (1959), Braginsky, Grosse, and Ring (1966), Goffman (1961), Levinson and Gallagher (1964), Rakusin and Fierman (1963), Szasz (1961, 1965), and Towbin (1966). Here schizophrenics are portrayed in terms usually reserved for neurotics and normal persons. Simply, the above authors subscribe to the beliefs that: (a)

[2] This statement is explicitly derived from formal theories of schizophrenia and not from clinical observations. It is obvious to some observers, however, that schizophrenics do attempt to manipulate others. The discrepancy between these observations and traditional theoretical assumptions about the nature of schizophrenics is rarely, if ever, reconciled.

the typical schizophrenic patient, as compared to normals, is not deficient, defective, or dissimilar in intrapsychic functioning; (b) the typical schizophrenic patient is not a victim of his illness; that is, it is assumed that he is not helpless and unable to control his behavior or significantly determine life outcomes; (c) the differences that some schizophrenic patients manifest (as compared to normals) are assumed to be more accurately understood in terms of differences in belief systems, goals, hierarchy of needs, and interpersonal strategies, rather than in terms of illness, helplessness, and deficient intrapsychic functioning. This orientation leads to the expectation that schizophrenic patients do try to achieve particular goals and, in the process, effectively manipulate other people.

There is some evidence in support of this viewpoint (e.g., Artiss, 1959; Braginsky, Holzberg, Finison, & Ring, 1967; Levinson & Gallagher, 1964). Furthermore, a recent study (Braginsky et al., 1966) demonstrated that schizophrenic patients responded, on a paper-and-pencil "mental status" test, in a manner that would protect their self-interests. Those who wanted to remain in the hospital (chronic patients) presented themselves as "sick," whereas those who desired to be discharged (first admissions) presented themselves as "healthy." That is, they effectively controlled the impressions they wished to make on others. Their manipulative performance, however, was mediated by an impersonal test.

Therefore, the following question is asked: Can schizophrenics engage in similar manipulative behaviors in a "face-to-face" interview with a psychologist? That is, will chronic schizophrenics who desire to remain in the hospital and live on open wards present themselves in an interview situation when they perceive that their open ward status is being questioned as (a) "healthy" and, therefore, eligible for open ward living, and in another interview situation when their residential status is being questioned as (b) "sick" and, therefore, ineligible for discharge? If so, are their performances convincing to a professional audience (i.e., psychiatrists)?

METHOD

A sample of 30 long-term (more than 2 continuous years of hospitalization) male schizophrenics living on open wards was randomly selected from ward rosters. Two days prior to the experiment the patients were told that they were scheduled for an interview with a staff psychologist. Although each patient was to be interviewed individually, all 30 were brought simultaneously to a waiting room. Each patient interviewed was not allowed to return to this room, to insure that patients who had participated would not communicate with those who had not.

Each patient was escorted to the interview room by an assistant, who casually informed the patient in a tone of confidentiality about the purpose of the interview (preinterview induction). Patients were randomly assigned by the assistant to one of three induction conditions (10 to each condition). The interviewer was unaware of the induction to which the patients were assigned, thereby eliminating interviewer bias.

Induction Conditions

Discharge induction. Patients were told: "I think the person you are going to see is interested in examining patients to see whether they might be ready for discharge."

Open ward induction.[3] Patients were told: "I think that the person you are going to see is interested in examining patients to see whether they should be on open or closed wards."

Mental status induction.[4] Patients were told: "I think the person you are going to see is interested in how you are feeling and getting along in the hospital."

After greeting each patient the interviewer asked: "How are you feeling?" Patients who responded only with physical descriptions were also asked: "How do you feel mentally?" whereas those who only gave descriptions of their mental state were asked: "How are you feeling physically?" The patients' responses were tape-recorded. The interview was terminated after 2 minutes,[5] whereupon the purpose of the experiment was disclosed.

Three staff psychiatrists from the same hospital separately rated each of the 30 tape-recorded interviews during two 40-minute sessions. The psychiatrists had no knowledge of the experiment, and they were unfamiliar with the patients; they were told by the experimenter that these were mental patients residing in the hospital and that as a group they represented a wide range of diagnostic categories.

The psychiatrists rated the patients on the following dimensions: (*a*)

---

[3] It may be suggested that the open ward induction was meaningless, since no patient enjoying open ward status would believe that he could be put on a closed ward on the basis of an interview. At the time this experiment was being conducted, however, this hospital was in the process of reorganization, and open and closed ward status was a salient and relevant issue.

[4] Mental status evelution interviews are typically conducted yearly. Thus, patients who have been in the hospital for more than a year expect to be interviewed for the purposes of determining their residency status.

[5] Although, admittedly, psychiatrists would never base decisions concerning mental status and discharge on a 2-minute interview, it was adequate for the purposes of this study (namely, to determine if mental patients effectively engage in impression management). The 2-minute response to the single question provided sufficient information for psychiatrists to form reliable impressions of the patients. Interestingly, the typical mental status interview conducted by these psychiatrists is rarely longer than 30 minutes.

the patient's degree of psychopathology, using a five-point scale ranging from "not at all ill" to "extremely ill"; (b) the amount of hospital control a patient needed, ranging on an eight-point scale from complete freedom ("discharge") to maximum control ("closed ward, continual observation"); and (c) the structural or qualitative aspects of the patient's speech, such as pressure of speech, affect, volume, etc. The score for each patient's speech characteristic was based on the sum of the psychiatrist's rating of 14 Lorr scale items (Lorr, 1953). Each item was rated on an eight-point scale ranging from not at all atypical to extremely atypical verbal behavior.

Predictions

If long-term patients are both motivated to live on open wards and to remain in the hospital and if, in addition, they effectively engage in impression management in order to realize these desires, then the following would be expected:

1. Psychiatrists will rate patients in the discharge and the mental status conditions as being similar with respect to psychopathology and need for hospital control. Mental status interviews are generally used by the hospital to evaluate patients for discharge; therefore, the mental status and discharge conditions offer the same potential consequences for patients. Thus, patients in both conditions will give the impression of being "sick" and in need of hospital control in order to decrease the probability of discharge. The purpose of including the discharge induction was to present the consequences of the interview as explicitly as in the open ward induction.

2. Psychiatrists will rate the patients in the open ward condition significantly less mentally ill and less in need of hospital control than patients in the discharge and mental status conditions. That is, patients in the open ward condition will give the impression of being "healthy" in order to maximize their chances of remaining on an open ward.

Subjects

The mean age of the patients was 47.4 years (SD = 8.36). The mean educational level of the group was 8.05 years of schooling (SD = 3.44). The median length of hospitalization was 10 years. In terms of diagnostic categories, 43% of the sample was diagnosed as chronic undifferentiated schizophrenic, 37% as paranoid schizophrenic, 10% as catatonic, and the remaining 10% as simple schizophrenic. There were no differences between the three experimental groups on any of the above variables.

RESULTS AND DISCUSSION

The reliability coefficients of the three psychiatrists' combined ratings of the patient interviews were as follows: (a) ratings of psychopathology —$r = .89$, $p < .01$; (b) need for hospital control—$r = .74$, $p < .01$; (c) normality of speech characteristics—$r = .65$, $p < .01$. Thus, it was concluded that there was significant agreement between the three psychiatrists.

The means of the psychopathology ratings by experimental condition are presented in Table 1. The ratings ranged 1-5. The analysis of variance of the data yielded a significant condition effect ($F = 9.38$, $p < .01$). The difference between the open ward and discharge conditions was statistically significant ($p < .01$; Tukey multiple-range test). In addition, the difference between the open ward and the mental status condition was significant ($p < .01$). As predicted, there was no significant difference between the discharge and mental status conditions.

The means of the ratings of need for hospital control are presented in Table 1. These ratings ranged 1-8. The analysis of these data indicated a significant difference between the means ($F = 3.85$, $p < .05$). Again, significant differences (beyond the .05 level) were obtained between the open ward and the discharge conditions, as well as between the open ward and mental status conditions. No difference was found between the discharge and mental status conditions.

TABLE 1 MEAN PSYCHOPATHOLOGY AND NEED-FOR-HOSPITAL-CONTROL RATINGS BY EXPERIMENTAL CONDITION

Rating	Open ward		Mental status		Discharge	
	M	SD	M	SD	M	SD
Psychopathology	2.63	.58	3.66	.65	3.70	.67
Need for hospital control	2.83	1.15	4.10	1.31	4.20	1.42

On the basis of these analyses it is clear that patients in the open ward condition appear significantly less mentally ill and in less need of hospital control than patients in either the discharge or mental status conditions. Obviously the patients in these conditions convey different impressions in the interview situation. In order to ascertain the manner by which the patients conveyed these different impressions, the following three manipulative tactics were examined: (*a*) number of positive statements patients made about themselves, (*b*) number of negative statements made about themselves, these include both physical and mental referents), and (*c*) normality of speech characteristics (i.e., how "sick" they sounded, independent of the content of speech). The first two indexes were obtained by counting the number of positive or negative self-referent statements a patient made during the interview. These counts were done by three judges independently, and the reliability coefficient was .95. The third index was based on the psychiatrists' ratings on 14 Lorr scale items of the speech characteristics of patients. A score was obtained for each patient by summing the ratings for the 14 scales.

Ratings of psychopathology and need for hospital control were, in part, determined by the frequency of positive and negative self-referent statements. The greater the frequency of positive statements made by a patient, the less ill he was perceived ($r = -.58$, $p < .01$) and the less in need of hospital control ($r = -.41$, $p < .05$). Conversely, the greater the frequency of negative statements, the more ill a patient was perceived ($r = .53$, $p < .01$) and the more in need of hospital control ($r = .37$, $p < .05$). It is notworthy that patients were consistent in their performances; that is, those who tended to say positive things about themselves tended not to say negative things ($r = -.55$, $p < .01$).

When self-referent statements were compared by condition, it was found that patients in the open ward condition presented themselves in a significantly more positive fashion than patients in the discharge and mental status conditions. Only 2 patients in the open ward condition reported having physical or mental problems, whereas 13 patients in the mental status and discharge conditions presented such complaints ($\chi^2 = 5.40$, $p < .05$).

The frequency of positive and negative self-referent statements, however, cannot account for important qualitative components of the impressions the patients attempted to convey. For example, a patient may give only one complaint, but it may be serious (e.g., he reports hallucinations), whereas another patient may state five complaints, all of which are relatively benign. In order to examine the severity of symptoms or complaints reported by patients, the number of "psychotic" complaints, namely, reports of hallucinations or bizzare delusions, was tallied. None of the patients in the open ward condition made reference to having had hallucinations or delusions, while nine patients in the discharge and mental status conditions spontaneously made such reference ($\chi^2 = 4.46$, $p < .05$).

In comparing the structural or qualitative aspects of patient speech no significant differences were obtained between experimental conditions. Patients "sounded" about the same in all three conditions. The majority of patients (80%) were rated as having relatively normal speech characteristics. Although there were no differences by condition, there was a significant inverse relationship ($r = -.35$, $p < .05$) between quality of speech and the number of positive statements made. That is, patients were consistent to the extent that those who sounded ill tended not to make positive self-referent statements.

In summary then, the hypotheses were confirmed. It is clear that patients responded to the inductions in a manner which maximized the chances of fulfilling their needs and goals. When their self-interests were at stake patients could present themselves in a face-to-face interaction as either "sick" or "healthy," whichever was more appropriate to the situation. In the context of this experiment "sick" impressions were conveyed when the patients were faced with the possibility of discharge. On the other hand, impressions of "health" were conveyed when the patients' open ward status was questioned. Moreover, the impressions they conveyed were convincing to an audience of experienced psychiatrists.

One may argue, however, that the differences between the groups were a function of differential anxiety generated by the inductions rather than a function of the patients' needs, goals, and manipulative strategies. More specifically, the discharge and the mental status conditions would generate more anxiety and, therefore, more pathological behavior than the open ward condition. As a result, the psychiatrist rated the patients in the discharge and mental status conditions as "sicker" than patients in the open ward condition. According to this argument, then, the patients who were rated as sick were, in fact, more disturbed, and those rated healthy were, in fact, less disturbed.

No differences, however, were found between conditions in terms of the amount of disturbed behavior during the interview. As was previously mentioned, the psychiatrists did not perceive any differences by condition in atypicality of verbal behavior. On the contrary, the patients were judged as sounding relatively normal. Thus, the psychiatrists' judgments of psychopathology were based primarily on the symptoms patients reported rather than on symptoms manifested. Patients did not behave in a disturbed manner; rather, they told the interviewer how disturbed they were.

The traditional set of assumptions concerning schizophrenics, which stresses their irrationality and interpersonal ineffectuality, would not only preclude the predictions made in this study, but would fail to explain parsimoniously the present observations. It is quite plausible and simple to view these findings in terms of the assumptions held about people in general; that is, schizophrenics, like normal persons are goal-oriented and are able to control the outcomes of their social encounters in a manner which satisfies their goals.

REFERENCES

Arieti, S. *American handbook of psychiatry*. New York: Basic Books, 1959.

Artiss, K. L. *The symp om as communication in schizophrenia*. New York: Grune & Stratton, 1959.

Becker, E. *The revolution in psychiatry*. London: Collier-Macmillan, 1964.

Bellak, C. *Schizophrenia: A review of the syndrome*. New York: Logos Press, 1958.

Braginsky, B., Grosse, M., & Ring, K. Controlling outcomes through impression-management: An experimental study of the manipulative tactics of mental patients. *J. Consult. Psychol.* 1966, 30, 295-300.

Braginsky, B., Holzberg, J., Finison, L., & Ring, K. Correlates of the mental patient's acquisition of hospital information. *J. Pers.* 1967, 35, 323-342.

Goffman, E. *The presentation of self in everyday life*. New York: Doubleday, 1959.

Goffman, E. *Asylums*. New York: Doubleday, 1961.

Joint Commission on Mental Illness and Health. *Action for mental health*. New York: Basic Books, 1961.

Levinson, D. S., & Gallagher, E. B. *Patienthood in the mental hospital*. Boston: Houghton-Mifflin, 1964.

Lorr, M. Multidimensional scale for rating psychiatric patients. *Veterans Administration Technical Bulletin*, 1953, 51, 119-127.

Rakusin, J. M., & Fierman, L. B. Five assumptions for treating chronic psychotics. *Ment. Hosp.*, 1963, 14, 140-148.

Redlich, F. C., & Friedman, D. X. *The theory and practice of psychiatry*. New York: Basic Books, 1966.

Schooler, C., & Parkel, D. The overt behavior of chronic schizophrenics and its relationship to their internal state and personal history. *Psychiatry*, 1966, 29, 67-77.

Searles, H. F. *Collected papers on schizophrenia and related subjects*. New York: International Universities Press, 1965.

Szasz, T. S. *The myth of mental illness*. New York: Hoeber-Harper, 1961.

Szasz, T. S. *Psychiatric justice*. New York: Macmillan, 1965.

Towbin, A. P. Understanding the mentally deranged. *Journal of Existentialism*, 1966, 7, 63-83.

PART 2

Alteration of Behavior

13. The Community and the Community Mental Health Center

M. Brewster Smith and Nicholas Hobbs

Certain official policies of the government of the United States are beginning to reflect the trend away from the narrow "disease" or "sickness" notion of mental illness. Perhaps the most tangible evidence of this position has been the creation of community mental health centers; these organizations have as their cornerstone the recognition that the "medical model" has been too restrictive. Flexibility and variety in care and treatment are the hallmarks of these new centers. They also reflect the fact that no one mental health discipline has a corner on the truth.

M. Brewster Smith, formerly Professor of Psychology and Director of the Institute of Human Development at the University of California, Berkeley, is now at the University of Chicago. He is Vice President of the Joint Commission on Mental Illness and Health and was formerly President of the Society for the Psychological Study of Social Issues and Editor of the *Journal of Abnormal and Social Psychology.*

Nicholas Hobbs is Provost of Vanderbilt University and Director of the John F. Kennedy Center for Research on Education and Human Development at Peabody College. He was Vice-Chairman of the Board of Trustees of the Joint Commission on Mental Illness and Health and is currently President of the American Psychological Association and Vice President of the Joint Commission on Mental Health of Children.

Throughout the country, states and communities are readying themselves to try the "bold new approach" called for by President John F. Kennedy to help the mentally ill and, hopefully, to reduce the frequency of mental disorders. The core of the plan is this: to move the care and treatment of the mentally ill back into the community so as to avoid the needless disruption of normal patterns of living, and the estrangement from these patterns, that often come from distant and prolonged hospitalization; to make the full range of help that the community has to offer readily available to the person in trouble; to increase the likelihood that trouble can be spotted and help provided early when it can do the most good; and to strengthen the resources of the community for the prevention of mental disorder.

This statement was adopted on March 12, 1966, by the Council of Representatives as an official position paper of the American Psychological Association, and published in *American Psychologist,* 21, 499-509, #6, June, 1966. Reprinted by permission of the authors and the American Psychological Association.

The community-based approach to mental illness and health attracted national attention as a result of the findings of the Joint Commission on Mental Illness and Health [See Selection 24] that was established by Congress under the Mental Health Study Act of 1955. After 5 years of careful study of the nation's problems of mental illness, the Commission recommended that an end be put to the construction of large mental hospitals, and that a flexible array of services be provided for the mentally ill in settings that disrupt as little as possible the patient's social relations in his community. The idea of the comprehensive community mental health center was a logical sequel.

In 1962, Congress appropriated funds to assist states in studying their needs and resources as a basis for developing comprehensive plans for mental health programs. Subsequently, in 1963, it authorized a substantial Federal contribution toward the cost of constructing community mental health centers proposed within the framework of state mental health plans. It appropriated $35,000,000 for use during fiscal year 1965. The authorization for 1966 is $50,000,000 and for 1967 $65,000,000. Recently, in 1965, it passed legislation to pay part of the cost of staffing the centers for an initial period of 5 years. In the meantime, 50 states and 3 territories have been drafting programs to meet the challenge of this imaginative sequence of Federal legislation.

In all the states and territories, psychologists have joined with other professionals, and with non-professional people concerned with mental health, to work out plans that hold promise of mitigating the serious national problems in the area of human well-being and effectiveness. In their participation in this planning, psychologists have contributed to the medley of ideas and proposals for translating the concept of comprehensive community mental health centers into specific programs. Some of the proposals seem likely to repeat past mistakes. Others are fresh, creative, stimulating innovations that exemplify the "bold new approach" that is needed.

Since the meaning of a "comprehensive community mental health center" is far from self-evident, the responsible citizen needs some guidelines or principles to help him assess the adequacy of the planning that may be underway in his own community, and in which he may perhaps participate. The guidelines and discussion that are offered here are addressed to community leaders who face the problem of deciding how their communities should respond to the opportunities that are opened by the new Federal and state programs. In drafting what follows, many sources have been drawn upon: the monographs and final report of the Joint Commission, testimony presented to Congress during the consideration of relevant legislation, official brochures of the National Institute of Mental Health, publications of the American Psychiatric Association, and recommendations from members of the American Psychological Association who have been involved in planning at local, state, and national levels.

The community mental health center, 1966 model, cannot be looked to for a unique or final solution to mental health problems: Varied patterns will need to be tried, plans revised in the light of evaluated experience, fossilized rigidity avoided. Even as plans are being drawn for the first comprehensive centers under the present Federal legislation, still other bold approaches to the fostering of human effectiveness are being promulgated under the egis of education and of economic opportunity programs. A single blueprint is bound to be inadequate and out of date at the moment it is sketched. The general approach underlying these guidelines may, it is hoped, have somewhat more enduring relevance.

Throughout, the comprehensive community mental health center is considered from the point of view of members of a community who are seeking good programs and are ultimately responsible for the kind of programs they get. The mental health professions are not to be regarded as guardians of mental health, but as agents of the community—among others—in developing and conserving its human resources and in restoring to more effective functioning people whose performance has been impaired. Professional people are valuable allies in the community's quest for the health and well-being of its members, but the responsibility for setting goals and major policies cannot be wisely delegated.

COMMUNITY INVOLVEMENT AND COMMUNITY CONTROL

For the comprehensive community mental health center to become an effective agency of the community, community control of center policy is essential.

The comprehensive community mental health center represents a fundamental shift in strategy in handling mental disorders. Historically, and still too much today, the preferred solution has been to separate the mentally ill person from society, to put him out of sight and mind, until, if he is lucky, he is restored to normal functioning. According to the old way, the community abandoned its responsibility for the "mental patient" to the distant mental hospital. According to the new way, the community accepts responsibility to come to the aid of the citizen who is in trouble. In the proposed new pattern, the person would remain in his own community, often not even leaving his home, close to family, to friends, and to the array of professional people he needs to help him. Nor would the center wait for serious psychological problems to develop and be referred. Its program of prevention, detection, and early intervention would involve it in many aspects of community life and in many institutions not normally considered as mental health agencies: the schools, churches, playgrounds, welfare agencies, the police, industry, the courts, and community councils.

This spread of professional commitment reflects in part a new conception of what constitutes mental illness. The new concept questions the appropriateness of the term "illness" in this context, in spite of recognition that much was gained from a humanitarian viewpoint in adopting the term. Mental disorders are in significant ways different from physical illnesses. Certainly mental disorder is not the private misery of an individual; it often grows out of and usually contributes to the breakdown of normal sources of social support and understanding, especially the family. It is not just an individual who has faltered; the social systems in which he is embedded through family, school, or job, through religious affiliation or through friendship, have failed to sustain him as an effective participant.

From this view of mental disorder as rooted in the social systems in which the troubled person participates, it follows that the objective of the center staff should be to help the various social systems of which the community is composed to function in ways that develop and sustain the effectiveness of the individuals who take part in them, and to help these community systems regroup their forces to support the person who runs into trouble. The community is not just a "catchment area" from which patients are drawn; the task of a community mental health center goes far beyond that of purveying professional services to disordered people on a local basis.

The more closely the proposed centers become integrated with the life and institutions of their communities, the less the community can afford to turn over to mental health professionals its responsibility for guiding the center's policies. Professional standards need to be established for the centers by Federal and state authorities, but goals and basic policies are a matter for local control. A broadly based responsible board of informed leaders should help to ensure that the center serves in deed, not just in name, as a focus of the community's varied efforts on behalf of the greater effectiveness and fulfillment of all its residents.

RANGE OF SERVICES

The community mental health center is "comprehensive" in the sense that it offers, probably not under one roof, a wide range of services, in-

cluding both direct care of troubled people and consultative, educational, and preventive services to the community.

According to the administrative regulations issued by the Public Health Service, a center must offer five "essential" services to qualify for Federal funds under the Community Mental Health Centers Act of 1963: (*a*) *inpatient care* for people who need intensive care or treatment around the clock; (*b*) *outpatient care* for adults, children, and families; (*c*) *partial hospitalization*, at least day care and treatment for patients able to return home evenings and weekends, perhaps also night care for patients able to work but needing limited support or lacking suitable home arrangements; (*d*) *emergency care* on a 24-hour basis by one of the three services just listed; and (*e*) *consultation and education* to community agencies and professional personnel. The regulations also specify five additional services which, together with the five "essential" ones, "complete" the comprehensive community mental health program: (*f*) *diagnostic service;* (*g*) *rehabilitative service* including both social and vocational rehabilitation; (*h*) *precare and aftercare*, including screening of patients prior to hospital admission and home visiting or halfway houses after hospitalization; (*i*) *training* for all types of mental health personnel; and (*j*) *research and evaluation* concerning the effectiveness of programs and the problems of mental illness and its treatment.

That the five essential services revolve around the medically traditional inpatient-outpatient core may emphasize the more traditional component of the comprehensive center idea somewhat at the expense of full justice to the new conceptions of what is crucial in community mental health. Partial hospitalization and emergency care represent highly desirable, indeed essential, extensions of the traditional clinical services in the direction of greater flexibility and less disruption in patterns of living. Yet the newer approach to community mental health through the social systems in which people are embedded (family, school, neighborhood, factory, etc.) has further implications. For the disturbed person, the goal of community mental health programs should be to help him and the social systems of which he is a member to function together as harmoniously and productively as possible. Such a goal is more practical, and more readily specified, than the elusive concept of "cure," which misses the point that for much mental disorder the trouble lies not within the skin of the individual but in the interpersonal systems through which he is related to others. The emphasis in the regulations upon consultation and public education goes beyond the extension of direct patient services to open wide vistas for imaginative experimentation.

The vanguard of the community approach to mental health seeks ways in which aspects of people's social environment can be changed in order to improve mental health significantly through impact on large groups. Just as a modern police or fire department tries to prevent the problems it must cure, so a good mental health center would look for ways of reducing the strains and troubles out of which much disorder arises. The center might conduct surveys and studies to locate the sources of these strains; it might conduct training programs for managers, for teachers, for ministers to help them deal with the problems that come to light. By providing consultation on mental health to the governing agencies of the community, to schools, courts, churches, to business and industry, the staff of the center can bring their special knowledge to bear in improving the the quality of community and family life for all citizens. Consultation can also be provided to the state mental hospitals to which the community sends patients, to assist these relics of the older dispensation in finding a constructive place in the new approach to mental health. Preferably, revitalized state hospitals will become integral parts of the comprehensive service to nearby communities.

In performing this important and difficult consultative role, the mental health professionals of the center staff do not make the presumptuous and foolish claim that they "know best" how the institutions of a community should operate. Rather, they contribute a special perspective and special competencies that can help the agencies and institutions of community life—the agencies and institutions through which people normally sustain and realize themselves—find ways in which to perform their functions more adequately. In this endeavor, the center staff needs to work in close cooperation with other key agencies that share a concern with community betterment but from different vantage points: councils of social agencies, poverty program councils, labor groups, business organizations, and the like. To promote coordination, representatives of such groups should normally be included in the board responsible for the center's policies.

Communities may find that they want and need to provide for a variety of services not specifically listed among the "additional services" in the regulations issued by the Public Health Service: for example, a special service for the aged, or a camping program, or, unfortunately, residences for people who do not respond to the best we can do for them. The regulations are permissive with respect to additional services, and communities will have to give close and realistic attention to their own needs and priorities. For many rural areas, on the other hand, and for communities in which existing mental health services are so grossly inadequate that the components of a comprehensive program must be assembled from scratch, the present regulations in regard to essential services may prove unduly restrictive. Communities without traditions of strong mental health services may need to start with something short of the full prescribed package. So long as their plan provides for both direct and indirect services, goes beyond the traditional inpatient-outpatient facility, and involves commitment to movement in the direction of greater comprehensiveness, the intent of the legislation might be regarded as fulfilled.

Many of the services that are relevant to mental health will naturally be developed under auspices other than the comprehensive center. That is desirable. Even the most comprehensive center will have a program that is more narrowly circumscribed than the community's full effort to promote human effectiveness. What is important is that the staff of the center be in good communication with related community efforts, and plan the center's own undertakings so as to strengthen the totality of the community's investment in the human effectiveness of its members.

FACILITIES

Facilities should be planned to fit a program and not vice versa.

The comprehensive community mental health center should not be thought of as a place, building, or collection of buildings—an easy misconception—but as a people-serving organization. New physical facilities will necessarily be required, but the mistake of constructing large, congregate institutions should not be repeated. The danger here is that new treatment facilities established in medical centers may only shift the old mental hospital from country to town, its architecture changed from stone and brick to glass and steel. New conceptions are needed even more than new facilities.

Small units of diverse design reflecting specific functions and located near users or near other services (such as a school or community center) might be indicated, and can often be constructed at a lesser cost than a centralized unit linked to a hospital. For example, most emotionally disturbed children who require residential treatment can be effectively served in small residential units in a neighborhood setting removed from the hospital center. Indeed, there is the possibility that the hospital with its tense and antiseptic atmosphere may confirm the child's worst fears about himself and set his deviant behavior.

Each community should work out the pattern of services and related facilities that reflects its own problems, resources, and solutions. The needs and resources of rural areas will differ radically from those of urban ones. Every state in the nation has its huge mental hospitals, grim monuments to what was once the latest word in treatment of the mentally ill, and a major force in shaping treatment programs ever since. It should not be necessary to build new monuments.

Continuity of Concern

Effective community action for mental health requires continuity of concern for the troubled individual in his involvements with society, regardless of awkward jurisdictional boundaries of agencies, institutions, and professions.

A major barrier to effective mental health programing is the historical precedent of separating mental health services from other people-serving agencies—schools, courts, welfare agencies, recreational programs, etc. This is partly a product of the way of thinking that follows from defining the problem as one of illness and thus establishing the place of treatment and the professional qualifications required to "treat" it. There are thus immense gaps in responsibility for giving help to people in trouble. Agencies tend to work in ignorance of each other's programs, or at cross purposes. For example, hospital programs for emotionally disturbed children often are operated with little contact with the child's school; a destitute alcoholic who would be hospitalized by one community agency is jailed by another.

Current recommendations that a person in trouble be admitted to the total mental health system and not to one component of it only fall short of coming to grips with the problem. The laudable aim of these recommendations is to facilitate movement of a person from one component to another—from hospital to outpatient clinic, for example, with minimum red tape and maximum communication among the professional people involved. Such freedom of movement and of communication within the mental health system is much to be desired. But freedom of movement and of communication between systems is quite as important as it is within a system.

No one system can comprise the range of mental health concerns to which we are committed in America, extending from serious neurological disorders to include the whole fabric of human experience from which serious—and not so serious—disorders of living may spring. Mental health is everyone's business, and no profession or family of professions has sufficient competence to deal with it whole. Nor can a mental health center, however comprehensive, encompass it. The center staff can and should engage in joint programing with the various other systems with whom "patients" and people on the verge of trouble are significantly involved—school, welfare, industry, justice [See Selection 3], and the rest. For such joint programing to reflect the continuity of concern for the individual that is needed, information must flow freely among all agencies and "systems." The staff of the center can play a crucial role in monitoring this flow to see to it that the walls that typically restrict communication between social agencies are broken down.

REACHING THOSE WHO MOST NEED HELP

Programs must be designed to reach the people who are hardly touched by our best current efforts, for it is actually those who present the major problems of mental health in America.

The programs of comprehensive community mental health centers must be deliberately designed to reach all of the people who need them. Yet the forces generated by professional orthodoxies and by the balance of public initiative or apathy in different segments of the community—forces that have shaped current "model" community mental health programs— will tend unless strenuously counteracted to restrict services to a favored few in the community. The poor, the dispossessed, the uneducated, the "poor treatment risk," will get less service—and less appropriate service —than their representation in the community warrants, and much, much less service than their disproportionate contribution to the bedrock problem of serious mental illness would demand.

The more advanced mental health services have tended to be a middle-class luxury; chronic mental hospital custody a lower-class horror. The relationship between the mental health helper and the helped has been governed by an affinity of the clean for the clean, the educated for the educated, the affluent for the affluent [See Selection 6]. Most of our therapeutic talent, often trained at public expense, has been invested not in solving our hard-core mental health problem—the psychotic of marginal competence and social status—but in treating the relatively well-to-do educated neurotic, usually in an urban center. Research has shown that if a person is poor, he is given some form of brief, mechanical, or chemical treatment; if his social, economic, and educational position is more favored, he is given long-term conversational psychotherapy. This disturbing state of affairs exists whether the patient is treated privately or in a community facility, or by a psychiatrist, psychologist, or other professional person. If the community representatives who take responsibility for policy in the new community mental health centers are indignant at this inequity, their indignation would seem to be justified on the reasonable assumption that mental health services provided at public expense ought to reach the people who most need help. Although regulations stipulate that people will not be barred from service because of inability to pay, the greatest threat to the integrity and usefulness of the proposed comprehensive centers is that they will nonetheless neglect the poor and disadvantaged, and that they will simply provide at public expense services that are now privately available to people of means.

Yet indignation and good will backed with power to set policy will not in themselves suffice to bring about a just apportionment of mental health services. Inventiveness and research will also be indispensable. Even when special efforts are made to bring psychotherapy to the disturbed poor, it appears that they tend not to understand it, to want it, or to benefit from it. They tend not to conceive of their difficulties in psychological terms or to realize that talk can be a "treatment" that can help. Vigorous experimentation is needed to discover ways of reaching the people whose mental health problems are most serious. Present indications suggest that methods hold most promise which emphasize actions rather than words, deal directly with the problems of living rather than with fantasies, and meet emergencies when they arise without interposing a waiting list. Much more attention should also be given to the development of nonprofessional roles for selected "indigenous" persons, who in numerous ways could help to bridge the gulf between the world of the mental health professional and that of the poor and uneducated where help is particularly needed.

INNOVATION

Since current patterns of mental health service are intrinsically and logistically inadequate to the task, responsible programing for the comprehensive community mental health center must emphasize and reward innovation.

What can the mental health specialist do to help people who are in trouble? A recent survey of 11 most advanced mental health centers, chosen to suggest what centers-in-planning might become, reveals that the treatment of choice remains individual psychotherapy, the 50-minute hour on a one-to-one basis. Yet 3 minutes with a sharp pencil will show that this cannot conceivably provide a realistic basis for a national mental health program. There simply are not enough therapists—nor will there ever be—to go around, nor are there enough hours, nor is the method suited to the people who constitute the bulk of the problem—the uneducated, the inarticulate. Given the bias of existing facilities toward serving a middle-class clientele, stubborn adherence to individual psychotherapy when a community can find and afford the staff to do it would still be understandable if there were clear-cut evidence of the superior effectiveness of the method with those who find it attractive or acceptable. But such evidence does not exist. The habits and traditions of the mental health professions are not a good enough reason for the prominence of one-to-one psychotherapy, whether by psychiatrists, psychologists, or social workers, in current practice and programing.

Innovations are clearly required. One possibility with which there has been considerable experience is group therapy; here the therapist multiplies his talents by a factor of six or eight. Another is crisis consultation: a few hours spent in active intervention when a person reaches the end of his own resources and the normal sources of support run out. A particularly imaginative instance of crisis consultation in which psychologists have pioneered is the suicide-prevention facility. Another very promising innovation is the use under professional direction of people without professional training to provide needed interpersonal contact and communication. Still other innovations, more radical in departure from the individual clinical approach, will be required if the major institutional settings of youth and adult life—school and job—are to be modified in ways that promote the constructive handling of life stresses on the part of large numbers of people.

Innovation will flourish when we accept the character of our national mental health problem and when lay and professional people recognize and reward creative attempts to solve it. Responsible encouragement of innovation, of course, implies commitment to and investment in evaluation research to appraise the merit of new practices.

CHILDREN

In contrast with current practice, major emphasis in the new comprehensive centers should go to services for children.

Mental health programs tend to neglect children, and the first plans submitted by states were conspicuous in their failure to provide a range of services to children. The 11 present community programs described as models were largely adult oriented. A recent (1965) conference to review progress in planning touched occasionally and lightly on problems of children. The Joint Commission on Mental Illness and Health bypassed the issue; currently a new Joint Commission on Mental Health of Children is about to embark upon its studies under Congressional auspices.

Most psychiatric and psychological training programs concentrate on adults. Individual psychotherapy through talk, the favored method in most mental health programs, is best suited to adults. What to do with an enraged child on a playground is not normally included in curricula for training mental health specialists. It would seem that our plans and programs are shaped more by our methods and predilections than by the problems to be solved.

Yet an analysis of the age profile of most communities—in conjunction with this relative neglect—would call for a radically different allocation of money, facilities, and mental health professionals. We do not know that early intervention with childhood problems can reduce later mental disorder, but it is a reasonable hypothesis, and we do know that the problems of children are receiving scant attention. Sound strategy would concentrate our innovative efforts upon the young, in programs for children and youth, for parents, and for teachers and others who work directly with children.

The less than encouraging experience of the child guidance clinic movement a generation and more ago should be a stimulus to new effort, not an occasion for turning away from services to children. The old clinics were small ventures, middle-class oriented, suffering from most of the deficiencies of therapeutic approach and outreach that have been touched upon above. A fresh approach to the problems of children is urgently needed.

We feel that fully half of our mental health resources—money, facilities, people—should be invested in programs for children and youth, for parents of young children, and for teachers and others who work directly with children. This would be the preferable course even if the remaining 50% were to permit only a holding action with respect to problems of adults. But our resources are such that if we care enough we can move forward on both fronts simultaneously.

The proposal to place the major investment of our mental health resources in programs for children will be resisted, however much sense it may make, for it will require a thoroughgoing reorientation of the mental health establishment. New facilities, new skills, new kinds of professional people, new patterns for the development of manpower will be required. And new and more effective ways must be found to reach and help children where they are—in families and schools—and to assist these critically important social systems in fostering the good development of children and in coming to the child's support when the developmental course goes astray. This is one reason why community leaders and other nonprofessionals concerned with the welfare and development of people should be centrally involved in establishing the goals of community mental health centers. They can and should demand that the character of the new centers be determined not by the present habits and skills of professional people but by the nature of the problem to be solved and the full range of resources available for its solution.

PLANNING FOR PROBLEM GROUPS THAT NOBODY WANTS

As a focus for community planning for mental health, the comprehensive center should assure that provision is made to deal with the mental health component in the problems of various difficult groups that are likely to "fall between the stools" of current programs.

Just as good community programing for mental health requires continuity of concern for the troubled individual, across the many agencies and services that are involved with him, so good programing also requires that no problem groups be excluded from attention just because their problems do not fit neatly into prevalent categories of professional interest, or because they are hard to treat.

There are a number of such groups of people, among whom problems of human ineffectiveness are obvious, yet whose difficulties cannot accurately or helpfully be described as mainly psychological: for example, addicts, alcoholics, the aging, delinquents, the mentally retarded. It would be presumptuous folly for mental health professionals to claim responsibility for solving the difficult social and biological problems that are implicated in these types of ineffectiveness. But it would also be irresponsible on the part of persons who are planning community mental health programs not to give explicit attention to the adequacy of services being provided to these difficult groups and to the adequacy of the attack that the community is making on those aspects of their problems that are accessible to community action.

Recently, and belatedly, national attention has been focused on the mentally retarded. This substantial handicapped group is likely to be provided for outside the framework of the mental health program as such, but a good community mental health plan should assure that adequate provision is in fact made for them, and the comprehensive center should accept responsibility for serving the mental health needs of the retarded and their families.

Some of the other problem groups just mentioned—e.g., the addicts and alcoholics—tend to get left out partly because treatment by psychiatric or psychological methods has been relatively unproductive. Naturally, the comprehensive center cannot be expected to achieve magical solutions where other agencies have failed. But if it takes the approach advocated here—that of focusing on the social systems in which problem behavior is embedded—it has an opportunity to contribute toward a rational attack on these problems. The skills that are required may be more those of the social scientist and community change agent than those of the clinician or therapist.

In planning its role with respect to such difficult groups, the staff of the center might bear two considerations in mind: In the network of community agencies, is humanly decent care being provided under one or another set of auspices? And does the system-focused approach of the center have a distinctive contribution to make toward collaborative community action on the underlying problems?

Manpower

The present and future shortage of trained mental health professionals requires experimentation with new approaches to mental health services and with new divisions of labor in providing these services.

The national effort to improve the quality of life for every individual —to alleviate poverty, to improve educational opportunities, to combat mental disorders—will tax our resources of professional manpower to the limit. In spite of expanded training efforts, mental health programs will face growing shortages of social workers, nurses, psychiatrists, psychologists, and other specialists. The new legislation to provide Federal assistance for the staffing of community mental health centers will not increase the supply of manpower but perhaps may result in some minor redistribution of personnel. If adequate pay and opportunities for part-time participation are provided, it is possible that some psychiatrists and psychologists now in private practice may join the public effort, adding to the services available to people without reference to their economic resources.

The manpower shortage must be faced realistically and with readiness for invention, for creative solutions. Officially recommended staffing patterns for community mental health centers (which projected nationally would require far more professionals than are being trained) should not be taken as setting rigid limitations. Pediatricians, general medical practitioners, social workers other than psychiatric ones, psychological and other technicians at nondoctoral levels should be drawn into the work of the center. Specific tasks sometimes assigned to highly trained professionals (such as administrative duties, follow-up contacts, or tutoring for a disturbed child) may be assigned to carefully selected adults with little or no technical training. Effective communication across barriers of education, social class, and race can be aided by the creation of new roles for specially talented members of deprived groups. New and important roles must be found for teachers, recreation workers, lawyers, clergymen.

Consultation, inservice training, staff conferences, and supervision are all devices that can be used to extend resources without sacrificing the quality of service.

Mental health centers should find ways of using responsible, paid volunteers, with limited or extended periods of service. There is a great reservoir of human talent among educated Americans who want to contribute their time and efforts to a significant enterprise. The Peace Corps, the Vista program, Project Head-Start have demonstrated to a previously skeptical public that high-level, dependable service can be rendered by this new-style volunteer. The contributions of unpaid volunteers—students, housewives, the retired—can be put to effective use as well.

PROFESSIONAL RESPONSIBILITY

Responsibility in the comprehensive community mental health center should depend upon competence in the jobs to be done.

The issue of who is to be responsible for mental health programs is complex, and not to be solved in the context of professional rivalries. The broad conception of mental health to which we have committed ourselves in America requires that responsibility for mental health programs be broadly shared. With good will, intelligence, and a willingness to minimize presumed prerogatives, professional people and lay board members can find ways of distributing responsibility that will substantially increase the effectiveness of a center's program. The tradition, of course, is that the director of a mental health center must be a psychiatrist. This is often the best solution, but other solutions may often be equally sensible or more so. A social worker, a psychologist, a pediatrician, a nurse, a public health administrator might be a more competent director for a particular center.

The issue of "clinical responsibility" is more complex but the principle is the same: Competence rather than professional identification should be the governing concern. The administration of drugs is clearly a competence-linked responsibility of a physician. Diagnostic testing is normally a competence-linked responsibility of a psychologist; however, there may be situations in which a psychiatrist or a social worker may have the competence to get the job done well. Responsibility for psychotherapy may be assumed by a social worker, psychiatrist, psychologist, or other trained person. The director of training or of research could reasonably come from one of a number of disciplines. The responsible community member, to whom these guidelines are addressed, should assure himself that there is a functional relationship in each instance between individual competence and the job to be done.

This issue has been given explicit and responsible attention by the Congress of the United States in its debates and hearings on the bill that authorizes funds for staffing community mental health centers. The intent of Congress is clear. As the Senate Committee on Labor and Public Welfare states in its report on the bill (Report No. 366, to accompany H.R. 2985, submitted June 24, 1965):

> There is no intent in any way in this bill to discriminate against any mental health professional group from carrying out its full potential within the realm of its recognized competence. Even further it is hoped that new and innovative tasks and roles will evolve from the broadly based concept of the community mental health services. Specifically, overall leadership of a community mental health center program may be carried out by any one of the major mental health professions. Many professions have vital roles to play in the prevention, treatment and rehabilitation of patients with mental illnesses.

Similar legislative intent was established in the debate on the measure in the House of Representatives.

Community members responsible for mental health centers should not countenance absentee directorships by which the fiction of responsibility is sustained while actual responsibility and initiative are dissipated. This is a device for the serving of professions, not of people.

TRAINING

The comprehensive community mental health center should provide a formal training program.

The need for centers to innovate in the development or reallocation of professional and subprofessional roles, which has been stressed above in line with Congressional intent, requires in every center an active and imaginative training program in which staff members can gain competence in their new roles. The larger centers will also have the self-interested obligation to participate in the training of other professionals. Well-supervised professional trainees not only contribute to the services of a center; their presence and the center's training responsibilities to them promote a desirable atmosphere of self-examination and openness to new ideas.

There should be a director of training who would be responsible for: (*a*) in-service training of the staff of the center, in the minimum case; and, in the larger centers, *(b)* center-sponsored training programs for a range of professional groups and including internships, field placements, postdoctoral fellowships, and partial or complete residency programs; and *(c)* university-sponsored training programs that require the facilities of the center to give their students practical experience. Between 5% and 10% of the center's budget should be explicitly allocated to training.

PROGRAM EVALUATION AND RESEARCH

The comprehensive community mental health center should devote an explicit portion of its budget to program evaluation. All centers should inculcate in their staff attention to and respect for research findings; the larger centers have an obligation to set a high priority on basic research and to give formal recognition to research as a legitimate part of the duties of staff members.

In the 11 "model" community programs that have been cited previously, both program evaluation and basic research are rarities; staff members are commonly overburdened by their service obligations. That their mental health services continue to emphasize one-to-one psychotherapy with middle-class adults may partly result from the small attention that their programs give to the evaluative study of program effectiveness. The programs of social agencies are seldom evaluated systematically and tend to continue in operation simply because they exist and no one has data to demonstrate whether they are useful or not. In this respect the "model" programs seem to be no better.

The whole burden of the preceding recommendations, with their emphasis on innovation and experimentation, cries out for substantial investment in program evaluation. Only through explicit appraisal of program effects can worthy approaches be retained and refined, ineffective ones dropped. Evaluative monitoring of program achievements may vary, of course, from the relatively informal to the systematic and quantitative, depending on the importance of the issue, the availability of resources, and the willingness of those responsible to take the risks of substituting informed judgment for evidence.

One approach to program evaluation that has been much neglected is hard-headed cost analysis. Alternative programs should be compared not only in terms of their effects, but of what they cost. Since almost any approach to service is likely to produce some good effects, mental health professionals may be too prone to use methods that they find most satisfying rather than those that yield the greatest return per dollar.

All community mental health centers need to plan for program evaluation; the larger ones should also engage in basic research on the nature and causes of mental disorder and on the processes of diagnosis, treatment, and prevention. The center that is fully integrated with its community setting will have unique opportunities to study aspects of these problems that elude investigation in traditional clinic and hospital settings. That a major investment be made in basic research on mental health problems was the recommendation to which the Joint Commission on Mental Illness and Health gave topmost priority.

The demands of service and of research are bound to be competitive. Because research skills, too, are scarce, it is not realistic to expect every community mental health center to have a staff equipped to undertake basic research. At the very least, however, the leadership in each center should inculcate in its training program an attitude of attentiveness to research findings and of readiness to use them to innovate and change the center's practices.

The larger centers, especially those that can establish affiliation with universities, have an obligation to contribute to fundamental knowledge in the area of their program operations. Such centers will normally have a director of research, and a substantial budget allocation in support of research, to be supplemented by grants from foundations and governmental agencies. By encouraging their staff members to engage in basic studies (and they must be sedulously protected from encroaching service obligations if they are to do so), these centers can make an appropriate return to the common fund of scientific and professional knowledge upon which they draw; they also serve their own more immediate interests in attracting and retaining top quality staff and in maintaining an atmosphere in which creativeness can thrive. As a rough yardstick, every center should devote between 5% and 10% of its budget to program evaluation and research.

Variety, Flexibility, and Realism

Since the plan for a comprehensive community mental health center must allocate scarce resources according to carefully considered priorities tailored to the unique situation of the particular community, wide variation among plans is to be expected and is desirable. Since decisions are fallible and community needs and opportunities change, provision should be made for flexibility and change in programs, including periodic review of policies and operations.

In spite of the stress in these guidelines on ideal requirements as touchstones against which particular plans can be appraised, no single comprehensive center can be all things to all men. Planning must be done in a realistic context of limited resources and imperfect human talent as well as of carefully evaluated community needs, and many hard decisions will have to be made in setting priorities. In rural areas, especially, major alterations in the current blueprint would seem to be called for if needed services are to be provided. As a result, the comprehensive community mental health centers that emerge should be as unique as the communities to whose needs and opportunities they are responsive. This is all to the good, for as it has been repeatedly emphasized, there is no well-tested and prefabricated model to be put into automatic operation. Variety among centers is required for suitability to local situations; it is desirable also for the richer experience that it should yield for the guidance of future programing.

The need for innovation has been stressed; the other side of the same coin is the need for adaptability to the lessons of experience and to changing requirements of the community. Flexibility and adaptiveness as a characteristic of social agencies does not "just happen"; it must be planned for. The natural course of events is for organizations to maintain themselves with as little change as possible, and there is no one more conservative than the proponent of an established, once-radical departure. Plans for the new centers should therefore provide for the periodic self-review of policies and operations, with participation by staff at all levels, and by outside consultants if possible. To the extent that active program evaluation is built intrinsically into the functioning of the center, the review process should be facilitated, and intelligent flexibility of policy promoted. Self-review by the center staff should feed into general review by the responsible board of community leaders, in which the board satisfies itself concerning the adequacy with which the policies that it has set have been carried out.

This final recommendation returns once more to the theme, introduced at the outset, that has been implicit in the entire discussion: the responsibility of the community for the quality and adequacy of the mental health services that it gets. The opportunities are now open for communities to employ the mechanism of the comprehensive mental health center to take major strides toward more intelligent, humane, and effective provision for their people. If communities rise to this opportunity, the implications for the national problem of mental health and for the quality of American life are immense.

———

The following people read an early draft of this statement and made suggestions for its improvement. Their assistance is gratefully acknowledged. They in no way share responsibility, of course, for errors of fact or judgment that may be in the paper.

George W. Albee
Roger Bibace
Arthur J. Bindman
Hedda Bolgar
Joseph E. Brewer
Mortimer Brown
John D. Cambareri
Robert C. Challman
Emory L. Cowen
Joseph J. DeLucia
Gordon F. Derner
Morton Deutsch
Paul R. Dingman
Herbert Dörken
Henry Dupont
J. Wilbert Edgerton
John C. Glidewell
Leonard D. Goodstein
Lee Gurel
Robert A. Harper
Ira Iscoe
Nelson C. Jackson
James G. Kelly
Oliver J. B. Kerner
Barbara A. Kirk
Lewis B. Klebanoff

Sheldon J. Korchin
Maurice Kott
Harry Levinson
John J. McMillan
Harry V. McNeill
Sherman E. Nelson
J. R. Newbrough
Nancy Orlinsky
Thomas F. A. Plaut
David B. Ray
Sheldon R. Roen
Joseph Samler
Bernard Saper
Guy Scott
Saleem A. Shah
Edwin S. Shneidman
Franklin C. Shontz
George A. Silver
Hans Strupp
Donald E. Super
Harold C. Taylor
Forrest B. Tyler
Mrs. Bernard Werthan
Stanley F. Yolles
Alvin Zander

14. Psychotherapy as a Learning Process

Albert Bandura

Many efforts have been made to explain the "how" of psychotherapy, that is, to arrive at the explanatory principles by which feelings, attitudes, and behavior are changed.

This review article brings together a host of studies which have focused on principles of learning as related to psychotherapeutic

Psychological Bulletin; 58: 143-159, 1961. Reprinted by permission of the author and the American Psychological Association. Prof. Bandura is a member of the Stanford University faculty.

changes. Note, however, that this article goes far beyond psychotherapy as *one process* by which behavior can be altered and raises
a much broader question: Can human behavior be modified through
psychological means and if so, what are the learning mechanisms that
mediate behavior change?

In this connection, then, the "brainwashing" techniques of the
Chinese Communists (Selection 7) would qualify for explanations by
principles of learning.

While it is customary to conceptualize psychotherapy as a learning
process, few therapists accept the full implications of this position. Indeed, this is best illustrated by the writings of the learning theorists
themselves. Most of our current methods of psychotherapy represent an
accumulation of more or less uncontrolled clinical experiences and, in
many instances, those who have written about psychotherapy in terms of
learning theory have merely substituted a new language; the practice remains essentially unchanged (Dollard, Auld, & White, 1954; Dollard &
Miller, 1950; Shoben, 1949).

If one seriously subscribes to the view that psychotherapy is a learning
process, the methods of treatment should be derived from our knowledge
of learning and motivation. Such an orientation is likely to yield new
techniques of treatment which, in many respects, may differ markedly
from the procedures currently in use.

Psychotherapy rests on a very simple but fundamental assumption, i.e.,
human behavior is modifiable through psychological procedures. When
skeptics raise the question, "Does psychotherapy work?" they may be responding in part to the mysticism that has come to surround the term.
Perhaps the more meaningful question, and one which avoids the surplus
meanings associated with the term "psychotherapy," is as follows: Can
human behavior be modified through psychological means and if so,
what are the learning mechanisms that mediate behavior change?

In the sections that follow, some of these learning mechanisms will be
discussed, and studies in which systematic attempts have been made to
apply these principles of learning to the area of psychotherapy will be
reviewed. Since learning theory itself is still somewhat incomplete, the
list of psychological processes by which changes in behavior can occur
should not be regarded as exhaustive, nor are they necessarily without
overlap.

COUNTERCONDITIONING

Of the various treatment methods derived from learning theory, those
based on the principle of counterconditioning have been elaborated in

greatest detail. Wolpe (1954, 1958, 1959) gives a thorough account of this method, and additional examples of cases treated in this manner are provided by Jones (1956), Lazarus and Rachman (1957), Meyer (1957), and Rachman (1959). Briefly, the principle involved is as follows: if strong responses which are incompatible with anxiety reactions can be made to occur in the presence of anxiety evoking cues, the incompatible responses will become attached to these cues and thereby weaken or eliminate the anxiety responses.

The first systematic psychotherapeutic application of this method was reported by Jones (1924b) in the treatment of Peter, a boy who showed severe phobic reactions to animals, fur objects, cotton, hair, and mechanical toys. Counterconditioning was achieved by feeding the child in the presence of initially small but gradually increasing anxiety-arousing stimuli. A rabbit in a cage was placed in the room at some distance so as not to disturb the boy's eating. Each day the rabbit was brought nearer to the table and eventually removed from the cage. During the final stage of treatment, the rabbit was placed on the feeding table and even in Peter's lap. Tests of generalization revealed that the fear responses had been effectively eliminated, not only toward the rabbit, but toward the previously feared furry objects as well.

In this connection, it would be interesting to speculate on the diagnosis and treatment Peter would have received had he been seen by Melanie Klein (1949) rather than by Mary Cover Jones!

It is interesting to note that while both Shoben (1949) and Wolpe (1958) propose a therapy based on the principle of counterconditioning, their treatment methods are radically different. According to Shoben, the patient discusses and thinks about stimulus situations that are anxiety provoking in the context of an interpersonal situation which simultaneously elicits positive affective responses from the patient. The therapeutic process consists in connecting the anxiety provoking stimuli, which are symbolically reproduced, with the comfort reaction made to the therapeutic relationship.

Shoben's paper represents primarily a counterconditioning interpretation of the behavior changes brought about through conventional forms of psychotherapy since, apart from high-lighting the role of positive emotional reactions in the treatment process, no new techniques deliberately designed to facilitate relearning through counterconditioning are proposed.

This is not the case with Wolpe, who has made a radical departure from tradition. In his treatment, which he calls reciprocal inhibition, Wolpe makes systematic use of three types of responses which are antagonistic to, and therefore inhibitory of, anxiety. These are: assertive or approach responses, sexual responses, and relaxation responses.

On the basis of historical information; interview data, and psychological test responses, the therapist constructs an anxiety hierarchy, a ranked list of stimuli to which the patient reacts with anxiety. In the case of desensitization based on relaxation, the patient is hypnotized and given relaxation suggestions. He is then asked to imagine a scene representing the weakest item on the anxiety hierarchy and, if the relaxation is unimpaired, this is followed by having the patient imagine the next item, on the list, and so on. Thus, the anxiety cues are gradually increased from session to session until the last phobic stimulus can be presented without impairing the relaxed state. Through this procedure, relaxation responses eventually come to be attached to the anxiety evoking stimuli.

Wolpe reports remarkable therapeutic success with a wide range of neurotic reactions treated on this counterconditioning principle. He also contends that the favorable outcomes achieved by the more conventional psychotherapeutic methods may result from the reciprocal inhibition of anxiety by strong positive responses evoked in the patient-therapist relationship.

Although the counterconditioning method has been employed most extensively in eliminating anxiety-motivated avoidance reactions and inhibitions, it has been used with some success in reducing maladaptive approach responses as well. In the latter case, the goal object is repeatedly associated with some form of aversive stimulus.

Raymond (1956), for example, used nausea as the aversion experience in the treatment of a patient who presented a fetish for handbags and perambulators which brought him into frequent contact with the law in that he repeatedly smeared mucus on ladies' handbags and destroyed perambulators by running into them with his motorcycle. Though the patient had undergone psychoanalytic treatment, and was fully aware of the origin and the sexual significance of his behavior, nevertheless, the fetish persisted.

The treatment consisted of showing the patient a collection of handbags, perambulators, and colored illustrations just before the onset of nausea produced by injections of apomorphine. The conditioning was repeated every 2 hours day and night for 1 week plus additional sessions 8 days and 6 months later.

Raymond reports that, not only was the fetish successfully eliminated, but also the patient showed a vast improvement in his social (and legal) relationships, was promoted to a more responsible position in his work, and no longer required the fetish fantasies to enable him to have sexual intercourse.

Nauseant drugs, especially emetine, have also been utilized as the unconditioned stimulus in the aversion treatment of alcoholism (Thirmann,

1949; Thompson & Bielinski, 1953; Voegtlen, 1940; Wallace, 1949). Usually 8 to 10 treatments in which the sight, smell, and taste of alcohol is associated with the onset of nausea is sufficient to produce abstinence. Of 1,000 or more cases on whom adequate follow-up data are reported, approximately 60% of the patients have been totally abstinent following the treatment. Voegtlen (1940) suggests that a few preventive treatments given at an interval of about 6 months may further improve the results yielded by this method.

Despite these encouraging findings, most psychotherapists are unlikely to be impressed since, in their opinion, the underlying causes for the alcoholism have in no way been modified by the conditioning procedure and, if anything, the mere removal of the alcoholism would tend to produce symptom substitution or other adverse effects. A full discussion of this issue will be presented later. In this particular context, however, several aspects of the Thompson and Bielinski (1953) data are worth noting. Among the alcoholic patients whom they treated, six "suffered from mental disorders not due to alcohol or associated deficiency states." It was planned, by the authors, to follow up the aversion treatment with psychotherapy for the underlying psychosis. This, however, proved unnecessary since all but one of the patients, a case of chronic mental deterioration, showed marked improvement and were in a state of remission.

Max (1935) employed a strong electric shock as the aversive stimulus in treating a patient who tended to display homosexual behavior following exposure to a fetishistic stimulus. Both the fetish and the homosexual behavior were removed through a series of avoidance conditioning sessions in which the patient was administered shock in the presence of the fetishistic object.

Wolpe (1958) has also reported favorable results with a similar procedure in the treatment of obsessions.

A further variation of the counterconditioning procedure has been developed by Mowrer and Mowrer (1938) for use with enuretic patients. The device consists of a wired bed pad which sets off a loud buzzer and awakens the child as soon as micturition begins. Bladder tension thus becomes a cue for waking up which, in turn, is followed by sphincter contraction. Once bladder pressure becomes a stimulus for the more remote sphincter control response, the child is able to remain dry for relatively long periods of time without wakening.

Mowrer and Mowrer (1938) report complete success with 30 children treated by this method; similarly, Davidson and Douglass (1950) achieved highly successful results with 20 chronic enuretic children (15 cured, 5 markedly improved); of 5 cases treated by Morgan and Witmer (1939), 4 of the children not only gained full sphincter control, but also made a significant improvement in their social behavior. The one child with whom the conditioning approach had failed was later found to have bladder difficulties which required medical attention.

Some additonal evidence for the efficacy of this method is provided by Martin and Kubly (1955) who obtained follow-up information from 118 of 220 parents who had treated their children at home with this type of conditioning apparatus. In 74% of the cases, according to the parents' replies, the treatment was successful.

EXTINCTION

"When a learned response is repeated without reinforcement the strength of the tendency to perform that response undergoes a progressive decrease" (Dollard & Miller, 1950). Extinction involves the development of inhibitory potential which is composed of two components. The evocation of any reaction generates reactive inhibition (I_r) which presumably dissipates with time. When reactive inhibition (fatigue, etc.) reaches a high point, the cessation of activity alleviates this negative motivational state and any stimuli associated with the cessation of the response become conditioned inhibitors ($_sI_r$).

One factor that has been shown to influence the rate of extinction of maladaptive and anxiety-motivated behavior is the interval between extinction trials. In general, there tends to be little diminution in the strength of fear-motivated behavior when extinction trials are widely distributed, whereas under massed trials, reactive inhibition builds up rapidly and consequently extinction is accelerated (Calvin, Clifford, Clifford, Bolden, & Harvey, 1956; Edmonson & Amsel, 1954).

An illustration of the application of this principle is provided by Yates (1958) in the treatment of tics. Yates demonstrated, in line with the findings from laboratory studies of extinction under massed and distributed practice, that massed sessions in which the patient performed tics voluntarily followed by prolonged rest to allow for the dissipation of reactive inhibition was the most effective procedure for extinguishing the tics.

It should be noted that the extinction procedure employed by Yates is very similar to Dunlap's method of negative practice, in which the subject reproduces the negative behaviors voluntarily without reinforcement (Dunlap, 1932; Lehner, 1954). This method has been applied most frequently, with varying degrees of success, to the treatment of speech disorders (Fishman, 1937; Meissner, 1946; Rutherford, 1940; Sheehan, 1951; Sheehan & Voas, 1957). If the effectiveness of this psychotherapeutic technique is due primarily to extinction, as suggested by Yates' study, the usual practice of terminating a treatment session before the subject becomes fatigued (Lehner, 1954), would have the effect of reducing the rate of extinction, and may in part account for the divergent results yielded by this method.

Additional examples of the therapeutic application of extinction procedures are provided by Jones (1955), and most recently by C. D. Williams (1959).

Most of the conventional forms of psychotherapy rely heavily on extinction effects although the therapist may not label these as such. For example, many therapists consider *permissiveness* to be a necessary condition of therapeutic change (Alexander, 1956; Dollard & Miller, 1950; Rogers, 1951). It is expected that when a patient expresses thoughts or feelings that provoke anxiety or guilt and the therapist does not disapprove, criticize, or withdraw interest, the fear or guilt will be gradually weakened or extinguished. The extinction effects are believed to generalize to thoughts concerning related topics that were originally inhibited, and to verbal and physical forms of behavior as well (Dollard & Miller, 1950).

Some evidence for the relationship between permissiveness and the extinction of anxiety is provided in two studies recently reported by Dittes (1957a, 1957b). In one study (1957b) involving an analysis of patient-therapist interaction sequences, Dittes found that permissive responses on the part of the therapist were followed by a corresponding decrease in the patient's anxiety (as measured by the GSR) and the occurrence of avoidance behaviors. A sequential analysis of the therapeutic sessions (Dittes, 1957a), revealed that, at the onset of treatment, sex expressions were accompanied by strong anxiety reactions; under the cumulative effects of permissiveness, the anxiety gradually extinguished.

In contrast to counterconditioning, extinction is likely to be a less effective and a more time consuming method for eliminating maladaptive behavior (Jones, 1924a; Dollard & Miller, 1950); in the case of conventional interview therapy, the relatively long intervals between interview sessions, and the ritualistic adherence to the 50-minute hour may further reduce the occurrence of extinction effects.

DISCRIMINATION LEARNING

Human functioning would be extremely difficult and inefficient if a person had to learn appropriate behavior for every specific situation he encountered. Fortunately, patterns of behavior learned in one situation will transfer or generalize to other similar situations. On the other hand, if a person overgeneralizes from one situation to another, or if the generalization is based on superficial or irrelevant cues, behavior becomes inappropriate and maladaptive.

In most theories of psychotherapy, therefore, discrimination learning, believed to be accomplished through the gaining of awareness or insight, receives emphasis (Dollard & Miller, 1950; Fenichel, 1941; Rogers, 1951; Sullivan, 1953). It is generally assumed that if a patient is aware of the cues producing his behavior, of the responses he is making, and of the reasons that he responds the way he does, his behavior will become more susceptible to verbally-mediated control. Voluntarily guided, discriminative behavior will replace the automatic, overgeneralized reactions.

While this view is widely accepted, as evidenced in the almost exclusive reliance on interview procedures and on interpretative or labeling techniques, a few therapists (Alexander & French, 1946) have questioned the importance attached to awareness in producing modifications in behavior. Whereas most psychoanalysts (Fenichel, 1941), as well as therapists representing other points of view (Fromm-Reichmann, 1950; Sullivan, 1953) consider insight a precondition of behavior change, Alexander and French consider insight or awareness a result of change rather than its cause. That is, as the patient's anxieties are gradually reduced through the permissive conditions of treatment, formerly inhibited thoughts are gradually restored to awareness.

Evidence obtained through controlled laboratory studies concerning the value of awareness in increasing the precision of discrimination has so far been largely negative or at least equivocal (Adams, 1957; Erikson, 1958; Razran, 1949). A study by Lacy and Smith (1954), in which they found aware subjects generalized anxiety reactions less extensively than did subjects who were unaware of the conditioned stimulus provides evidence that awareness may aid discrimination. However, other aspects of their findings (e.g., the magnitude of the anxiety reactions to the generalization stimuli were greater than they were to the conditioned stimulus itself) indicate the need for replication.

If future research continues to demonstrate that awareness exerts little influence on the acquisition, generalization, and modification of behavior, such negative results would cast serious doubt on the value of currently popular psychotherapeutic procedures whose primary aim is the development of insight.

METHODS OF REWARD

Most theories of psychotherapy are based on the assumption that the patient has a repertoire of previously learned positive habits available to him, but that these adaptive patterns are inhibited or blocked by competing responses motivated by anxiety or guilt. The goal of therapy, then, is to reduce the severity of the internal inhibitory controls, thus allowing the healthy patterns of behavior to emerge. Hence, the role of the therapist is to create permissive conditions under which the patient's "normal growth potentialities" are set free (Rogers, 1951). The fact that most. of our theories of personality and therapeutic procedures have been developed primarily through work with oversocialized, neurotic patients may account in part for the prevalence of this view.

There is a large class of disorders (the undersocialized, antisocial personalities whose behavior reflects a failure of the socialization process) for whom this model of personality and accompanying techniques of treatment are quite inappropriate (Bandura & Walters, 1959; Schmideberg, 1959). Such antisocial personalities are likely to present *learning deficits*, consequently the goal of therapy is the acquisition of secondary motives and the development of internal restraint habits. That antisocial patients prove unresponsive to psychotherapeutic methods developed for the treatment of oversocialized neurotics has been demonstrated in a number of studies comparing patients who remain in treatment with those who terminate treatment prematurely (Rubenstein & Lorr, 1956). It is for this class of patients that the greatest departures from traditional treatment methods is needed.

While counterconditioning, extinction, and discrimination learning may be effective ways of removing neurotic inhibitions, these methods may be of relatively little value in developing new positive habits. Primary and secondary rewards in the form of the therapist's interest and approval may play an important, if not indispensable, role in the treatment process. Once the patient has learned to want the interest and approval of the therapist, these rewards may then be used to promote the acquisition of new patterns of behavior. For certain classes of patients such as schizophrenics (Atkinson, 1957; Peters, 1953; Robinson, 1957) and delinquents (Cairns, 1959), who are either unresponsive to, or fearful of, social rewards, the therapist may have to rely initially on primary rewards in the treatment process.

An ingenious study by Peters and Jenkins (1954) illustrates the application of this principle in the treatment of schizophrenic patients. Chronic patients from closed wards were administered subshock injections of insulin designed to induce the hunger drive. The patients were then encouraged to solve a series of graded problem tasks with fudge as the reward. This program was followed 5 days a week for 3 months.

Initially the tasks involved simple mazes and obstruction problems in which the patients obtained the food reward directly upon successful completion of the problem. Tasks of gradually increasing difficulty were then administered involving multiple-choice learning and verbal-reasoning problems in which the experimenter personally mediated the primary rewards. After several weeks of such problem solving activities the insulin injections were discontinued and social rewards, which by this time had become more effective, were used in solving interpersonal problems that the patients were likely to encounter in their daily activities both inside and outside the hospital setting.

Comparison of the treated group with control groups, designed to isolate the effects of insulin and special attention, revealed that the patients in the reward group improved significantly in their social relationships in the hospital, whereas the patients in the control groups showed no such change.

King and Armitage (1958) report a somewhat similar study in which severely withdrawn schizophrenic patients were treated with operant conditioning methods; candy and cigarettes served as the primary rewards for eliciting and maintaining increasingly complex forms of behavior, i.e., psychomotor, verbal, and interpersonal responses. Unlike the Peters and Jenkins study, no attempt was made to manipulate the level of primary motivation.

An interesting feature of the experimental design was the inclusion of a group of patients who were treated with conventional interview therapy, as well as a recreational therapy and a no-therapy control group. It was found that the operant group, in relation to similar patients in the three control groups, made significantly more clinical improvement.

Skinner (1956b) and Lindsley (1956) working with adult psychotics, and Ferster (1959) working with autistic children, have been successful in developing substantial amounts of reality-oriented behavior in their patients through the use of reward. So far their work has been concerned primarily with the effect of schedules of reinforcement on the rate of evocation of simple impersonal reactions. There is every indication, however, that by varying the contingency of the reward (e.g., the patient must respond in certain specified ways to the behavior of another individual in order to produce the reward) adaptive interpersonal behaviors can be developed as well (Azrin & Lindsley, 1956).

The effectiveness of social reinforcers in modifying behavior has been demonstrated repeatedly in verbal conditioning experiments (Krasner, 1958; Salzinger, 1959). Encouraged by these findings, several therapists have begun to experiment with operant conditioning as a method of treatment in its own right (Tilton, 1956; Ullman, Krasner, & Collins, in press; R. I. Williams, 1959); the operant conditioning studies cited earlier are also illustrative of this trend.

So far the study of generalization and permanence of behavior changes brought about through operant conditioning methods has received relatively little attention and the scanty data available are equivocal (Rogers, 1960; Sarason, 1957; Weide, 1959). The lack of consistency in results is hardly surprising considering that the experimental manipulations in many of the conditioning studies are barely sufficient to demonstrate conditioning effects, let alone generalization of changes to new situations. On the other hand, investigators who have conducted more intensive reinforcement sessions, in an effort to test the efficacy of operant conditioning methods as a therapeutic technique, have found significant changes in patients' interpersonal behavior in extra-experimental situations (King & Armitage, 1958; Peters & Jenkins, 1954; Ullman et al., in press). These findings are particularly noteworthy since the response classes involved are similar to those psychotherapists are primarily concerned in modifying through interview forms of treatment. If the favorable results yielded by these studies are replicated in future investigations, it is likely that the next few years will witness an increasing reliance on conditioning forms of psychotherapy, particularly in the treatment of psychotic patients.

At this point it might also be noted that, consistent with the results from verbal conditioning experiments, content analyses of psychotherapeutic interviews (Bandura, Lipsher, & Miller, 1960; Murray, 1956) suggest that many of the changes observed in psychotherapy, at least insofar as the patients' verbal behavior is concerned, can be accounted for in terms of the therapists' direct, although usually unwitting, reward and punishment of the patients' expressions.

PUNISHMENT

While positive habits can be readily developed through reward, the elimination of socially disapproved habits, which becomes very much an issue in the treatment of antisocial personalities, poses a far more complex problem.

The elimination of socially disapproved behaviors can be accomplished in several ways. They may be consistently unrewarded and thus extinguished. However, antisocial behavior, particularly of an extreme form, cannot simply be ignored in the hope that it will gradually extinguish. Furthermore, since the successful execution of antisocial acts may bring substantial material rewards as well as the approval and admiration of associates, it is extremely unlikely that such behavior would ever extinguish.

Although punishment may lead to the rapid disappearance of socially disapproved behavior, its effects are far more complex (Estes, 1944; Solomon, Kamin, & Wynne, 1953). If a person is punished for some socially disapproved habit, the impulse to perform the act becomes through its association with punishment, a stimulus for anxiety. This anxiety then motivates competing responses which, if sufficiently strong, prevent the occurrence of, or inhibit, the disapproved behavior. Inhibited responses may not, however, thereby lose their strength, and may reappear in situations where the threat of punishment is weaker. Punishment may, in fact, prevent the extinction of a habit; if a habit is completely inhibited, it cannot occur and therefore cannot go unrewarded.

Several other factors point to the futility of punishment as a means of correcting many antisocial patterns. The threat of punishment is very likely to elicit conformity; indeed, the patient may obligingly do whatever he is told to do in order to avoid immediate difficulties. This does not mean, however, that he has acquired a set of sanctions that will be of service to him once he is outside the treatment situation. In fact, rather than leading to the development of internal controls, such methods are likely only to increase the patient's reliance on external restraints. Moreover, under these conditions, the majority of patients will develop the attitude that they will do only what they are told to do—and then often only half-heartedly—and that they will do as they please once they are free from the therapist's supervision (Bandura & Walters, 1959).

In addition, punishment may serve only to intensify hostility and other negative motivations and thus may further instigate the antisocial person to display the very behaviors that the punishment was intended to bring under control.

Mild aversive stimuli have been utilized, of course, in the treatment of voluntary patients who express a desire to rid themselves of specific debilitating conditions.

Liversedge and Sylvester (1955), for example, successfully treated seven cases of writer's cramp by means of a retraining procedure involving electric shock. In order to remove tremors, one component of the motor disorder, the patients were required to insert a stylus into a series of progressively smaller holes; each time the stylus made contact with the side of the hole the patients received a mild shock. The removal of the spasm component of the disorder was obtained in two ways. First, the patients traced various line patterns (similar to the movements required in writing) on a metal plate with a stylus, and any deviation from the path produced a shock. Following training on the apparatus, the subjects then wrote with an electrified pen which delivered a shock whenever excessive thumb pressure was applied.

Liversedge and Sylvester report that following the retraining the patients were able to resume work; a follow-up several months later indicated that the improvement was being maintained.

The aversive forms of therapy, described earlier in the section on counterconditioning procedures, also make use of mild punishment.

SOCIAL IMITATION

Although a certain amount of learning takes place through direct training and reward, a good deal of a person's behavior repertoire may be acquired through imitation of what he observes in others. If this is the case, social imitation may serve as an effective vehicle for the transmission of prosocial behavior patterns in the treatment of antisocial patients.

Merely providing a model for imitation is not, however, sufficient. Even though the therapist exhibits the kinds of behaviors that he wants the patient to learn, this is likely to have little influence on him if he rejects the therapist as a model. Affectional nurturance is believed to be an important precondition for imitative learning to occur, in that affectional rewards increase the secondary reinforcing properties of the model, and thus predispose the imitator to pattern his behavior after the rewarding person (Mowrer, 1950; Sears, 1957; Whiting, 1954). Some positive evidence for the influence of social rewards on imitation is provided by Bandura and Huston (in press) in a recent study of identification as a process of incidental imitation.

In this investigation preschool children performed an orienting task but, unlike most incidental learning studies, the experimenter performed the diverting task as well, and the extent to which the subjects patterned their behavior after that of the experimenter-model was measured.

A two-choice discrimination problem similar to the one employed by Miller and Dollard (1941) in their experiments of social imitation was used as the diverting task. On each trial, one of two boxes was loaded with two rewards (small multicolor pictures of animals) and the object of the game was to guess which box contained the stickers. The experimenter-model (M) always had her turn first and in each instance chose the reward box. During M's trial, the subject remained at the starting point where he could observe the M's behavior. On each discrimination trial M exhibited certain verbal, motor, and aggressive patterns of behavior that were totally irrelevant to the task to which the subject's attention was directed. At the starting point, for example, M made a verbal response and then marched slowly toward the box containing the stickers, repeating, "March, march, march." On the lid of each box was a rubber doll which M knocked off aggressively when she reached the designated box. She then paused briefly, remarked, "Open the box," removed one sticker, and pasted it on a pastoral scene which hung on the wall immediately behind the boxes. The subject then took his turn and the number of M's behaviors performed by the subject was recorded.

A control group was included in order to (a) provide a check on whether the subjects' performances reflected genuine imitative learning or merely the chance occurrence of behaviors high in the subjects' response hierarchies, and (b) to determine whether subjects would adopt certain aspects of M's behavior which involved considerable delay in reward. With the controls, therefore, M walked to the box, choosing a highly circuitous route along the sides of the experimental room; instead of aggressing toward the doll, she lifted it gently off the container.

The results of this study indicate that, insofar as preschool children are concerned, a good deal of incidental imitation of the behaviors displayed by an adult model does occur. Of the subjects in the experimental group, 88% adopted the M's aggressive behavior, 44% imitated the marching, and 28% reproduced M's verbalizations. In contrast, none of the control subjects behaved aggressively, marched, or verbalized, while 75% of the controls imitated the circuitous route to the containers.

In order to test the hypothesis that children who experience a rewarding relationship with an adult model adopt more of the model's behavior than do children who experience a relatively distant and cold relationship, half the subjects in the experiment were assigned to a nurturant condition; the other half of the subjects to a nonnurturant condition. During the nurturant sessions, which preceded the incidental learning, M played with subject, she responded readily to the subject's bids for attention, and in other ways fostered a consistently warm and rewarding interaction with the child. In contrast, during the nonnurturant sessions, the subject played alone while M busied herself with paperwork at a desk in the far corner of the room.

Consistent with the hypothesis, it was found that subjects who experienced the rewarding interaction with M adopted significantly more of M's behavior than did subjects who were in the nonnurturance condition.

A more crucial test of the transmission of behavior patterns through the process of social imitation involves the delayed generalization of imitative responses to new situations in which the model is absent. A study of this type just completed, provides strong evidence that observation of the cues produced by the behavior of others is an effective means of eliciting responses for which the original probability is very low (Bandura, Ross, & Ross, in press).

Empirical studies of the correlates of strong and weak identification with parents, lend additional support to the theory that rewards promote imitative learning. Boys whose fathers are highly rewarding and affectionate have been found to adopt the father-role in doll-play activities (Sears, 1953), to show father-son similarity in response to items on a personality questionnaire (Payne & Mussen, 1956), and to display masculine behaviors (Mussen & Distler, 1956, 1960) to a greater extent than boys whose fathers are relatively cold and non-rewarding.

The treatment of older unsocialized delinquents is a difficult task, since they are relatively self-sufficient and do not readily seek involvement with a therapist. In many cases, socialization can be accomplished only through residential care and treatment. In the treatment home, the therapist can personally administer many of the primary rewards and mediate between the boys' needs and gratifications. Through the repeated association with rewarding experiences for the boy, many of the therapist's attitudes and actions will acquire secondary reward value, and thus the patient will be motivated to reproduce these attitudes and actions in himself. Once these attitudes and values have been thus accepted, the boy's inhibition of antisocial tendencies will function independently of the therapist.

While treatment through social imitation has been suggested as a method for modifying antisocial patterns, it can be an effective procedure for the treatment of other forms of disorders as well. Jones (1924a), for example, found that the social example of children reacting normally to stimuli feared by another child was effective, in some instances, in eliminating such phobic reactions. In fact, next to counterconditioning, the method of social imitation proved to be most effective in eliminating inappropriate fears.

There is some suggestive evidence that by providing high prestige models and thus increasing the reinforcement value of the imitatee's behavior, the effectiveness of this method in promoting favorable adjustive patterns of behavior may be further increased (Jones, 1924a; Mausner, 1953, 1954; Miller & Dollard, 1941).

During the course of conventional psychotherapy, the patient is exposed to many incidental cues involving the therapist's values, attitudes, and patterns of behavior. They are incidental only because they are usually considered secondary or irrelevant to the task of resolving the patient's problems. Nevertheless, some of the changes observed in the patient's behavior may result, not so much from the intentional interaction between the patient and the therapist, but rather from active learning by the patient of the therapist's attitudes and values which the therapist never directly attempted to transmit. This is partially corroborated by Rosenthal (1955) who found that, in spite of the usual precautions taken by therapists to avoid imposing their values on their clients, the patients who were judged as showing the greatest improvement changed their moral values (in the areas of sex, aggression, and authority) in the direction of the values of their therapists, whereas patients who were unimproved became less like the therapist in values.

FACTORS IMPEDING INTEGRATION

In reviewing the literature on psychotherapy, it becomes clearly evident that learning theory and general psychology have exerted a remarkably minor influence on the practice of psychotherapy and, apart from the recent interest in Skinner's operant conditioning methods (Krasner, 1955; Skinner, 1953), most of the recent serious attempts to apply learning principles to clinical practice have been made by European psychotherapists (Jones, 1956; Lazarus & Rachman, 1957; Liversedge & Sylvester, 1955; Meyer, 1957; Rachman, 1959; Raymond, 1956; Wolpe, 1958; Yates, 1958). This isolation of the methods of treatment from our knowledge of learning and motivation will continue to exist for some time since there are several prevalent attitudes that impede adequate integration.

In the first place, the deliberate use of the principles of learning in the modification of human behavior implies, for most psychotherapists, manipulation and control of the patient, and control is seen by them as antihumanistic and, therefore, bad. Thus, advocates of a learning approach to psychotherapy are often charged with treating human beings as though they were rats or pigeons, and of leading on the road to Orwell's *1984*.

This does not mean that psychotherapists do not influence and control their patients' behavior. On the contrary. In any interpersonal interaction, and psychotherapy is no exception, people influence and control one another (Frank, 1959; Skinner, 1956a). Although the patient's control of the therapist has not as yet been studied (such control is evident when patients subtly reward the therapist with interesting historical material and thereby avoid the discussion of their current interpersonal problems), there is considerable evidence that the therapist exercises personal control over his patients. A brief examination of interview protocols of patients treated by therapists representing differing theoretical orientations, clearly reveals that the patients have been thoroughly conditioned in their therapists' idiosyncratic languages. Client-centered patients, for example, tend to produce the client-centered terminology, theory, and goals, and their interview content shows little or no overlap with that of patients seen in psychoanalysis who, in turn, tend to speak the language of psychoanalytic theory (Heine, 1950). Even more direct evidence of the therapists' controlling influence is provided in studies of patient-therapist interactions (Bandura et al., 1960; Murray, 1956; Rogers, 1960). The results of these studies show that the therapist not only controls the patient by rewarding him with interest and approval when the patient behaves in a fashion the therapist desires, but that he also controls through punishment, in the form of mild disapproval and withdrawal of interest, when the patient behaves in ways that are threatening to the therapist or run counter to his goals.

One difficulty in understanding the changes that occur in the course of psychotherapy is that the independent variable, i.e., the therapist's behavior, is often vaguely or only partially defined. In an effort to minimize or to deny the therapist's directive influence on the patient, the therapist is typically depicted as a "catalyst" who, in some mysterious way, sets free positive adjustive patterns of behavior or similar outcomes usually described in very general and highly socially desirable terms.

It has been suggested, in the material presented in the preceding sections, that many of the changes that occur in psychotherapy derive from the unwitting application of well-known principles of learning. However, the occurrence of the necessary conditions for learning is more by accident than by intent and, perhaps, a more deliberate application of our knowledge of the learning process to psychotherapy would yield far more effective results.

The predominant approach in the development of psychotherapeutic procedures has been the "school" approach. A similar trend is noted in the treatment methods being derived from learning theory. Wolpe, for example, has selected the principle of counterconditioning and built a "school" of psychotherapy around it; Dollard and Miller have focused on extinction and discrimination learning; and the followers of Skinner rely almost entirely on methods of reward. This stress on a few learning principles at the expense of neglecting other relevant ones will serve only to limit the effectiveness of psychotherapy.

A second factor that may account for the discontinuity between general psychology and psychotherapeutic practice is that the model of personality to which most therapists subscribe is somewhat dissonant with the currently developing principles of behavior.

In their formulations of personality functioning, psychotherapists are inclined to appeal to a variety of inner explanatory processes. In contrast, learning theorists view the organism as a far more mechanistic and simpler system, and consequently their formulations tend to be expressed for the most part in terms of antecedent-consequent relationships without reference to inner states.

> Symptoms are learned S-R connections; once they are extinguished or deconditioned treatment is complete. Such treatment is based exclusively on present factors; like Lewin's theory, this one is a-historical. Non-verbal methods are favored over verbal ones, although a minor place is reserved for verbal methods of extinction and reconditioning. Concern is with *function*, not with *content*. The main difference between the two theories arises over the question of "symp-

tomatic" treatment. According to orthodox theory, this is useless unless the underlying complexes are attacked. According to the present theory, there is no evidence for these putative complexes, and symptomatic treatment is all that is required (Eysenck, 1957, pp. 267-268). (Quoted by permission of Frederick A. Praeger, Inc.)

Changes in behavior brought about through such methods as counterconditioning are apt to be viewed by the "dynamically-oriented" therapist, as being not only superficial, "symptomatic" treatment, in that the basic underlying instigators of the behavior remain unchanged, but also potentially dangerous, since the direct elimination of a symptom may precipitate more seriously disturbed behavior.

This expectation receives little support from the generally favorable outcomes reported in the studies reviewed in this paper. In most cases where follow-up data were available to assess the long-term effects of the therapy, the patients, many of whom had been treated by conventional methods with little benefit, had evidently become considerably more effective in their social, vocational, and psychosexual adjustment. On the whole the evidence, while open to error, suggests that no matter what the origin of the maladaptive behavior may be, a change in behavior brought about through learning procedures may be all that is necessary for the alleviation of most forms of emotional disorders.

As Mowrer (1950) very aptly points out, the "symptom-underlying cause" formulation may represent inappropriate medical analogizing. Whether or not a given behavior will be considered normal or a symptom of an underlying disturbance will depend on whether or not somebody objects to the behavior. For example, aggressiveness on the part of children may be encouraged and considered a sign of healthy development by the parents, while the same behavior is viewed by school authorities and society as a symptom of a personality disorder (Bandura & Walters, 1959). Furthermore, behavior considered to be normal at one stage in development may be regarded as a "symptom of a personality disturbance" at a later period. In this connection it is very appropriate to repeat Mowrer's (1950) query: "And when does persisting behavior of this kind suddenly cease to be normal and become a symptom" (p. 474).

Thus, while a high fever is generally considered a sign of an underlying disease process regardless of when or where it occurs, whether a specific behavior will be viewed as normal or as a symptom of an underlying pathology is not independent of who makes the judgment, the social context in which the behavior occurs, the age of the person, as well as many other factors.

Another important difference between physical pathology and behavior pathology usually overlooked is that, in the case of most behavior disorders, it is not the underlying motivations that need to be altered or removed, but rather the ways in which the patient has learned to gratify his needs (Rotter, 1954). Thus, for example, if a patient displays deviant sexual behavior, the goal is not the removal of the underlying causes, i.e., sexual motivation, but rather the substitution of more socially approved instrumental and goal responses.

It might also be mentioned in passing, that, in the currently popular forms of psychotherapy, the role assumed by the therapist may bring him a good many direct or fantasied personal gratifications. In the course of treatment the patient may express considerable affection and admiration for the therapist, he may assign the therapist an omniscient status, and the reconstruction of the patient's history may be an intellectually stimulating activity. On the other hand, the methods derived from learning theory place the therapist in a less glamorous role, and this in itself may create some reluctance on the part of psychotherapists to part with the procedures currently in use.

Which of the two conceptual theories of personality—the psychodynamic or the social learning theory—is the more useful in generating effective procedures for the modification of human behavior remains to be demonstrated. While it is possible to present logical arguments and impressive clinical evidence for the efficiency of either approach, the best proving ground is the laboratory.

In evaluating psychotherapeutic methods, the common practice is to compare changes in a treated group with those of a nontreated control group. One drawback of this approach is that, while it answers the question as to whether or not a particular treatment is more effective than no intervention in producing changes along specific dimensions for certain classes of patients, it does not provide evidence concerning the relative effectiveness of alternative forms of psychotherapy.

It would be far more informative if, in future psychotherapy research, radically different forms of treatment were compared (King & Armitage, 1958; Rogers, 1959), since this approach would lead to a more rapid discarding of those of our cherished psychotherapeutic rituals that prove to be ineffective in, or even a handicap to, the successful treatment of emotional disorders.

REFERENCES

Adams, J. K. Laboratory studies of behavior without awareness. *Psychol. Bull.*, 1957, 54, 393-405.

Alexander, F. *Psychoanalysis and psychotherapy.* New York: Norton, 1956.

Alexander, F., & French, M. T. *Psychoanalytic therapy.* New York: Ronald, 1946.

Atkinson, Rita L. Paired-associate learning by schizophrenic and normal subjects under conditions of verbal reward and verbal punishment. Unpublished doctoral dissertation, Indiana University, 1957.

Azrin, N. H., & Lindsley, O. R. The reinforcement of cooperation between children. *J. abnorm. soc. Psychol.*, 1956, 52, 100-102.

Bandura, A., & Huston, Aletha, C. Identification as a process of incidental learning. *J. abnorm. soc. Psychol.*, in press.

Bandura, A., Lipsher, D. H., & Miller, Paula, E. Psychotherapists' approach-avoidance reactions to patients' expressions of hostility. *J. consult. Psychol.*, 1960, 24, 1-8.

Bandura, A., Ross, Dorothea, & Ross, Sheila, A. Transmission of aggression through imitation of aggressive models. *J. abnorm. soc. Psychol.*, 1961, 63, #3, 575-582.

Bandura, A., & Walters, R. H. *Adolescent aggression.* New York: Ronald, 1959.

Cairns, R. B. The influence of dependency-anxiety on the effectiveness of social reinforcers. Unpublished doctoral dissertation, Stanford University, 1959.

Calvin, A. D., Clifford, L. T., Clifford, B., Bolden, L., & Harvey, J. Experimental validation of conditioned inhibition. *Psychol. Rep.*, 1956, 2, 51-56.

Davidson, J. R., & Douglass, E. Nocturnal enuresis: A special approach to treatment. *British med. J.*, 1950, 1, 1345-1347.

Dittes, J. E. Extinction during psychotherapy of GSR accompanying "embarrassing" statements. *J. abnorm. soc. Psychol.*, 1957, 54, 187-191. (a)

Dittes, J. E. Galvanic skin responses as a measure of patient's reaction to therapist's permissiveness. *J. abnorm. soc. Psychol.*, 1957, 55, 295-303. (b)

Dollard, J., Auld, F., & White, A. M. *Steps in psychotherapy.* New York: Macmillan, 1954.

Dollard, J., & Miller, N. E. *Personality and psychotherapy.* New York: McGraw-Hill, 1950.

Dunlap, K. *Habits, their making and unmaking.* New York: Liveright, 1932.

Edmondson, B. W., & Amsel, A. The effects of massing and distribution of extinction trials on the persistence of a fear-motivated instrumental response. *J. comp. physiol. Psychol.*, 1954, 47, 117-123.

Erikson, C. W. Unconscious processes. In M. R. Jones (Ed.), *Nebraska symposium on motivation.* Lincoln: Univer. Nebraska Press, 1958.

Estes, W. K. An experimental study of punishment. *Psychol. Monogr.*, 1944, 57 (3, Whole No. 363).

Eysenck, H. J. *The dynamics of anxiety and hysteria.* New York: Praeger, 1957.

Fenichel, O. *Problems of psychoanalytic technique.* (Trans. by D. Brunswick) New York: Psychoanalytic Quarterly, 1941.

Ferster, C. B. Development of normal behavioral processes in autistic children. *Res. relat. Child.*, 1959, No. 9, 30. (Abstract)

Fishman, H. C. A study of the efficiency of negative practice as a corrective for stammering. *J. speech Dis.* 1937, 2, 67-72.

Frank, J. D. The dynamics of the psychotherapeutic relationship. *Psychiatry*, 1959, 22, 17-39.

Fromm-Reichmann, Frieda. *Principle of intensive psychotherapy.* Chicago: Univer. Chicago Press, 1950.

Heine, R. W. An investigation of the relationship between change in personality from psychotherapy as reported by patients and the factors seen by patients as producing change. Unpublished doctoral dissertation, University of Chicago, 1950.

Jones, E. L. Exploration of experimental extinction and spontaneous recovery in stuttering. In W. Johnson (Ed.), *Stuttering in children and adults.* Minneapolis: Univer. Minnesota Press, 1955.

Jones, H. G. The application of conditioning and learning techniques to the treatment of a psychiatric patient. *J. abnorm. soc. Psychol.*, 1956, **52**, 414-419.

Jones, Mary C. The elimination of children's fears. *J. exp. Psychol.*, 1924, **7**, 382-390. (a)

Jones, Mary C. A laboratory study of fear: The case of Peter. *J. genet. Psychol.*, 1924, **31**, 308-315. (b)

King, G. F., & Armitage, S. G. An operant-interpersonal therapeutic approach to schizophrenics of extreme pathology. *Amer. Psychologist*, 1958, **13**, 358. (Abstract)

Klein, Melanie. *The psycho-analysis of children*. London: Hogarth, 1949.

Krasner, L. The use of generalized reinforcers in psychotherapy research. *Psychol. Rep.*, 1955, **1**, 19-25.

Krasner, L. Studies of the conditioning of verbal behavior. *Psychol. Bull.*, 1958, **55**, 148-170.

Lacey, J. I., & Smith, R. I. Conditioning and generalization of unconscious anxiety. *Science*, 1954, **120**, 1-8.

Lazarus, A. A., & Rachman, S. The use of systematic desensitization in psychotherapy, *S. Afr. med. J.*, 1957, **32**, 934-937.

Lehner, G. F. J. Negative practice as a psychotherapeutic technique. *J. gen. Psychol.*, 1954, **51**, 69-82.

Lindsley, O. R. Operant conditioning methods applied to research in chronic schizophrenia. *Psychiat. res. Rep.*, 1956, **5**, 118-138.

Liversedge, L. A., & Sylvester, J. D. Conditioning techniques in the treatment of writer's cramp. *Lancet*, 1955, **1**, 1147-1149.

Martin, B., & Kubly, Delores. Results of treatment of enuresis by a conditioned response method. *J. consult. Psychol.*, 1955, **19**, 71-73.

Mausner, B. Studies in social interaction: III. The effect of variation in one partner's prestige on the interaction of observer pairs. *J. appl. Psychol.*, 1953, **37**, 391-393.

Mausner, B. The effect of one partner's success in a relevant task on the interaction of observer pairs. *J. abnorm. soc. Psychol.*, 1954, **49**, 557-560.

Max, L. W. Breaking up a homosexual fixation by the conditioned reaction technique: A case study. *Psychol. Bull.*, 1935, **32**, 734.

Meissner, J. H. The relationship between voluntary nonfluency and stuttering. *J. speech Dis.*, 1946, **11**, 13-33.

Meyer, V. The treatment of two phobic patients on the basis of learning principles: Case report. *J. abnorm. soc. Psychol.*, 1957, **55**, 261-266.

Miller, N. E., & Dollard, J. *Social learning and imitation*. New Haven: Yale Univer. Press, 1941.

Morgan, J. J. B., & Witmer, F. J. The treatment of enuresis by the conditioned reaction technique. *J. genet. Psychol.*, 1939, **55**, 59-65.

Mowrer, O. H. *Learning theory and personality dynamics*. New York: Ronald, 1950.

Mowrer, O. H., & Mowrer, W. M. Enuresis—a method for its study and treatment. *Amer. J. Orthopsychiat.*, 1938, **8**, 436-459.

Murray, E. J. The content-analysis method of studying psychotherapy. *Psychol. Monogr.*, 1956, **70** (13, Whole No. 420).

Mussen, P., & Distler, L. M. Masculinity, identification, and father-son relationships. *J. abnorm. soc. Psychol.*, 1959, **59**, 350-356.

Mussen, P., & Distler, L. M. Child-rearing antecedents of masculine identification in kindergarten boys. *Child Develpm.*, 1960, **31**, 89-100.

Payne, D. E., & Mussen, P. H. Parent-child relationships and father identification among adolescent boys. *J. abnorm. soc. Psychol.*, 1956, **52**, 358-362.

Peters, H. N. Multiple choice learning in the chronic schizophrenic. *J. clin. Psychol.*, 1953, **9**, 328-333.

PETERS, H. N., & JENKINS, R. L. Improvement of chronic schizophrenic patients with guided problem-solving motivated by hunger. *Psychiat. Quart. Suppl.*, 1954, **28**, 84-101.

Rachman, S. The treatment of anxiety and phobic reactions by systematic desensitization psychotherapy. *J. abnorm. soc. Psychol.*, 1959, **58**, 259-263.

Raymond, M. S. Case of fetishism treated by aversion therapy. *Brit. med. J.*, 1956, **2**, 854-857.

Razran, G. Stimulus generalization of conditioned responses. *Psychol. Bull.*, 1949, **46**, 337-365.

Robinson, Nancy M. Paired-associate learning by schizophrenic subjects under conditions of personal and impersonal reward and punishment. Unpublished doctoral dissertation, Stanford University, 1957.

Rogers, C. R. *Client-centered therapy.* Boston: Houghton Mifflin, 1951.

Rogers, C. R. Group discussion: Problems of controls. In E. H. Rubinstein & M. B. Parloff (Eds.), *Research in psychotherapy.* Washington, D.C.: American Psychological Association, 1959.

Rogers, J. M. Operant conditioning in a quasi-therapy setting. *J. abnorm. soc. Psychol.*, 1960, **60**, 247-252.

Rosenthal, D. Changes in some moral values following psychotherapy. *J. consult. Psychol.*, 1955, **19**, 431-436.

Rotter, J. B. *Social learning and clinical psychology.* Englewood Cliffs, N. J.: Prentice-Hall, 1954.

Rubenstein, E. A., & Lorr, M. A comparison of terminators and remainers in outpatient psychotherapy. *J. clin. Psychol.*, 1956, **12**, 345-349.

Rutherford, B. R. The use of negative practice in speech therapy with children handicapped by cerebral palsy, athetoid type. *J. speech Dis.*, 1940, **5**, 259-264.

Salzinger, K. Experimental manipulation of verbal behavior: A review. *J. gen. Psychol.*, 1959, **61**, 65-94.

Sarason, Barbara R. The effects of verbally conditioned response classes on post-conditioning tasks. *Dissertation Abstr.*, 1957, **12**, 679.

Schmidberg, Melitta. Psychotherapy of juvenile delinquents. *Int. ment. hlth. res. Newsltr.*, 1959, **1**, 1-2.

Sears, Pauline S. Child-rearing factors related to playing of sex-typed roles. *Amer. Psychologist*, 1953, **8**, 431. (Abstract)

Sears, R. R. Identification as a form of behavioral development. In D. B. Harris (Ed.), *The concept of development: An issue in the study of human behavior.* Minneapolis: Univer. Minnesota Press, 1957.

Sheehan, J. G. The modification of stuttering through non-reinforcement. *J. abnorm. soc. Psychol.*, 1951, **46**, 51-63.

Sheehan, J. G., & Voas, R. B. Stuttering as conflict: I. Comparison of therapy techniques involving approach and avoidance. *J. speech Dis.*, 1957, **22**, 714-723.

Shoben, E. J. Psychotherapy as a problem in learning theory. *Psychol. Bull.*, 1949, **46**, 366-392.

Skinner, B. F. *Science and human behavior.* New York: Macmillan, 1953.

Skinner, B. F. Some issues concerning the control of human behavior. *Science*, 1956, **124**, 1057-1066. (a)

Skinner, B. F. What is psychotic behavior? In, *Theory and treatment of psychosis: Some newer aspects*. St. Louis: Washington Univer. Stud., 1956. (b)

Solomon, R. L., Kamin, L. J., & Wynne, L. C. Traumatic avoidance learning: The outcomes of several extinction procedures with dogs. *J. abnorm. soc. Psychol.*, 1953, 48, 291-302.

Sullivan, H. S. *The interpersonal theory of psychiatry*. New York: Norton, 1953.

Thirmann, J. Conditioned-reflex treatment of alcoholism. *New Engl. J. Med.*, 1949, 241, 368-370, 406-410.

Thompson, G. N., & Bielinski, B. Improvement in psychosis following conditioned reflex treatment in alcoholism. *J. nerv. ment. Dis.*, 1953, 117, 537-543.

Tilton, J. R. The use of instrumental motor and verbal learning techniques in the treatment of chronic schizophrenics. Unpublished doctoral dissertation, Michigan State University, 1956.

Ullman, L. P., Krasner, L., & Collins, Beverly J. Modification of behavior in group therapy associated with verbal conditioning. *J. abnorm. soc. Psychol.*, in press.

Voegtlen, W. L. The treatment of alcoholism by establishing a conditioned reflex. *Amer. J. med. Sci.*, 1940, 119, 802-810.

Wallace, J. A. The treatment of alcoholics by the conditioned reflex method. *J. Tenn. Med. Ass.*, 1949, 42, 125-128.

Weide, T. N. Conditioning and generalization of the use of affect-relevant words. Unpublished doctoral dissertation, Stanford University, 1959.

Whiting, J. W. M. The research program of the Laboratory of Human Development: The development of self-control. Cambridge: Harvard University, 1954. (Mimeo)

Williams, C. D. The elimination of tantrum behaviors by extinction procedures. *J. abnorm. soc. Psychol.*, 1959, 59, 269.

Williams, R. I. Verbal conditioning in psychotherapy. *Amer. Psychologist*, 1959, 14, 388. (Abstract)

Wolpe, J. Reciprocal inhibition as the main basis of psychotherapeutic effects. *AMA Arch. Neurol. Psychiat.*, 1954, 72, 205-226.

Wolpe, J. *Psychotherapy by reciprocal inhibition*. Stanford: Stanford Univer. Press, 1958.

Wolpe, J. Psychotherapy based on the principle of reciprocal inhibition. In A. Burton (Ed.), *Case studies in counseling and psychotherapy*. Englewood Cliffs, N. J.: Prentice-Hall, 1959.

Yates, A. J. The application of learning theory to the treatment of tics. *J. abnorm. soc. Psychol.*, 1958, 56, 175-182.

(Received January 21, 1960)

15.   Systematic Desensitization

S. Rachman

Whereas the previous selection discussed learning principles in a general sort of way as they apply to altering behavior, this paper by Dr. Rachman of the Institute of Psychiatry, University of London, focuses upon a specific technique of behavior therapy. Systematic Desensitization is the most prominent of the learning approaches to the modification of deviant adult behavior.

Systematic desensitization is the most widely used method of behavior therapy. It was derived from and is closely connected with experimental psychology. Moreover, its operations and effects can be explicitly described and properly examined. The purpose of the present paper is to consider the experimental and clinical justification for this procedure.

Desensitization was developed by Joseph Wolpe in the early 1950s. He arrived at this method, which may be described as a gradual deconditioning of anxiety responses, in the following manner: Dissatisfied with the results which he was obtaining with the prevailing forms of psychotherapy, Wolpe returned to an examination of experimentally induced neurotic disturbances. At the time, two promising leads were those provided by the work of Pavlov and his successors on artificial neuroses, and the early but neglected work of Watson and Jones on the genesis and elimination of children's fears. Wolpe (1958) carried out a series of experiments on the artifical induction of neurotic disturbance in cats and came to the conclusion that the most satisfactory way of treating these neurotic animals was by gradual deconditioning along the lines proposed by Jones in 1924. Wolpe began by feeding the neurotic cats in an environmental situation which was distinctly dissimilar from the original traumatic environment. Wolpe then proceeded gradually, through a series of carefully worked-out stages, to situations which approximated more and more to the original traumatic situation. He found that in this way he was able to overcome the animal's neurotic reactions and restore them to apparent normality. It was obvious, however, that feeding responses would not be particularly effec-

Psychological Bulletin, 67, 93-103, #2, February, 1967. Reprinted by permission of the author and the American Psychological Association.

tive in the treatment of adult neurotic patients. His search for responses which would be antagonistic to anxiety led him to the work of Jacobson (1938), who recommended the use of relaxation as a treatment for neurotic disorders. Wolpe decided to substitute relaxation for feeding as the major incompatible response which would dampen the anxiety reactions. As will be made evident in this paper, there are ample data to show that the imposition of antagonistic responses (feeding, relaxation, etc.) upon anxiety will, in definable circumstances, reduce the intensity of the anxiety reaction.

At first he attempted to relax his patients in the presence of the actual anxiety-provoking objects. This method, he soon discovered, was both tedious and impractical since it involved amassing a large collection of objects for the treatment of each patient. Furthermore, as some patients did not experience anxiety in the presence of discrete and tangible objects, it meant that he would either have to refuse such patients treatment or develop some new method. He then began experimenting with the imaginary evocation of the anxiety-producing stimuli and soon found that it provided a very effective substitute for the real object. In other words, instead of attempting to treat a patient complaining of a phobia of dogs with an accumulation of photographs and models of dogs, he simply asked the patient to imagine these objects while relaxing in the consulting room. This method produced results and was easy to manipulate in the consulting room. It also allowed the therapist a high degree of flexibility in the planning of treatment.

Very simply, this is how the method of desensitization works. The patient is relaxed and then requested to imagine the anxiety-producing stimuli in a very mild and attenuated form. When the image is obtained vividly, a small amount of anxiety is usually elicited. The therapist then relaxes the patient again and instructs him to stop imagining the scene and to continue relaxing. The full sequence is: relax, imagine, relax, stop imagining, relax. The superimposition of relaxation on the anxiety reaction produces a dissipation of anxiety (reciprocal inhibition). This process is then repeated with the same stimulus or with a stimulus which is slightly more disturbing. The patient is again relaxed and the next stimulus is then presented and dissipated. With each evocation and subsequent dampening of the anxiety response, conditioned inhibition is built up (Wolpe, 1958). Eventually the patient is able to imagine even the previously most anxiety-provoking stimulus with tranquility, and this tranquility then generalizes to the real-life situation. The transfer of improvements from the consulting room to real-life situations usually accompanies each stage of the treatment program in a regular, temporal fashion. When the person is able to envisage the previously disturbing stimulus in the consulting room without anxiety, he generally finds that he is able to cope with the actual stimulus in the real-life situation without difficulty. Naturally, before the systematic desensitization proper commences, various preliminary steps have to be taken. In the first place, a full history of the patient's current disorder and his general history are obtained. Second, an attempt is made to reduce or eliminate any conflicts or anxiety-provoking situations which prevail at the time of treatment. If, for example, the patient's parents or spouse are exposing him to anxiety-producing situations, an attempt is made to alter their behavior (see Wolpe, 1958, for clinical examples). Third, the patient is trained in the methods of progressive relaxation as described by Jacobson. Fourth, a hierarchy or group of hierarchies containing the anxiety-producing stimuli is established by the therapist and patient as a result of detailed therapeutic discussions. In these discussions, the therapist, with the aid of the patient, builds up a series of situations which might produce anxiety in the patient. The patient is then required to rank them from the most disturbing to the least disturbing situation. When all these steps have been completed, the desensitization itself may proceed. Accounts of the actual technique are provided by Wolpe (1958, 1961), Lazarus (1964), Eysenck and Rachman (1965), and Paul (1966), and a selection of cases is available in Eysenck (1960, 1964).

The method of desensitization, and the other therapeutic procedures used by Wolpe (1958), are all based on the following general principle, as stated by him:

> If a response antagonistic to anxiety can be made to occur in the presence of anxiety-provoking stimuli so that it is accompanied by a complete or partial suppression of the anxiety responses, the bond between the stimuli and the anxiety responses will be weakened [p. 71].

The clinical effectiveness of desensitization has been discussed by Wolpe (1958, 1961), Eysenck and Rachman (1965), and Rachman (1965b). The success rates reported with behavior therapy (in which desensitization usually features very prominently) are usually in the region of 75%. The three most recent clinical reports have all yielded a similar outcome (Hain, Butcher, & Stevenson, 1966; Marks & Gelder, 1966; Meyer & Crisp, 1966). It would appear that Rachman's (1965a) conclusion regarding behavior therapy in general, can be applied with equal merit to desensitization—"It is a promising technique which is virtually certain to be effective in a large number of phobic and anxiety states but the treatment of severe, chronic patients needs to be improved." In the present paper, however, we shall be considering primarily the experimental use of systematic desensitization.

Some of the most important experimental work on this subject has been carried out by Lang and Lazovik. In 1963, they reported on the results of an experiment carried out on nonpsychiatric subjects who suffered from an excessive fear of snakes. This pioneer experiment was carefully and elaborately prepared and the experimental design and execution were of a high quality. The stringent controls which they applied enhanced the significance of their findings. The aims of the experiment were described by Lang and Lazovik (1963) as follows:

1. To evaluate the changes in snake phobic behavior that occur over time, particularly the effect of repeated exposure to the phobic object.

2. Compare these changes with those that follow systematic desensitization therapy.

3. Determine the changes in behavior that are a direct function of the desensitization process.

Lang and Lazovik chose to study snake phobia because of its fairly common occurrence (Geer, 1965) and also because of the assumed symbolic sexual significance attributed to snakes (e.g., Brill, 1949; Hendrick, 1948). Twenty-four college student volunteers were finally selected by a combination of interview, questionnaire, and direct exposure to a nonpoisonous snake. Only those subjects who rated their fears as intense and whose behavior in the presence of the snake confirmed the subjective report were used in the experiment. The subjects were divided into two matched groups, an experimental group ($n = 13$) and a control group ($n = 11$). The experimental treatment comprised two essential parts: training, and desensitization proper. The training procedure consisted of 5 sessions of 45 minutes duration, during which an anxiety hierarchy consisting of 20 situations involving snakes was constructed. The subjects were then trained in deep relaxation and taught how to visualize the feared scenes vividly while under hypnosis.

Following this training period, the experimental subjects were given 11 sessions of systematic desensitization, during which they were hypnotized and instructed to relax deeply. The anxiety items from the hierarchy were then presented, starting with the least frightening scenes and working up the scale to the most frightening scenes. As the experimental design demanded that each treated subject receive only 11 treatment sessions, some of the subjects were not desensitized to all of the items in the hierarchy. In order to assess the effectiveness of reality training, half of the experimental subjects were exposed to the snake before treatment on a number of occasions. The control subjects did not participate in desensitization but were evaluated at the same time as their opposite numbers in the experimental series, and their behavior in the presence of the snake was ascertained at the beginning and the end of the experiment. All of the available subjects were seen and evaluated 6 months after the completion of therapy.

The authors summarized their results in the following way:

The results of the present experiment demonstrate that the experimental analogue of desensitization therapy effectively reduces phobic behavior. Both subjective rating of fear and overt avoidance behavior were modified, and gains [compared to the control group] were maintained or increased at the 6-months follow up. The results of objective measures were in turn supported by extensive interview material. Close questioning could not persuade any of the experimental subjects that a desire to please the experimenter had been a significant factor in their change. Furthermore, in none of these interviews was there any evidence that other symptoms appeared to replace the phobic behavior.

The fact that no significant change was associated with the pretherapy training argues that hypnosis and general muscle relaxation were not in themselves vehicles of change. Similarly, the basic suggestibility of the subjects must be excluded. . . . Clearly, the responsibility for the reduction in phobic behavior must be assigned to the desensitization process itself [p. 524].

Lang and Lazovik also found a very close connection between the degree of improvement and the amount of progress made in the desensitization of hierarchy items within the 11 sessions provided by the experiment. They also made three general points on the basis of their results. First, as has been argued on previous occasions (see Eysenck & Rachman, 1965), it is not necessary to "explore with the subject, the factors contributing to the learning of a phobia or its unconscious meaning in order to eliminate the fear behavior." Second, they were not able to find any evidence to support the presumed claim that symptom substitution will arise if the symptoms are treated directly. Third, they pointed out that in reducing phobic behavior, it is not necessary to alter the basic attitudes, values, or personality of the subject.

Lang, Lazovik, and Reynolds (1965) recently reported further developments with this experimental procedure. They completed a study which included the experimental treatment of 23 subjects by systematic desensitization, 11 untreated controls, and 10 subjects who participated in "pseudotherapy." This last group of subjects is a particularly important addition since they received the same preliminary training as the desensitization group and participated in the same number of interview sessions. The major difference was that the pseudotherapy group was relaxed in the interview sessions but not desensitized—instead the therapist carefully avoided presenting any anxiety-provoking stimuli. These subjects were under the impression that they were being given a form of dynamic or interpretative therapy. The essential difference in the treated and pseudotherapy groups lay then in the use of systematic desensitization. Consequently, any difference in the treatment outcome had to be attributed to the use of this behavior therapy technique. The results were clear-cut and indicated that the subjects treated by systematic desensitization showed significant reductions in phobic behavior. The untreated subjects and the subjects who participated in pseudotherapy showed no improvement whatever. Among the subsidiary observations made by Lang *et al.*, the following are of particular interest: (*a*) None of the successfully treated subjects showed signs of developing substitute symptoms. (*b*) Again, it was found to be unnecessary to delve into the presumed basic causes of their fear of snakes. (*c*) Simply being in a therapeutic relationship with the therapist was not sufficient to effect significant changes in the phobia (see also Paul, 1966). (*d*) Successful behavior therapy was completely independent of the subject's basic suggestibility (as assesed on the Stanford scale). (*e*) The systematic desensitization of the specific fear generalized positively to other fears and an all-around improvement was observed.

Substantially confirmatory results were also reported in an experiment by Paul (1966). He investigated the effectiveness of desensitization in reducing interpersonal performance anxiety (actually, fear of public speaking). Five groups of carefully matched students were randomly allotted to the following groups: (*a*) systematic desensitization ($n = 15$), (*b*) insight therapy ($n = 15$), (*c*) attention placebo ($n = 15$), (*d*) no treatment control ($n = 29$), and (*e*) no contact ($n = 22$). Each of the 74 students comprising the first four groups was assessed before and after the completion of the experiment on three different types of scales. These measures included a number of self-report questionnaires, physiological measures (pulse rate and palmar sweating), and a rating of their behavior in a real-life stress situation (which involved speaking in public). Five experienced therapists participated in the experiment after having received brief but intensive training in the desensitization technique. One of the interesting sidelights to emerge from this experiment was the apparent success with which these predominantly interpretative or nondirective therapists acquired the ability to use desensitization treatment. Each therapist was allotted patients from the three treatment groups (i.e., desensitization, insight, attention placebo). On the completion of a comparatively short period of treatment (5 hours over 6 weeks), all subjects, including the nontreatment controls, were retested. Subjects who had received desensitization treatment showed a significantly better response to treatment than any of the other subjects. This superiority was evident on all three types of measurement—subjective report, physiological arousal, and reaction to stress. The superiority of the desensitized group was maintained at the 6-week follow-up period. Like the experiments conducted by Lang and Lazovik (1963), the work of Paul (1966) indicates that it is possible to bring about significant reductions in fear, even long-standing fears, by the use of systematic desensitization. It also indicates that fears can be eliminated without any exploration in depth. It should be pointed out, however, that this study by Paul is best regarded as an investigation of the effectiveness of desensitization in its own right, and not as a demonstration of the superiority of this technique over other forms of therapy, particularly interpretative or insight treatment. Such a brief period of treatment cannot be regarded as a fair test of "insight therapy" which, by general agreement, is a procedure requiring a great deal of time to execute. Paul anticipated this objection by referring to reports of the success of brief psychotherapy and counseling and by pointing out that most patients suffering from anxiety currently receive *brief* therapy. These arguments are of practical importance and well-taken. Nevertheless, it seems to be unfair to long-term therapies such as psychoanalysis to refer to the procedure as "insight" treatment; "brief psychotherapy" is perhaps a more accurate description of Paul's procedure. Furthermore, Paul's use of the term "follow-up" to denote the reassessment carried out 6 weeks after the completion of the experiment can be misleading. This is not in the ordinary sense a follow-up, but should be regarded more correctly as a posttreatment assessment. Only 1 of the 10 assessment procedures was readministered *twice* after treatment had been completed. The stability of changes induced by desensitization therapy was better tested by other studies such as those carried out by Lang and Lazovik (1963). Nevertheless, the corroborative value of Paul's study is impressive.

In a recent development of this study, Paul and Shannon (1966) demonstrated that systematic desensitization "can be efficiently combined with group discussion and administered in groups without loss of effectiveness in the treatment of interpersonal performance anxiety." Ten chronically anxious students were treated in two groups of five each: nine weekly sessions were given. Significant improvements were obtained at the completion of group treatment; the 10 subjects were shown to be considerably less anxious than the 10 untreated control subjects with whom they were compared. A comparison between the group-treatment results with the individual-desensitization-treatment results obtained in Paul's (1966) earlier study indicated that "the changes obtained for the group treatment equalled or excelled those obtained for individual treatments on every scale."

A very tightly controlled investigation of the effect of desensitization was recently carried out by Davison (1965). He had two main aims in designing his study. First, he wanted to examine the overall effect of desensitization treatment when compared with a no-treatment group. Second, he was interested in teasing out the effective elements of desensitization treatment. He used 28 non-psychiatric female subjects, all of whom complained of, and demonstrated, excessive fear of snakes. The subjects were divided into four matched groups on the basis of their behavior in the presence of real snakes. The four groups were treated in the following manner: Group 1 received desensitization under relaxation, in the usual manner. Group 2 received relaxation training, but during the treatment sessions these subjects were given irrelevant images to consider while under deep relaxation. Group 3 was given desensitization without either receiving training in relaxation or being relaxed in the actual treatment sessions. Group 4 received no active treatment but was merely assessed prior to and after the completion of the experiment. The subjects in Groups 2 and 3 were "yoked" to the systematic desensitization subjects, thereby ensuring that all of the girls who received treatment of any kind received the same number and durations of exposure to imaginary stimuli. The same therapist acted for all the subjects. At the completion of treatment, the retest avoidance exposures showed that the "desensitization under relaxation" group showed greater improvements than the other three groups, which did not differ. It was also observed that the subjects who were asked to imagine the anxiety-evoking stimuli without first being relaxed signalled anxiety far more often during treatment sessions than the other subjects. The importance of this study, apart from providing another demonstration of the effectiveness of desensitization in eliminating or reducing fears, is that it helps to isolate the mechanisms which produce the reductions in fear. Davison has demonstrated in this experiment that it is neither relaxation alone nor desensitization alone which produces the improvements. Rather, it is a combination of desensitization *and* relaxation which reduces fear. Apart from its practical importance, this experimental result goes partway towards confirming Wolpe's theoretical account of his treatment procedure. One would predict on the basis of his ideas of reciprocal inhibition that neither desensitization nor relaxation would in themselves be adequate procedures for eliminating fear.

A very similar result was also reported by Rachman (1965b). In this study, four small groups of spider phobic, nonpsychiatric subjects were allocated to the following experimental groups: desensitization with relaxation, desensitization without relaxation, relaxation only, no-treatment controls. The purpose of the experiment was "further to explore the effective mechanism contained in the treatment called 'systematic desensitization' based on relaxation":

> What are the necessary parts of the treatment procedure? Three specific questions are framed; is the treatment more effective than no-treatment? Is the treatment more effective than relaxation alone? Is the treatment more effective than desensitization without relaxation? [p. 256]

The effects of treatment were assessed by subjective reports, avoidance tests, and fear estimates. Marked reductions in fear were obtained only in the desensitization-with-relaxation group, and it was concluded that the combined effects of relaxation and desensitization were greater than their separate effects. Commenting on the results, Rachman (1965b) said that

> neither relaxation nor desensitization is effective in its own right. The catalytic effect of the two procedures is greater than their separate actions. It means also that the learning process involved is probably conditioned inhibition rather than extinction. This is not meant to imply that extinction is never responsible for the reduction of fear. In the present context however, inhibition is a more effective process [p. 250].

Like Davison, Paul, and Lang and Lazovik, Rachman could adduce no evidence of symptom substitution. Moreover, the improvements in phobic behavior observed at the end of treatment were found to be reassuringly stable over a 3-month follow-up period.

The fact that desensitization (i.e., graded and gradual exposures to the fearful stimuli) without relaxation is less effective than the same procedure carried out under relaxation supports Wolpe's conception of the effects of this treatment. He regards reciprocal *inhibition* as the main basis for the reduction and elimination of anxiety. In a stimulating article on this subject, Lomont (1965) argued that extinction rather than counterconditioning may be the process underlying the observed reductions in fear. In a reexamination of a number of experiments with animals, he could find only two studies in which the introduction of an inhibiting counterresponse appeared to produce superior results. An experiment by Gale, Strumfels, and Gale (1966) clearly indicates the superiority of the inhibition technique. Three groups of rats were matched on the basis of their acquisition of a conditioned emotional reaction and then subjected to extinction treatment, inhibition treatment, and no treatment, respectively. The addition of a feeding response during the repeated and progressive introduction of the fear stimulus (inhibition treatment) produced a quicker and greater reduction in fear. As mentioned above (Gale *et al.*, 1966, pp. 6–15), the evidence from analogue studies on human subjects also points to the superiority of the inhibition procedure.

In a recent study, Lomont and Edwards (1967) subjected some of Lomont's theoretical deductions to an experimental test. In particular, they attempted to answer two questions:

> (1) Is the efficacy of systematic desensitization due at all to the contiguity of muscular relaxation with anxiety stimulus visualization?
> (2) Can the efficacy of the technique be more satisfactorily ex-

plained in terms of reciprocal inhibition than on the basis of extinction?

The aims of the study are of course similar to those of Rachman's (1965b) investigation, and likewise the experimental procedure is comparable. Two groups of snake-phobic students (n = 11, each group) were treated. The first group received desensitization treatment with relaxation and the second group was given desensitization without relaxation (extinction procedure). On three out of five measures of snake-phobia change, systematic desensitization "produced significantly greater, or very nearly significantly greater, fear reduction than the extinction procedure [which appeared to be] totally ineffective."

This experimental outcome is consistent with the results reported by Rachman (1965b) and by Davison (1965) in their comparable investigations. At the very least, these three studies now justify the conclusion that reciprocal inhibition produced by relaxation is superior to extinction as a method for reducing fear.

It should be remembered, however, and Lomont's (1965) article demonstrates this lucidly, that extinction procedures can and do effect reductions in fear. The assumed operation of extinction processes is indeed an important feature of the learning theory view of neurotic disorders proposed by Eysenck and Rachman (1965). Among other things, it was said to be largely responsible for the frequent occurrence of spontaneous remissions of neurotic disturbances. This view was also expressed by Lomont.

Cooke (1966) compared the relative effectiveness of two types of desensitization treatments—imaginal desensitizing versus real-life desensitizing. He employed three groups of nonpsychiatric subjects with excessive fears of rats. Each group consisted of four subjects, and their fear reactions were ascertained by avoidance tests in the usual manner (see Lang & Lazovik, 1963; Paul, 1966). The first group was relaxed and then exposed in a graded and gradual manner to real rats, while the second group was relaxed and desensitized to similar items in imagination only. The third group consisted of a no-treatment control. Cooke found no overall difference between the two types of treatment, both of which produced significant decreases in fear (compared to the control group). He showed, however, that highly anxious subjects showed more fear reduction when treated in the Wolpeian fashion with imaginal stimuli. This difference in the response to treatment of slightly and highly anxious subjects is of some interest because of the clinical reports which have suggested that anxious patients do not respond to behavior therapy as well as less anxious patients (see Lazarus, 1963; Marks & Gelder, 1966; Wolpe, Salter, & Reyna, 1965). In a sense, Cooke's results run counter to these clinical findings which all tend to show that anxious subjects respond more slowly to behavior therapy. Clearly this is a point which needs further investigation. Some other findings to emerge from Cooke's study and which are of interest include the fact that no symptom substitution was observed nor were any increases in anxiety noted after treatment. Cooke also remarked on the consistency and reliability of the avoidance test scores and the subjective fear estimates.

Two other aspects of desensitization treatment which have received recent attention are the distribution of treatment sessions and the speed of generalization from imaginal desensitization to real-life behavior. Ramsay, Barends, Breuker, and Kruseman (1966) compared the effectiveness of massed and spaced treatment sessions. Twenty nonpsychiatric subjects with fears of various animals were given desensitization treatment under conditions of massed and spaced practice. In the spaced practice condition, each subject was given four fear-hierarchy stimuli to imagine in a 20-minute period. Four such treatment sessions were given. For the massed practice group, each treatment session contained eight items and the session lasted for 40 minutes. Two of these prolonged sessions were administered. In this way, the subjects in the two groups received the same amount of time in treatment and the same number of item presentations. The results showed a highly significant drop in fear due to the treatment, and that the learned reductions in fear were more efficiently induced under the distributed practice condition. In passing, Ramsay et al. (1966) commented on the ease with which the experimental therapists (with no previous experience of desensitization) acquired the necessary skill in successfully administering the treatment.

Rachman (1966) described an exploratory investigation into the speed of generalization from desensitization-treatment conditions to real-life situations. The two aims of the study were to "search for time lags and to pin down the time at which the generalization occurs." A subsidiary purpose in carrying out the investigation was to see if it could throw any light on the occurrence of relapse after desensitization treatment. The basic design of the study consisted of the following steps: (a) The subject was exposed to an anxiety-provoking stimulus involving spiders and asked to estimate the degree of fear which developed. (b) This pretreatment assessment was immediately followed by desensitization treatment usually lasting approximately 15 minutes. In every case, the subject was desensitized to an imaginal representation of the identical stimulus used in the pretreatment avoidance test. (c) Immediately after the completion of the desensitization, the subject was reexposed to the original stimulus in vivo. (d) This avoidance test was then repeated 24 hours later and, once more, 3 days or 1 week later. Measurements of the subject's reaction to the phobic stimulus were thus obtained on four occasions: immediately before treatment, immediately after treatment, 24 hours later, and 1 week later. It was found that the reductions in fear transferred from the imaginal desensitization session almost immediately. Spontaneous recovery of some degree of fear (i.e., relapse) occurred on slightly less than 50% of the occasions tested. The last finding is consistent with the clinical observations reported by Agras (1965). It is to be hoped that the design used in this experiment will be repeated and extended with a view to investigating the possible causes of clinical relapse. It is also of interest in demonstrating not only the frequency with which generalization does occur, but also, fairly precisely, when such transfer takes place.

A slightly atypical experiment was carried out by Lazarus in 1961 and also affords some evidence in support of the effectiveness of systematic desensitization. This study was unusual in that the treatment was carried out in groups rather than in individual treatment sessions and because of the heterogeneity of the sample used. The group desensitization technique had never been used before so that Lazarus' study to a large extent was exploratory rather than confirmatory. The results were nevertheless favorable to the desensitization approach and have now received a measure of support from the experiment recently reported by Paul and Shannon (1966). Altogether, Lazarus treated 17 control subjects and 18 experimental subjects. The samples consisted of four types of patients. These were 11 acrophobics, 15 claustrophobics, 5 cases of impotence, and 4 mixed disorders. The experimental subjects were treated in four separate groups, varying in size from two to five subjects, and the control subjects were treated in groups of no less than three subjects at a time. The experimental subjects were trained in relaxation and were given desensitization training and, eventually, desensitization treatment. The first control group was given group interpretative therapy, and the second control group (consisting of eight patients) received interpretative therapy and relaxation. Although the subjects treated by Lazarus were not drawn from a psychiatric population, they were nevertheless severely limited in their social relationships and general psychological adjustment because of their complaints. Before commencing treatment, each subject was interviewed and given psychometric tests and, where possible, was observed in a real-life fear situation. The assessment of the treatment effect was carried out by the interview method and also by a further excursion into the relevant feared situation. The results showed that a high degree of success was obtained with the group desensitization method, whereas those patients who received interpretative treatment did not show any recoveries. Of the eight patients treated by group interpretative therapy and relaxation, only two recovered. Follow-up studies were conducted on all the patients who had shown any sign of recovery. The follow-ups were carried out by means of a questionnaire, and any patient who revealed even a slight phobic recurrence was considered to have relapsed. Although Lazarus paid attention to the question of possible symptom substitution, no evidence of this phenomenon was encountered. Lazarus summarized his results this way:

> Group desensitization was applied to 18 patients of whom 13 initially recovered and three subsequently relapsed. Group interpretation was applied to nine patients. There were no recoveries in this group. Group interpretation plus relaxation was applied to eight patients of whom two recovered and one subsequently relapsed. The 15 patients who had not benefitted from the interpretative procedures were then treated by group desensitization. There were 10 recoveries of whom two subsequently relapsed [p. 508].

Of the 18 subjects who were treated by group desensitization, 13 recovered in a mean of 20.4 sessions. The 15 patients who were not symptom-free after undergoing interpretative group therapy and who were treated by desensitization showed a 66% recovery rate after a mean of only 10.1 sessions. Lazarus suggested that the fact that these patients recovered in a shorter time than did the original experimental subjects indicates that they may have received some form of nonspecific benefit from either the relaxation training or from the relaxation training in association with the interpretative therapy. Unfortunately, Lazarus's results cannot be accepted without reserve because the experimental design contained some weaknesses. The possibility that rater contamination and experimenter bias distorted the results cannot be ruled out because both the treatment and assessments were carried out by Lazarus himself.

In an experiment on a small group of asthmatic patients who acted as their own controls, Moore (1965) obtained a greater degree of improvement with desensitization treatment than that recorded when the patients received either relaxation or relaxation and suggestion. An interesting aspect of the treatment outcome in this study was that when the subjects were merely relaxed, their subjective reports suggested some improvements in their condition, whereas the physiological measurements (respiratory flow) reflected little change. The results obtained revealed significant improvements after systematic desensitization, apparently attributable to the *desensitization* procedure. In the case of this procedure, subjective reports and physiological tests improved together. For this reason, and because of the intrinsic clinical interest of this study, replications and extensions of this experiment would be extremely useful.

The present state of the experimental evidence on desensitization permits the following conclusions: (*a*) Desensitization therapy effectively reduces phobic behavior. (*b*) The elimination of phobic behavior is analogous to the elimination of other responses from the subject's repertoire. (*c*) Although it is often useful clinically, the *experimental* studies show that it is not essential to ascertain the origin of a phobia in order to eliminate it and neither is it necessary to change the subject's basic attitudes or to modify his personality. (d) The elimination of a phobia is not followed by symptom substitution. (e) The response to treatment is not related to suggestibility. (f) Relaxation alone or hypnosis alone does not reduce the phobia. (g) Relaxation and hypnosis accompanied by pseudotherapeutic interviews do not reduce the phobia. (h) The establishment of a therapeutic relationship with the patient does not in itself reduce the phobia—at best it produces marginal improvements. (i) Desensitization administered in the absence of relaxation appears to be less effective than systematic desensitization treatment. (j) Interpretative therapy combined with relaxation does not reduce phobic behavior. (k) A limited number of observations raise the possibility that reductions in fears which are produced by desensitization occur almost immediately; in a large minority of instances, a proportion of the fear-reduction accomplished in experimental treatment sessions reappears within 24 hours.

Although some of these conclusions are still tentative (the last two in particular), as a body they constitute a very important advance in our ability to reduce phobias. It is clear nevertheless that there is a great deal which still needs to be investigated and understood. Perhaps the most immediate need is for further experimental studies which attempt to apply these findings to psychiatric patients. While it is true that the clinical reports which have been published to date are, with some exceptions, consistent with the experimental evidence discussed in this paper, there remains a need for careful experimental investigation of the clinical application of desensitization. The recent study reported by Marks and Gelder (1966) is an example of the type of application which is required. The bulk of the work which has been reported so far has of course been carried out on phobic subjects. There is therefore a need for further investigation of both psychiatric and nonpsychiatric subjects who suffer from complaints other than excessive fears or phobias. Clearly, it is necessary to find other psychiatric and nonpsychiatric analogies on which to carry out similar experiments to those already described. One such example is the study carried out by Moore (1965) on asthmatic patients. From an experimental point of view, the full range of applicability of desensitization treatment remains to be explored. One of the specific problems which will have to be reexamined in clinical experiments is the role of anxiety in facilitating or impeding the progress of desensitization treatment. The clinical reports tend on the whole to indicate that the presence of high anxiety impedes or entirely prevents the progress of desensitization treatment (Eysenck & Rachman, 1965). On the other hand, the experiment reported by Cooke (1966) suggests that, in certain instances at least, the presence of high anxiety might be associated with a speedy response to desensitization. Closely allied to this problem is the question of the role of depression in desensitization treatment. Several clinical reports (e.g., Hain, Butcher, & Stevenson, 1966; Meyer & Crisp, 1966) have pointed out that the presence of depression in psychiatric patients tends to interfere, often quite seriously, with desensitization treatment. The comparative effectiveness of different therapists is another matter which needs to be examined. In the main, the results available from the experiments in which this variable has featured tend to suggest that intertherapist differences are of minor significance—at least where nonpsychiatric phobic subjects are concerned. However, it may well be that in the management of severely disturbed patients the ability (or personality?) of the therapist may be of some significance. It must be pointed out, however, that there have been some surprising indications from the experiments on nonpsychiatric subjects suggesting that it is possible to bring about the reduction or elimination of excessive fears with comparatively little training in the desensitization procedure. Needless to say, the management of psychiatric patients would by its very nature require more prolonged training and experience. In their retrospective analysis of the effects of behavior therapy in general, Marks and Gelder (1964) adduced some evidence to indicate that clinical experience was an important factor in determining the outcome of such treatment. On the technical side, two aspects of the desensitization procedure which would bear further examination are the optimum number and duration of scene presentations during the actual treatment sessions. Another possibility which has not received the attention which one might have expected is the use of drugs to facilitate the treatment procedure. A modification of the desensitization treatment recently described by Friedman (1966a, 1966b) is particularly interesting. In this method, the patient is relaxed by the injection of methohexitone sodium (Brietal) and then desensitized. The apparent advantages offered by this chemical technique are that it is capable of inducing rapid and deep relaxation without in any way impairing the patient's ability to image the anxiety-evoking stimuli. It is possible in this way to eliminate not only the preliminary training in relaxation but also to reduce the duration of each session. Moreover, it enables treatment to be offered to even those patients who experience difficulty in acquiring skill in relaxation. The replication and extension of Friedman's technique appears to be a very worthwhile undertaking. Obviously, any such examination should make due allowance for the possible effect of the drug as such, and it will probably be necessary to provide controls for the effect of the Brietal acting independently of any desensitization procedure.

Another methodological innovation which merits clinical investigation is the administration of group desensitization. The experiments of Lazarus (1961), of Paul and Shannon (1966), and the author's personal experience of group treatment suggest that it may prove to be as effective as individual treatment.

Finally, two theoretical advances are worth noting. When behavior therapy was first introduced, numerous objections were raised, particularly in psychoanalytic circles, and two of the most serious and widely expressed criticisms were these: first, it was argued that the tendency of behavior therapists to treat manifest neurotic behavior would, if successful, lead to symptom substitution; that is, the patient would develop new and possibly even worse symptoms if the so-called defensive reactions were removed by the behavior therapist. This phenomenon of symptom substitution has in the event proved to be of minimum importance and occurs very rarely. In none of the experiments described above was symptom substitution observed, even though it was in almost all cases carefully sought. In the clinical reports the occurrence of symptom substitution is also rare (see Eysenck & Rachman, 1965; Rachman, 1965).

A second objection which was raised was that it is impossible to bring about the reduction or elimination of neurotic symptoms and behavior unless one first eliminated the presumed basic causes of the illness. It was said that behavior therapy could not succeed because it was directing its attention to the wrong idea. This objection, too, has now been firmly eliminated. In the experimental investigations and in the clinical reports there is overwhelming evidence that substantial improvements in neurotic behavior can be obtained by systematic desensitization (and other methods of behavior therapy) even when little or no attention is paid to the possible or presumed underlying causes of the illness.

REFERENCES

Agras, W. S. An investigation of the decrement of anxiety responses during systematic desensitization therapy. *Behav. Res. & Ther.*, 1965, **2**, 267-270.

Brill, A. A. *Basic principles of psychoanalysis.* New York: Doubleday, 1949.

Cooke, G. The efficacy of two desensitization procedures: An analogue study. *Behav. Res. & Ther.*, 1966, **4**, 17-24.

Davison, G. The influence of systematic desensitization, relaxation, and graded exposure to imaginal stimuli in the modification of phobic behavior. Unpublished doctoral dissertation, Stanford University, 1965.

Eysenck, H. J. (Ed.) *Behavior therapy and the neuroses.* Oxford: Pergamon Press, 1960.

Eysenck, H. J. (Ed.) *Experiments in behaviour therapy.* Oxford: Pergamon Press, 1964.

Eysenck, H. J., & Rachman, S. *The causes and cures of neurosis.* London: Routledge & Kegan Paul, 1965.

Friedman, D. A new technique for the systematic desensitization of phobic symptoms. *Behav. Res. & Ther.*, 1966, **4**, 139-140. (a)

Friedman, D. Treatment of a case of dog phobia in a deaf mute by behaviour therapy. *Behav. Res. & Ther.*, 1966, **4**, 141-142. (b)

Gale, D. S., Sturmfels, G., & Gale, E. N. A comparison of reciprocal inhibition and experimental extinction in the therapeutic process. *Behav. Res. & Ther.*, 1966, 4, #4, 149-155.

Geer, J. H. The development of a scale to measure fear. *Behav. Res. & Ther.*, 1965, 3, 45-53.

Hain, J., Butcher, R., & Stevenson, I. Systematic desensitization therapy: An Analysis of results in twenty-seven patients. *Brit. J. Psychiat.*, 1966, 112, 295-308.

Hendrick, I. *Facts and theories of psychoanalysis.* (2nd ed.) New York: Knopf, 1948.

Jacobson, E. *Progressive relaxation.* Chicago: Chicago University Press, 1938.

Lang, P. J., & Lazovik, A. D. The experimental desensitization of a phobia. *J. abnorm. soc. Psychol.*, 1963, 66, 519-525.

Lang, P., Lazovik, A. D., & Reynolds, D. J. Desensitization, suggestibility and pseudotherapy. *J. abnorm. soc. Psychol.*, 1965, 70, 395-402.

Lazarus, A. A. Group therapy of phobic disorders by systematic desensitization. *J. abnorm. soc. Psychol.*, 1961, 63, 504-510.

Lazarus, A. A. The results of behaviour therapy in 126 cases of severe neurosis. *Behav. Res. & Ther.*, 1963, 1, 69-79.

Lazarus, A. A. Crucial procedural factors in desensitization therapy. *Behav. Res. & Ther.*, 1964, 2, 59-64.

Lomont, J. F. Reciprocal inhibition or extinction? *Behav. Res. & Ther.*, 1965, 3, 209-220.

Lomont, J. F., & Edwards, J. E. The role of relaxation in systematic desensitization. *Behav. Res. & Ther.*, 1967, 5, #1, 11-25.

Marks, I., & Gelder, M. A controlled retrospective study of behaviour therapy in phobic patients. *Brit. J. Psychiat.*, 1965, 111, 561-573.

Marks, I., & Gelder, M. Severe agoraphobia. A controlled prospective trial of behaviour therapy. *Brit. J. Psychiat.*, 1966, 112, 309-320.

Meyer, V., & Crisp., A. H. Some problems of behaviour therapy. *Brit. J. Psychiat.*, 1966, 112, 367-382.

Moore, N. Behaviour therapy in bronchial asthma: A controlled study. *J. Psychosom. Res.*, 1965, 9, 257-274.

Paul, G. L. *Insight versus desensitization in psychotherapy.* Stanford: Stanford University Press, 1966.

Paul, G. L., & Shannon, D. T. Treatment of anxiety through systematic desensitization in therapy groups. *J. abnorm. Psychol.*, 1966, 71, 124-135.

Rachman, S. The current status of behaviour therapy. *Arch. gen. Psychiat.*, 1965, 13, 418-423. (a)

Rachman, S. Studies in desensitization: I. The separate effects of relaxation and desensitization. *Behav. Res. & Ther.*, 1965, 3, 245-252. (b)

Rachman, S. Studies in desensitization: III. The speed of generalization. *Behav. Res. & Ther.*, 1966, 4, 7-16.

Ramsay, R., Barends, J., Breuker, J., & Kruseman, A. Massed versus spaced desensitization of fear. *Behav. Res. & Ther.*, 1966, 4, 205-208.

Wolpe, J. *Psychotherapy by reciprocal inhibition.* Stanford: Standford University Press, 1958.

Wolpe, J. The systematic desensitization treatment of neuroses. *J. Nerv. Ment. Dis.*, 1961, 132, 189-203.

Wolpe, J., Salter, A., & Reyna, J. *The conditioning therapies: The challenge in psychotherapy.* New York: Holt, Rinehart & Winston, 1964.

16.   Group Psychotherapy on Television: An Innovation with Hospitalized Patients

Frederick H. Stoller

> Moving away from conceptualizing certain behavior as being deter-
> mined by "sickness" or "illness" has resulted, also, in attempting differ-
> ent approaches in care or "treatment." Group psychotherapy is not
> new, but the introduction of television into it is new. Moreover, the
> secrecy in treatment which was long advocated can, of course, no
> longer be maintained when television is utilized.
>   The author of this article was formerly Senior Psychologist at Cam-
> arillo State Hospital, Camarillo, California, and is currently at the
> Youth Studies Center, University of Southern California.

A recent innovation in the conduct of group therapy in a mental hospital setting took advantage of the presence of a closed-circuit television
system. Regularly scheduled group therapy was conducted within the
television studio and the proceedings broadcast to the television sets on the
various wards. Participants in the groups were chronic hospitalized patients, who, in the opinion of the staff, were not making any progress
toward leaving the hospital. These patients were fairly representative of
the largely chronic group of patients who have not responded to most
efforts at rehabilitation. This paper will deal with the initial experience of
conducting psychotherapy under such circumstances and will explore
some of the implications of psychotherapy in an open, public setting.

A few words about the closed-circuit television station are in order and
will provide an appropriate background for this innovation. Within the
last few years, Camarillo State Hospital set up a television studio, operated
under the auspices of the Rehabilitation Service for the purpose of creating
and broadcasting programs of its own. The entire operation is handled
by patients supervised and trained by two staff members.[1] During the

American Psychologist, 22, 158-162, #2, February, 1967. Reprinted by permission
of the author and the American Psychological Association.

[1] The author wishes to express his gratitude to Tom Emmitt, supervisor of CSH-TV,
whose active cooperation and encouragement made this innovation as successful as
it was. The patient staff of CSH-TV also deserves particular commendation for the
enthusiasm and resourcefulness they displayed in what was a novel and extremely
difficult technical task. Special thanks is also due Larry Fielder who, in his former
capacity of helping supervise the hospital television station in its formative years,
also played a special role in helping set up this innovation.

morning and afternoon hours of weekdays, this station has a regular schedule of programs imparting information, participant entertainment, and similar programs. Its purpose has been to serve the special needs of the hospital population rather than to supplant the programming of commercial television. It has a double role: as a highly successful industrial therapy detail for a number of patients who work at the studio, and as an increasing part of the educational-recreational-therapeutic program of the hospital.

The idea of utilizing television for psychotherapy emerged from the author's experience in conducting a series of discussion groups on television. These groups followed the filming of movies on mental illness and consisted of rather abstract discussions of some of the problems outlined in the movies. Patients who participated in these discussions were relatively articulate and more likely to be in various stages of remission than in a chronic phase. In the experience of both the author and the participating patients, it was noted that the anticipatory anxiety so common with public performance was soon overcome once the actual performance commenced. The participants tended to conduct themselves in a highly creditable manner, somewhat to their own surprise. It would seem that performance of this sort tend to bring out the potential of individuals; that people tend to rise to the occasion when they are on public display. Within the context of providing continuity between behavior and self-expectancy, a successful series of performances could contribute to a dramatic alteration of the self-image held by individuals with histories of repeated failures.

With the idea that exposure plus the excitement involved in the conduct of television would provide an enhancement for the persons involved, a group of patients was sought whom it was felt would particularly benefit from such an arrangement. The chronically hospitalized individual, particularly the chronic schizophrenic, constitutes a group whose characteristic self-debasement and retreat from social engagement represents elements which might be particularly well modified in such a setting. Initially, a group of 10 female patients were assembled, all of whom were chronically hospitalized, and many of whom were quite severely regressed. The public nature of the setting was exploited and interaction between the members of the group and the television staff was invited. Wards were invited to watch the proceedings, particularly the home wards of the patients. Initially, hand microphones were used and these had to be held up close to the mouth. It was felt that the close proximity of the microphone and television camera had a compelling effect and so would make withdrawal and silence less likely. At the beginning of the session, each of the participants was asked to introduce himself to the audience. This helped break the ice immediately.

Because of their unique quality, physical arrangements require a special note. The patients and the therapist sat in a tight circle and two television cameras constantly circled around the periphery of the circle, shifting to the various members of the group. In addition to the two cameramen, cable handlers accompanied each camera and another man handled the overhead microphone. Directors and other television staff occupied a control booth and, at any particular session, many visitors might be present. More often than not, 10 or more people were in the immediate environment of the group.

For the most part, the therapist focused the direction of therapy toward enhancing the interaction between individuals in the group and toward others in their environment, toward their static situation in the hospital, and toward steps they could take to remedy this as well as the self-image they had of themselves. Individuals were urged to take specific steps such as pursuing off-ward work details or approaching appropriate personnel concerning the initiating of leave planning. It was repeatedly emphasized that their present predicament was a function of their own passivity.

It should be emphasized that these patients were among the more regressed on their wards. Some had been hospitalized for as many as 14 years, others had rarely spoken for almost as many years. Some were actively delusional and all had exhausted the therapeutic efforts of the staff. As an example of the level of maturity at which they tended to function, one patient suggested, as an appropriate activity for the first session, that they pretend they were part of a big department store and that the therapist play he was store owner and tell everyone what to do. For a number of patients, saying anything at all was an achievement. One young woman, of about 24 years of age, who had been hospitalized since the age of about 11, rarely uttered a word at any time.

Anyone who has attempted therapy with patients of this genre will know how difficult it is to obtain response of any kind from them. It was, therefore, quite gratifying to note the nature of the response induced through the modality of television. There was no question that a marked enhancement in the response of these patients over and above the usual format had occurred. Everyone responded to some degree and, as time went on, the increasing involvement of some individuals was quite marked. The response that they received from their home ward was one of excitement and recognition, a feature which was hardly part of their usual routine. Both ward personnel and fellow patients remarked on how well they had done and looked. The staff's perception of many of the patients changed remarkably because their actual behavior contradicted expectations most vividly.

As the number of sessions increased, and although novelty of the television medium wore off, its effectiveness as a therapeutic adjunct continued on a high level. The therapy session became the highlight of the week for the patients in a way in which routine group therapy rarely achieves. Concrete evidence of movement was apparent, not only in the manner in which the group functioned, but also in individual acts outside the therapeutic sessions. Some moved into off-ward work details and began to explore activities in the hospital about which they had not previously evidenced any awareness. Others began to seek out some ward activities in contrast to their previous inactivity. Some have left the hospital or are working on plans for leaving the hospital.

As some of the patients dropped out, a number of male patients were added so as to make a mixed group. As a group, the males received less feedback from their home wards than the initial female patients had and showed less dramatic evidence of movement. But even here, they responded in ways which were more gratifying than would have likely been the case had they been engaged in a group within a different context. One of these men froze the first few sessions, and appeared unable to say a word. Gentle pressure was exerted upon him every session, both by the therapist and by other patients who began to become adept at stimulating their fellow members into responding. After about three or four sessions in this manner, he suddenly began to talk in a free and open manner, to everyone's surprise.

Uncomfortable incidents were quite infrequent. At one time one of the patients began to cry openly and the therapist encouraged the group to handle her feelings in a very supportive manner. On many occasions patients have openly spoken in delusional fashion. However, it was the therapist's observation that psychotic verbalizing tended to decrease in frequency as the sessions became an established part of their routine. Most striking of all was the increased spontaneity of the group. During the initial session, the therapist did most of the talking and would direct himself toward individual patients a good deal of the time. The cameramen would maneuver their cameras wherever they saw the therapist direct his attention and so were able to focus the cameras on the appropriate speaker with relatively little difficulty. However, by the fourth and fifth sessions, the amount of spontaneity had increased to such a degree that the cameramen and director had difficulty anticipating who was going to speak next and often missed the initial parts of an interchange. While this was partly in response to the therapist's insistence that the members of the group address themselves to each other and the emphasis be placed on mutual help, it was also a function of the increasing ease with which these patients saw themselves in the framework of the television studio, broadcasting, and their growing involvement in the activity.

Subsequently, another group has been initiated with some slight changes in format. This group, while almost as chronic in terms of the number of years of hospitalization, tended to be somewhat younger in age and not quite as regressed. However, they were equally hopeless in the eyes of the staff and their status had become pretty well stabilized. Four males and five females constituted the second group and their spontaneity has moved with even greater speed than the first. Because of an improved sound system, the hand microphones used with the first group were dispensed with at no noticeable loss to the group's responsiveness.

A further innovation was attempted with this second group which shows very important promise. The first four sessions of this were videotaped and following the third session, the group was invited to remain and view themselves. They accepted the invitation with great enthusiasm and watched a playback of the whole session. No attempt was made to deal with their feelings or impressions as they viewed themselves, but the matter was taken up with them during the next week's session. One patient remarked that he thought that he was speaking too much (he was) and he made a marked attempt to moderate his defensive verbosity. Another patient felt she had not spoken enough and made a visible attempt to increase her spontaneity. The use of videotape presents a possibility for immediate self-viewing and self-evaluation of one's impact on others which is unequalled by any other modality. The urge to look at oneself is apparently an irresistible one and even patients who seemed to have abandoned a considerable amount of their self-esteem cannot turn away from this. Its use in this fashion, although rather crude, would seem to hold a great deal of promise if accompanied by meaningful group discussion.

Subsequent work with videotape feedback has utilized what can be termed "focused feedback." It had been noted that when self-viewing is done in a passive fashion, patients tend to concentrate on aspects of their physical appearance rather than on meaningful elements of their interpersonal impact. By having the therapist focus on what he considers to be significant aspects of their manner of interacting, it was found that patients had the opportunity to see themselves within a meaningful framework. Under these circumstances, the opportunity for self-perception is unsurpassed. Videotape has the distinct advantage of immediate playback; the more this is delayed, the more chance of diluting the immediacy of this type of self-viewing.

One of the more surprising features of group therapy in a television studio is the degree of concentration which the members of the group tend to give to the group itself despite the multitudinous distractions which are an inherent part of the scene. Considering that we are dealing with chronic schizophrenics, whose general tangentiality, limited attention span, and tendency toward avoidance of interpersonal situations are such prominent characteristics, their degree of involvement suggests that some relatively unique phenomenon is operating.

In analyzing social functioning, Goffman (1959) has used the analogue of the theatrical performance, pointing out that social roles can be likened to performances before an audience. He refers to groups of individuals banded together to maintain a common impression before a larger social group as teams. In this sense, the chronic hospital patient can be viewed as a one-man team rather than belonging to a multi-individual team. It may be that the television group compels the patient to participate in a team which is literally performing before an audience. Such a multi-individual team is concerned about maintaining its performance and collective impression so that individuals within the team who damage the team image tend to be corrected by the other members. This phenomenon greatly resembles Bach's (1954) observation that groups tend to push their members away from pathology. While this phenomenon is not absent in psychotic groups, the context of television seems to enhance it.

In this kind of an analysis, the therapist is very much a part of the team. He differs from the others only in that he may be more explicit about maintaining the performance and also provides a model for doing this. It should be emphasized that, in Goffman's terms, team performance is a ubiquitous and natural social phenomenon and that the schizophrenic differs only in the degree to which he tends to avoid such participation. Viewed in this context, the presentation of group therapy in open sessions, before seen and unseen audiences, may not be as far removed from actual life situations as a first impression might imply.

Open therapy, that is, therapy conducted in a public forum, as opposed to the conventional closed-door private setting, has many implications for the manner in which the therapy is conducted. Moreno (1946) has utilized audiences in psychodrama and very often the observers were used as part of the interaction. However, in television therapy, the only immediate interaction is with the studio staff and some observers within the studio. In Goffman's terms, the therapy group and the studio staff form a team for presenting a particular kind of social performance and, therefore, participate in mutual efforts to support a particular impression before the larger audience. The unseen viewers represent an audience with which no immediate interaction is possible but does, in many ways, represent the larger social scene we all face. Participating in the televised group gives the patient the opportunity to cooperate with others in performing before the world at large.

Mowrer (1963) is one of the few who has seriously questioned the implication of privacy in the therapeutic endeavor. He has noted that privacy implies withdrawal and denial, a practice most patients have been engaging in for many years. He portrays conventional therapy in terms of a patient revealing long-hidden sins to another individual who will be equally as secretive about them as he was, perpetuating the attitude towards these sins. In actuality, a good portion of the psychotherapeutic movement has veered away from what Berne (1961) has referred to as the game of "Archaeology," namely "digging up significant material." As Rotter (1963) has stated in looking at recent trends:

> The general overall trend is toward less emphasis on investigation of the past and interpretation of symbolic manifestations of the unconscious and more emphasis on dealing with the present, using the patient's relationship to the therapist in therapy as a source of learning. More recently, there has been increased interest in conceiving of the patient's difficulties in terms of inadequate solution of problems [p. 821].

This is particularly true for the field of group therapy, about which Rotter states:

> The tendency is no longer to regard group therapy as a kind of mass situation with the same goals as individual psychotherapy. Rather it is regarded as a special situation where the patient has the opportunity to learn group norms, where he can be reinforced for social interest, and where he is able to learn about others' reactions to his own social behavior [p. 819].

Under the circumstances thus enumerated, the necessity for privacy and confidentiality can be challenged. In much of contemporary psychotherapy there is little attempt to unearth embarrassing facts about the patient nor to have him reveal aspects of himself which are ordinarily secretive or taboo. Rather, the kind of image he presents to the world is made explicit to the patient together with its consequences in terms of the kind of treatment he generally receives from the world (this is one specific reason why the use of videotape has such attraction as a possible technical enhancement to group therapy). With this approach to therapy the need for privacy and confidentiality is greatly reduced.

An undesirable concomitant of the usual secretive circumstances under which psychotherapy is generally conducted is the often negative misconceptions of the process that many individuals develop. It would be an impossible task to determine the proportion of persons who could profit from certain features of group therapy but who veer away from it under the mistaken impression that their personalities will be taken away from them or that their inherent weaknesses and inadequacies would be revealed in a destructive manner. The open exposure of psychotherapy, as it is actually conducted, would demonstrate to many that the process is far different from the general conception and that it is hardly the devastating and mysterious experience they anticipate. Unwittingly, many psychotherapists have perpetuated the conception of therapy as an arcane art so as to perpetuate their own omnipotent and magical image.

The impact of televised therapy on the audience is now being investigated. Informal inquiries have suggested there is an appreciable impact upon the audience by regularly observing group therapy. In many ways, television, with its intense close-ups that view the individual from a far closer vantage point than is customary in ordinary interaction, can foster intense identification. One should not underestimate the possible effect of this identification by chronic hospitalized patients when observing a group like themselves who struggle with their own inarticulateness and passivity and move toward more effectiveness. It has been observed that the patient TV staff has a tendency to respond to increased tension in the group with more erratic functioning in their various jobs, suggesting considerable impact.

There is much likelihood that by having patients regularly observe televised group therapy, a more efficient utilization of trained therapists could be achieved. However, the probability is that it would be most effectively utilized if integrated with some more inclusive program. Television can only be a medium which educates and influences. It cannot be a substitute for personal interaction.

Group therapy on television is an innovation which has already shown evidence that it enhances the effectiveness of psychotherapy with the chronic schizophrenic. Exploration with a wider range of groups and the development of techniques exploiting the unique features of videotape are being undertaken. Training in psychotherapy as well as general education about therapy is also being explored. Perhaps, most important of all, is the light it casts on group processes by wrenching this common technique from its customary seclusiveness into an open, public setting.

REFERENCES

Bach, G. R. *Intensive group psychotherapy.* New York: Ronald Press, 1954.
Berne, E. *Transactional analysis in psychotherapy.* New York: Grove Press, 1961.
Goffman, E. *The presentation of self in everyday life.* New York: Doubleday Anchor, 1959.

Moreno, J. L. Psychodrama and group psychotherapy. *Sociometry*, 1946, **9**, 249-253.

Mowrer, O. H. Payment or repayment? The problem of private practice. *Amer. Psychologist*, 1963, 18, 577-580.

Rotter, J. B. A historical and theoretical analysis of some broad trends in clinical psychology. In S. Koch (Ed.), *Psychology: A study of a science*. Vol. 5. *The process areas, the person, and some applied fields: Their place in psychology and in science*. New York: McGraw-Hill, 1963. Pp. 780-830.

17.   A Review of Psychiatric Developments in Family Diagnosis and Family Therapy

Don D. Jackson and Virginia Satir

One of the recent trends in the observation and care of the "mentally ill" is *family therapy*—it has come on the scene only within the past ten years or so. Family therapy is a radical innovation from the traditional psychotherapeutic approaches; succinctly, it means that all members of a nuclear family are seen together at the same time by the same therapist.

This article outlines the major historical forces and events which have been responsible for the development of family therapy. Too, it provides the rationale upon which the approach is based.

We are presenting our brief observations on the history of family diagnosis and therapy, we trust, more in the spirit of Toynbee than in the style of the *Encyclopaedia Brittannica*.

We must begin by defining what we are including under the rubric "family diagnosis and therapy" because the designation of "family" as a treatment unit, in contrast to a uniform understanding of the individual as the treatment unit, means different things to different people. A family approach, we believe, requires an orientation stressing sociocultural forces and explicitly acknowledging more diagnostic and prognostic implications of the "here and now" situation than might be subscribed to by clinical therapists generally.

Technically, using the family as a treatment unit has been interpreted differently by different clinicians. The different approaches seem to fall into the following general categories:

From *Exploring the Base for Family Therapy* (edited by Nathan W. Ackerman, Francis L. Beatman, and Sanford Sherman); Family Service Association of America, 215 Park Avenue South, New York 3, New York, pages 29-49, 1961. Reprinted by permission of the authors and the Family Association of America. Dr. Jackson was Director of the Mental Research Institute, Palo Alto, California. Virginia Satir was a member of the staff.

1. The members of a biological or nuclear family are treated conjointly, which means that all family members are seen together at the same time by the same therapist. The members of the family include parents, children, other significant relatives such as grandparents and aunts or uncles, and other significant non-relative people, with the selection dependent on relationships and not necessarily on blood ties. This is our approach at the Mental Research Institute.

2. The members of a family are seen conjointly for diagnostic purposes, and family members are then assigned on an individual basis to different therapists who will work collaboratively. Another variation is to select one member for individual psychotherapy after a family diagnosis has been made. It is our impression that this latter practice is generally used when geographical circumstances, such as the patient's being in a hospital some distance from his home, necessitate it.

3. Family members are seen individually from the outset by a single therapist who then pieces together the picture of family interaction and continues to treat the family members individually. Family members may also be seen individually from the outset, each by a different therapist. The therapists then sit down together to pool their findings to try to arrive at a picture of family interaction—perhaps in much the same spirit as the family itself might do—with subsequent individual treatment. The family interaction is observed primarily at the level of collaboration.

All the above approaches are predicated on the necessity for viewing the symptoms of the identified patient or patients within the total family interaction, with the explicit theoretical belief that there is a relationship between the symptom of the identified patient and the total family interaction. The extent to which the therapist "believes" in family therapy will determine his emphasis on techniques that convey this orientation to the patient.

4. In another form of working with the family, the identified patient is seen in individual psychotherapy and family members are seen occasionally to determine how best to elicit their aid, or simply to urge them not to interfere with the patient's progress. We feel the utility of this method is limited. It is based on the theoretical concept that the patient alone is a sick unit, and that the other family members are well and capable of change in the interest of the patient. This approach emphasizes the existence of two units within the family—the identified patient as the sick unit and the other family members as the well unit.

It seems to us that, for clarity's sake, "family" should refer to parents and children (or other persons who are a part of the immediate social family), and the terms "diagnosis" and "therapy," and "concurrent," "conjoint," or "collaborative" should be employed to designate the exact nature of the technique being used.

A search of the *Cumulus Medicus* for the past thirty years for papers in which the noun "family" appears, reveals that this designation relates to methods of study or treatment that can be considered "family oriented." We believe the terms "family diagnosis" and "therapy" should be restricted to those systems of study where the therapist's impression of state X in subject A carries probability statements about subject B; if B is in the same nuclear family and at a different level, A's inferences about B change A's probable state (behavior, motivation, and so on) from X to X_1, X_2, and so on. In individual therapy, the focus tends to be on how A feels about B or about himself, without shifting levels.

One final point in connection with terminology. Although it is possible to label what is meant by "the family," and to label the approaches used to the family as a unit, the language used in theoretical descriptions about family interaction reveals the need to find new and more appropriate terminology that may correctly define the concepts. Writers attempting to explain concepts of family interaction seem to be struggling to apply to family interaction terminology that is useful in describing individual therapy, with resulting unclear conclusions. At the present time, if we were able to find a common denominator in all the literature about description and analysis of family interaction, we would have a greater pool of common observations and probably greater agreement about their significance.

SOME INFLUENTIAL FACTORS

The following general factors seem to us crucial in contributing to the development of family-oriented rather than individually-oriented psychological observation and treatment.

1. Psychiatry, since the late 19th century, has been gradually losing its fraternal position to medicine and is becoming instead a cousin who, though a blood relative, springs from a different family. Psychology, sociology, and anthropology are increasingly influencing the kind of psychological data obtained and the nature of the interpretation given these data. For example, it has been recently reported that eldest sons of Indian families living in Singapore are many times more vulnerable to a schizophrenic psychosis than any other member of the Indian family or any of the members of the Chinese or Malayan families who constitute

the other two main ethnic groups.[27] * Such a finding surely must eventually influence the diagnostic and therapeutic approach to the patient who is an Indian eldest son. Thus, in this simple example, we see how anthropology and sociology may make direct contributions to the etiology of emotional illness and consequently influence psychiatric practice.

2. The child guidance movement, which was initially developed through efforts of the juvenile court to treat delinquent children specifically, rather naturally expanded to look for and include expeditious and economical means to diagnose and treat neurotic and psychotic children. Experience, especially on the part of social workers, has led to the conclusion that treating the child is not enough and, more recently, that treating the child and the mother may not be enough. In 1942, Mildred Burgum published a paper[9] in which she demonstrated by statistics from a child guidance clinic that the father's role was ignored in the early approach to the family and that this fact might account for a high dropout rate. Such findings have gradually become incorporated in child guidance practices. If the clinic is to keep the father involved, however, it means further manpower problems for the clinic and thus a push in the direction of family therapy. Our own group has discovered that the child who is labeled by the family as the patient is not necessarily the "sickest" in the family. Such datum casts doubt on the wisdom of seeing only the identified patient and the mother. A family approach thus comes to offer increased data that were not always available under the older methods, as well as possibilities for increased economy and research.

3. The psychoanalytic movement, which has been so largely responsible for loosening the ties between classical medicine and psychiatry, has been a prime influence in family diagnosis. Flügel, in *The Psycho-Analytic Study of the Family*, the first book of its kind, states, "It is probable that the chief practical gain that may result from the study of the psychology of the family will ensue more or less directly from the mere increase in understanding the nature of, and interactions between, the mental processes that are involved in family relationships."[11]

a. Although psychoanalysis is a system that focuses on the individual, reference to the family has been appearing since Freud's case of little Hans. The classical Oedipus situation, originally an intrapsychic construct, has become increasingly interpersonal especially as the mother's pregenital influence has come to be recognized. The sociologist, Parsons, and others have expanded Freud's original notion into the broader frame-

* In this article the reference numbers refer to the bibliography at the end of the article.

work of anthropology and sociology. The emphasis on ego psychology since the 1920's and the writings of the so-called neo-Freudian psychoanalysts have become increasingly interactive or transactional and thus have focused on the patient's significance to others, usually his family. Even the emphasis on intrapsychic objects by Klein, Fairbairn, Windicott, and others stirs a curiosity to discover these objects in the real world.

b. Freud's extreme position in relation to the relatives of the patient has led to a re-examination of his position and, on the part of some analysts, to a search for more workable arrangements. Freud issued an urgent warning against any attempt to engage the confidence or support of parents or relatives, confessing that he had little faith in any individual treatment of them. It was inevitable that individuals like Mittelman and Oberndorf would be challenged to test these dicta and thus lead to further developments toward a family concept.

c. Another influence toward family studies, which has indirectly stemmed from the psychoanalytic movement, has to do with the disappointment in the results of this expensive and time-consuming technique and the possible relation of results to a change in the type of clinical material with which psychoanalysts deal. The shift in emphasis from symptom neuroses to character, marital, and child guidance problems has resulted in a broadening of analytic techniques with an emphasis on parameters and on psychoanalytically oriented psychotherapy.

d. Child analysis failed to fulfil its initial promises as analysts discovered that even five one-hour sessions a week could not keep up, in most cases, with the influences of the remaining 163 hours at home. The number of child analysts who have stuck to their last is surprisingly small, and this fact must have had some influence in giving tacit approval for others to seek new techniques in treating children.

Thus, psychoanalysis has acted both in a positive and in a negative sense to expedite the family movement and it is obvious that many of the authorities on family diagnosis and therapy are psychoanalytically trained. This latter factor has contributed to a complication of which we shall speak later—the current lack of a language for family diagnosis and therapy.

4. Gradually an awareness has been developing of the existence of health within the same framework in which pathology exists, which has led to a beginning re-evaluation of the prognosis of emotional illness. The concept of "adaptation" has helped focus on the "why" of the illness rather than on fixed psychopathological symptoms. Jahoda's recent book on mental health and mental illness[18] introduces dimensions of health and emphasizes the needs to see the "sick person" or "sick family" in dimensions of health as well as illness. A diagnosis of a sick person de-

scribed entirely in terms of pathology often presents a dreary, hopeless picture. None but the most brave, foolish, or dedicated would attempt the apparently hopeless. However, a visit to the home, a session with the whole family, can reveal to the therapist unsuspected pockets of ability of family members to relate, to share a joke, or even to be a little kind to each other.

5. Another important factor in the development of a family approach has emerged from the psychotherapy of schizophrenia which blossomed in the thirties and underwent an increased growth rate during the forties. Federn and others thought that the schizophrenic's irrepressible id created an atmosphere in which the therapist needed to focus on current situations and actual experience. Sullivan, from a somewhat different point of view, advised the same procedure and cautioned that reality factors existed as a kernel in all the patient's distorted productions. These points of view brought the therapist more in contact with the patient's real experience within his family, and this practice was strengthened by the eloquent writings of Fromm-Reichmann. In addition, the hospital management of schizophrenics involved visits from relatives and led to a suspicion that these relatives were difficult people to handle. It is interesting that a recent report by G. W. Brown of the Maudsley Hospital confirms the validity of this early suspicion.[8] He demonstrated that the success or failure of chronic schizophrenic patients after leaving the hospital depended on whether they returned to their parents or spouse, or were able to live alone in a lodging or with siblings. The highest failure was in those returning to their parents and in those returning to a spouse and *was not related to their diagnosis or to their prognosis on admission.* On the other hand, if a married patient was able to return to his spouse and remain outside the hospital over three months, he achieved a higher level of social adjustment than any of the other schizophrenics studied. Other recent studies have revealed that the single most significant correlate with the patient's length of stay in the hospital was the number of visits he received during his first two months of hospitalization.[10, 37] In the face of such discoveries, it becomes increasingly difficult for the therapist of the schizophrenic to remain purely patient-oriented.

6. A final factor is an augmentation of point 1, concerning the growth of anthropology, psychology, and sociology and their increasing clinical orientation. A psychiatrist interested in the family would not think of ignoring the work of Parsons and Bales,[28] any more than he would overlook Ackerman's recent book.[1] Two of the most promising avenues of exploration of family interaction lie in the field of social psychology and its study of small groups and in the field of communication and information theory, largely peopled by experimental and clinical psychologists.

The factors that we have mentioned are not mutually exclusive and interdigitate in a way that makes it difficult to tease them apart. For example, the child mental health program was largely conducted in clinics where non-psychiatrists did the bulk of the work and where finances were of great moment. In the search for efficacious brief methods it was a recognized fact that a social worker could more properly interview parents than could a psychoanalyst since the latter would be uncomfortable in crossing tradition-bound lines that dedicated him to a single patient. On the other hand, the fact that a good deal of family work has evolved from interest in schizophrenia is due to slightly different combinations of circumstances. Schizophrenia, an increasingly important illness with no predictable means of cure, was psychologically everyone's baby but no one's baby, and therefore analysts, psychiatrists, and social scientists were free to contribute to and experiment in its treatment.

Whatever the various factors contributing to the evolution of family diagnosis and therapy, one thread runs rather clearly through the history of modern psychoanalytically-oriented psychiatry. This is the gradual development of concepts from a monadic viewpoint to dyadic and currently, triadic or larger. Even though Flügel saw the need of studying family members, he used his study of individual family members and of family systems in order to increase the knowledge of the individual. His approach, therefore, is essentially monadic. We have not come a great distance from his position, as witness the words of Spiegel and Bell:

> Practice may or may not follow theory faithfully. The dynamic theories of psychopathology and the findings derived through their use have been largely individual-centered. However, these theories have been constructed in such a way that the individual is conceived as a self-contained system becoming relatively closed early in life. Even the social and cultural variance of these theories share this assumption. *We do not find evidence that treatment procedures vary significantly* from what one would expect on the basis of theory. In the context of the habitual lip-service paid to the family as a whole, isolated groups or individuals have attempted to maintain a focus on a family unit in diagnostic formulations and treatment procedures but attempts to bring the family to the forefront have not been established.[39]

The one portion of this statement we wish to disagree with is the authors' claim that there are no treatment procedures that vary significantly. It seems to us that Nathan Ackerman's treatment of a family at the Family Mental Health Clinic and our own approach at the Mental Research Institute are significantly different from any recognized method of individual therapy. It is possible that some therapists would be shocked at what goes on in family therapy because the approach is so much a transactional one rather than a careful hovering attention to the individual's apparent thoughts and feelings.

The literature reveals relatively little that could be described as organized formulations that would set the theoretical base of those who diagnose and treat emotional illness of a labeled patient as a part of sick family interaction, apart from the theory underlying the treatment of an individual. The reason may be that concepts surrounding individual diagnoses and treatment are pretty universally accepted and form the primary content of respectable professional training. Much of the writing deals with the family in relation to schizophrenia, a disorder that is set apart from neuroses and has not had an important part in psychoanalytic theory. Any resemblance between interaction in families where schizophrenia exists and interaction in families where other forms of emotional illness exist is difficult for some individuals to accept. In the same vein, these same individuals make a sharp distinction between the techniques of treating schizophrenic patients and non-psychotic patients.

EVENTS LEADING TO ACCEPTANCE OF CONJOINT TREATMENT

After some soul-searching and much library searching we would like to present some of the events that we believe have played an important part in the relatively new idea of conjoint family diagnosis and therapy. We use schizophrenia as a model for simplicity's sake and because of our greater familiarity with this subject.

The following events are some of the high spots in the approach to conjoint work with the families of schizophrenics—a type of treatment that is apparently less than ten years of age.

1911: Freud wrote his famous Schreber case.[13] The dynamics of paranoia were discussed and were seen to have defensive aspects and underlying dynamics which made schizophrenia more than a cerebral defect. Incidentally, in the description of this case are allusions to "wife" and "mother" which are of interest to students of schizophrenia.

1916: Rudin's monograph on the genetics of schizophrenia appeared.[34] Patients' families were interviewed and a connection was made between their difficulties and the patients'. During the twenties and thirties some of Rudin's students published further studies of the families of schizophrenic index cases. Especially important were those studies in which the children of schizophrenic parents were examined and found to evince many mental disorders including neuroses and manic-depressive disorder. Although the approach was biological, the schizophrenic and his family were nevertheless brought together for study and the lack of nice Mendelian findings raised the question of social forces.

1920: Moreno and others began group psychotherapy with hospitalized patients.[26] The whole group therapy movement has had a definite, if not obvious, effect on family theory and therapy, since it pointed up the value of analyzing interaction as it occurred between individuals. Through witnessing interaction, the group therapist was able to improve his diagnosis. Identifying interaction and interpreting this interaction in terms of motivation were means by which psychological growth was enhanced.

1927: Sullivan reported on his spectacular work with schizophrenics at the Sheppard and Enoch Pratt Hospital,[41] where the transactions that went on between the hospital personnel and the patients were seen to lead to behavioral changes when the response on the part of the staff member was changed so that it did not meet the patient's usual expectations as he had come to experience this in his own family. Sullivan saw that, in the patient's mind, the staff was an extension of his family and that he responded and dealt with them in the same way. Thus, Sullivan emphasized the importance of the hospital family, that is the physician, nurses, and aides, in contributing to the patient's recovery.

1934: Kasinin and his colleagues described the parent-child relationship of some schizophrenics and implied that this relationship was an important and specific etiological factor.[20] Later Kasinin described a pair of identical twins discordant for schizophrenia and described differences in their relationship vis-à-vis the family.

1934: Hallowell published an article on culture and mental disorder,[14] one of the early attempts to demonstrate the importance of social factors in psychoses.

1938: Ackerman wrote on "The Unity of the Family,"[2] conceptualizing a clinical purpose in viewing the family as an entity when dealing with individual disturbance.

1939: Beaglehole published a ten-year study of schizophrenia in New Zealand[5] comparing the incidence in the white and native Maori populations. The difference was great enough to invite the citing of family and culture as possible causative factors.

1939: Pollack and others published *Heredity and Environmental Factors in the Causation of Manic-Depressive Psychoses and Dementia Praecox.*[31] Among other things, this volume indicated that schizophrenic patients might have a special position in the family, for example, being the more financially dependent.

1939: Abram Kardiner's book, *The Individual and His Family,* appeared.[19]

1943: Sherman and Kraines published an article entitled "Environmental and Personality Factors in Psychoses."[36]

1944: L. S. Penrose described mental illness in husband and wife as a contribution to the study of associative mating, where essentially it was postulated that mate selection might be a means of groping for health.[29]

1945: Richardson brought forth his book, *Patients Have Families.*[33] This was in part an attempt to formulate some family diagnoses rather than treating the individual vis-à-vis his family group.

1950: Reichard and Tillman published an article entitled "Patterns of Parent-Child Relationships in Schizophrenia."[32]

1950: Ackerman and Sobel wrote "Family Diagnosis: An Approach to the Pre-School Child,"[3] which inverted the typical child guidance approach and highlighted the understanding of family processes as a means of understanding the young child.

1951: Ruesch and Bateson published their famous book, *Communication, the Social Matrix of Psychiatry.*[35] Many of their contributions foreshadowed the current interest in communication, information theory, and feedback mechanisms.

1954: Stanton and Schwartz published *The Mental Hospital.*[40] Among other important contributions was their discovery that acute upsets in schizophrenic patients' therapy coincided with a covert disagreement between the administrator and the therapist. A similar phenomenon in the family context was discussed recently in a paper by Weakland and Jackson.[43]

1954: Wahl described antecedent factors in the histories of 392 schizophrenics.[42] The importance of psychological and family events stood out clearly in this group of young males hospitalized while in the military service.

1954: John Spiegel published a paper, "New Perspectives in the Study of the Family."[38] A later report of the Committee on the Family of the Group for the Advancement of Psychiatry, prepared by Kluckhohn and Spiegel,[21] has become a classic in this field.

1954: Jackson presented a paper to the American Psychiatric Association entitled "The Question of Family Homeostasis,"[17] in which he described some psychological upsets occurring in family members in relation to improvement on the part of the identified patient. Parental interaction patterns were tentatively related to specific symptoms in the patient and the concept "schizophrenogenic mother" was rejected as being incomplete and misleading.

1956: Bateson and others presented some ideas on a communication theory of schizophrenia which were based, in part, on conjoint therapy with schizophrenic patients and their families.[4]

1957: Bowen presented a paper at the American Orthopsychiatric Association entitled "Study and Treatment of Five Hospitalized Family Groups Each with a Psychotic Member."[7] His findings, based on the most intensive family study ever undertaken, supported the findings of Lidz and others who had observed the fluctuating nature of symptoms from one family member to another as changes within the family interaction were taking place. Further, there was the observation that the nature and kind of symptom bore a strong resemblance to the content and nature of the total family interaction.

1957: Midelfort published *The Family in Psychotherapy.*[25] Working in a small Wisconsin community, he capitalized on the hospital's traditional use of relatives to assist in the care of the patients, by involving families of schizophrenics and depressed patients in brief therapy.

1957: Lidz and his co-workers published "The Intrafamilial Environment of the Schizophrenic Patient."[24] They have subsequently published a number of outstanding papers in this area.

1958: Wynne and others described "Pseudo-Mutuality in the Family Relationships of Schizophrenics"[45] in which they stressed the discrepancy between a superficial and a deeper look at these families.

The way in which ideas about family therapy and diagnosis have come about is clearly evolutionary rather than revolutionary. The impetus was provided by the continuing search for further knowledge about the causes of mental and emotional illness and a more effective means of treatment.

As one looks over the literature of the last fifty years, one notes the patchwork pattern, in a chronological sense, of reports of successful treatment results that came about through a new method of treatment or new knowledge about the causes of illness. When one assembles and analyzes these reports, the direction toward our present concepts about treating illness as an integral part of the total family interaction can be seen as slowly evolving and inevitable.

At the present time there is not yet a well-defined, total, conceptual framework for diagnosis and treatment of the family, but some isolated brave souls have provided us with important experiences and research findings which, if integrated, may well be the beginning of a validatable conceptual framework.

SPECIAL CONTRIBUTIONS

Since 1958, the number of contributions that could be listed would more than equal the brief and incomplete list already given. From the above chronological list we have omitted several names only to offer them special mention. They are Eugen Bleuler, Adolph Meyer, and Manfred Bleuler. Among them, they have exerted tremendous influence in bridging the vast gulf in conceptualizing relative influences on human behavior from neurone to family. Bleuler devoted more of his famous book[6] to the so-called secondary symptoms of schizophrenia than to the primary ones, and laid the basis for psychological therapy in this disorder, particularly by his humanitarian approach and his observations on the patients' response to human contact. Adolph Meyer, originally a neuropathologist, stressed the individual's experiences, present and past, and helped bring schizophrenia out from under the microscope. The life history form that Meyer evolved must have brought parental characteristics to the attention of his students even though the parents were not present in the flesh. Many American psychiatrists have stressed their debt to Meyer, including Sullivan and two of his students, Leo Kanner. and Theodore Lidz, and have contributed much to our understanding of family interaction in the schizophrenic disorders. Finally, to Manfred Bleuler goes the credit for synthesizing the methods of population genetics, and he and Böök have removed the focus of the schizophrenic genetic study from the index case to the epidemiology of local populations. Bleuler's interest is indicated by the fact that when one of his associates discovered eight of the families of fifty schizophrenic index cases were reported in the hospital chart as normal, he went to visit them in their homes and made his own observations. He was, needless to say, disillusioned about the good impression they had made at the hospital.

The early association of the schizophrenic family, via the suggestion of poor protoplasm, with mental illness, mental deficiency, criminality, epilepsy, and tuberculosis has undergone sweeping changes, and yet these very studies unwittingly helped us focus on the "family" as an object of study. As evidence for the hereditary or infectious etiology of mental and social disorders waned, it was a natural step to ask, "All right, but why do they appear to be familial?" Perhaps the familial incidence of pellagra and the subsequent discovery of its relation to family eating habits played a part in this shift of emphasis.

It is obvious then that the family approach owes much to many and that these contributors have been from both the biological and the psychological sides of the fence. We realize that it is not considered good form to dichotomize; yet such dichotomy does very strongly exist in our science. Using the family as a treatment unit seems to us to be a recognition that the patient does not get sick alone, nor does he get well alone. Furthermore, it is consistent with a common observation: that people direct love, hate, fear, and destructiveness toward someone, which implies interaction; done by oneself, such action does not count for much.

Conjoint family therapy validates the widely accepted personality theory that the learning about handling love, hate, anger, and fear takes place in the nuclear family. In our opinion this learning then becomes the basis upon which any family interaction is shaped. By the nature of things, it influences the development of individual self-esteem and consequently the individual's behavior.

PREDICTIONS AND PORTENTS

Since no red-blooded historian these days is content merely to report, we shall take the liberty of naming current trends and possible future trends that we feel will be important in shaping the development and outcome of family diagnosis and therapy. These trends will be listed under certain topics for the sake of convenience.

1. Psychoanalysis

We feel that just as events point to increasing union between psychiatry, the family, and social science, there will be no such union in the main current of psychoanalysis for some time to come. Although there is a small group of psychoanalysts who are interested in participating in family studies and research, there is a much larger group who do not consider this work immediately relevant to their own interests, and even a rather hard-bitten group who feel that current family approaches are superficial and tangential and can in no way be compared scientifically with the depth analysis of psychoanalytic therapy. There is also a group of well meaning psychoanalysts who are attempting to correlate and collate family data with their own observations as individuals, but who unwittingly do the family movement a disservice. This is because some of them feel that knowledge about family individuals is old stuff and is now merely being refurbished. Their descriptions of family work are largely couched in the monadic framework of psychoanalytic terminology and are still essentially individual. They have not yet become convinced that the parts are greater than the whole; their main tenet is that the treatment of a family is theoretically impractical because of the difficulty the therapist has in handling more than one transference at the same time. This latter observation is part of the reason why family diagnosis and therapy needs a new terminology since the concept of transference cannot be carried over in its entirety from monadic encounters on the couch to experiences a single therapist has with multiple family members.

We feel that the concept of family diagnosis and therapy owes much of its current position to psychoanalysis. We predict that there will be an increasing divergence between the two groups. The divergence is due partly to the inapplicability of psychoanalytic terminology to family work, and partly to the fact that the majority of analysts will probably remain interested in their own line of endeavor and find the shift to a family orientation rather difficult to make. This situation has not been unknown to science previously. Witness the findings in electromagnetics of Clark and Maxwell, and the change in concepts following Einstein's contributions. The observations of the electromagnetic theorists were not rejected because a broader conceptualization made its appearance. The current scene reveals evidence of friction and we hope the struggle will not produce a generation of fence-sitters who are waiting to see how the whole business comes out, but will instead serve to stimulate all clinicians to look at all new data rationally and objectively.

2. The Social Sciences

In contrast to its relationship with psychoanalysis, the future of the diagnosis and therapy of the family through its linkage with the social sciences appears very promising. Several recent and current efforts point up possible avenues for exploration.

a. The family is seen as the unit of health, both physical and psychological, a concept crystallized by the publication of Richardson's book, *Patients Have Families*.[33] We all have experienced or have been aware of episodic outbreaks of various illnesses in families. Even such an obvious factor as contagion does not always explain these outbreaks and many times there appear to be inexplicable combinations of infections, psychosomatic disorders, and "accidents." Just as we know little about the siblings of the identified patient, we know next to nothing about family disease patterns.

b. Foote and Cottrell in *Identity and Interpersonal Competence*,[12] and Parsons and Bales in their volume on family interaction[28] have pioneered efforts to devise operational definitions and measurements describing families.

c. Spiegel and Kluckhohn have focused on family cultural patterns and taught us not to mix our observations indiscriminately. It appears that the family researcher has to be pro-segregation or his generalizations will not hold up.

d. Similarly in the socioeconomic arena, Kohn and Clausen,[22] Hollingshead and Redlich,[16] and others have indicated important differences in families as far as their socioeconomic level and their beliefs, values, and child-rearing practices are concerned. Kohn has found in his Washington studies that the mother is the accepted head of the household in most of his lower-class material.[*] What adjustments, then, must one make in using the term "Oedipus complex" if he would generalize from lower- to middle-class families?

e. Pollak, in his work at the Jewish Board of Guardians, has demonstrated how invaluable the efforts of a sociologist may be in shaping psychopathological concepts.[30] His approach escapes from the closed system of psychiatric nosology and his concepts lend themselves to further expansion by other workers.

f. Westley and Epstein at McGill University are demonstrating the importance of choosing a healthy index case rather than the traditional sick one.[44] If their conclusions are verified—for example, that some of their healthy subjects come from homes wherein the parents maintain an atrocious sex life—then some of the basic concepts we have borrowed from psychoanalysis and indiscriminately used in studying the family need careful scrutiny.

g. Finally, I want to mention one of the outstanding and certainly most indefatigable workers in the family area, Reuben Hill.[15] He and his associates at the University of Minnesota are assaying the entire literature of marriage and the family with the idea of organizing concepts, pointing up promising leads, and outlining areas of conflicting data.

CONCLUSION

None of us knows what system or systems will be worked out in the area of family diagnosis and therapy, but without doubt they will differ greatly from anything that currently appears in psychiatric textbooks. The possibilities are legion, but the current emphasis on data-processing via machines will probably influence the development of family description.

The importance of social sciences in this area probably means a greater

* Melvin L. Kohn, personal communication.

focus on systems of health, rather than disease, which has been the traditional occupation of psychiatrists. Current promising concepts include family homeostasis, coalitions within the family and their stability, role-playing, acquisition of family models, three-generation theory, the theoretical applications of the game theory, decision-making, recognition of resemblance, and so on.

In our own work at the Mental Research Institute, we have been tremendously impressed with such a simple matter as the difference in goal-directedness of healthy versus psychologically sick families. During a structured interview, the family is asked to plan something together—a trip, a vacation, an acquisition, anything. The healthier family seems to operate on the premise that the good of the individual rests in the greatest good for all. Even lively sparks of sibling rivalry fail to get the family machinery off its course; the operation seems unequivocally focused on the goal, rather than on the relationships between the family members who are trying to achieve that goal. The sicker families have difficulty even in fantasying that they might plan something as a group; should they attempt a plan, one member is apt to comment at a meta level about another's suggestion. That is, it becomes not a question of whether A prefers the beach. There is great harkening back to the past and even jumping to the future with the implication that it doesn't make any difference since it will not work out anyhow. Such processes as co-operation, collaboration, and compromise can be studied microscopically in small sections of recorded interviews and related to the enormous literature in social psychology on the nature of small group process. Family movies help us discover learned mannerisms, disqualifications, via nonverbal behavior, and so on.

Another way of studying family interaction is to adumbrate a set of explicit and implicit rules under which the family appears to be operating, which can be observed clinically in terms of what family members may or may not overtly expect of each other. If this notion has any value, we eventually hope to find differences in rules, and rules about rules, in psychologically healthy versus psychologically ill families. For example, it is our impression that the family of the chronic schizophrenic is guided by a rigid set of rules which are largely covert. These families do not like to think of themselves as being rigid and they do not explicitly acknowledge what the rules are. When a rule is made more explicit, it automatically is called into question and this produces family anxiety. Rules may be called into question if they are stated too overtly. A may challenge a particular rule and B will then point out how this particular rule does not fit in this particular instance. Rules may be called into question if a member threatens withdrawal from the group. It may be one of the covert rules not to acknowledge the possibility of independence. Withdrawal may be interpreted as rebellion against certain rules. The particular rule that A is alleged to be rebelling against may be revealed by the kind of implication the other family members attribute to his reason for withdrawal. Rules are called into question if they are exposed to an outsider's opinion; for example, the opinion of the therapist. This may mean some tricky foot work for the therapist if he is to keep the show on the road.

On the other hand, if rules are too closely followed, then a skew will result because the enforcement of each rule becomes a caricature of previous rules and a model for future ones. This was observed during the 1930's by Lasswell in his work with large companies.[23] He noted that if the boss was a short man with a bow tie and a cigar, the assistant boss would be even shorter with an even bigger cigar. Similarly, the schizophrenic patient is apt to caricature the rules in his family. It is this behavior that becomes labeled as "sick" by the family and may provoke both laughter and anger on their part. Generally, the sick family will attribute the greatest evil possible to the breaking of a rule, but at the same time they may excuse it. This contradictory behavior is not unknown in government. If a citizen complains, he may be labeled as unpatriotic and a scoundrel; if he does not complain he may suffer from gross inequities. Rationalizations are invaluable in handling such situations whether they are claims that the opposition is trying to cause trouble or, as in a family, the parents claim that the school system is outmoded and additionally that their child happened to get the worst teacher in school. All these maneuvers result in denying and obscuring the facts. A family governed by a rigid set of covert rules finds itself unable to deal with the vicissitudes of life, whether pleasurable or painful, and yet the family pact to hold to the rules may give to outsiders the illusion of strength. The inadequacy of the rules is shown by their not being discussed or debated and by the family's rationalizing each unfortunate happening as a separate chance matter. This concept of rules can be very directly translated into the therapeutic effort. For example, one family had a rule that the mother treasured loyalty above all else and had a right to feel hurt if a family member were critical of her, especially if this should happen within earshot of an outsider. A therapist was able to convince the husband that *true* loyalty demanded that he be able to be critical of his wife (if only via thought), since true loyalty consists in relating to the total person including both his assets and liabilities. To relate only to the assumed assets would be merely blind following.

When communication within the family is studied, data about health and pathology become available. The social scientist, lacking the bias toward disease that is part of medical training, is in a better position than the psychiatrist to do research in this area.

SUMMARY

In general, it is our impression that family diagnosis and therapy have come a long way from the classic monadic descriptions of early psycho-analysis. The trend, influenced by many contributions from many fields, has been toward a horizontal and a vertical expansion. Horizontally, more members have been included, more cultures and more socio-economic data. Vertically, levels of interaction, communication, and information have been taken into consideration to replace a simple stimulus-response description, or more colloquially, a "who did *what* to whom" orientation.

Currently, the crying need seems to be for a useful language to de-scribe multilevel interaction. Even a single message is multileveled, and the response is multileveled and related in a complex way to the first message. The context adds at least another level.

With regard to therapy specifically, we feel that all psychotherapies are related to change and growth and that conjoint family therapy offers one of the most impressive laboratories for studying growth and change available to the researcher. In only the last few years, many aspects of the individual's emotional growth or lack of it that would previously have been labeled "constitutional" have been interpreted as part of the matrix of family interaction.

REFERENCES

1. Nathan W. Ackerman. *The Psychodynamics of Family Life*. New York: Basic Books, 1958.
2. ————. "The Unity of the Family." *Archives of Pediatrics*, Vol. LV, No. 1 (1938), pp. 51-62.
3. ———— and Raymond Sobel. "Family Diagnosis: An Approach to the Pre-School Child." *American Journal of Orthopsychiatry*, Vol. XX, No. 4 (1950), pp. 744-753.
4. Gregory Bateson, Don D. Jackson, Jay Haley, and John H. Weakland. "Toward a Theory of Schizophrenia." *Behavioral Science*, Vol 1, No. 4 (1956), pp. 251-264.
5. Ernest Beaglehole. *Social Change in the South Pacific*. New York: Mac-millan Co., 1958.
6. Eugene Bleuler. *Dementia Praecox, or the Group of Schizophrenias*. New York: International Universities Press, 1952.
7. Murray Bowen, Robert H. Dysinger, Warren M. Brodey, and Betty Basa-mania. "Study and Treatment of Five Hospitalized Family Groups Each with a Psychotic Member." Read at the Annual Meeting of the American Orthopsychiatric Association, Chicago, Ill., March 8, 1957.
8. George W. Brown. "Experiences of Discharged Chronic Schizophrenic Patients in Various Types of Living Group." *Milbank Memorial Fund Quarterly*, Vol. XXXVII, No. 2 (1959), pp. 105-131.

9. Mildred Burgum. "The Father Gets Worse: A Child Guidance Probelm." *American Journal of Orthopsychiatry*, Vol. XII, No. 3 (1942), pp. 474-485.
10. G. Morris Carstairs, and G. W. Brown, (Maudsley Hospital, London, England). "A Census of Psychiatric Cases in Two Contrasting Communities," *Journal of Mental Science*, Vol. CIV, No. 434 (1958), pp. 72-81.
11. J. C. Flügel. *The Psycho-Analytic Study of the Family*. London: Hogarth Press, 1921, p. 217.
12. Nelson Foote and Leonard S. Cottrell, Jr. *Identity and Interpersonal Competence*. Chicago: University of Chicago Press, 1955.
13. Sigmund Freud. "Psycho-Analytic Notes upon an Autobiographical Account of a Case of Paranoia." *Vol. III. Collected Papers*. New York: Basic Books, 1959, pp. 387-416.
14. A. Irving Hallowell. "Culture and Mental Disorder." *Journal of Abnormal and Social Psychiatry*, Vol. XXIX, No. 1 (1934), pp. 1-9.
15. Reuben Hill. "A Critique of Contemporary Marriage and Family Research." *Social Forces*, Vol. XXXIII, No. 3 (1955), pp. 268-277.
16. August B. Hollingshead and Frederick C. Redlich. *Social Class and Mental Illness*. New York: John Wiley and Sons, 1958.
17. Don D. Jackson. "The Question of Family Homeostasis." *Psychiatric Quarterly Supplement*, Vol. XXXI, No. 1 (1957), pp. 79-90.
18. Marie Jahoda. *Current Concepts of Positive Mental Health*. New York: Basic Books, 1958.
19. Abram Kardiner. *The Individual and His Family*. New York: Columbia University Press, 1939.
20. Jacob Kasinin, Elizabeth Knight, and Priscilla Sage. "The Parent-Child Relationship in Schizophrenia." *Journal of Nervous and Mental Disease*, Vol. LXXIX, No. 3 (1934), pp. 249-263.
21. Florence R. Kluckhohn and John P. Spiegel. "Integration and Conflict in Family Behavior," Report No. 27. Topeka, Kansas: Group for the Advancement of Psychiatry, 1954.
22. Melvin L. Kohn and John A. Clausen. "Social Isolation and Schizophrenia." *American Sociological Review*, Vol. XX, No. 3 (1955), pp. 265-273.
23. Harold D. Lasswell. *The Psychopathology of Politics*. Chicago: University of Chicago Press, 1930.
24. Theodore Lidz, *et al.* "The Intrafamilial Environment of the Schizophrenic Patient, I. The Father." *Psychiatry*, Vol. XX, No. 4 (1957), pp. 329-342.
25. Christian F. Midelfort. *The Family in Psychotherapy*. New York: McGraw-Hill, 1957.
26. Jacob L. Moreno. *The First Book on Group Psychotherapy*, 5th ed. New York: Beacon House, 1957.
27. H. B. M. Murphy. "Culture and Mental Disorder in Singapore." *Culture and Mental Health*, Marvin K. Opler (ed.). New York: Macmillan Co., 1959, pp. 291-316.
28. Talcott Parsons and Robert F. Bales. *Family Socialization and Interaction Process*. Glencoe, Ill.: Free Press, 1955.
29. Lionel S. Penrose. "Mental Illness in Husband and Wife: A Contribution to the Study of Associative Mating." *Psychiatric Quarterly Supplement*, Vol. XVIII, No. 2 (1944), pp. 161-166.

30. Otto Pollak. *Integrative Sociological and Psychoanalytic Concepts.* New York: Russell Sage Foundation, 1956.
31. Horatio M. Pollock, *et al. Heredity and Environmental Factors in the Causation of Manic-Depressive Psychoses and Dementia Praecox.* Utica, New York: State Hospitals Press, 1939.
32. Suzanne Reichard and Carl Tillman. "Patterns of Parent-Child Relationships in Schizophrenia." *Psychiatry,* Vol. XIII, No. 2 (1950), pp. 247-257.
33. Henry B. Richardson. *Patients Have Families.* New York: Commonwealth Fund, 1945.
34. E. Rudin. "Vererbung und Enstehung geistiger Störungen, I. Zur Vererbung und Neuentstehung der Dementia Praecox," *Monographien aus dem Gesamt-Gebiete der Neurologie und Psychiatrie,* Vol. XII. Berlin: Springer, 1916.
35. Jurgen Ruesch and Gregory Bateson. *Communication, the Social Matrix of Psychiatry.* New York: W. W. Norton, 1951.
36. Irene C. Sherman and Samuel S. Kraines. "Environmental and Personality Factors in Psychoses." *Journal of Nervous and Mental Disease,* Vol. XCVII, No. 6 (1943), pp. 676-691.
37. Robert Sommer. "Visitors to Mental Hospitals." *Mental Hygiene,* Vol. XL, No. 1 (1959), pp. 8-15.
38. John P. Spiegel. "New Perspectives in the Study of the Family." *Marriage and Family Living,* Vol. XVI, No. 1 (1954), pp. 4-12.
39. ———— and Norman W. Bell. "The Family of the Psychiatric Patient." *American Handbook of Psychiatry,* Vol. I. New York: Basic Books, 1959, p. 134.
40. Alfred H. Stanton and Morris S. Schwartz. *The Mental Hospital.* New York: Basic Books, 1954.
41. Harry Stack Sullivan. "The Onset of Schizophrenia." *American Journal of Psychiatry,* Vol. VII, (1927), pp. 105-134.
42. Charles W. Wahl. "Some Antecedent Factors in the Family Histories of 392 Schizophrenics." *American Journal of Psychiatry,* Vol. CX, No. 9 (1954), pp. 668-676.
43. John H. Weakland and Don D. Jackson. "Patient and Therapist Observations on the Circumstances of a Schizophrenic Episode." *American Medical Association Archives of Neurology and Psychiatry,* Vol. LXXIX, No. 4, (1958), pp. 554-574.
44. William A. Westley. "Emotionally Healthy Adolescents and Their Family Backgrounds," *The Family in Contemporary Society.* Iago Galdston (ed.). New York: International Universities Press, 1958, pp. 131-147.
45. Lyman C. Wynne, *et al.* "Psuedo-Mutuality in the Family Relationships of Schizophrenics." *Psychiatry,* Vol. XXI, No. 2 (1958), pp. 205-220.

18.   Justified and Unjustified Alarm Over Behavioral Control

Israel Goldiamond

The alteration of deviant behavior may be thought of as "behavior control" (teaching may be thought of in this fashion, too). As the techniques are improved and utilized with more and more people, there are some individuals who become concerned about such questions as: (1) can man be made to perform acts against his own interests and (2) to what extent might conformity and automaton behavior be produced within the social order?

Dr. Goldiamond argues in this paper that much of the current alarm is irrelevant to the issue of the scientific control of behavior, for much of it is based upon misunderstanding of modern scientific advances in behavioral control and in the nature of the science of behavior itself.

As you read certain of the illustrations of behavior control which Dr. Goldiamond cites—operant conditioning applied to stuttering and to psychotic behavior—contrast both the purposes of those pursuits and the context in which they are applied to the "brainwashing" activities of the Chinese Communists (Selection 7).

Concern is currently being expressed over the possibilities of control of human behavior in the same sense that other natural phenomena are currently being controlled. The causes for this concern are varied. One form of concern involves the replacement of man by the control devices he is creating. Such concern during the early Industrial Revolution led to action by the Luddites, who smashed the machines which were replacing them. At the other (literary) extreme, machines replaced man in Capek's post-World War I drama, R.U.R. (Rossum's Universal Robots), which introduced the term *robot*, from the Slavic root for work. (The human

Paper presented at a symposium entitled "Social Responsibilities of the Psychologist," *The American Psychological Association*, 1963 Annual Convention, Philadelphia. Used by permission. This paper was written while the author was on a Research Career Development Award, 1963-1968, N. I. M. H., at the Institute for Behavioral Research, Silver Spring, Maryland, and on appointment as Professor of Psychology, Arizona State University, Tempe. It was written under contract between the Washington School of Psychiatry and the Office of the Surgeon General, U.S. Army Medical Research and Development Command. Contract No. DA-49-193-MD-2448. The views presented are those of the author and do not necessarily reflect the views of either contracting agency. Dr. Goldiamond is currently at the University of Chicago.

race, however, was re-established since, in the process of producing progressively more human robots, the scientists had produced a pair with procreative powers, an Adam and Eve.) The new cybernetic revolution of the last ten years, with its resultant automation, is producing another surge of technological unemployment. Our concern with this technology of decision and control functions will not be with this aspect but rather with its effects upon a science and technology of behavior. These are currently being perceived as threatening the robotization of man and as creating the possibility of his being controlled, thereby losing his freedom.

The cybernetic and electronic discoveries of the past decade have provided new instruments and methods of investigation which enable us to ask new scientific questions and, often, to get new answers. The effects of such investigative tools upon science may be exemplified by the microscope, a trivial application of optics once magnification was known. There was nothing in the history of medicine which could have logically predicted such an instrument since it arose out of developments in the unrelated field of optics. Nevertheless, this instrument enabled Pasteur to ask questions about small forms of life and to find the answer now generally known as the germ theory of disease. Without such instrumentation, the theory would have been merely speculation. New developments in the instrumentation of today are providing tools for asking questions which could not have been stated before. Included in the "spin-off" from space research, where miniaturized equipment is generated by the space constraints of space vehicles, has been equipment currently being implanted in living organisms for purposes of analysis and control. Turning to more mundane developments, new instruments created in electronics and allied sciences have led in many areas to having control of behavior replace its prediction. The relay provides for instantaneous delivery of reinforcement, and the relay rack and various open-faced switching circuits provide the opportunity to associate these reinforcements in a very literal way with a variety of behaviors and other conditions and to schedule and program these events.

That behavioral control is with us is no longer debatable. Chimpanzees are currently being trained in binary notation and are solving problems their species had never encountered before (Ferster, 1964). Man is not only becoming a geological force but may also be becoming a zoological one. We may well ask why humans have difficulty with such mathematical languages. The process of programming such changes in chimpanzees may provide clues for application to humans of linguistic and mathematical problems. We have not only had our astronauts but also our astrochimps, whose behavior in space was controlled by scientists on earth—a kind of telecontrol which involved procedures drawn right from the book (Rohles, Grunzke, and Reynolds, 1963). Pigeons have been trained for quality control in the selection of pills and other products (Verhave, 1959). They, thereby, replace human quality control and create the possibility of what might be called "bestiological unemployment." We have heard of programmed instruction and forthcoming changes in education. These are often extensions from animal research of the type described. Very recently, related procedures were applied to students from the lowest third of their graduating high school classes in a state university in an effort to restore them to the academic community (Cohen, 1964). Currently, projects are under way involving the controlled alteration and elimination of stuttering (Goldiamond, 1964) and behavioral deficits such as autism in children (Ferster and DeMyer, 1961). Extensions are being made to marital and scholastic counseling. A ward in a mental hospital has been put under similar environmental control, and some of the patients are now working as attendants in other wards (Ayllon & Azrin, 1964; Mishler, 1964).

A textbook on theories of learning (Hilgard, 1956) remarks that of all the theories of learning in the book, Skinner's position is the only one whereby the instructor can take an animal and train him to perform directly in front of a class. The author wonders to what extent this demonstration of control will prove applicable to human behavior. The caveat now turns out to be unnecessary. Indeed, we recently directly applied to children a new laboratory procedure whereby pigeons were taught very rapidly to discriminate forms which had hitherto taken thousands of trials (Terrace, 1963a,b). In this case, preschool children were taught, almost without error, to discriminate forms and letters whose learning was otherwise accompanied by errors and failures (Moore & Goldiamond, 1964). The procedures could also be extended to the establishment of errorless discrimination of verbal concepts by adults (Goldiamond, 1964).

Such books as Huxley's *Brave New World* (and his revisit), Orwell's *1984*, Skinner's *Walden Two*, and Krutch's *Man the Measure* take sides with regard to the possibility and implications of control of human behavior. The concern over control may be classified according to the following issues:

(1) Is control over behavior possible? That grave implications are perceived in this possibility suggests that to many authors the possibility is an actuality, either at present or in the not-too-distant and science-unfiction future.

(2) If such control is possible, can it be used, on a practical level, to make man perform acts in the interests of the controller and, especially,

where such interests are against his own? A subsidiary question is whether such control can be used socially to produce conformity, automaton behavior, and robotization of man and his society.

At least two assumptions are corollaries of the latter subsidiary question. These are that (a) man's past technological advances in the natural sciences have produced homogeneity and uniformity in the fields in which they have been applied and (b) it is to the interests of a social controller to produce automaton behavior.

The perception of control as related to conformity, which is implied in the subsidiary question raised, may be related to the equation of freedom with individual differences and, with the equation of scientific control, with the absence of freedom. This raises the third issue.

(3) If such control is possible, what are the philosophic implications with regard to human nature, man's conceptualization of man, and man's treatment of man? As was indicated in the foregoing paragraph, one set of implications may be drawn if certain assumptions are made relating freedom and individuality and freedom and control.

These questions are often raised against a background of man's struggles against tyranny and changing philosophic views of man, which are considered relevant to present-day social problems and procedures for their alleviation. They have also become entangled in the issue of determinism and responsibility. An important newspaper, for example, recently editorialized that a major factor responsible for current immorality was acceptance of the philosophy of determinism. Social scientists were considering the behavior of lawbreakers as being environmentally determined. The lawbreakers were, therefore, not being held accountable for their actions; the enusing absence of punitive measures was increasing lawlessness.

A philosophical paradox which has been raised as a kind of divertissement is: if man's behavior is determined and can be controlled by a controller, is the controller then an exception? What controls him? While this may be a philosophical paradox, on a practical level it has been suggested that social control be established over him. The possibility of a moratorium on research in behavioral control has also been suggested, a kind of twentieth-century Luddite movement.

The arguments to be presented in the current discussion are that much of the alarm generated is irrelevant to the issue of the scientific control of behavior; the alarm may be based upon a misunderstanding of the nature of the science of behavior itself; the implications of these advances have not only eluded literate members of our society but often those literate members of our society known as scientists. Another contention of the present discussion will be that the alarm which is expressed may be based upon an extension from formulations in psychology which preceded the advent of the current decade and which may be obsolete at present. Had these formulations held up, then the cries of alarm would have been only too justified. Stated otherwise, if the recent developments, where control is demonstrable, were a logical outgrowth of previous systematizations which lacked such control, then there would be cause for alarm. Developments in science and in other areas as well have a way of leaving their systematizers behind, and I hope to document this assertion in the course of this argument.

Fundamentally, the issue can be related to C. P. Snow's (1959, 1963) postulation of two literate audiences. One of these is the scientific audience, and the other is the standard literate audience. There is an intransitivity between the languages they speak: if the physicist does not understand the novelist, it is because he does not read him. But he could understand him, were he to read, as many do. His training has included the possibility of such understanding. If the novelist cannot read the physicist, it is because he cannot understand him. The differences in their training has precluded such understanding. An example of the differences in inclusiveness of training is cited by Isaac Asimov, who not only writes charming science fiction but is also an excellent chemist. He reported a recent university faculty meeting where one of the English professors stated: "After looking at my roll today, I discovered a John Milton in my class." Everyone laughed. A physicist then remarked: "Now, isn't that a coincidence. I have a Frederick Gauss in my class." Only the scientists laughed. This is an easily remedied difference in education, but other differences in training are not remedied as easily. Scientific conclusions have a way of getting themselves written in the mother tongue, and a literate reader may assume that he understands the conclusion, inasmuch as it is written in English and conforms to the laws of grammar which he has been taught as well as the scientist. However, *the acceptability of any scientific conclusion must rest upon the validity of the empirical and logical procedures used to obtain that conclusion,* and very often the only person capable of ascertaining the validity of procedures used is someone engaged in active research in that area. This has created islands of noncommunication within scientific disciplines as well as between the two cultures defined by Snow. Presenting a stimulus for 2.05 seconds may make all the difference from presenting it for 1.00 seconds. What may seem to be an alarming conclusion may turn out upon examination of the procedures used to obtain them to be either trivial or inconclusive. The literate person (and the other-islander scientist) may be at the mercy of faith in the written word or what friends he consults in any scientific controversy.

SUBLIMINAL PERCEPTION

As the first case study of this type of difficulty, and one which bears upon the present issue of behavioral control, we shall present the issue of subliminal perception. It will be recalled that about seven years ago, the possibility was raised that somebody might, using a screen, or radio, or television, project stimuli too faint to be seen or heard but which would, nevertheless, control or influence behavior. More than one company was formed to exploit this possibility, which was called subliminal perception —the word "subliminal" being the Latin term for "below the threshold." The hue and cry was immediate. The *Saturday Review of Literature* (1957) devoted a full-page editorial to the subject, stating that the subconscious mind was not to be sullied to increase the sales of popcorn. In indignant terms, it urged that the apparatus be put on a warhead of an atomic bomb and exploded on the Bikini atoll. The *Christian Century* (1957) warned ministers not to use this nefarious device, even for such good ends as subliminally flashing: Rally for Christ tonight. A commission was formed by the legislature of a prominent eastern state, to investigate this possibility and the need to protect its citizens (1959). In contrast to the alarm expressed by these humanistic quarters, the technical journals, by and large, stuck to the facts, reporting the results as claims made by their proponents.

This alarm was clearly related to classical formulations written in language which has now become part of our literate culture. For example, Fenichel (1945) related unconscious phenomena to experiments in subliminal perception, which area William James (1902) considered as one source of material leading to mental "incursions . . . of which the subject does not guess the source, and which, therefore take for him the form of unaccountable impulses to act." Understood in terms of this background, commercial exploitation of subliminal projection does pose a grave threat, and one newspaper writer raised the possibility of its use in political campaigns. These are members of our literate culture. An analysis in terms of recent advances in the branch of perception known as signal detection (Swets, Tanner, & Birdsall, 1961; Goldiamond, 1958, 1962) involving an understanding of the experimental and logical *procedures* underlying the research, provides an interpretation considerably at variance from the claims of the commercial would-be exploiters and from the understanding of the literate audience which accepted them.

Where is subliminal perception today? What happened to it? Why is it not being used? The conclusion that subliminal perception could be used in the manner indicated by its commercial sponsors *was not validated by the procedures used to obtain those conclusions* and involves technical excursions into the Theory of Signal Detection and mathematical decision theory which are beyond the scope of this paper. Nevertheless, in common language, if we examine the procedures of subliminal perception carefully, we discover that the experiments can be subsumed under the following paradigm: The experimenter asks the subject if he perceives a stimulus, which is decreased in magnitude or duration, until the subject says "No." At that stimulus level or below it, the subject is required to respond some other way. This behavior demonstrates that he is still being influenced by the stimulus. The occurrence of such influence upon his behavior at a stimulus level which he reports is unperceived is interpreted in what seems to be a straightforward manner, namely, that the subject can be influenced by what he does not know or does not consciously perceive. Stated otherwise, he is capable of being influenced unconsciously. This interpretation makes several interesting assumptions: that the subject can define what he perceives, that when he reports this he has exhausted his definition of his perception, and that such report by the subject validly defines perception to the experimenter. Another assumption is that there is such a thing as a threshold, and another is that there is such a thing as a subconscious mind. Finally, it is assumed that the procedures link all of these.

In actuality, the data can be explained not only more parsimoniously but in a manner which leads to producing the behaviors desired, by reference to two different classes of behavior. One class involves stating that the stimulus was perceived or unperceived. Another class involves describing the stimulus or reacting to it in some way other than such report. Although both classes of behavior will vary as the stimulus is being varied, they can also be manipulated independently of each other and of the stimulus. Stated otherwise, they are governable by different variables. It is as though a voltmeter and ammeter were in line on the same varying current. The voltmeter had an *additional* variable, namely, some steel filings in its bearings. At a high current level both needles moved, but at a low current level only the ammeter recorded, since the voltmeter was stuck at this point. This would give us the extraordinary phenomenon of *current without voltage*, exactly parallel to the *discrimination without awareness* of the subliminal research. In physics, no one would rush into print with this unusual finding but would seek to investigate what variables were involved. A similar procedure is required in the analysis of behavior, and labeling the phenomenon unconscious is no substitute for an explanation. As was mentioned earlier, such an explanation has been provided by the Theory of Signal Detection, which is an outgrowth of classical psychophysics. Interestingly, the work of Fechner, one of the founders of psychophysics, was regarded as trivial by William James (1890), and the field was derogated by others as "brass instrument psychology." The suggestion here is that the current lack of communication between literary culture and scientific culture, which defines its phenomena in relation to its procedures (brass instruments), was also characteristic of the last century. This has been noted as well by Snow. What is more relevant to the current discussion is that by rejecting the scientific procedural language, as James did, the literary culture may lose some ability to evaluate the impact upon society of a developing science and technology and may become alarmed when there is no cause or may be quiescent where there is cause. In all events, it may not be able to evaluate the validity of the conclusions reached by investigators—James regarded early research in areas related to subliminal perception as among the greatest advances and potential contributions to the young discipline of psychology.

The misunderstandings are further complicated. The case of subliminal perception cited rests upon the assumption that a stimulus has a kind of simple mechanical control over behavior. This assumption is often made in other areas of communications as well. We are told that if only our propaganda were correct, we could influence foreign nations. If only we could use the appropriate language, if only we could state our advertisements appropriately, if only we would use the appropriate colors or the appropriate lighting, then we could "sell" the behavior we want. John Milton, in contrast, wrote in prison, under highly inappropriate conditions, but, then again, he was an exceptional person. What may be involved in this ubiquitous lawfulness which is accompanied by exceptions granted to exceptional people is a confusion between early formulations of respondent conditioning and current operant research, which continually recurs in discussions of brain-washing, another form of control.

It will be recalled that Pavlov got a dog to salivate by pairing a tone with citric acid, and after many pairings of these two the tone alone elicited salivation. It was then assumed by some interpreters that this was the scientific explanation of association and that if association of stimuli was appropriately handled, one would get the appropriate behavior. The human organism, or for that matter any other organism, was considered a simple device governed by this simple stimulus-response relation. The appellation, *S-R psychology*, was given to this position; like *brass-instrument psychology* it had pejorative connotations and was rejected by many members of our literate culture. This rejection was extended to an experimental psychology allegedly based on S-R relations (but, interestingly, implicit acceptance of the S-R relation explicitly rejected by the literate culture underlay its alarm over subliminal perception). In actuality, this is a misinterpretation of much of experimental psychology, including the Pavlovian branch, which rejects the S-R relation given as an oversimplification. Such rejection by experimental psychologists also enters into their questioning of subliminal perception.

As the Theory of Signal Detection indicates, things are not quite that simple, even in perception. The perceptual response in a threshold task is not in simple relation to the stimulus presented for judgment. The response is also governed by its consequences, like any other decision. The experimenter may manipulate the consequences, using a decision matrix, and thereby obtain any number of thresholds for the same stimulus presentations.

The analysis of behavior in terms of its consequences is the subject of much research in operant laboratories, which we shall now consider. It is the successful application of operant research to various human and animal behaviors that leads us to Case II of the hue and cry over the control of behavior.

Operant Conditioning

Operant behavior is defined as behavior whose rate or form is governed by its consequences. For example, a pigeon pecks at a disc. If, when the disc is pecked, food is produced (the pigeon having been deprived of food for a considerable amount of time), then the rate of pecking will be observed to increase. If food is not produced, then the rate of pecking will decrease. Some consequences may increase behavior, and some may decrease them. Nature is often merciless in its application of these consequences. The child learning to ride a bike exemplifies this. If he leans over too much in one direction, the consequence will be falling. If he moves his front wheel in the direction of the fall, the consequence will be staying erect. In a short time, the appropriate behaviors will be established, and we state that the child has learned to ride. Considerable lawfulness has emerged from the laboratory where these phenomena are studied under carefully controlled conditions. In the laboratory, a specified response is stipulated, and the equipment is set up to schedule consequences of different kinds immediately and in different sequences and with other variations so that relationships between the consequence, the behavior, and the other conditions can be carefully analyzed.

A characteristic of most operant research which is particularly relevant to the current alarm is its use of *control*, rather than *prediction*, to validate its findings. Related to the use of control rather than prediction is the emphasis upon *procedural* control rather than *statistical* control, and the use of *single* organisms rather than *groups*. The predictive-statistical-groups procedure when applied to a question of learning, might attempt to validate a theory by predicting from it that a certain variable would affect learning (therapy, or what have you). Two groups of subjects might be run, which are differentiated on the basis of the variable. If one group averages, say, 60 per cent on the criterion behavior and the other 75 per cent, and the difference between them is statistically significant and in the right direction, the theory might be considered validated. The control-procedure-individual approach, applied to the same problem would be an attempt to answer the following question: How can we get *every* single organism to attain 100 per cent of the criterion behavior? The emphasis is on procedures which produce the results required in each case, rather than predicting what the average will do, with a given individual's behavior indeterminate. This, of course, is control, and it is this aspect of operant research which has made it amenable for application to the solution of practical problems and which bids to establish a technology of behavior in the same sense that technologies have developed in the natural sciences. The control established may be utilized to gain theoretical knowledge. Once the phenomenon is under control, that is, it varies in functional relation with the independent variable, one can attempt to describe the lawful relation, its relation to other relations, and the constraining conditions under which it holds. If such analysis is unsuccessful, procedures for change and control are nevertheless bequeathed to their wielder. There has been lamentation in recent psychological journals that few studies are repeated. Operant conditioning research is characterized by such continual repetition, inasmuch as procedures developed in one investigation are incorporated into the next.

At least one law or major generality has emerged out of such research. This is the procedure of Differential Reinforcement. What this procedure states is that if different reinforcements (A and B) are systematically applied to different behaviors (a and b), then there will be differential effects upon the rates or other descriptions of that behavior. For example, one can get pigeons who normally peck on the ground to peck high in the air. This is done by supplying reinforcement whenever the pigeon raises his head and not when he lowers it. Eventually he will stretch his head and peck like a woodpecker. In this manner, a variety of skills can be programmed. One can also attach differential reinforcement to the same response in the presence of different stimuli. For example, if when the disc is green the peck is reinforced and when the disc is red the peck is not reinforced, the pigeon will quickly come to respond when the green light appears but will not when the red light is on. He who controls the light switch can control behavior—getting a peck when green appears and none with red. We can also attach differential reinforcement to more complex cases in which both different behaviors and different stimuli are systematically related, as when different behaviors are appropriate for different conditions. Various types of reinforcements have been used, such as food, water, sex, words, money, attention, change in temperature; the recent use of electrical brain stimulation has led to all kinds of lurid pictures in popular magazines. Varieties of subjects have been used, ranging from frogs to people, and varieties of behavior on a human level have been altered, ranging from tics to reading.

Considerable attention has been devoted to the variables and conditions maintaining ongoing behavior, and precise relations between behavior and the environment have been established. To elucidate these relations, a controlled environment has been established, in which extraneous fluctuations have been minimized. For a pigeon, this is the familiar insulated picnic icebox. Use of such highly controlled environments has led to the conclusion that in order to get the behaviors we want, we need a highly controlled environment (i.e. a box or, on the human level, a prison cell). Since such control is generally unavailable, there have come about, on the one hand, a questioning of the applicability of operant procedures to less controlled conditions and, on the other hand, a quest for more control in applied situations.

At the Institute for Behavioral Research, we have been treated to two extremes on the control continuum. One has involved Project ECHO, Environmental Control Human Organism, in which a human being lived for five months in a large controlled environment made habitable from a walk-in ice box, the logical extension of the picnic box for the pigeon (Findley, Migler, and Brady, 1964). The other has involved a departure from such complete control and observation.

In the experiment in which chimpanzees are taught binary arithmetic (Ferster, 1964), two chimpanzees live in a considerably uncontrolled environment. They have a space larger than in most zoos, in which they swing, jump, and engage in free activity. When, however, one wants some food from his environment, he must work for it. To do so, he enters a small screened enclosure on the premises and works at binary notation. Successful solution provides food; when he wishes to, he leaves. The other animal is visible and often engages in vigorous behavior while one animal works. This situation is quite similar to that of the native African habitat. If a chimpanzee wants a banana, he must approach it in a certain way; and if he wants a nut, in another way. The ways in which he approaches a banana are governed by the past symbiosis between chimpanzees and bananas. In the present case, the relationship of the chimp and his environment is being programmed by man, rather than by accidents of evolution, and this involves learning binary notation.

Environments which require complex behaviors may generate such behaviors, and those requiring simple behaviors may generate such behaviors. In our laboratory course at Arizona State University, students work to shape individual rats. After two weeks, the rat picks up a marble upon call and carries it to an appropriate place. Often, in every class of thirty-two, two students will state that they have a feeble-minded rat who cannot learn. The rat is then given to a better team of students, and the rat is found not to be feeble-minded after all. Similarly, Harold Cohen, chairman of the Design Department at Southern Illinois University, took students who were in the lowest third of the high school class and who would have not been normally admitted into the university system of Illinois. He set up a special environment for them and made rather strong demands in terms of the number of books read, records listened to, and the like. The students responded rather well to this challenging environment. Procedures which were derived from the animal laboratory, to maintain study behaviors, were successfully applied.

BEHAVIORAL ANALYSIS AND CYBERNETICS

Can we program the environment to get the behaviors we want? This is one of the critical questions of this day. The environment can be programmed to produce stupid behaviors and can also be programmed to produce highly complex behaviors. One of the basic problems involved is to define the behavior we want in a manner which enables us to work with it. It is here that behavior analysis and cybernetics have a commonality. The age of cybernetics can be said to have started with the definition of thinking. Rather than defining thinking in terms of processes imputed to the thinker, the original group decided to define thinking in terms of the behaviors of the observers. Stated otherwise, the cybernetic definition of thinking was: What does a person have to do, and when, for us to state that he thinks. Or, stated more formally, *what behaviors under what conditions define thinking?* A machine could be constructed which exhibited those behaviors and which thought, by this definition.

One investigator may define thinking as the occurrence of behavior A under condition Z. Another may define thinking as the occurrence of behaviors A, B, C, under Y, Z, a broader definition than the preceding one. They both, however, define thinking in terms of the observer rather than processes of the thinker. Elsewhere, I have called this approach the Basic Behavioral Question. This Basic Behavioral Question can be applied to areas other than thinking. It can be applied to memory (producing as an output, upon call, certain inputs previously presented, by which definition, libraries and record players are memory devices). It can be applied to visual perception (differential responding to reflected wave lengths, by which definition, radar networks see), to decision-making (optimizing net gain in accord with a specified matrix, by which definition an advanced computer system can decide), and to other "higher mental processes" in general.

The Basic Behavioral Question is also shared by modern behavioral analysis or a newer behaviorism. It supplies us with a definition of the problem, stated in the terms of the observer. There may be many definitions of a term which share this approach. The different definitions and answers can coexist without conflict since the observations which differ, and which define the term, are explicitly differentiable. The Basic Behavioral Question also supplies us with a criterion to aim for. For example, if we define abstraction as displaying certain specified behaviors under certain specified conditions and the behaviors do not occur when we establish the conditions, we can then try to develop procedures to get the organism in question to emit these behaviors under these conditions. We can thereby train a pigeon to abstract as defined. To the extent that the definition of abstraction is relevant to the common usage of the term with human organisms, the procedures we develop with pigeons may be useful to develop abstraction in children. By analyzing what it is that maintains such behavior or alters it, we may then learn the variables involved in the maintenance and elimination of such behavior (and processes). Accordingly, we may then not only develop procedures for control but also develop an analysis of the problem; that is, we may develop theoretical knowledge.

Definitions according to the BBQ differ from operational definitions to the extent that they more readily reflect common usage. A scientist may define mother love operationally as the number of kisses a mother gives a child. The Basic Behavioral Question asks: "When people use the term, *mother love*, what behaviors of the mother are they talking about and what are the conditions under which these behaviors must occur for them to use this term?" The attempt is made to have contact with the usage of the term by the social community. To the extent that the social usage of the term contains undefinable or contradictory elements or is an open set, the Basic Behavioral definition may differ from the social definition; but in that case the social definition may contain questionable elements. To the extent that a technology is unavailable to answer some of the questions raised in the social definition, the BBQ may omit these questions and possibly only temporarily. In this case, the definition suggests what instrumentation is needed. These differences between operational and behavioral definitions may be differences in degree and may pertain only to the more usual use of operationism in psychology, but they can lead to differences in procedures.

Cybernetics and behavioral analysis differ in that in one case we construct a device in accord with the BBQ, but in the other case we are given a biological organism and must change it through what may be some other means in accord with the linguistic analysis. It is probably in this difference that the main limitations upon drawing analogies from cybernetic machine systems to biological systems reside. The machine is constructed, but the organism may be given constraints attached to its reconstruction.

The Basic Behavioral Question may also be applied where the "meanings of the behavior" differentiate them. For example, the objectively similar behaviors of bumping blindly into a chair, are classified as different when engaged in by a malingerer, a hysterically blind person, or a genuinely blind one. If we deal with a BBQ based on topography of the response alone, the behaviors are the same: blindness involves lack of differential responding to reflected wave-lengths within a certain spectrum. However, if we try to alter the behaviors, three different procedures will have to be used. This control definition is implied in the clinician's statement that the difference in meanings of the behavior is important, since differences in meaning will presume different treatments. The behaviors can be said to differ in terms of the consequences which maintain them. The blind behaviors of the malingerer will have the consequence of keeping him out of the Army, and the blind behaviors of the hysteric will have other consequences subsumed under the term "secondary gain." That the behavior of the genuinely blind person can not be altered by the consequences and that his behavior is not considered a psychological problem suggests that control of consequences is relevant to psychology as defined by clinical practice. There is a further suggestion that the BBQ definition of one of the uses of meaning is the *consequences* of the behavior. Stated otherwise, the study of this use of meaning may involve the analysis of operant behavior.

The approach can be used to answer questions considerably removed from the connotations of automata and mechanism. Let us, for example, examine the term "creativity." Rather than ask what happens to the creator when he creates, let us ask ourselves what characterizes the person whom we define as creative. It turns out that most creative people are (1) highly competent in their subject matter, examples being Einstein, Bach, or Auden. However, competence alone is not enough, since the pedant may also be competent. The creative person is also one (2) who handles his subject manner in a new way. Needless to say, novelty is not enough, although to some educators, who encourage children to "create," this seems sufficient. The combination of novelty with competence is also not enough, since some psychotics are competent in a novel way. The behavior must also (3) tie in with the reinforcements of some community (sometimes a community of one!). Given this definition of creativity, we can attempt to program an environment which will optimize creative behaviors or people who engage in novel responses in their area of competence which tie in with the reinforcements of a community.

FREEDOM AND BEHAVIORAL ANALYSIS

The Basic Behavioral Question can be applied to the definition of *freedom*. In this case, we start off asking ourselves this question: "Given two people, one of whom we agree has more freedom than the other, what are the behaviors and conditions which differentiate them?" A person who is "compelled" does not have many response alternatives available to him during the conditions of his compulsion. We may be able to alter his behaviors, so that when the hitherto compelling conditions are now presented, a variety of responses may occur, that is, more response alternatives are available. When we define freedom in terms of the number of response alternatives available (this is only a partial definition), we can then actually program the environment to increase freedom and also to provide the person with greater freedom in other environments as well. The issue becomes one of knowing how to do this, and a determinate science of behavior can increase freedom. Indeed, there is nothing novel to this thought, since effective psychiatrists and others interested in clinical problems have been increasing the patient's range of responses, his degree of freedom, his responsibility, and his effectiveness.

Freedom has often been implicitly equated with sloppiness of control, as was the case in the Austria of Dolfuss, which was popularly described as "dictatorship mitigated by sloppiness." Indeed, one implication of this implicit definition may underlie the objection to operant control, that by being efficient it is dictatorial. Closer examination, however, reveals that freedom may not be synonymous with sloppiness. The child who responds, "In just a minute, Daddy," when called to brush his teeth, may not be more free than one who responds immediately. He may be watching a television show whose reinforcements are controlling watching behavior. His behavior may be under effective environmental control. Fundamentally, the subject at issue between obeying the paternal command and not obeying it may not even be one of sloppy control versus good control but rather one of *whose* control is involved. In this sense, freedom is an irrelevant term, as it is in the case of freedom from physical laws.

However, if we are to examine the usage of the term, freedom, carefully, we may discover that a BBQ definition may, in the commonly used sense of the term, help us to preserve it. A person who is more free than another may have more types of alternate consequences contingent upon his differing behaviors and may, therefore, have more response alternatives than the other person. It is in this sense that a well-educated person, who can get support in a variety of ways, is freer than someone who can only dig ditches for a living. This definition of freedom is not incompatible with control of behavior and, by alerting us to the sources of reinforcement in a community, may alert us how to program our environment to maintain and even to extend freedom; it may make us effective *as well as* well-meaning.

SELF-CONTROL

A further extension of operant conditioning of human affairs involves self-control. The Greek maxim, "know thyself" can be translated behaviorally into: "Know what behaviors thou wantest from thyself, and know the conditions which optimize their occurrence, and set up these conditions." In this manner, Ferster, (Ferster, Nurnberger, and Levitt, 1962) was able to get obese nurses to reduce. Normally, when one reduces, the goading stimulus is fear of the consequences of overweight. As the overweight goes down, this goading stimulus is attenuated, finally being eliminated upon the completion of the crash program, and the person may start overeating again. Rather than telling the nurses that they must *will* to reduce, the investigators analyzed the conditions which controlled their overeating and taught the nurses how to control these conditions. They were taught a very effective form of self-control. Similarly, I have been engaged in an attempt to apply such procedures to other forms of counselling for students whose study behaviors were inadequate to keep them in school and for marital pairs whose marital behaviors were inadequate to maintain a successful marriage. It is useless to tell people that they should be more decent to each other, since they know this already. New Year's resolutions, which are characterized by the will to change, are also characterized by their ineffectiveness. The will to come to work early expressed in such a resolution may be unsuccessful, but if an alarm clock is purchased—a simple change in the environment— the person may get up in the morning. The road to divorce is paved with good intentions. The cases I have worked with have involved people who have been adequate in many areas in their lives but have not exhibited the behaviors to make their marriage go. The procedures involved are basically training in the analysis of behavior and in attempting to have the individuals involved apply the analysis to the problem at hand. The significant environment here, of course, is the environment which each partner creates for the other. Counselling sessions become "research conferences" between counsellor and client, the subject being the expert in the content of his life, the behaviors he wants, and the conditions we can capitalize upon.

Two examples will be cited in the marital counselling situations. In the first case, the husband reported to me one day that the whole procedure would not work since his wife needed him less than he needed her; that is, the influence upon each other was not reciprocal. He was asked how he knew, and he said it was evident. He was then asked to restate this behaviorally, namely, that his wife was behaving in a certain way less than he behaved in that way, and was asked to specify the behaviors (BBQ) he was talking about. He then stated that she did not exhibit such dependency behaviors as asking him to do things for her. I asked, "When was the last time she asked you to do something for her?" He said, "Yesterday she asked me to change the burnt-out bulb in the kitchen." "Did you do this?" Answer: "No." "Well?" I said. The point then dawned on him that if he wanted such behaviors he was to reinforce them, and the classical way to maintain and establish dependency is to provide continual help. There ensued a discussion of needs, personality, and related inferences. "If by personality, all that is meant is my behavior, then my personality changes from one moment to the next, because my behavior changes," he stated. "I should hope so," I said. "Well, what is my true personality; what is the true me?" he asked. "Do you have a true behavior?" I asked. He said: "Hummmmmmmmmm, I don't—that is interesting," and he proceeded to take notes. Incidently, I sat back and watched him take notes throughout, a reversal of the usual procedures.

The next week he came in and stated, "I did something last week that I have never done before in my life. When I teach in classrooms, I am able to manage my classroom; but when I talk to tradespeople, I find I am very timid and allow myself to be cheated. Well, last week my carburetor gave out. I knew if I went to the garage they would make me buy a new one even though I have a one-year's guarantee. I sent my wife down to the garage instead. She is a real scrapper. She came back with a new carburetor without it costing us a cent. Why should I have to be all things to all men? In school I control things, but with tradespeople I don't. So what?"

Another case involved a husband and wife whose problem was the lack of affectionate behaviors on the part of the husband. One of her later comments to me was: "I am at my wits end as to how to shape his behavior. I don't know what reinforcements I have. The characteristic of a good reinforcement is that it can be applied immediately and is immediately consumed. I could withhold supper, but that is not a good reinforcer because I can't turn it off and on. I can't apply deprivation, because that's my problem. I don't know what to do." I mention this merely to illustrate how a problem may be formulated in these research conferences, in which subjects of the conferences are applying behavioral analysis to the problems on hand. Both husband and wife were fully in on the discussions, they tried out various procedures, and finally they, themselves, came up with the one which worked. Stated otherwise, they were the experts in the content of the marriage; I was simply a consultant on abstract procedures. Together we tried to make the procedures fit their particular terrain.

One of the local clinical psychologists discussed my counselling procedures with me and commented, "You know, I don't believe in marital counselling." I asked why not, and she stated, "Because I think that marital problems are merely symptomatic of a deeper underlying problem; their solution, for all you know, may involve breaking up the marriage." "Oh," I said. "Let me cite an abstract case: my garage door is stuck. I call in a carpenter to fix the door and leave him with the keys. When I return, I discover that my house has been dismantled and my lot chopped up, with a high rise apartment in one corner and a sunken garage underneath. I did not ask the carpenter to change my house; it was perfectly adequate the way it was. I only asked him to change the garage door. The carpenter's behavior is highly unethical and unwarranted. Fortunately, you are not as effective as the carpenter."

The aim in behavioral modification of the type we have been using is to alter those behaviors about which a contractual agreement has been made implicitly or explicitly. By being able to specify the behaviors in question, focus can be made upon those behaviors. One of our stuttering subjects, for example, was suicidal and had tried shock and other treatments to eliminate stuttering, without success. Within two weeks, in exact accord with the program utilized, she was reading in the booth without stuttering and was also able to read bedtime stories to her children. Her home life changed in accord. Rather than the stuttering being a symptom of underlying disturbances, the other behavioral disturbances could be considered symptoms of stuttering! The term, symptom, can be defined behaviorally rather then mystically. When the dermatologist states that a skin rash is a symptom of a blood imbalance, he is stating that he will treat something other than the presenting complaint. Analogously, where a behavior is defined as a symptom, this implies that something else (possibly some other behavior) will be treated rather than the problem behavior. The BBQ may be applied to the problem in the following manner: What are the behaviors (or behavioral deficits) and the conditions which define the problem for us in this individual? What procedures do we have to utilize to alter them?

Assuming that we can develop remedial procedures to alter behavior, what are the implications for prevention? What about etiology? Cause and etiology are not necessarily scientifically synonymous. One of the marital patients started on his childhood, and was cut off. "But doesn't it affect me now?" he asked. "Look," I said, "a bridge with a load limit of three tons opens in 1903. The next day, a farmer drives eighteen tons over it; it cracks. The bridge collapses in 1963. What caused the collapse?" "The farmer in 1903," he said. "Wrong," I said, "the bridge collapses in 1963 because of the cracks that day. Had they been filled in the preceding day, it would not have collapsed. Let's discuss the cracks in your marriage." The same treatment will serve to put out a forest fire started by a match, lightning, or spontaneous combustion. To prevent a fire, though, do we have to know what started it? We can consider forest fires as maintained by a volatile combustible, oxygen, and a concentration of heat. Control of any of these will control the fire. These we can discover in the laboratory, but not necessarily in the forest, where a gust of wind may accentuate *or* attenuate the fire. We can now ask ourselves what specific forms these are likely to take in the natural ecology. Since forests are wood and grow in air, a likely source of control is the concentration of heat. This is likely to be in the form of common matches, campfires, lightning, or areas of undergrowth which build up heat. Accordingly, we can control matches and campfires, clean out undergrowth, watch for lightning, and thereby *prevent* forest fires. Analysis of behavior in terms of its maintaining variables may be used both for remediation and prevention.

With regard to the marital counselling and study counselling that we have been doing, the net outcome has been that the people involved have learned to lick their own problems and have learned to utilize procedures which may stand them in good stead in other areas of behavior. They began applying the procedures elsewhere in many ways, trying to shape others, like the beginning graduate student. If this does not define the self-enhancement and the self-actualization that Carl Rogers talks about, I don't know what does. Thus, "paradoxically," application of self-control procedures derived from controlled laboratory research can fulfill the aims of those clinical psychologists who pride themselves on effecting change through providing greater freedom for the client. The notion that extension of operant conditioning to counselling involves manipulation of the patient, whereas a client-centered approach involves having the patient learn for himself, is an invalid distinction which ignores the fact that operant procedures can be used for self-control.

If this application of self-control procedures to counselling problems restores some human dignity to people who had lost self-confidence through the inability to control their own problems, the application of direct control procedures may have a similar effect. I am referring to the work of Ayllon and Azrin at Anna State Hospital, where a complete ward has been turned over to operant procedures. The investigators have drawn up lists of behaviors they want from the patients and behaviors which the patients like to engage in, and they make the latter contingent upon the former through a token system. The patient gets a token for brushing her teeth, making her bed, and so on. With these tokens, she can rent a pass to go out, buy cigarettes, get a better bed, and so on. The ward has lost its stinking schizophrenic smell. Choices, decisions, and dignity have now been restored to the patients; they no longer must await the whim of a nurse before they go outdoors, but can decide on their own.

This system was, of course, imposed upon the patients without their consent, but in this it does not differ from the current social mission of the hospital, which is to discharge the patients as cured, whether they want to be cured or not. The distinction is that the system works according to explicitly specifiable procedures. And choice and dignity have been restored to the patients by focus upon their behaviors, rather than upon some assumed underlying state.

The self-control process may be applied not only by the person to set up his own environment to get the behaviors that he wants, but may also be a solution to the problem of brain-washing. The person who learns to control his own behavior can also learn how to keep his behavior from being controlled and to apply counter-control. If the inquisitor doesn't possess this knowledge, then the captive who has been trained in it will have the upper hand. If the inquisitor has the knowledge but the captive doesn't, the latter will be putty. The race will be to the one who knows the most and possesses the greater means to apply the knowledge. When was it otherwise?

Accordingly, it seems to us at the Institute for Behavioral Research that it is quite vital to train people in the analysis of behavior, so that professionals in other disciplines may draw from it that which they find useful in their own area. We are attempting to program such a course at the Institute. This programmed course must not be confused with the programmed instruction which involves blanks in textbooks. Rather, the programmed course involves standard articles and chapters as well as programmed texts, laboratory exercises, discussions at stipulated points in the sequence, all of which constitute progression through the course. When the subject has gone through so much, he earns the right to take up the instructor's time. This reinforcement works rather effectively. The basic philosophy involved here is that when one shapes a pigeon, one is guided in the application of the next step by the behavior of the pigeon in the preceding step. If the pigeon raises his head, he is reinforced; and if he lowers his head, there is no reinforcement. Where the pigeon controls the experimenter's behavior, laboratory control over the learning of pigeons is superb. Equally good learning on a human level also involves having the teacher govern his behavior by the progress of the student. In the laboratory, the payoff to the experimenter for being guided by the pigeon is the research report. Unfortunately, in the university, the payoffs to the instructor are usually not attached to being controlled by the behavior of the learner.

There is reciprocal control here. It is the experimenter who sets the criteria to be approached or the terminal behaviors he wishes from the learner. These terminal behaviors are the experimenter's BBQ definition of knowledge. To establish these behaviors, he must put himself under the control of the learner, modifying his own behaviors in accord with the learner's behaviors, so that the criterion behavior is shaped. There has been too much emphasis in discussing conditioning on control *over* the learner (or the patient) and not enough emphasis on control *by* the learner (or patient). Experimental analysis of behavior suggests that we be sensitive to such reciprocal control.

We are attempting to establish a program which incorporates these features, and the specification and progression of the *behaviors* we require of the students is basically the program of the course. The textual and other materials used are relevant only insofar as they contribute to the progression of the student's behavior toward the criterion behavior. We believe this emphasis upon behavior rather than content is the meaning underlying the progressive educator's statement that he is "interested in teaching the child rather than the subject matter."

As we stated earlier, it is our hope to make this program available to professionals in other areas so that they may draw from the available procedures developed in behavioral analysis those procedures which they consider applicable to their disciplines. What we are stating is that the physicist or the psychiatrist or the marital partner knows the content of his own area far better than we do. Further, he is on the spot to apply procedures when they are most critically effective. Hence, the program of extension. There is a reverse side to this program, which involves the contributions to behavior analysis from disciplines with different orientations and procedures for control.

BEHAVIOR TECHNOLOGY AND CONFORMITY

Modern technology now reverses rivers. Although the humorist likes to assert that highways now take up all available space and all rivers are dammed, in actuality this is not so. Granted, stupidity and cupidity have had their say, but these are not inventions of modern technology. In general, we have constructed highways and dammed rivers where it has been socially useful and economically feasible to do so. I would suggest that when a technology of behavior is firmly established, the same principle will apply, namely, that we shall control those behaviors which we find it socially useful and economically feasible to control. We would certainly like to see our children come out of schools having learned what they are supposed to learn. We would like to see our prisoners rehabilitated and our mentally ill behaving appropriately.

The notion that behavioral technology will mean a prison state or manipulation of behavior on a total scale ignores some of the more recent developments in the experimental analysis of behavior and in self-control. When one starts to apply experimental analysis to practical problems, the procedures which develop in practice differ considerably from those which may be projected from a theoretical understanding.

Brave New World and *1984* project upon the future behaviors which are fundamentally like the behaviors of today. It is this anomaly which produces the irony and sting of these works. As literature, they may have merit, but as predictions of the future, their prophesies must be questioned. *Brave New World* depicts a society which is so technologically advanced that babies are reared in test tubes. This is a technology which is far beyond what we possess today, but not beyond the bounds of reason. A level of technology this advanced will contain stimuli that at present we can not even conceive of. If we assume behavior to be under stimulus control, as I do, the assumption that given all these novel stimuli of the future the behaviors that emerge are going to be the behaviors of today leads to a far more pessimistic view of the future of the human race than anything Huxley or Orwell could have dreamed of. If our behavior does not conform to the new stimuli but stays the same way it is today, we will become extinct more rapidly than did the dinosaurs. This point is missed by those who cite the paradox of who will control the controller. The controller will be controlled by his subjects, who will also be controlled by him, and the loop is never closed but is always subject to opening and revision by the new stimuli being explosively created by our expanding technology. Sociologists charge the Ford with being a major influence in the changed sexual mores of today—something certainly not foreseen by Ford nor by the sociologists. It will be recalled that the germ theory of disease rests upon the development of the microscope from the telescope, something alien to medicine. The behavior of tomorrow will be similar to the behavior of today to the extent that the controlling stimuli are similar; to the extent that these will change, behavior will change. Inasmuch as I cannot predict what future stimuli will be created, I can not predict what behavioral or societal developments will occur. I would suggest, however, that we keep our eyes open and try to understand what is going on, especially in the scientific community.

The notion that modern technology has produced mass conformity forgets the conformities produced by the absence of knowledge and by superstition. In the absence of good medicine, the children of a backward society may have straight, knock-kneed, or bowlegs of different heights and at picturesque angles. Given such picturesque and crippled legs, one can engage in only a very few locomotive behaviors. Given missing teeth, one can eat only mush. Given, however, modern technology, one can use one's straight legs to climb mountains and one's straight teeth to eat steak or mush. In a backward society, behavior is extremely predictable. The son of a peasant will be a peasant. How to keep his son down on the farm is a problem faced by farmers. In our society, among the most predictable people is the compulsive who washes his hands every five minutes. Applying behavioral analysis to get him out of the hospital will make his behavior predictably less predictable.

The issue has also been raised of responsibility, ethics, freedom, and man's concept of man if his behavior is under environmental control. I would submit that the issue of determinism is irrelevant to the issue of responsibility. The Puritan was a Calvinist and lived in a highly responsible world. One can imagine the Puritan chicken thief coming before a Puritan judge and claiming that he was not to blame, since a stern Deity had preordained that he steal the chicken. And one can imagine the judge stating with equal firmness that it hath also been written that he should be punished in such a manner that he would never sin again. Determinism and the use of consequences to alter behavior are not incompatible with each other. It is up to society to learn how to use consequences appropriately to minimize the likelihood of certain behaviors and to maintain others. If behavioral psychology does not allow the criminal the out of escaping the consequences of his act by referring to events which were beyond his control, neither does it allow the teacher to escape the consequences of his sloppy training procedures by placing the blame on the inabilities of his students. Rather, it places upon all of us the responsibility of trying to gain more knowledge in the area of behavior and trying to apply what we know.

In a recent science fiction story, a baby was given a revolver to play with. The analogy was modern man, with his advanced technology in physical sciences but with no control over his behavior. If the human race does have a future, it may be in the development of a science and technology of a behavior at least equal to that which we possess in the physical sciences. It should be pointed out that the use and misuse of any advance is *behavior*. If we can understand and control behavior, perhaps we can understand and control the misuse of other sciences. Whether or not this occurs in time is problematic, but at least it offers us some ray of hope.

The scientific analysis of behavior requires attention to scientific method and procedures, and its results are often surprising. They are especially surprising to those who equate control with automata and a concept of mechanism which they can understand. The various physical and biological sciences have changed so radically in the past few years that one physicist has remarked that most of the major concepts he learned in college are now obsolete. While this has not yet occurred to this extent in the analysis of behavior, the likelihood that a literate person trained in the psychology of yesteryear can understand current developments is becoming increasingly remote. The two languages of C. P. Snow are advancing upon this area as well. This poses the danger that what is a genuine danger and requires social control will be unrecognized while that which is not a danger will be attacked. Such was the case with subliminal perception, where a discrepancy of two behaviors was related to the literately understandable concept of unconscious control. Such is the case with experimental analysis and control of ongoing behavior, where control is associated with the literately understandable concept of lack of freedom and dignity.

This discussion has mainly stressed the unjustified alarm over behavioral control. The *justified* alarm is occasioned by the growing existence of two languages in an area of vital concern to man—*his own behavior*. Much of the current alienation of the literate person from his culture of today may be related to a past history of ignoring or being ignorant of the developing sciences and their associated technologies. The literary culture is being increasingly shaped by stimuli they never created. If history is not to repeat, that is, if alienation is not to occur precisely in that area which has occupied so many of the considerable talents of the literate culture, namely, human behavior, communication is necessary. It is the possibility of the disruption of such communication that may provide justified alarm—not over behavioral control, but over the possibility of alienation from the developing analysis and technology of behavioral control.

The British scientist, Dingle, recently reported a paradox in science and its relation to society. He stated that philosophers discovered some time ago that when they used the same terms, these same terms often had different meanings. Accordingly, laboratories were established in which the terms were defined in a standard and limited way. Such limitations turned out, paradoxically, to be extremely applicable in understanding and controlling the limitless world outside the laboratory. The paradox resolves itself if we regard science as a representational system in which the scientist communicates representations of his observations. These representations are admittedly limitations. I would like to raise the argument that most communication involves representation and is therefore limited. In the scientific representational systems, we try to be explicit about the limitations that we impose upon ourselves. Other representational systems may assume that they are unlimited (or deal with the totality or the total personality or what have you), and yet others may acknowledge the fact that they are limited but do not attempt to make explicit the nature of their limitations. Given, now, two competing systems, both of them limited, but with one of them having an awareness of its limitations and attempting to state them explicitly and the other either not aware of the fact that it is limited or unaware of what its limitations are, the race will obviously be to the system whose wielders know what they are doing. Science may be awkward, slow, bumbling, time-consuming, and narrow; but its contributions rest upon the difference mentioned. Through such awareness of his limitations, man has become a geological force which changes the course of rivers and a zoological force which changes the ecology. Through the application of scientific method to behavior, he is becoming a behavioral force which, hopefully, can be applied to the self-control of his own behavior.

REFERENCES

Ayllon, T. and Azrin, N. H. Reinforcement and instructions with mental patients. *J. exp. Anal. Behavior*, 1964, 7, 327-331.

Christian Century, 1957, 74, p. 1157.

Cohen, H. L. Behavioral architecture. *Architectural Association Journal*, 1964, 80, No. 883, 7-11.

Commission for the Study of Subliminal Projection. Final Report Trenton, N. J.: State Supt. Public Documents, 1959.

Dingle, Review of H. C. W. Churchman and P. Ratooth (Eds.) Measurement: definitions and theories. *Scientific Amer.*, 1960, 203, No. 6, 189.

Fenichel, O. *The psychoanalytic theory of neurosis.* New York: Norton, 1945.

Ferster, C. B. Arithmetic behavior in chimpanzees. *Scientific American*, 1964, 210, No. 5, 98-106.

Ferster, C. B. and DeMyer, M. K. The development of performances in autistic children in an automatically controlled environment. *J. chron. Diseases*, 1961, 13, 312-345.

Ferster, C. B., Nurnberger, J. I., and Levitt, E. B. The control of eating. *J. Mathetics*, 1962, 1, No. 1, 87-109.

Findley, J. D., Migler, B. M., and Brady, J. V. A long-term study of human performance in a continuously programmed experimental environment. *J. exp. Anal. Behavior*, 1964, (in press).

Goldiamond, I. A research and demonstration procedure in stimulus control, abstraction, and environmental programming. *J. exp. Anal. Behavior*, 1964, 7, 216.

Goldiamond, I. Indicators of perception: I. Subliminal perception, subception, unconscious perception: an analysis in terms of psychophysical indicator methodology. *Psychol. Bull.*, 1958, 55, 373-411.

Goldiamond, I. Perception. In Bachrach, A. J. (Ed.). The experimental foundations of clinical psychology. New York: Basic Books, 1962.

Goldiamond, I. Stuttering and fluency as manipulable operant response classes. In Krasner, L., and Ulmann, L. P. (Eds.). Research in Behavior Modification. New York: Holt, Rinehart, and Winston, 1965.

Hilgard, E. R. Theories of Learning. New York: Appleton-Century-Crofts, 1956 (Second ed.).

James, William. The Principles of Psychology, Vol. I, New York: Holt, 1890.

James, William. The varieties of religious experience. New York: Longmans Green, 1902.

Mishler, K. B. Of people and pigeons. SKEF Psychiatric Reporter, 1964, 15, 9-12.

Moore, R., and Goldiamond, I. Errorless establishment of visual discrimination using fading procedures. J. exp. Anal. Behavior, 1964, 7, 269-272.

Rohles, F. H. Jr., Grunske, M. E., and Reynolds, H. H. Chimpanzee performance during the ballistic and orbital project Mercury flights. J. compar. physiol. Psychol., 1963, 56, 2-10.

Saturday Review, 1957, 40, No. 40, p. 20.

Snow, C. P. The two cultures: and a second look. Cambridge: Cambridge University Press, 1959, expansion, 1963.

Swets, J. A., Tanner, W. P., Jr., and Birdsall, T. G. Decision processes in perception. Psycholog. Rev., 1961, 68, 301-340.

Terrace, H. S. Discrimination learning with and without "errors." J. exper. Anal. Behavior, 1963, 6, 1-27. (a).

Terrace, H. S. Errorless transfer of a discrimination across two continua. J. exp. Anal. Behavior, 1963, 6, 223-232. (b).

Verhave, T. Recent developments in the experimental analysis of behavior. Proc. Eleventh Research Council, Amer. Meat Institution Found., Chicago, 1959, 113-136.

19. Personal Responsibility, Determinism, and the Burden of Understanding

Edward Joseph Shoben, Jr.

As was cited on page 4, Nicholas Hobbs testified before a Congressional Committee:

Historically, a great step forward was made when mental disorders were declared to be an illness, and the sufferer to be in need of treatment rather than punishment. . . .

In this selection, Dr. Shoben, formerly of the Department of Psychological Foundations and Services, Teachers College, Columbia University and Director of Clinical Training, and now at SUNY, Buffalo first elaborates the significance of that great step:

Like those beset by consumption, gout, and the plague, the insane were thought of with sympathy, dealt with considerately, and looked

Antioch Review, Winter, 1960-61. Reprinted by permission.

upon as victimized by some external and naturalistic process of a
pathological character. . . .

And further:

As Freud gave shape to these patterns of ideas a hundred years
later, they acquired the explicitly deterministic and non-evaluative
character which typifies the social science of the twentieth century.
So far as behavioral abnormalities are concerned, they are interpreted
as products of knowable (if not known) outcomes of heredity and
environmental interactions.

Secondly, Dr. Shoben examines a view which is currently overlooked or ignored, in the main—*the concept of individual responsibility.*

For those of us who are steeped in the methods and outlook of
science, Dr. Shoben's comments may be both difficult to grasp and
at marked variance with many of our beliefs. What he has to say
about *individual responsibility* deserves our consideration for several
reasons: (1) "mental illness" is a very broad term (Selection 1); (2)
during recent years such concepts as "will power" have been receiving
attention by other social scientists; (3) the views of social science (or
of any man-made "institution," for that matter) are by no means fixed
—sometimes our conceptual models must change if knowledge is to
advance.

In 1793, Pinel struck the chains from the inmates of the Bicetre, stak-
ing his job and his reputation on the conception that the insane were sick
human beings.[1] While his ideas were not without precedent, his action
provides a useful symbol of the ending of one era in man's thinking about
man and the beginning of another. For with the links of iron, there fell a
set of conceptions that had long guided men's efforts to understand the
emotional troubles to which they are heir.

The predominant notions that had previously governed thought about
disturbances of behavior were supernaturalistic and moralistic in tone
and often cruel in their implications. The deviant person was by definition one who had offended God, been possessed by the devil, committed
some major sin, surrendered his humanity in some voluntary way, or had
been "born that way" in the sense of having been forever out of grace by
destiny. Beating with chains, scourging, and the ducking stool were combined with prayer as methods of eliminating the devil's agents from the
soul of the patient or providing a means of atonement for the commission
of sins. Repentance and "being made clean again" were the goals of what
would now be called mental health. Even in so enlightened an earlier
period as the Renaissance, the outright psychotics were regarded as less

[1] This major event in the history of psychiatry and social thought is well described
in a number of reliable sources. One such source is [7].

than human and consequently as legitimate objects of mixed fear and derision. Tom o' Bedlam in *King Lear* embodies that status of the mental patient at such a time.

With Pinel, however, things changed. Psychotics—and, by extension, other sufferers from behavioral disorders—were to be considered as people entitled to humane treatment. Further, their difference from others was to be conceived as medical in nature, analogous to the differences observable as a result of bodily diseases. Like those beset by consumption, gout, and the plague, the insane were to be thought of with sympathy, dealt with considerately, and looked upon as victimized by some external and naturalistic process of a pathological character.

This point of view was in harmony, of course, with two developing traditions that have been enormously influential and useful in the modern world. One was the tradition of physical and biological science, receiving its impetus in large part from Newton and Harvey and growing in vogue as its applicability to immediately practical affairs became apparent through the industrial revolution. The other was the tradition of naturalistic and liberal social thought as expressed in the *philosophie* and given currency in the American and French revolutions of which Pinel was a contemporary. As Freud gave shape to these patterns of ideas a hundred years later, they acquired the explicitly deterministic and non-evaluative character which typifies the social science of the twentieth century. So far as behavioral abnormalities are concerned, they are interpreted as products of knowable (if not known) outcomes of heredity and environmental interactions. They are defined as problems only with reference to some kind of cultural or societal context on the ground that neurotics and psychotics do not fit productively into the social scheme of things. When the troubles of any individual classify him as such a problem, he is to be regarded as "sick" and subjected to therapy in order to correct the pathogenic influences of his history. If treatment fails, then he is removed to an institution in which he will be cared for as humanely as finances will permit while society functions without the disruption of his presence in it.

THE POINT OF VIEW EXAMINED

The essence of this point of view, which seems so thoroughly appropriate if not downright inevitable to at least the educated in today's Western world, is its basis in the outlook and methods of science. Human disorders are conceived, like other phenomena, to be outgrowths of naturalistic processes occurring in orderly if complex sequences. What happens later in the sequence is determined by what happened earlier. Since the sequences are lawful, knowledge of them is possible and affords a predictive understanding of their outcomes. If ways can be devised to intervene in the sequences, manipulating them in some selected fashion, then their results can be controlled as well as predictively understood.

The great advantages of the scientific *Weltanschaung* in physics and biology are both evident and incontestable. Especially in its application to technology and medicine has science proved its utility beyond question. Moreover, it seems fair to assert that the only route to genuine public knowledge is that provided by science. In the behavioral disciplines, science has in large degree replaced authority, prejudice, and unbridled speculation in the comprehension of human affairs. Substantial knowledge of such processes as learning and perception, of such important groups as women and racial stocks, and of such relationships as those between parents and children and between social structures and character formation has been recently developed with happy changes both in the general intellectual climate and in social policy. Thus, poverty is no longer regarded as a proper object for moral censure but a function of complex societal processes and individual characteristics. Similarly, delinquents and neurotics are more likely to be pitied for their illness than condemned for their sin. Programs aimed at alleviating such conditions as poverty, crime, and emotional disorder seem much more effective by virtue of their grounding in basic knowledge rather than in moralistic judgments often a bit whimsical in their nature.

But it must be noted that the growth of science in the study of behavior has had two very different kinds of consequences. First, as in physics and biology, the social sciences have acquired high instrumental utility. Given a particular objective, the knowledge generated by psychology, sociology, anthropolgy, and economics often provides an answer to the question of how to attain it. Sometimes the answer is highly applicable; sometimes less so. Over a wide range of problems, however, the contribution of behavioral science is consistently to reduce the error in estimates of how to achieve an agreed-upon goal.

On the other hand, behavioral science has produced changes in the values men hold as well as showing them how to achieve some of those they cherish. It has already been pointed out how the development of a naturalistic and deterministic science altered the view of psychotics and neurotics in a more humanitarian direction. No member of the helping professions is likely to argue that such a change in valuational attitudes is undesirable. Yet it is legitimate to ask if modifications of this sort have taken place without the slighting of some significant features of human life.

A New Set of Villains

In rising to the challenge of this question, one may wonder, first of all, if some of the humanitarian attitudes concomitant to science have not been correlated with other values that are not entirely consonant with it. To take only one of the many possible examples, the tendency of clinicians, quite in keeping with a deterministic logic, is to search for the roots of emotional disorder in their patients through examining their histories, especially the histories of their relationships with parents and similar significant figures. Because parent-child frictions appear with high frequency under such conditions, clinical workers tend to conceive of parents as the villains of the pathological piece, the latter-day devils whose possession of the psyche of their youngster accounts for his delinquent actions or his neurotic anxieties. Certainly, it is not uncommon in the counseling or psychotherapy of young adults for inferences about the parents to be used in explaining the client's conduct in spite of two facts: The clinician has often not seen the parents, and he is generally quite willing to assert *abstractly* that patients are seldom objective informants about those who play significant roles in their lives.

It is quite possible that parents wear the cloven hoof more frequently than other people. But the attitude that is under discussion as an outgrowth of the sophisticated contemporary view of human behavior entails some embarrassing contradictions. First of all, it overlooks the implication of a kind of infinite regress in accounting for psychological malaise. If the troubles of a given client are the result of his parents' neuroses, were not they products of *their* parents' disorders? And so on, back through the family line? If the scheme is admissible at all, there is little room for devils in it, and no generation is more blameworthy than any other. True, one can argue, not without cogency, that blame is beside the point; but this argument seems honored at least as much in the breach as in the observance, and it presents problems when one hears clinicians discuss the desirability of a patient's expressing his negative and hostile feelings toward his parents or their surrogates as a condition of his improvement.

Second, this view of things ignores the concept of individual responsibility. While it is quite possible to make out a case under the banner of determinism for the irrelevance of such a notion, it is worth remarking that nobody behaves as if he believed such a case were true. Judgments of responsibility are shot through the warp of social life, and the ubiquitousness of such judgments is as much a part of humanity as are thought and its vehicle, language. Perhaps this observation justifies a brief scanning of the concept in relation to the problem under scrutiny.

As a term, "responsibility" refers to two different things.[2] One has to do with a logical and deterministic relationship between observations or constructs. Thus, it makes perfectly good sense to speak, for example, of previous frustrations as "responsible" in some degree for one's present aggressions. In such a context, responsibility is defined by the extent to which one may logically or empirically explain one variable in terms of another. The other meaning of "responsibility," however, is concerned descriptively with a pattern of behavior. There seem to be essentially three types of actions involved in "responsibility" in this sense: the keeping of both explicit and implied promises, the acknowledgement of error, and a tendency to act *as if* one were to a significant extent the master of one's own destiny. A kind of prototypically responsible person, therefore, is one who can be relied upon to keep his word and to act in accordance with the rules he has acknowledged as binding on him, who admits his mistakes, and who shows attitudinal evidence of regarding his future as somewhat in his own discharge. Like all trait names, "responsibility" implies a dimension along which people can be ordered in terms of more or less, and no one probably fits one extreme or the other with exactness. But the central point is that the concept can be construed in a purely behavioral way, and the construction seems to identify a class of conduct that is vitally important in human relationships.

THE NEGLECTED RESOURCE

The basic charge implied in these comments is that contemporary behavioral science has been unconcerned with the self-determining characteristics and potentialities of the person. As a result, it occupies a curious position both philosophically and programmatically. In its outlook, it has substituted a kind of fatalism of events for the fatalism of divinity typical of older points of view. Demon possession, failure of divine election, or a state of being out of grace have given way to parental mishandling, an unhealthy ordering of society, or faulty education. But while these latter explanations of disturbed conduct are presumably more susceptible to correction, and while they clearly support a gentler and more humane approach to troubled people, they neither suggest any promising basis for remedial or developmental work with the individual case; nor do they take into account that characteristic human tendency, so central in the judgments of men about each other, to regard oneself and one's fellows as something more than pawns on the genetic and environmental chessboard. In a sense, the discarding of the notion of sin along with the supernatural overtones it carried in the days before Pinel may have

---

[2] The distinction drawn here is similar to that in [2].

amounted to a dumping of the baby with the bath water. If sin implied a punitive kind of treatment, it also acknowledged personal responsibility and self-determination as a human attribute. One need not defend cruelty to find a meaningful challenge in recollecting that exposure to the scourge and the ducking stool was sometimes associated with behavioral improvement, just as, among modern patients, there is a moderate correlation between behavioral improvement and exposure to various shock therapies, many of which are terrifying to those who undergo them.

This oversimplification of determinism into a fatalism of events and this neglect of the self-determining quality of human character may have had noteworthy programmatic consequences. Among other things, much research has been devoted to identifying the explanatory antecedents of criminal or psychopathological tendencies (the "sins" of yesteryear), neglecting the value systems associated with such tendencies or the problem of how such values are learned and modified. As a result, quite a good deal is known about troubled and disordered personalities but very little about zestful and contentedly vigorous ways of life and how they may be facilitated. Similarly, in concentrating on the adverse and unfortunate effects of punitive methods of child care, education, and treatment, behavioral science has not yet come to grips with the problem of how people respond to challenges, the extent to which they find standards useful in the achievement of maturity, and the degree to which their self-worth is dependent on an acquired sense of integrity, a relatively clear set of principles by which their lives are guided, and the formulation of ideals. It is as if the "virtuous" were merely the "non-sinful"—as if normality or maturity were merely the absence of pathological traits or symptoms. Since the *forms* that pathology takes are often determined by their cultural or social context, such a conception leads to the implication that the normal person is simply the innocuous conformist who creates a minimum of trouble for his group. Recent attacks on the behavioral sciences as advocating a kind of spineless "adjustment"[3] to the immediate social world, while quite wrong headed, are the understandable spawn of this omission in the research and service programs of psychology, sociology, education, and their intellectual kin.

The Humanities as Hypotheses

It is important to be clear: Nothing said here is to be construed as a stricture on science as a way of knowing or as a way of studying human affairs. Indeed, it may be well to repeat the earlier assertion that science is the *only* route to public knowledge that man has available. In its in-

[3] One of the best known and most clearly symptomatic of these attacks is [6].

vestigations of personality and behavior, however, science may have been limited by two factors, (1) the *Zeitgeist* within which it has operated and (2) its declaration of independence from the wisdom men have accumulated over their history. On the one hand, the sciences of behavior, dealing as they do with people and society—the things that matter most— have been pressed into the service of the liberal social ideas that both yield the rich and precious heritage of free expression and the value of the individual person and occasionally degenerate into license, irresponsibility, and sentimentality. The problems that have been chosen for investigation reflect in large part the emphasis on impulse release and the denial of authority that animated Pinel's time and flowered in the *fin-de-siècle* revolt for which Freud was a perhaps unwitting but certainly eloquent spokesman. A fascinating chore in the sociology of knowledge would be that of evaluating research in personality dynamics against the dominant values of the first half of the twentieth century. It seems at least a tenable hypothesis that the work done has been a reflection of such social themes as naturalism, a high premium placed on impulse gratification, anti-authoritarianism, and opposition to rules and conventions. Like other cultural products, behavioral science is likely, at least in its content, to embody in significant degree its milieu. Such a state of affairs is quite comprehensible, but it remains limiting.

Similarly, the technological power of science and its growth in prestige has led scientists to divorce themselves from the humanistic traditions represented in history, literature, and philosophy. This conflict is only symbolized by, not restricted to, the tension between behavioral scientists and professors in the humanities on university campuses.[4] While it is true that the humanistic traditions embody conservative as well as liberal conceptions and, like any tradition, tend to crystallize at times into bigotry and closed-mindedness, they also are the carriers of recurrent insights and ideas about the most rewarding relationships between man and man, man and society, and—for those who are interested—man and those Powers other than himself that he perceives in the universe. Such ideas, confused and contradictory as they sometimes are, constitute the basis for wisdom, guides evolved over history to the choices men must make in living out their lives. They represent the behavioral prescriptions in varied and often incompatible terms that define the varieties of the "good life" that the social sciences can be instrumental in achieving but which science itself cannot define.

If this reading of things has any merit, then it is obvious that a critical clarity about possible humanistic objectives and a creative hardheadedness about the methods of science must be combined if knowledge about

---

[4] This issue is discussed from different angles of regard and with consistent cogency in [4].

human behavior and the potentialities of human personality is to be expanded in ways less limited by the *Zeitgeist* and more relevant to some of the issues that beset modern men. For example, it is possible to regard some of the great historical documents—the Bible, the Nichomachean Ethics, Shakespeare's tragedies—as a congeries of hypotheses about the relationship of particular life styles to such affects as guilt or security, fear or joy, self-esteem or self-derogation. Similarly, one finds in such cultural records hints that may be useful in establishing criteria of normality, emotional maturity, or positive mental health—criteria which cannot be evolved from within a scientific frame of reference alone, but which must be made explicit if research on psychological and social well being is to take a more useful turn. Still more important, the humanistic account of man's experience that these documents present abounds in theories—metaphorical in language, literary in form, and devoted to the particular case, but potentially translatable—of the self-determining character of personality. The relative utility of these theories can only be tested in the crucible of systematic and controlled observation by the methods of science. But science must be familiar with them and must attend to the task of rendering them into propositions susceptible to research and precise examination.

The Burden of Understanding

But there is another way in which the traditions of the humanities bear upon the business of behavioral science, and it is nowhere clearer than in relation to the crucial and poignant problem of mental health. There has been a strong tendency recently, only illustrated by the work of Szasz [5], to challenge the whole notion of psychopathology and the behavior disorders as "disease states," lying within the province of psychology and the medical sciences for their study and control. In spite of the advantages of this post-Pinel position, it seems quite inconsistent with the usual and accepted concepts of disease. What are known as psychiatric disturbances involve complex problems in living that bear little resemblance to tuberculosis or smallpox. The latter entail physiological and physico-chemical events which the physician observes, classifies (diagnoses), and treats from outside. The disorders of behavior, on the other hand, imply social and psychological occurrences of which the therapist, within the treatment situation, is an inevitable part. It was the perception of this truth that led Harry Stack Sullivan to characterize the work of the psychiatrist, in contrast to that of other physicians, as that of a "participant observer."

The same perception accounts for Davis's conclusion, based on a careful analysis of the mental hygiene movement, that the role of those concerned with the prevention and therapy of psychopathology is "not that of a scientist but that of a practising moralist in a scientific, mobile world" [1]. Considerations of mental health are considerations of man's struggle with the problem of how he *should* live, the moral problem of how conflicting needs and values may best be reconciled within individuals and between persons and groups, the ethical problem of how a man may properly judge the "rightness" or "goodness" of his own conduct and that of his fellows. These questions of what constitutes appropriate and desirable ways of life are the traditional domain of philosophy, religion, and literature. They are *not*, by the disclaimers of many scientists themselves, the domain of science.

It is not that science is beside the point, of course. But one's goals, the criteria for the style of life that one aspires to follow, and the moral values that one espouses and lives by cannot be derived from the structure of psychology or sociology. The decisions that are required here can only come from a discriminating appraisal of human experience. To the extent that a man is familiar with the reflected-upon grapplings of his kind with similar problems, he possesses both a richer stock of the relevant data and the techniques of thought by which to evaluate them. Clearly, neither scholarship nor intellectualism is at issue. What does seem central is the degree to which one has become a part of a tradition that emphasizes the critical examination of values in human action. Much of contemporary psychotherapy, like much of contemporary education, is willy-nilly devoted, sometimes competently and sometimes blunderingly, to aiding the individual to accept more fully his humanistic heritage.

It is well to be reminded here of Susanne Langer's wise observations:

> Because our moral life is negotiated so largely by symbols, it is more oppressive than the morality of animals . . . animals react only to the deed that is done or is actually imminent; . . . whereas we control each other's merely incipient behavior with fantasies of force . . . the power of symbols enables us not only to limit each other's actions, but to command them; not only to *restrain* one another, but to *constrain*. . . . The story of man's martyrdom is a sequel to the story of his intelligence, his power of symbolical envisagement.
>
> For good or evil, man has this power of envisagement, which puts on him a burden that purely alert, realistic creatures do not bear—the burden of understanding. . . . So he must conceive a world and a law of the world, a pattern of life, and a way of meeting death [3].

This view applies as much to the personal situation as to the human condition generally. To a large extent, a man controls his own behavior through his envisagement of goals and the consequences of attempting their attainment. His conduct is a significant reflection of the way he has conceived the world and its law, the pattern of his life, and the way that death can best be met. This inevitable burden of understanding can at times grow unsupportable, and the traveler falls.

But the only means available for strengthening him is greater understanding. The major alternative is the view that men live out their destinies in worlds fashioned from the impersonal interaction of their genes and their environments, worlds in which they themselves exert little influence and no creativity. Attractively, such a conception permits the harried and lonely individual to plead irresponsibility when chivvied, as he often is, by apparently insuperable difficulties of one kind or another. But the relief born of dodging responsibility—the responsibility for implementing moral values—is short lived. It remains significant that psychotherapists, regardless of the theoretical language that they speak, typically characterize their patients as being, in some way and in some crucial segments of their lives, irresponsible and self-deluding.

In carrying the burden of understanding, the sciences of behavior can be a basic asset. Knowledge of a precise and systematic kind is closely relevant and even essential to responsible moral criticism. The discriminative scanning of values is more effective to the degree that it is more informed, more bulwarked by the tested, public propositions about events that science—and, probably, only science—can give. But science is not an alternative to the evaluation of goals, norms, and the criteria of sanity and desirable solutions to the recurrent problems of living that men must face.

Hilaire Belloc has somewhere written a couplet that seems oddly apropos:

> Always keep ahold of nurse
> For fear of finding something worse.

In the present context, the nurse is that insistent propensity, sometimes unselfconscious and sometimes highly sophisticated, for men to act as if their fate were in their own discharge and to think discriminatingly about how they may most wisely meet their responsibility. The exercising of this propensity is the heart of the humanistic tradition. It is the job of the behavioral sciences to strengthen it and to make it more widely available to men whose burden of understanding is currently extremely heavy.

REFERENCES

1. Davis, K. Mental hygiene and the class structure. *Psychiatry*, 1938, *1*, 65.
2. Fingarette, H. Psychoanalytic perspectives on moral guilt and responsibility. *Phil. phenomenol. Res.*, 1955, *16*, 18-36.

3. Langer, Susanne. *Philosophy in a new key.* New York: Mentor Books, 1954.
4. Riesman, D. *Constraint and variety in American education.* Lincoln, Neb.: University of Nebraska Press, 1956.
5. Szasz, T. S. The myth of mental illness. *Amer. Psychologist,* 1960, *15,* 113-118.
6. Whyte, W. H. *The organization man.* New York: Simon and Schuster, 1956.
7. Zilboorg, G. *A history of medical psychology.* New York: Norton, 1941.

20. Patient Role and Social Uncertainty: A Dilemma of the Mentally Ill

Kai T. Erikson

> As you may remember from the large-scale survey—*Americans View Their Mental Health* (Selection 1, page 14) it was found that few people were prepared to be told that they must accept at least a share of the responsibility for their mental and emotional troubles.
>
> The present article deals with the dilemma of persons in mental hospitals as a result of those institutions being operated on the basis of the medical model. According to Dr. Erikson, a member of the Department of Psychiatry, Emory University:

> Thus it should be a matter of small surprise if the analogy is taken too seriously and patients enter the therapeutic setting with the passive attitude that they have come to be "fixed," or with the comfortable notion that mental illness is something which·has happened to them, something in which they are only indirectly implicated, like an "enemy" invasion of germs.

> If, as Szasz has pointed out (Selection 2), mental illness is really a matter of "problems in living," it is no wonder that little help is received for them in a mental hospital which operates in much the same fashion as one does for regular medical problems.

The concept of role has become widely used in the field of mental health to relate the behavior of mental patients to the social setting of their illness. The literature in which this concept has appeared, however, has been largely concerned with the specialized culture of the mental

Psychiatry; 20: 263-274, 1957. Reprinted by special permission of The William Alanson White Psychiatric Foundation, Inc. and by the author. Copyright 1957, The William Alanson White Psychiatric Foundation, Inc. The research on which this paper is based was supported by a Fellowship from the Grant Foundation and was conducted under the auspices of the Family Study Center, University of Chicago. I am grateful to Nelson N. Foote, Director of the Family Study Center, for many helpful criticisms and to Robert P. Knight, M.D., Medical Director of the Austen Riggs Center, Stockbridge, Mass., for the opportunity to do this study. David Rapaport of the Austen Riggs Center offered me his wise counsel throughout and this paper is deeply indebted to him.

hospital—the formal and informal structures of ward life—almost as if the universe to which a patient relates when he enacts a "patient role" is neatly contained within hospital walls.[1] To the sociologist, who generally uses the concept of role in a broader social context, this tends to place a one-sided emphasis on the institution itself as the essential focus of the patient's social life.

When a person enters a mental hospital for treatment, to be sure, he abandons many of the social ties which anchored him to a definite place in society. However, the act of becoming a mental patient effects a fundamental *change* in the person's relationship to the ongoing processes of society, not a complete withdrawal from them; and while the forms of his participation are altered, he remains acutely sensitive to outer influences. Even in the relative isolation of the hospital ward, then, the patient's behavior to some extent articulates his relationship to the larger society and reflects the social position which he feels is reserved for him in its organizational structure. It is this aspect of the role of the patient which the present paper will consider.

DEFINITIONS

Role usually is used to designate a set of behaviors or values about behavior which is commonly considered appropriate for persons occupying given statuses or positions in society. For the purposes of this paper, it will be useful to consider that the acquisition of roles by a person involves two basic processes: *role-validation* and *role-commitment*. Role-validation takes place when a community "gives" a person certain expectations to live up to, providing him with distinct notions as to the conduct it considers appropriate or valid for him in his position.[2] Role-

---

[1] See, for example, the following: J. F. Bateman and H. W. Dunham, "The State Hospital as a Specialized Community Experience," *Amer. J. Psychology* (1948) 105:445-448; William Caudill, Fredrick C. Redlich, Helen R. Gilmore, and Eugene B. Brody, "Social Structure and Interaction Processes on a Psychiatric Ward," *Amer. J. Orthopsychiatry* (1952) 22: 314-334; George Devereux, "The Social Structure of the Hospital as a Factor in Total Therapy," *Amer. J. Orthopsychiatry* (1949) 19: 493-500; Howard Rowland, "Interactional Processes in a State Hospital," *Psychiatry* (1938) 1:323-337; Alfred Stanton and Morris S. Schwartz, "Medical Opinion and the Social Context in the Mental Hospital," *Psychiatry* (1949) 12:243-249; Stanton and Schwartz, *The Mental Hospital*; New York, Basic Books, 1954.

[2] Validation, it might be pointed out, is meant to be more than a community's attempt to impose its moral preferences upon members. The community may validate certain behavior as appropriate for certain individuals even while remaining completely outraged by it. By naming a criminal "habitual" or "confirmed," for instance, people declare their intention of punishing him, not because his conduct *violates* their expectations or is "unlike" him, but precisely because it *is* like him and is thus the valid way for him to act.

commitment is the complementary process whereby a person adopts certain styles of behavior as his own, committing himself to role themes that best represent the kind of person he assumes himself to be, and best reflect the social position he considers himself to occupy.

Normally, of course, these processes take place simultaneously and are seldom overtly distinguished in the relationship between the person and his community. The person learns to accept the image that the group holds up to him as a more or less accurate reflection of himself, is able to accept as his own the position which the group provides for him, and thus becomes more or less committed to the behavior values which the group poses as valid for him. The merit of making a distinction between these two processes, then, is solely to visualize what happens in marginal situations in which conflict does occur—in which the person develops behavior patterns which the community regards as invalid for him, or the community entertains expectations which the person feels unable to realize. Sociologists, traditional specialists in this aspect of deviance, have generally been more concerned with the process of validation than that of commitment, concentrating on the mechanisms which groups employ to persuade individuals that roles validated for them deserve their personal commitment.

In so doing, sociologists have largely overlooked the extent to which a person can *engineer* a change in the role expectations held in his behalf, rather than passively waiting for others to "allocate" or "assign" roles to him. This he does by being so persistent in his commitment to certain modes of behavior, and so convincing in his portrayal of them, that the community is persuaded to accept these modes as the basis for a new set of expectations on its part.

Thus the process by which persons acquire a recognized role may, at times, involve long and delicate negotiations between the individual and his community. The individual presents himself in behavior styles that express his personal sense of identity and continuity;[3] the group validates role models for him that fit its own functional needs.[4] The negotiation is concluded when a mutually satisfactory definition of the individual is reached and a position established for him in the group structure—or when the issue becomes stalemated and suppressive sanctions against deviance are called into play.

The argument to be presented here is that such a negotiation is likely to follow a mental patient's admission to a mental hospital, particularly if he does not qualify as a "certified" patient with a circumscribed disease. In accepting hospitalization, the patient is often caught in the pull of

[3] See in this connection, Erik H. Erikson, "The Problem of Ego Identity," *J. Amer. Psychoanal. Assn.* (1956) 4: 56-121.

[4] See Talcott Parsons, *The Social System*; Glencoe, Ill., The Free Press, 1951.

divergent sets of expectations: on the one hand, he is exposed to psychiatry's demand that he make a wholehearted commitment to the process of treatment, and, on the other, he is confronted by a larger society which is often unwilling to validate these commitments. He is left, then, with no consistent and durable social role, with no clear-cut social models upon which to fashion his behavior. The patient is thus often persuaded by the logic of psychiatric institutions to attempt to engineer validation in the role this society provides for the *medical* patient—in which, to be sure, distinctly psychotic patients are presumed to belong. To establish his eligibility for this conventional role, the mental patient must negotiate, using his illness as an instrumentality. He must present his illness to others in a form which they recognize as legitimate, perhaps even exaggerating his portrayal of those behaviors which qualify medical patients for their role. In having to do so, the argument continues, he is often left with little choice but to become sicker or more chronically sick.

The Patient

This section is based primarily on data collected in a small, "open" psychiatric hospital which offered analytically oriented psychotherapy for a fairly selective group of patients. Diagnoses in this population ranged, for the most part, from the severe psychoneuroses to borderline psychoses. The institutional setting lacked the scheduled rigidity of closed hospital routines and allowed for an unusual degree of personal initiative. Since the patients received almost daily individual therapy and were, in a certain respect, volunteers for treatment who recognized the implications of their patienthood, they could hardly be considered representative of the average ward population. But the experienced clinician will be able to determine to what extent generalizations made from observation of this group apply to patients in custodial institutions, whose contacts with the outside world are more limited. No doubt many of the same social forces act upon patients in any hospital situation, even where behavior is more strictly routinized and confined within the limiting boundaries of a closed ward so that it may seem to reflect the common setting in which it took place rather than the common motivations which produced it. Thus it is possible that the uniqueness of the therapeutic setting in which these observations took place simply affords a more spontaneous picture of social forces operating in any psychiatric hospital.

While doing some sociological work in this setting, the writer took a brief inventory of behavior themes which seemed characteristic of the patient group and which appeared to be among the central motifs of the patients' role behavior.

One may begin by noting certain contradictions implicit in the very act of becoming a mental patient. By accepting hospitalization, the patient makes a contractual agreement to cooperate in a therapeutic partnership: he agrees to want and to appreciate treatment, to be realistic about his need for help to volunteer relevant information, and to act as reliably as possible upon the recommendations of his therapist. Yet it is widely considered a condition of his illness that he is unable to make meaningful contact with any reality, therapeutic or otherwise. In the grip of these discrepant expectations, his behavior is likely to be a curious mixture of the active and the passive, a mosaic of acts which tend to confirm his competence and acts which tend to dramatize his helplessness. He must test the limits of his own uncertain controls and look for consistent expectations to guide him, as the following fragment from a case history illustrates:

> One of the outstanding characteristics of this patient is his absolute uncertainty about his illness and what is expected of him in the institution and in therapy. He is uncertain whether he actively produces his hysterical states or whether they come upon him without his being able to do anything about them. He does not know whether he is supposed to show his symptoms or suppress them, to "let go" of his impulses and act out or to exert active self-control and "put the lid on." He is afraid that if he does the former, he is psychotic and will be considered too sick for the open institutional setting here; if he does the latter, he will be a pretending psychopath and considered too well to continue treatment here at all. He does not know what he should expect from himself, from other patients, from his sickness, from other people he knows, or even from his therapist. Perhaps his most crucial problem at the moment is to define for himself what are the conditions of his stay here as a patient.

This fragment sums up the bewildering social situation in which the patient must act, and it is not difficult to understand how the final assumption of a consistent social role might represent to him a clarification and partial adjustment. To demonstrate this, it might be interesting to isolate a few strands of behavior from this complicated fabric.

All children are taught in this culture that it is impolite to stare at or make reference to the infirmities of cripples. So it is interesting to note that the generous impulse of outsiders to overlook a patient's less visible infirmities is likely to put the patient in an instant state of alarm, and to bring urgent assurances on his part that he is severely sick and in serious need of treatment. Patients often bring this topic into conversation on scant provocation and continue to talk about it even when fairly vigorous attempts are made by visitors to change the subject. The patient is likely to describe this as "accepting the realities of his illness," by which he means that he frankly admits the seriousness of his sickness and refuses to take refuge in some convenient defense that might deny it. Yet to the observer it often appears that this is an attempt to convince *others* of these realities as well as to remind himself, as if he were afraid they would be overlooked entirely. The patient seems to feel it crucial that his illness be accepted as a fundamental fact about himself, the premise on which he enters into relations with others.

Side by side with this severe "honesty," the patient can develop a considerable degree of responsibility in carrying out the therapeutic recommendations of his therapist. And if the hospital tries to foster the patient's social initiative, he may respond with resources that even the therapist did not know were at his disposal. Such initiative is usually in evidence only during certain hospital activities and sometimes appears to belie the very weaknesses which the patient, at other times, displays so insistently. Patients at the hospital in question, for instance, have organized and produced dramatic plays before outside audiences, performing with a skill that surprised professional dramatic observers, and succeeding even when the therapists themselves had severe reservations about the outcome. At a prizewinning performance in a neighboring city, some of the audience were and remained under the impression that the players were members of the medical staff rather than patients of the institution.

Yet as one records this accomplishment, it must be noted that such positive efforts can sometimes be as deceptive as they are surprising, and that, at times, they can produce negative undercurrents that threaten to cancel out the accomplishment altogether. In reporting on the plays performed at the hospital, one journalist noted that the patients produce and act in plays before paying audiences with a competence equal to that of any good amateur group. At the same time, the reporter said, one of the doctors had remarked ruefully, "I was very upset when one of my patients, after doing a fine job in the play, went back to the patients' dormitory and tried to set fire to it."

The example is extreme, but it illustrates the conflict a patient encounters in committing himself to positive and constructive activity. Like Penelope, who wove a cloak by day only to unravel it at night, the mental patient often portrays the insecurity of his position by staging, after every advance of this kind, a dramatic retreat into impulsivity and destruction.

Thus at once the patient accepts responsibility for a type of performance rarely asked of the average person, yet is unable to control actions which, in the light of the earlier accomplishment, would seem to be well within his realm of mastery. This seeming paradox is a recurring motif that runs through the whole complex of the patient's role behavior. As has been shown in the case abstract that introduced this section, the patient has potentialities for activity and passivity, for resourcefulness and helplessness, in any given area of action. To organize these into a coherent role pattern, it seems, the patient partitions his hospital world into areas where he considers one or the other of these potential responses specifically appropriate.

In some decisive situations, as has been described, the patient faces his hospital life with remarkable initiative. Yet in others, an overwhelming theme of helplessness seems to dominate his behavior. He is likely to insist, in terms far stronger than the situation would appear to necessitate, that he is unable to control his behavior and must be given a wide license for conduct that is certainly unconventional according to the values prevalent outside the hospital. A patient was asked "Why did you do that?" His answer, "How should I know? If I knew these things, I wouldn't be here," reflects the values thus emerging in the patient role pattern. Patients have been heard comforting one another by saying, "Of course you can't do it." This process of "giving up defenses" is, of course, presumed to be essential for successful treatment, particularly in intensive analytic therapy, and a certain license for impulsivity and acting out seems to be part of much of psychotherapy in general. But the patient often seems to reserve his right for such license with what appear to be unnecessary claims that he "can't help it."

One might add that whereas clinical evidence indicates that patients often feel a strong guilt at "having let others down," the values of the patient group seldom allow its overt expression—and even supply convenient channels for its projection elsewhere. It is not uncommon for patients to bitterly indict their parents, often for the same weakness they themselves "can't help," sometimes talking as if a kind of deliberate conspiracy was involved in the events that led to their own illness. The weakness of this logic seems evident even to those who use it most persistently, which again indicates that the social usages which allow its expression must have an important social function to the patient group. If a little harsh, it may be one way to deny one's responsibility for being sick, while nevertheless accounting for one's illness in terms that are current outside the hospital walls.

The point is that most of the persons a patient encounters in the hospital, certainly the other patients, are perfectly willing to acknowledge that ego deficiencies are not his "fault" and that he is often compelled to act without the benefit of sufficient controls. To what audience, then, does he address his continual protest that he has the *right* to some license and cannot help the fact that he is sick? Largely, one begins to think, these assertions are broadcast not to the audience assembled in the confined orbit of the hospital at all—but to the omnipresent public which, as shall be seen, fails to validate his commitment to therapy. To assume that hospital walls or the implicit ideology of psychiatric institutions protect the patient from this audience would be an unfortunate oversight. The image of the public audience is firmly incorporated within the patient himself, and this image is constantly reinforced by newspapers, movies, radio, and television. The specialized values which psychiatry introduces into the hospital setting cannot entirely overcome the fact that the patient remains sensitive to current public notions about mental illness, and, on certain levels of awareness, even shares them in substance.

What does the outside audience ask of the patient—and its internalized image make him ask of himself? Essentially, he is asked to justify his voluntary retirement to a hospital by demonstrating that he *needs* it, by displaying a distinct illness requiring highly specialized help. The reason for a person's therapy in a residental setting is obviously the wish on everybody's part that he develop adjustive initiative. Yet if large parts of society doubt his claim to illness when he appears to have a certain competence—when, for instance, he rehearses healthy modes of behavior on or off the stage—he is left in the exposed position of one who has to *look* incompetent even while learning to become the exact opposite. A few minutes before going on the stage, a patient-actor announced, "It is a tradition here that the show *never* goes on!" This tradition is of particular interest because it has no basis in fact whatever. The show in question did go on, as had all of its predecessors. Yet even in the act of positive accomplishment the patient feels it important to repeat that failure is the norm among mental patients, for he always anticipates the question, "Look, if you can do these things so well, why are you here?"

This prominent theme of helplessness which runs through the patient's verbal and behavioral repertoire again reasserts the basic paradox. For while much of the time he may display a passivity that almost suggests disability; he shows a certain ingenuity in organizing his passive behavior strategically; he can put considerable energy into maneuvers which show him to be helpless; in short, he can go to ample expense to give the impression of one who has nothing to expend. This does not imply, of course, that the patient is deliberately staging a deceptive performance. On the contrary, it suggests that the psychological needs which motivate such behavior are as compelling, in a certain way, as those considered to be anchored somewhere in the dynamics and genetics of his illness, and, in fact, tend to reinforce them.

In the absence of clear-cut organic symptoms, a "real" illness which "can't be helped" is the most precious commodity such patients have in their bargaining with society for a stable patient role. It is the most substantial credential available in their application for equal rights with the medical patient, and as such, may come to have an important social value to them. The fatal logic of this may be that the patient will find his social situation better structured for him if he gives in to his illness and helps others to create an unofficial hospital structure which supports the perpetuation of patienthood.

SOCIAL UNCERTAINTY

Although all human groups rely heavily upon the mechanisms they develop to suppress deviant behavior, among the most crucial measures of any society are the provisions it makes for absorbing certain kinds of deviance into its structure. Societies often accomplish this by placing given individuals—usually those whose deviancy is not considered deliberate—in special statuses where their otherwise invalid behavior becomes the expected and legitimate mode of conduct.

In a well-known analysis, Talcott Parsons argues that illness is a form of deviance which the culture shelters in this manner.[5] By setting role expectations for the ill person which both exempt him from his usual social duties and assure that he will return to them as soon as possible, society effectively neutralizes the onus his failure to perform would otherwise imply. The conditions of this special sick role, as Parsons sees them, are four: First, the sick person is exempted from certain of his normal social obligations. Second, the sick person is considered unable to recover by an act of conscious will; that is, he "can't help it." Third, the sick person is considered obligated to want to get well, to cooperate with a physician in achieving recovery, and to accept the protection of the sick role only so long as it is therapeutically necessary. Fourth, the sick person is regarded as in need of technically competent help, which implies that accepting the status of "sick person" is conditional upon accepting the status of "patient."

When sociologists speak about societies "doing" something—providing roles, entertaining expectations, and so on—they take for granted that the acts in question are matters of general public agreement, are institutionalized by consensus. One might ask, then, on the basis of what criteria do persons qualify for the sick role? Like the military physician who must determine from day to day which of the many men who report to him are really sick, the public at large must have some generally accepted standards for deciding who is eligible for the sick role exemptions. The sick role, of course, is not granted only out of sympathy for a person's dis-

---

[5] Talcott Parsons, "Illness and the Role of the Physician: A Sociological Perspective," Amer. J. Orthopsychiatry (1951) 21: 452-460.

comfort: it is granted as factual recognition that the person is, in fact, *unable* to carry out his normal duties. The first of these criteria, then, to follow Parsons' logic, is that the person must be at least partially disabled either because of the severity of the illness or the requirements for cure. Furthermore, the patient's disability must be considered one that he is unable to erase by a deliberate exercise of will, his willingness and ability to "get well as soon as possible" must remain unquestioned, and his condition must be regarded as within the province of a qualified therapeutic profession. In fact, in most medical practice it is the physician, acting in the name of society, who certifies his patient as "really" ill.

This brings up an uncomfortable argument. Although the public generally accepts the physician's verbal certificate as indication of legitimate physical sickness, it continues to doubt the medical legitimacy of many forms of mental illness and often fails to accept the mental patient as a qualified candidate for the sick role.

Recent evidence indicates that, despite the public's growing acceptance of psychiatry, current attitudes toward mental illness fall considerably short of the enlightened attitudes promoted in popular publications. The results of these studies have not yet been made available except in scattered summaries, but certain conclusions can be drawn from them that throw the present situation of psychiatry specifically and the field of mental health generally into a fairly harsh focus.[6]

It appears that on the surface the public has developed reasonably tolerant attitudes toward the mentally ill and even a hesitant respect for the practice of psychiatry. People understand the need for increased psychiatric facilities, appreciate the enormity of the mental health problem, and agree that mental illness is a condition requiring specialized treatment and competently trained help. Yet underneath the pleasant surface of these enlightened principles, people have little idea how to recognize the concrete problems that these principles encompass.

The average person, it seems, cannot identify mental illness when he sees it, cannot recognize the symptoms that indicate it, and remains quite uncertain about the very meaning of the term when pressed for a definition. He continues to resist the notion that a person can be mentally ill and not entirely "out of his mind," although willing to accept illness as

---

[6] The reference here is to a study conducted by the National Opinion Research Center, University of Chicago. It is based on 3,500 intensive interviews with a representative cross section of the American public. A book describing the results of this study is being prepared by Shirley A. Star, Senior Study Director of the NORC, but in the meantime two short reviews of the general findings are available: Shirley A. Star, "The Public Ideas about Mental Illness," a paper presented to the Annual Meeting of the National Association for Mental Health, Indianapolis, November 5, 1955; Shirley A. Star, a report on public attitudes in *Psychiatry, the Press and the Public*; Washington, D.C., Amer. Psychiat. Assn., 1956; pp. 1-5.

legitimate if the patient is a potential danger to the community and is securely committed to a custodial institution.[7]

> In practice, people make it clear that they do not generally regard behavior as proof of mental illness, unless three interrelated conditions obtain. First of all, they look for a breakdown of intellect, an almost complete loss of cognitive functioning or, in short, a loss of reason. . . . Second, people expect, almost as a necessary consequence of this loss of rationality, that the behavior called mental illness must represent a serious loss of self-control, usually to the point of dangerous violence against others and certainly to the point of *not being responsible for one's acts*. . . . Finally, people feel that, to qualify as mental illness, behavior should be inappropriate—that is, neither reasonable nor expected under the particular circumstances in which the person finds himself.[8]

There seems to be some public agreement that persons not totally psychotic may have "nervous disorders" or other behavioral difficulties. But it is generally felt that these conditions do not amount to "real" sickness—one of the tests being, apparently, that mental illness is not legitimate if one can recover from it—and do not require any specialized help other than consultation or simple encouragement. For this purpose, competent help is available from friends, ministers, and general medical practitioners as well as psychiatrists—perhaps in that order of importance.

Thus the psychiatrist continues to deal with his patient in a context of rather general public uncertainty, if not outright mistrust. He cannot share the physician's license for simply naming his patient to the sick role, confident that the patient's community will substantiate the claim. The psychiatrist can only proceed tentatively: his assurances about a patient's condition or need for special attention, particularly if that patient has not slipped off into a state of colorful sickness visible to the untutored eye, are often contradicted, often ignored, and seldom regarded as the final word of a specialized authority.

Traditional medicine, of course, has had centuries to attract the respect of society and can point to a continued series of new and successful forms of treatment. But it may take more than just time for such authority to be transferred to psychiatry. For it may well be that the very

---

[7] This raises a further problem of interest, which the present paper cannot take time to discuss. In a certain sense it is true that severely psychotic patients may be considered legitimately ill by the general public, but this is at best a special case of the sick role. For it is widely held that mental illness is not legitimate if recovery is possible. Thus, commitment to a custodial institution is regarded far more as leading to a state of permanent constraint than to a provisional role which the patient takes while under treatment which will result in a resumption of normal social obligations.

[8] Shirley A. Star, "The Public's Ideas about Mental Illness," reference footnote 6. The italics are mine.

conceptual frameworks which society has acquired through its acceptance of medical and other scientific phenomena do not lend themselves
to an understanding of psychiatric subject matter. Injury or disease is
conceived as something which has palpable substance, can be located
somewhere on the physical organism, can be diagnosed according to an
existing body of knowledge, and can be treated with fairly standard instruments in fairly standard ways. In comparison with this set of expectations concerning medical care, the psychiatrist can offer very little. In his
role as therapist, he specifically deals with the symbolic, the unique, the
personal aspects of human experience, and while his medical arsenal can
supply a few standard diagnostic tests, some somatic therapies, and an
increasing variety of pills, there is nothing approximating a blueprint
after which he can fashion his treatment. When he deals with the dynamics of mental illness, every step he takes is novel and without a precise precedent. As a consequence, many strata of society cannot regard
mental therapy as an honest concern of medicine, which, after all, in its
traditional objectivity, is supposed to be oriented to substantial and material matters rather than to the intangibles of human experience. If the
public makes this distinction too readily, it is using criteria to do so
which medicine has advocated for centuries.

The ill person, then, in committing himself to psychiatric treatment
and in trying to develop a systematic patient role, is taking on modes of
behavior which make little sense to those he adopts them for. It is clear
that the public remains skeptical about his claims of sickness, and leaves
him in the uncertain position of having to engineer new kinds of access
to a legitimate sick role, or, perhaps, turning away altogether into other
channels of expression for his deviant motivational needs. How many are
shuffled off into marginal areas of society to find a deviant group setting
—into criminal gangs, religious sects of one sort or another, into "artists"
colonies or hobo camps—one can only guess. However, every physician
will agree that an impressive clue to the alternatives of becoming a mental patient is provided by the number of persons who have to translate
their discomfort into physical ailments before they are able to recognize
it at all.

THE DILEMMA

This problem may gain in relevance if one turns from the broader organizational aspect of the patient role and inquires briefly about the
social career of the particular patient.

The sick role which Parsons visualizes is a transitory one. It is easy to
acquire if eligibility is established, easy to abandon once its functional

value is exhausted, so that the experience of being sick poses no necessarily abrupt breaks in the continuity of the medical patient's life. But the mental patient is in double jeopardy. He acquires recognition as a "sick" person only at a considerable emotional pride, if at all; later, he is able to withdraw from this recognition only with extreme difficulty, for he then faces the widespread conviction that legitimate mental illness cannot be completely cured anyway.[9] Moreover, the mental patient's treatment is often designed to effect comprehensive ego changes rather than simply to restore him to his former state of health, so that on several counts his experience with sickness may become crucial to his developing sense of direction and identity. The danger is that patienthood may become a model for his image of the future rather than a provisional shelter in which he resets himself for a life already in progress. In some cases of lifelong difficulty, the patient's efforts to be recognized as a patient may be the first definite attempts he has ever made to establish himself in a clear-cut social identity, while his adjustment to the hospital community may be the first successful one he has ever made.

For when the patient has to seek definition as acutely sick and helpless in order to achieve a measure of public validation for his illness—and simultaneously has to use all his remaining strengths to struggle against that illness—a dilemma is posed which he may resolve by simply giving up the struggle altogether and submerging himself in the sick definition permanently. The temptation to embrace such a definition, despite its lack of social approval—perhaps even because of it!—may be quite persuasive, as one of Dostoievski's characters points out:

> Oh, if I had done nothing simply from laziness! Heavens, how I should have respected myself then! I should have respected myself because I should at least have been capable of being lazy; there would at least have been one positive quality, as it were, in me, in which I could have believed myself. Question: What is he? Answer: A sluggard. How very pleasant it would have been to hear that of oneself! It would mean that I was positively defined, it would mean that there was something to say about me. "Sluggard"—why, it is a calling and vocation, it is a career. . . . I should have found for myself a form of activity in keeping with it. . . .[10]

This poses a further dilemma for psychiatry. The medical conditions which, it is currently believed, provide the optimal clinical setting for treatment may at the same time be social conditions which put a stamp

[9] An interesting fictional account of this difficulty can be found in Eileen Bassing, *Home Before Dark*; New York, Random House, 1957.

[10] F. M. Dostoievski, "Notes from Underground," pp. 442-537; in *A Treasury of Russian Literature*, edited by Bernard Guilbert Guerney; New York, Vanguard, 1943; p. 454.

of permanence on the illness. The danger that the patient will find himself a permanent "form of activity in keeping with" his momentary patienthood, while trying to engineer access to the medical patient role which psychiatry advocates for him, cannot be overlooked when psychiatrists consider their high readmission rates and their constant struggle with chronicity. It is important to realize that the patient's tendency to see himself as a medical responsibility and make symbolic application for the allowance this implies receives its initial impetus and support from psychiatry, even as psychiatry struggles for its own recognition within medicine. Practically every term in psychiatric usage which identifies patients, treatment, therapeutic settings, and hospital organization is borrowed from medical practice. Certainly a great number of psychiatric procedures are fashioned after medical models, while the physical facilities provided for the treatment of mental patients often duplicate those of the conventional hospital. To the psychiatrist himself, this may be largely a matter of convenience and training, but to the patient it is likely to have an implicit social logic: given the setting, it is only appropriate that he entertain the role expectations of any medical patient.

Perhaps even more important is the manner in which mental mechanisms are likely to be conceptualized by the psychiatrist and his patient alike, providing these mechanisms with an illusion of substance that renders them akin to anatomical organs. In constructing a workable model of psychic processes, psychiatry has tended to visualize the human mind by the use of intricate structural analogies—beginning, perhaps, with Freud's use of topographical terms and continuing throughout a literature in which the ego is likened to a building or machine and disorder is likened to a failure of supports, a weakening or collapse of foundations, and so on. These analogies may well serve the needs of psychiatry to order the dynamic problems it encounters; but they also tend to buttress the patient's already strong tendency to attribute to his illness—in those cases where he cannot actually blame verifiable organic changes—a quasiorganic structure and substance. Substantial disorders, of course, traditionally lie in the province of the surgeon or the practitioner who coaches the organism back to health. Thus, it should be a matter of small surprise if the analogy is taken too seriously and patients enter the therapeutic setting with the passive attitude that they have come to be "fixed," or with the comfortable notion that mental illness is something which has "happened" to them, something in which they are only indirectly implicated, like an "enemy" invasion of germs.

When this disparity between popular attitudes and medical values in psychiatry is pointed out, it is usually proposed that a massive program of public education be initiated in order to create public attitudes receptive to psychiatric realities, thereby creating a consistent patient role for the mentally ill. However, the sociologist may well suggest that these proposals be considered in the light of two crucial issues.

The first of these is the simplest. Would psychiatry be adequately serving its own interests if it *were* able to promote the mental patient's eligibility for the conventional sick role? This role has its roots in a fairly precise line of demarcation between the sick and the well, in that those people who are considered ill enough to need specific exemption are set aside into an identifying social status and expected to perform a fairly well established social role. Medically speaking, there may be some reality to this largely artificial distinction: the physician's practice, at least, is not unduly hampered if the community recognizes different sets of expectations for those whom he regards as his patients. However, to make this clear a social distinction between mental health and mental illness, between the mental patient and the normal citizen, not only puts the psychiatrist in the uncomfortable position of revealing the uncertainty of his knowledge about these groups of phenomena; it puts the patient who does not and should not wish to claim considerable disability into a position of grave jeopardy. Psychiatrists usually prefer to visualize human behavior as falling on a spectrum, in which degrees of illness are recognized as gradations between the polar states of ideal health and total collapse, and thus psychiatrists should be acutely sensitive to the dangers of marking some point on this spectrum as the line between health and illness.[11] Many of them hope to provide preventive and other services to those who remain on the healthier end of the spectrum, for example, and will have every reason to resist the implication that those regarded as in some degree "ill" require special social license. At the present state of knowledge, psychiatrists may find it to their advantage if the state of *being sick enough to need help* and the state of *needing exemptions from normal social duties* are not articulated too clearly within the same role.[12]

The second issue is whether or not psychiatry, especially as it branches out into child guidance and preventive psychiatry, can ever support the contention that it remains an ideological branch of medicine. This is not to question who should carry the *legal* responsibilities for treatment of mental disorders, but to consider how effective scientific analogies are for public education. The public's skepticism about psychiatry as a medical tradition, it must be realized, is not simply a consequence of ignorance

[11] See, in this connection, a report by John Spiegel in *Psychiatry, the Press and the Public*, reference footnote 6, pp. 13-18.

[12] This is of outstanding importance in military psychiatry, for instance, where *failure* to offer exemptions to clearly sick persons is often regarded as the best therapeutic measure available. This point was made by Bruce L. Bushard in "The Army's Mental Hygiene Consultation Service," a paper read to the Symposium on Preventive and Social Psychiatry, held under the auspices of the National Research Council and the Walter Reed Army Institute of Research, Washington, D.C., April 15-18, 1957.

or emotional resistance; it has a fairly wide basis in fact and is presented in a framework of fairly sound logic. It cannot be the purpose of this paper to cite the fundamental differences which exist between psychiatric and medical practice on the one hand, and between the mental and medical patient on the other. I am here talking about the *social forms* which the public creates to handle the problem of illness, and considering whether or not a convincing enough logic is available to persuade the public that mental illness belongs to the same social classification as the distinctly organic. Such a logic would have to explain why most medical treatments can become increasingly routinized while psychotherapy must remain individualized and personal. It would have to explain why the objects of physical and mental therapy are basically different, the former restoring the patient to an earlier state of health, the latter changing the very resources with which the patient faces life. Most important, it would have to establish a certain number of predictive criteria, on the basis of which society could estimate the likelihood of recovery in particular cases, the length of treatment required, and the pain or complication the patient could reasonably expect in the meantime. For the sick role is issued by society to help maintain the functional coherence of social processes. It is provisionally assigned, with an implicit expiration date in mind which can be at least vaguely anticipated. To the patient's community, therefore, it is a matter of profound importance whether he asks for a certain period of exemption to recover from an illness or seeks a blank check in order to undergo the uncertainties of psychiatric treatment. The latter instance changes the whole basic relevance of the sick role to the social group which validates its use.

True, psychiatric procedures may, in time, achieve a degree of standardization and a body of knowledge which will make this grouping of medical and mental patients into a single social category reasonable from the public's point of view. Even if one avoids the argument as to whether such a degree of standardization can ever be achieved—or will be good therapeutic practice if it is—it is clear that in the meantime psychiatry's continued attempt to use medical values in the treatment of mental illness may result in continued patient insecurity.

It may then be argued that the time has come for psychiatry to review and perhaps revise its general approach so as to create a more realistic position for the mental patient in society, one which relies less heavily on medical claims and instead takes more firmly into account the social realities that underlie public resistance to the whole ideology of psychiatric practice.

This might call for the sort of re-evaluation which appears to be taking place in certain European treatment centers and is spreading with the growth of the field of social psychiatry. In such centers psychiatrists have joined with social workers, psychologists, and other specialists in the field of social relations to produce a therapeutic atmosphere which relies less on medical analogies than is generally common in the United States. The emphasis seems to be on *re-education* and *resocialization* rather than on therapy, on *development and training* rather than on reintegration of ego processes, on the *therapeutic community* with its roots in outside society rather than on the hospital with its specialized culture. Certain European institutions, notably the day-hospital which has spread throughout England and the Netherlands, expose patients to a schedule in certain respects far nearer to that of a student than that of a medical patient, while special trade schools and training centers, supervised by clinicians, take over a large bulk of the borderline and even chronically psychotic cases which might be permanently hospitalized or neglected altogether in the United States. It may be that this combination of an educational approach to mental illness and its complementary role of *special student* will provide the richest clue to a clear-cut social position for those now regarded as mentally ill.

It must be admitted in conclusion that the sociologist looks at the patient from a special viewpoint, burdening rather slim threads of evidence with heavy arguments and enjoying a speculative freedom which cannot be shared by those who take the actual and continuing responsibility for treating mental illness. However, the clinician's understanding of the therapeutic environment he creates for his patient may be sharpened by the concepts of the social sciences, particularly where these concepts help to view both patient and psychiatry as participants in the cultural context of social life. The sociologist must point out that whenever a psychiatrist makes the clinical diagnosis of an existing need for treatment, society makes the social diagnosis of a changed status for one of its members. And while the clinician must insist that the treatment which follows and the setting provided for it have to be geared to the inner-dynamic realities of the patient's illness, the sociologist proposes that recovery may also depend upon gearing the ongoing treatment to the social realities of the patient's changed status.

21.   The Hospital as a Therapeutic Instrument

Robert A. Cohen

Ever since their creation American mental hospitals have tended to be prison-like in appearance and operation—belying the title "hospital." Prominent features have been, and continue to be, barred windows and locked doors. With rare exception this is almost as true of the small exclusive private ones as the large over-crowded state operated ones. During the past few years the appearance has improved to some extent in that the window bars have been replaced by ingeniously constructed screens; these serve the identical purpose as do the steel bars.

It is even trite to mention that people under these circumstances and regimes can take little responsibility for their own behavior. Perhaps of greater significance is the fact that such bastions may serve to convince the public that "mental illness" is *a thing* which happens to people and will be "fixed" within the hospital.

In the present selection, Dr. Cohen describes two "open-door" hospitals, as they have come to be called, in England. As you will see in *Action for Mental Health* (Selection 24) one of the recommendations of the *Joint Commission* is that "open-door" hospitals be utilized here in the United States.

One of the more important goals of psychotherapy, aside from that of contributing to the relief of the patient's tension and to the furthering of his emotional development, is to provide information concerning the nature of the needs and interpersonal events without which normal personality growth cannot occur. On the basis of such knowledge, treatment methods which have largely developed from empirical experience in relatively inflexible institutional settings can be modified by building into

Psychiatry; 21: 29-35, 1958. Reprinted by special permission of The William Alanson White Psychiatric Foundation, Inc. and by permission of the author. Copyright 1958, The William Alanson White Psychiatric Foundation, Inc. Robert A. Cohen is S.B. Univ. of Chicago 30; Ph.D. and M.D. 35; Asst. in Physiology, Univ. of Chicago 31-35; Clin. Intern, Michael Reese Hosp., Chicago 36-37; House Officer, Henry Phipps Psychiatric Clin. 37-38; Jr. Phys. 38-39, Asst. Phys. 40-41, Sheppard and Enoch Pratt Hosp.; Senior Fellow, Inst. for Juvenile Res., Chicago 39-40; Commander (MC) USNR 41-46; Assoc. Phys., Chestnut Lodge Sanitarium 46-48, Clinical Dir. 48-53; Dir., Clinical Investigations, NIHM 53-. Diplomate, Amer. Board of Psychiatry and Neurology 43. Member, Sigma Xi, Amer. Psychiatric Assoc., Amer. Psychoanalytic Assoc. This is an expanded version of a paper presented at the meeting of the Washington Psychiatric Society on October 25, 1957.

them what has been discovered to be important in the course of intensive psychotherapy.

The Stanton-Schwartz study[1] of the mental hospital ward is an outstanding example of a germinal project in this direction. It was a logical development of the trend which Dexter Bullard started at Chestnut Lodge when he brought Frieda Fromm-Reichmann to the mental hospital to apply psychoanalytic principles to work with psychotic patients, and afforded Harry Stack Sullivan further opportunities for the scope of his studies of interpersonal relations. An early innovation in hospital therapy which resulted from this collaboration was the division of certain therapeutic functions between the psychotherapist and the administrative psychiatrist as inaugurated by Morse and Noble, and by Bullard.[2] In his work with aggressive children at the National Institute of Mental Health, Redl has extended this study of the administrative and intensive psychotherapeutic areas of therapy to include the school and activity programs. He has demonstrated that it is possible to plan interventions in these areas with a degree of sophisticated goal direction equal to that employed in individual psychoanalytic therapy.[3] In the field of child therapy the importance of treating the mother and child simultaneously has long been recognized, but the dynamics of the relationship between the child's symptoms and the parents' personalities were only recently brought to light in the pioneer work of Szurek, Johnson, and their co-workers.[4] More recently these observations from child therapy have been extended in the United States to the study of the schizophrenic patient and his family by Bateson and Jackson, Bowen, Lidz, and Wynne, and of the normal family by Spiegel;[5] in England the Tavistock group has considered like problems.

[1] Alfred H. Stanton and Morris S. Schwartz, The Mental Hospital; New York, Basic Books, 1954.

[2] R. T. Morse and T. D. Noble, "Joint Endeavors of the Administrative Physician and Psychotherapist," Psychiatric Quart. (1942) 16: 578-585. Dexter M. Bullard, "The Application of Psychoanalytic Psychiatry to the Psychoses," Psychoanalytic Rev. (1939) 26: 526-534.

[3] Fritz Redl, "Child Study in a New Setting," Children (1954) 1: 15-20.

[4] S. A. Szurek and Adelaide M. Johnson, "Etiology of Anti-Social Behavior in Delinquents and Psychopaths," J. Amer. Med. Assoc. (1954) 154: 814-817, S. A. Szurek, "The Family and the Staff in Hospital Psychiatric Therapy of Children," Amer. J. Orthopsychiatry (1951) 21: 597-611.

[5] Gregory Bateson, D. D. Jackson, J. Haley, and J. Weakland, "Toward a Theory of Schizophrenia," Behavioral Science (1956) 1: 251-264. M. Bowen, "Family Participation in Schizophrenia," paper presented at the Annual Meeting of the American Psychiatric Association, Chicago, Illinois, May 15, 1957. Ruth W. Lidz and Theodore Lidz, "The Family Environment of Schizophrenic Patients," Amer. J. Psychiatry (1949) 106: 332-345. Lyman Wynne, Irving M. Ryckoff, J. Day, and S. I. Hirsch, "Pseudo-Mutuality in the Family Relations of Schizophrenia," paper presented at the Annual Meeting of the American Psychiatric Association, Chicago, Illinois, May, 1956. John P. Spiegel, "The Resolution of Role Conflict Within the Family," PSYCHIATRY (1957) 20: 1-16.

Perhaps the most dramatic application of knowledge gained from individual therapy to treatment plans has occurred in the armed services. During World War II the first efforts at treatment of those patients with war neuroses who were judged to have favorable prognoses involved sending them to convalescent hospitals in the beautiful but isolated national parks in continental United States. By the end of the war the treatment plan had gradually evolved from a program of relaxation and amusement, through one of work and assigned responsibilities in hospitals located near large cities, and finally to assignment—not on the sick list—with other returning units to retraining commands. By the end of the Korean conflict, treatment which had begun as far away from combat as possible was brought to the front lines; consideration was given to the stress on the combat unit as a whole; psychotherapy was given without admitting the patient to the sick list, and the incidence of hospitalization was cut to a fraction of the World War II figure.

But despite these very substantial applications of principles learned from intensive individual psychotherapy, it is probably still fair to say that most of those who get training in such therapy do not make the broader applications. Some have become professors in medical schools or medical directors of specialized hospitals, but relatively few have returned to the large state hospital or the community mental hygiene clinic where the great mass of psychiatric patients are forced to turn for treatment.

For some years now European psychiatrists have been carrying out interesting innovations in the general area of social psychiatry which, although empirically based, anticipate what may prove to be the natural trend of the work referred to above. As contrasted to the United States, there has been relatively greater attention paid to new uses of existing resources, and less to large-scale efforts to increase the numbers of psychiatrists, nurses, social workers, and other therapeutic personnel. Instead of trying to build more hospitals and to provide more psychotherapy time, efforts are being made—as in current military psychiatry—to see the patient in the community as early as possible, to keep him there as long as possible, and, in those cases to which major therapeutic intervention proves necessary, to return him to the community as soon as possible. Attempts are made to develop and utilize community resources in the treatment plan. Sivadon has described one such effort, Maxwell Jones another, and Querido's program in Amsterdam was recently referred to in an Editorial Note in PSYCHIATRY.[6] From these and other studies, it is

[6] Paul Daniel Sivadon, "Techniques of Sociotherapy," PSYCHIATRY (1957) 20: 205-210. Maxwell Jones, "The Treatment of Personality Disorders in a Therapeutic Community," PSYCHIATRY (1957) 20: 211-220. Editorial Notes: "A Community Psychiatric Program—the Amsterdam Experience," PSYCHIATRY (1956) 19: 95-96.

claimed that these social psychiatric efforts have proved to be unexpectedly promising. Not only are many persons able to carry on without serious difficulties, but a gradual revolution is taking place in the character of the hospital itself. Patients are being given increasing responsibility for the direction of their daily activities; the locked ward is being opened; the atmosphere of the hospital is changing from that of a restrictive custodial institution to one of a rehabilitation center to which patients come voluntarily for help.

I recently had an opportunity to visit two "open-door" hospitals in Great Britain: the Dingleton Hospital at Melrose, Scotland, where George M. Bell is Physician-Superintendent, and the Mapperley Hospital at Nottingham, England, directed by Duncan Macmillan. I am going to devote most of my remarks to a description of Mapperley, mainly because it is a relatively large hospital located in a city with a population of 312,000 and is thus relatively comparable to county and smaller state hospitals in the United States. Dingleton has only 418 beds, is located in a rural area, and is not as favorably situated for the development of an integrated mental health program as is Mapperley. Each hospital has now successfully maintained an open-door policy for a number of years. Apparently they developed in this direction quite independently, although Bell actually has priority, having been, I believe, the first superintendent in Great Britain to break the custodial convention.

Mapperley is the regional mental hospital for the city and county of Nottingham. It is 77 years old, located within the city limits, and has approximately 1,100 beds. Although it receives all patients from the area regardless of the nature and extent of their illness, it has been a completely open hospital without any locked doors for 5 years. Only one committed patient was admitted in 1956; he came from prison and was committed by the court. In 1929 every patient was committed, and most of the wards were locked. During 1956, 1,360 patients were discharged as recovered or improved—this out of a total of 1,554 admissions; 194 patients died during the year, of whom 165 were age 65 or older. Relatively small numbers received insulin or electric shock treatments, and the tranquilizing drugs were used in markedly smaller amounts than is customary in the United States. The admission rate has risen steadily since the open-door policy was instituted: in 1949 there were 540; in 1955 there were 921; and, as stated before, in 1956 there were 1,554. This program is carried out by 13 physicians who, in addition to their hospital work, spend half their time in various clinics outside Mapperley Hospital proper. Their intramural work includes four half-day clinics at Mapperley, and in addition they provide psychiatric services for 30 other half-day clinics in a variety of institutions throughout the city. Among these are marriage counseling and child guidance centers, juvenile delinquency clinics, after-care and rehabilitation units, clinics in each of the general hospitals, plus a steadily growing domiciliary visitation service. As a result of this arrangement, in the past two years relatively few patients have been admitted to Mapperley Hospital without first having been seen by a hospital physician in a clinic away from the hospital. In the case of geriatric patients, the doctor has usually made one or two home visits as well, and such home visits by both a physician and social worker are the next goal of the program for all patients.

Within the hospital, the open-door policy was inaugurated by Macmillan as soon as he became physician-superintendent during the war years; it proceeded gradually but steadily until the last ward was opened in 1951. We discussed at some length the problems which were encountered in bringing this about and the methods employed in meeting them. I shall pass these by, except to mention that he did not open any wards until the nursing staff was ready and willing to do so, in one instance waiting some 6 months—not entirely without applying pressure—beyond the point when he felt the move could have been made.

It is generally felt that the open-door policy has resulted in a remarkable change in the hospital atmosphere. Since patients will not be secluded or kept in the hospital against their will, staff attitudes and procedures have necessarily undergone an almost complete transformation. Problems which were previously dealt with by restraint, transfer to a disturbed ward, or other authoritarian measures must now be resolved by changes in personal relationships between patients and staff. The surrender of the key by the staff has resulted in a different attitude toward patients; and this in turn has altered the patients' traditional attitude toward the hospital and staff. Without much regard for theory or technique, the staff has developed an operational interest and concern in human problems which in the United States is seen most often in the better-staffed teaching or specialized therapeutic institutions.

It is of special significance that in Nottingham the open door has not been a goal in itself, but is rather an essential element in a total attitude toward behavioral problems. While he does not specifically formulate it in this way, Macmillan's approach assumes that disturbed behavior is in large measure a social phenomenon which can be dealt with by altering the dynamics of the social situation. Although he started working within the hospital itself, his goal has been to establish contact with patients as early as possible—even before the behavioral difficulties reach the proportions of mental illness. He also tacitly assumes that extramural management and the maintenance of the patient in his customary social setting is far more desirable than hospitalization. Accordingly, he looks upon the hospital as a link in a chain of treatment settings, one which he uses as sparingly and for as short a time as possible.

Macmillan and his chief social worker took me with them on domiciliary visits to five elderly persons who were having great difficulty, and were disturbing not only their own families but the neighbors as well. Several of these people had been seen previously and had refused either to visit the day hospital or to come into Mapperley for a two-week period of examination and evaluation. Macmillan explained that he preferred to make many such home visits if necessary—the record was 40—rather than force a patient into the hospital. On this occasion, three of the five patients we visited consented to spend their days at the rehabilitation center—to be called for and brought back home each day by the bus. One was finally persuaded to enter the hospital for a two-week period, and one for a four-week stay. In each of these situations my own impulse would have been to suggest indefinite hospitalization, and this, I think, is the clue to an essential aspect of Macmillan's approach. It is his belief, and his experience, that despite considerable organic changes or quite marked stresses in the family relationships, the families and the patients do better with either a limited period of hospital care, or the six- to eight-hour change of routine which is afforded by visits to the day-care center. If at the end of the stipulated two- to four-week period further hospital care is necessary, it is offered, but again with a specified time limit. The idea of indefinite hospitalization has been largely abandoned.

Does this scheme work? It is my impression that it is a highly effective plan, and that it is supplying an increasingly excellent standard of psychiatric care to the community. The hospital has become a community hospital in the true sense of the term. The custodial atmosphere which it must have had ten years ago has largely disappeared. The guidance clinic, the week-end ward, and the after-care centers provide a series of treatment settings which are designed to suit a wide variety of situations and which are particularly effective because the same psychiatric staff is responsible for each of these treatment areas. The social workers attached to the city mental health service come to regularly scheduled staff meetings at the hospital. In turn, the hospital staff consistently utilizes the social work services in outpatient contacts. Each of the hospital nurses has had a three-week assignment to the social work group, and has made domiciliary visits with them. Consequently, there is a strong feeling of unity in the entire staff.

Does this approach really cure mental illness or is it simply an effective method for maintaining the *status quo*? Instead of concentrating ineffective persons in the hospital, are they dispersed throughout the community where each becomes a focus of family tensions? Is the rest of the family group, then, pressed down to a just bearable level of misery in order to achieve an exciting trend in hospital discharge statistics? These are highly pertinent questions which I cannot answer on the basis of a brief visit. The tendency in American psychiatry has been to assume that without psychotherapy there will be little personality growth. According to this view, these patients would tend toward a social recovery, and would remain vulnerable should they be unfortunate enough to encounter difficulties similar to those which precipitated the first illness. Both the Mapperley and Dingleton approaches do contain large measures of support, reassurance, and encouragement. Although the patient is given considerable responsibility for the ordering of his own life and for the continuation of treatment, insight in the conventional sense is not a goal or is there any talk of personality change. But personality change is a concept which derives from intensive individual therapy, and there are difficulties in applying it to the study of social psychiatric methods. And, further, the one approach is probably not to be regarded as a cheap substitute for the other, but rather as a method of treatment with indications and contraindications in its own right.

Perhaps some inferences as to the nature of the results of these particular therapies can be made by a consideration of the personalities of Bell and Macmillan themselves. Macmillan is pleasant, self-contained, and by United States standards rather reserved. Bell is simple, direct, and somewhat more outgoing. In contacts with staff and patients, Macmillan kept some distance, but was very obviously looked up to with respect and with confidence that he knew what he was about. Bell, although not lacking this respect and confidence, had slightly more of the relationship of the trusted family doctor. In terms of my experiences in the United States with men who have instituted innovations and departures from convention, I was surprised to find that neither of the two was aggressive nor did either show the type of self-awareness often found in leaders. The last sentence does not convey just what I mean, nor will this one: Obviously men who have instituted and carried through programs such as these are not ordinary physician-superintendents, yet there was a quality of ordinariness about them. Some people lead by having ideas no one else could ever think of; Macmillan and Bell lead by making one feel that he could have accomplished what they did, only they happened to get the idea first.

I took it as characteristic of Bell that during my visit he called the Admiralty in London to make certain that a patient who was to remain in the hospital a week longer than was originally expected would not be transferred from his old ship when he returned to duty. Then, instead of relaying the affirmative answer through his secretary or a nurse, he took it upon himself to tell the patient personally that the matter had been arranged. He spoke with unhappiness about certain changes which came with the introduction of lay business administrators into the hospital, saying that certain economies which had been instituted cost too much in terms of patients' welfare. At one time he had seen to it that every year each male patient received one suit made to measure and each female patient one dress made to order—I should emphasize that these were inexpensive by United States standards. He felt that this expense was more than justified by the sense of personal importance made-to-measure clothing would bring each patient. Macmillan, in describing his program, did not advance only his own impressions. He showed me reports sent to him by the nurses after their three-week tours with the social work group, each of which he reads and comments on personally.

At the psychiatric congress in Zurich I was chatting about Mapperley with the Commissioner of Mental Hygiene of an American state hospital system. He had visited the hospital for a shorter period than I and was as favorably impressed. However, he felt that such a program could not easily be duplicated in the United States because their nursing and aide staff was of a higher caliber and had more pride in and devotion to the work than was commonly true here. This seems superficially true—but one would expect to find such a group in a setting where the staff's readiness for a program is taken into account in the inauguration of a change; where staff and patients participate in decisions as to changes and improvements in the wards; where the staff gains broader experience through new assignments on which they personally report to the superintendent; and where all levels of staff share in interpreting the hospital to the community. Both Macmillan and Bell shun the limelight more than most pioneers; their leadership has a quality which makes it possible for their staffs to achieve as high a degree of identification with their programs as with them, and to make, and feel that they have made, essential contributions to those programs.

With these remarks I have tried to convey something of the nature of the setting in which these patients are treated. Perhaps one can extrapolate these impressions to gain some idea of the nature of the personality changes which are apt to occur in such a setting. To return first to the question of the impact on the family group of the early return of the patient to the community: the domiciliary visits reminded me vividly of the reports of the centrifugal effect on the family produced typically by the handicapped child. Obviously each of these five families was under considerable stress, and the effectiveness of each member was seriously impaired—hence my impulse to recommend indefinite hospitalization. But the question might legitimately be raised as to whether a ready recourse to prolonged hospitalization is not an acting-out based on identification with the family's despair. Perhaps the open-door policy and the recent work on treatment of the family unit is an attempt to handle this family anxiety therapeutically; when such efforts are successful, it may be that the symptom complex in the patient alters as well. In other words, certain aspects of the patient's illness may not be the cause of the family tensions but either the result of them, or coincident with them.

It is my impression that these treatment programs, as presently organized, do tend to foster transference improvements which are less stable than improvements which result from personality growth. That this might be at least partly true is indicated by the fact that 853 out of the 1,554 admissions to Mapperley in 1956 were readmissions; of these, 183 had been admitted on more than one occasion previously. However, it was Macmillan's feeling that the trend was in a favorable direction; he was willing to accept the possibility that as many as half of his patients might return to the hospital once and that far fewer might return twice, but he believed that the number who would have to return three or more times would be insignificant. And since the community attitude toward the hospital has shifted to a notable degree, such readmissions no longer carry a stigma. There can be no doubt about the fact that he has been able to keep many people in the community who had previously been incarcerated in the hospital, and many of them are engaged in productive work. What remains to be seen is whether there will be further improvement as the recently extended services of the operation begin to exert a noticeable effect in the next few years.

I believe that it would be an error to assume that even the majority of the improvements are essentially social recoveries. This may indeed be true, but I would take seriously the description of the staff given by the Commissioner of Mental Hygiene referred to earlier. It is my impression that the staffs have developed to this level by virtue of the atmosphere I have described, and I assume that equal growth would tend to occur in the patient group. Although these programs are not without flaws, they did impress me as providing to a high degree the types of experience which, from intensive psychotherapy studies, one would consider necessary for optimal personality functioning.

In conclusion, then, I have tried to report some developments in social psychiatry, consideration of which might lead to some useful modifications in traditional procedures. Unfortunately, as in most operating systems, the pressure for service is so great that the recordings at Mapperley and Dingleton are not adequate for a critical research evaluation of results. But the Mapperley program particularly provides an opportunity for research studies which can hardly be equalled elsewhere. These services are well accepted by the community. The opportunity of seeing the patient in his home with his family about him made me realize how much one misses in an office or clinic interview. The unusually well-integrated day-care and after-care plans provide for an extended contact with patients which could make available data concerning the natural history of emotional disorders which cannot be acquired in the clinical settings with which I am familiar. If this type of program could be combined with psychotherapy as offered in many clinics in the United States, one might then achieve a level of psychiatric care superior to any which has yet been attained.

22.   The Society of the Streets

> As you saw in the article *Mental Disorders and Status Based on Race* (Selection 5), the incidence of "mental illness" is highest in the lower classes. Moreover, the manifestations of emotional disturbance are different in people from those classes.
>
> These studies from the booklet *The Society of the Streets* illustrate some of the experimentation which is being conducted in an effort to find ways of dealing with or of providing "treatment" for these people.
>
> Note particularly in the section titled "Experiment in Reform" how radically different the approach is from classical "psychotherapy."

From Gang to Club

The Henry Horner Boys Club is in a public-housing project on Chicago's West Side. In an area where gang violence once was rife, citizens walk the streets unafraid and gang fights have given way to sports events.

The Horner Club has done much to bring about this transformation, not so much by its facilities and activities inside the clubhouse, but by its work on the streets outside. Through an extension program, it has reached out into the neighborhood to bring youngsters into the club, rather than waiting passively for them to join on their own initiative.

Because there were lessons to be learned from the program, and because the neighborhood is typical of many slum districts across the nation where delinquency is a problem, the Ford Foundation in 1960 granted $875,000 to the Chicago Boys Clubs, of which the Horner Club is one, for a six-year experiment in delinquency prevention in three areas.

"As the population of our cities increases," says David R. Hunter, head of the Foundation's youth-development work, "thousands who can afford to do so move to the expanding suburbs. Into the deteriorating sections of real estate they leave behind flock the racial minorities and others who have not made the grade in our competitive society.

The Society of the Streets is a booklet published by the Ford Foundation, Office of Reports, 477 Madison Avenue, New York 22, New York, pages 5-14 and 37-42, June, 1962. Reprinted by permission.

"The adolescents in these areas are victims of a paradox. The goals of our society are predominantly middle-class. Portraying 'the American dream' of unlimited opportunity and material success, movies, newspapers, and television extol the man with wealth, status and education.

"At the same time, society denies slum youngsters the chance to achieve its goals. Middle-class children are brought up to expect success, are helped by their parents to achieve it, and are taught to subordinate present satisfactions to long-range opportunities. But adolescents in depressed urban neighborhoods have little direct contact with successful persons, often lack an adequate family life, and are unsure about finding legitimate ways to achieve recognition.

"Frustrated, these youngsters seek alternative methods of satisfaction. If society will not give them the status they seek, they will look for it within smaller groups with goals they *can* achieve. The values of such groups are often directly contrary to those of society. Status may depend on prowess in gang fights, in flouting authority, and in taking by stealth what cannot be obtained legitimately.

"Foundation-assisted experiments in delinquency control in the slum areas of several big cities are aimed at giving such youngsters legitimate opportunities for life."

The Horner Club, forerunner of the Chicago experiment, consisted in 1956 of three cellar rooms without windows or plumbing. The director at that time, Cressy Larson, began studying the youths in the neighborhood, and trying to talk to them. Most of the boys had quit school, and had little home life. The gang was their refuge from a hostile world.

John Ray, who is still with the club, joined Larson later that year. Within three months he knew a hundred teen-agers by name or sight. Gradually, they began turning to him for advice. He arbitrated their disputes, appeared in court in their behalf, and talked to school principals to help solve some of the youths' problems.

Gang members gradually turned to more constructive forms of activity. Groups gradually transformed themselves and began organizing meetings, dances, and sports events. The club program, for boys aged six to eighteen, added a photography group, summer camp, woodshop, library, and game room. Many gang members returned to high school. Others found jobs and completed their high-school requirements in the club library.

Ray revived an idea successfully introduced by Larson—the Honor Guard, consisting of drill teams with a drum and bugle corps and drum majorette units. Ray found that the drill teams, organized on the basis of existing groups, quickened the transformation of gangs into social clubs.

The boys were proud of their ability to master tricky drill movements. Their skill gave them something they wanted—adult support and praise.

Later, Ray organized a youth council that set behavior standards for social-club affairs. The council received complaints about excessive drinking and other social offenses, and the representative of the club concerned was expected to make sure the offender was disciplined.

Adult groups were also formed. Volunteer drill instructors for the Honor Guard were organized into groups of "fathers of the Guards." The women who met to alter the uniforms for the Guard became a ladies' auxiliary. Soon, adults were sponsoring weekend outings with busloads of children and parents. The Henry Horner Parents Neighborhood Council was set up, with members mainly from the housing project.

Out of this experience came the idea of a resource coordinator who would work for the boys within the community. He would contact local industry to find employment possibilities. He would work with such neighborhood agencies as churches, schools, and the police to develop a joint approach to pressing youth problems. And he would work with such community groups as block organizations and parents' groups.

The Foundation-supported experiment aims at a thorough test of this extension-work effort to provide socially acceptable outlets for the drive and energies of slum-area teen-agers. In addition, a new emphasis is being placed on the organization of community resources to provide jobs and opportunities for personal development.

The experiment covers two test areas besides the predominantly Negro Horner section. One, the Jane Addams Boys Club area, also has Mexican, Italian, and Puerto Rican families. The other, the Lincoln Club area, has Negro, German, Italian, Puerto Rican, and Hungarian groups. Also, three control areas were selected, each similar to one of the test areas in housing, ethnic, and delinquency patterns. A comparison between the test and control areas will measure the experiment's effectiveness.

The Chicago Boys Clubs recruited more extension workers and resource coordinators, not only to test the Horner approach, but also to mobilize other Chicago agencies in a concerted attack on youth problems.

Research, an integral part of the Chicago experiment, is conducted by the University of Michigan. A University sociologist, Hans W. Mattick, is field director of the project—watching, questioning, and collecting and assessing data on the spot. In Ann Arbor, Professor Ronald Lippitt and his staff at the University's Center for Research in Group Dynamics collate the reports, and keep in constant touch with the Chicago staff. If extension work plus community-resource coordination can produce results in three neighborhoods with different racial patterns, the lessons should be applicable to many other cities.

Al Collier of Los Angeles is a Senior Deputy Probation Officer—to the tough teen-agers he deals with every day, "a cop." But, like the social workers in Chicago, Collier and others in the Los Angeles County Probation Department believe that prevention is a sounder long-range solution to delinquency than correction.

"Correction by itself can never keep pace with juvenile delinquency," says Nort Sanders, director of the Department's Delinquency Prevention Service Office. "Crime and violence are commonplace in our slums. We estimate that at least 20,000 teen-agers belong to street gangs. Marijuana, heroin, and illegally-obtained barbiturates are widely used."

Collier heads Group Guidance, a specialized service in which twelve deputy probation officers work with the hard-core city gangs that are not handled by conventional youth-serving agencies. Since it started in 1943, Group Guidance has centered on three basic goals: establishing an individual-counseling relationship with gang members; using this relationship in influencing the gang; and introducing family and neighborhood influences directly into work with gangs.

In approaching a gang, a Group Guidance deputy begins with an activity program to attract and hold the interest of its members. He gradually gets to know the gang members as individuals and tailors his activities to their needs. He is available equally to gang members, police, parents, and school and other agency personnel. As his influence increases, the orientation of the gang changes, organized sports and social activities increase, and, hopefully, delinquency and gang conflicts lessen.

Group Guidance also works with parents of the gang members—with varied success. "The parents proved much more difficult to work with than the youth," one officer reported. "They wanted to blame everyone but themselves for the gang activity their youth became involved in—the deputy sheriffs, the school officials, and, most of all, the rival gang." But Group Guidance presses home the fact that parents can handle many of the youngsters' problems.

Although Collier's deputies are not social workers in the ordinary sense, they receive training to deal with sociological problems. "Also," says Collier, "a lot of training comes on the job. If a deputy has an affinity for working with gang members, he'll learn to deal with them on their own level. And no amount of theoretical training will tell you how to deal with a kid who comes at you with a knife."

Furthermore, a deputy is what the sociologists call an "unambiguous authority figure." "These kids respect the masculine image," Collier states. "They know where they are. First, they know the deputy is a cop. But they also think, 'Here is a cop who likes me.'"

The point is especially important for the many youths who come from homes without fathers. Gang activity, some authorities claim, is due partially to a "compulsive masculinity," an acting out of the male role that has no counterpart in the home. If this is true, a strong male authority figure could be an important influence in reducing delinquency.

This is one of the points to be evaluated in a four-year experiment supported by the Ford Foundation. A $133,000 grant to the Los Angeles Probation Department will test the Group Guidance approach in one of the toughest areas of the city. Gang trouble is expected to become more severe unless steps are taken to deal with it. To ensure a thorough test, the number of Group Guidance workers in the area will be increased. Researchers will collect data on delinquency rates in the area and compare them with other areas of Los Angeles County.

The deputies will concentrate on "building bridges" between gang members and neighborhood institutions and agencies. They will also work with parents' groups to stimulate family interest in the youths' welfare, and will help gang members find jobs and recognize employment as a desirable objective.

Experiment in Reform

A dozen boys troop into the basement of a house near the Brigham Young University campus in Provo, Utah. They have spent the day digging ditches, and all wear heavy, mud-stained boots. They are healthy and tanned from prolonged work out of doors. They take their places on couches and a few straight-backed chairs. LaMar T. Empey, associate professor of sociology at the University, switches on a tape recorder, the signal for an unusual meeting to begin.

The boys are part of an experiment in rehabilitation that has so far shown chances of success beyond normal correction methods. Adjudged delinquent by a court, these youths—instead of being sent to a reformatory or placed on probation—have been assigned to "the Pinehills program." They live at home and work on city projects, such as tree-planting, litter-clearing, and street maintenance. Late every afternoon they attend a meeting at the house in the Pinehills area for a discussion of their problems.

Unlike reformatory inmates, the youths are not told how much time they will spend in the Pinehills program. Indeed, a boy's first impression is one of bewilderment at the absence of regulation. He soon finds that he cannot earn his release by outwardly conforming to a set of rules, because there are no apparent rules to conform to. He learns that the only way out is through the group meeting. He must prove, not only to the authorities but also to his fellow delinquents, that he is fit to be released. The final decision is theirs.

The method was pioneered at the Highfields Residential Group Center in New Jersey and is known as the "Highfields approach." To test the effectiveness of the method, the Ford Foundation made a grant of $182,000 to Brigham Young University for a six-year experiment. Similar Foundation-sponsored experiments are being carried out in Kentucky and New Jersey.

"The Highfields and Pinehills approaches are based on the view that, while some delinquents need personal psychotherapy, most are members of a delinquent system with its own values," Professor Empey says. "They rely on this system to give them recognition they cannot obtain in the larger society, where even the schools regard them as undesirable.

"Hence the problem: to bring the delinquent to accept the conventional system by making the delinquent and conventional alternatives clear and by making the conventional system have some value for him."

The meeting at Pinehills illustrates how delinquents may be brought along this path. The center of discussion today is Joe, a rebellious fifteen-year-old. He has been in the program for two months, and has apparently made little progress in changing his antagonistic attitude toward society. Joe is sullen, not too talkative. He is sure of only one thing—he doesn't want to be rejected by the program and sent to Ogden, the state industrial school, where he would be kept inside the walls.

Professor Empey usually says little at these meetings. Occasionally he subtly guides the discussion to keep it on the subject, but normally he is content to let the youths carry the ball.

In this case, the group is generally critical of Joe's behavior since he entered the Pinehills program. As one of them puts it: "He should drop his tough-guy role." The group thinks that Joe has a chip on his shoulder, that he is overaggressive because he has to prove something. Several point out that he is unfriendly—they have tried to talk to him while on a work project and he hasn't given them a civil answer. They say Joe "messes around," and does nothing to help later arrivals at Pinehills.

Joe is puzzled. He admits he is a "tough guy." Other boys were tough with him, so he naturally had to defend himself. Gradually, in self-defense as he sees it, he built his reputation, and the boys he has beaten in a fair fight now show him respect. What happens if he gives up being a "tough guy"? To Joe, the answer is obvious: He will lose the respect of the boys he has beaten and will have to fight them all over again.

Joe is in a dilemma as the meeting ends: Change his ways or be sent to Ogden—either seems a distasteful prospect. But the session has at least pinpointed Joe's problem, and it is now out in the open. The chances are good that it will eventually be solved, for studies show that delinquents discharged from the Pinehills program return to their old habits less often than those discharged from conventional reform institutions.

Delinquents at Pinehills are from fifteen to seventeen years of age, and are all repeated offenders. Their crimes include vandalism, shoplifting, car theft, and burglary. Up to twenty boys are assigned to the program at one time; when one leaves, another is assigned to the group. The length of stay is usually from five to eight months. In addition to taking part in discussion sessions, some boys work and others attend school.

From the start, each delinquent is forced to turn to the other boys for guidance since the adult staff members deliberately offer little help. The boy is surprised to find that his fellows demand complete honesty; if he is not honest, the other youths interpret it as a lack of faith in their discretion. Before they will help him solve his problems, they require him to disclose his entire delinquent history. This usually means telling much more than is known to police and court.

Furthermore, the boy sees that he must either make a sincere effort to change or be sent to a reformatory. Like Joe, he becomes worried. He has access to no adult counseling, only to the group. He becomes confused and hostile. The program staff considers this a *good* sign. The boy is *not* in command of the situation, and is therefore amenable to change. In terms of the theory described above, the boy is unsure that the delinquent system can furnish what he really wants. He is being forced into a comparison of the delinquent and conventional systems.

The group discussion permits the boy to vent his feelings of anger and hostility and gives the group a chance to analyze his behavior. Eventually, the meetings enable the group to decide whether his attitude is changed sufficiently to warrant his release.

After release, the boy continues to meet with members of his group, who help him solve new problems and serve as a check on his behavior. Efforts are made to keep him in school and teach him a trade. If he leaves school, a citizens' advisory council tries to find the boy a job.

The Pinehills experiment is being evaluated by continuous research, interviews, and questionnaires. The progress of delinquents who have been through the Pinehills program is being compared with that of two control groups—one on probation, the other in a reformatory—selected at random by Judge Monroe J. Paxman of Utah County Juvenile Court.

The results so far indicate that the program is not only cheaper but more effective than the reformatory system as a method of rehabilitation.

23. Daytop Lodge—A New Treatment Approach for Drug Addicts

Joseph A. Shelly and Alexander Bassin

Drug addiction, classified as one of the Character Disorders or Conduct Disorders, has defied conventional means of treatment. In the middle of the 1930's, narcotic addiction was recognized officially as an "illness" with the creation of the United States Public Health Service Hospitals at Lexington, Kentucky, and Fort Worth, Texas. In the intervening years, thousands of narcotic addicts have received treatment based upon the "medical model." As these authors point out, the results have been dismal.

The study reported here commits major violence on the "medical model," but the results appear to be promising—see particularly "Postscript 1969" at the end of this selection.

Mr. Shelly is Chief Probation Officer, the Supreme Court, Brooklyn, while Dr. Bassin, formerly on the staff of the Civic Center there, is now at Florida State University.

It hardly seems necessary to beat kettledrums of alarm about the seriousness of the drug addiction problem. Let it suffice to note that at the White House Conference on Narcotic and Drug Abuse, Mayor Wagner of New York startled the gathering by estimating that the city's addicts steal up to a billion dollars worth of merchandise a year to support their habit. In other words, an addict constitutes a one-man crime wave, committing burglaries, larcenies, frauds and/or prostitution to acquire the wherewithal to engage in a strictly cash-on-the-barrelhead business transaction, the purchase of narcotics.

Addicts fill about half the cells of the New York Penitentiary on Riker's Island. They constitute a sizable percentage of the population of the state prisons. They pillage and plunder the community. Their activities deteriorate neighborhoods, impoverish families and demoralize parents, wives and children.

Thus far, efforts to treat this disorder by conventional means have been consistently and grossly ineffective. Riverside Hospital, a New York facility for adolescent addicts, in operation for a decade, has been able to report only a handful of abstainers over a five-year period, leading some

Corrective Psychiatry and Journal of Social Therapy, 11: 186-195, #4, 1965. Reprinted by permission of the authors and the Journal.

wag to estimate that each cure cost close to a million dollars. Statistics emanating from the U.S. Public Health Service Hospitals at Lexington, Kentucky, and Fort Worth, Texas, are equally discouraging. Followup studies indicate that many addicts do not display the simple decency— merely out of respect for the $40-a-day treatment taxpayers provide for them at these excellent medical facilities, if nothing else—of at least waiting 48 hours after their release before taking an initial shot of heroin.

Nevertheless, probation departments have a reality problem in this area. Despite the fearfully poor prognosis, men are placed on probation and they almost invariably start "chipping" (occasional usage) on weekends, gradually building up an increased dependence on drugs until they are fully hooked and thoroughly committed to the whirlwind of crime and depredation to support their habit.

Several years ago we heard of the use of Nalline by the correction authorities on the West Coast to provide early detection of the use of heroin, and we reasoned that perhaps such a system of examination of probationers would enable us to determine at an early stage of usage what the situation was so that remedial steps could be taken to nip the habit before it devastated the user. Furthermore, we reasoned that, if the probationer became aware that our department had a surefire means of detection, he would be less inclined to start experimenting with the use of drugs.

To obtain funds for such an experiment we proposed to the National Institute of Mental Health that a program of Nalline testing be initiated. Dr. Carl Anderson replied with the suggestion that (a) there might be a better detection procedure than Nalline; thin-layer chromatography, for example, and (b) perhaps we should consider the use of a halfway house as a therapeutic community to alter the addict's value system.

At Dr. Anderson's suggestion, we made a study of the treatment and detection procedures throughout the United States. In the company of the eminent criminologist, Dr. Herbert A. Bloch of Brooklyn College, and a psychiatrist with many years' experience in attempting to treat drug addicts, Dr. Daniel Casriel, we visited facilities in different parts of the country but found nothing particularly impressive. Nothing at all, that is, until we came upon the somewhat down-at-the-heel, offbeat operation on the West Coast called Synanon, which made a deep impression on us. We examined the procedures employed at that institution and decided that some of the features could be incorporated into a small facility operated under the auspices of a court bureaucracy.

A number of the free-flowing, spontaneous aspects of Synanon could not be grafted into the somewhat rigid corpus of a court structure. We finally hammered out a research proposal which we trusted would enable us (a) to establish a halfway house for the treatment of drug addicts on probation, (b) to evaluate the rehabilitative effects of such an institution in comparison with results of supervising drug addicts on probation in a small specialized caseload and a large general caseload, (c) to formulate and operate a program of activity designed to provide the addict in the halfway house with a value system and status organization leading to his eventual and reasonably speedy integration into normal society, (d) to employ a testing procedure, thin-layer chromatography, to quantify the progress of an abstinence program among the subjects involved in this experiment and to determine if this chemical procedure may perhaps of itself be an inhibitory mechanism in keeping the addict from returning to the use of narcotics.

NIMH, on the heels of the White House conference, provided a grant of $390,000 to be expended over a five-year period for this purpose. As many before us involved in demonstration research have discovered, we found that there is many a slip between the neat promulgation of a program within the safe covers of a document and its eventual execution in the tough world of reality. Real estate was our first problem. We finally located a white elephant millionaire's mansion consisting of 20 rooms in a suburban section of the New York area on a seven-acre wooded lot overlooking Raritan Bay. But our difficulties with real estate paled to insignificance when we began to wrestle with the problem of management.

During the first year we went through some four managers, all of whom were well-meaning but who simply expired under the strain of attempting to cope with the population of the most skillful manipulators, liars and con-men our civilization seems to be able to produce. Nevertheless, despite ups and downs and a daily crisis situation, the project seemed to be doing well. In contrast with most prison and hospital situations, our men impressed all, including even their closest relatives, as having become remarkably friendly, outgoing, self-possessed. We administered thin-layer chromatography examinations regularly and, although occasionally we obtained a positive or questionable test finding, we were able to resolve most of the situations without difficulty. Because of "splits" (unauthorized departures) we were unable during the first year of operation to obtain the 25 residents the program permitted. As a new probationer was admitted, another resident would depart for one reason or another.

But our over-all evaluation of the situation, the undeniable spirit of hope and confidence that we observed at every visit, gave us the confident spirit that we were on the road to pioneering a new and significant treatment methodology for the addict.

Last October we were finally able to obtain the services of a Synanon graduate, David Deitch, who had a history of some 14 years of heroin addiction. Deitch installed two assistants, fellow drug addicts he had trained at Synanon, and with his bride of a few months, Sue, a wonderfully warm-hearted girl of 24, a graduate of Brandeis University, who became acquainted with Deitch when he was director of the Westport facility of Synanon, moved in as the new manager of Daytop Lodge.

Intake Interview

All features of our treatment approach were described in the original proposal to NIMH, but seemed to take on new meaning and direction under the supervision of Deitch. The first step in the basic process occurs when it is established that a particular defendant meets the basic eligibility requirements for admission to Daytop Lodge. He is presented to the judge on the basis of a presentence investigation with a recommendation that he be given an opportunity to attempt to enter our research facility. We explain to the judge that we have no control over the operation; it is entirely up to the man to prove to the management of the halfway house that he sincerely wishes to give up the habit and reform. The man is released from jail, makes his way across the street to our office, where he receives a short interview, a hand-written copy of directions for reaching Daytop and a dollar bill to cover his expenses on the way.

When the man arrives at Daytop, after a ferry and bus ride, he is usually told to sit on a chair in a veranda, and he usually remains there with no one speaking to him for as long as two hours. He finds himself in the midst of the easy-going camaraderie of men, but he observes that the atmosphere is completely different from what he has experienced in the past in hospitals, prisons and other institutions. What shakes him the most, however, is to see former associates with whom he might have shot up in alleyways, perhaps sharing the same spike, who seem not to see him, who look through him as if he were not there. He remains sitting before an open, unlocked door, but somehow does not get up to leave. He thus passes successfully the first step in the initiation procedure to enter the Daytop fraternity.

Finally, the applicant is called into the office for an interview. The office is comfortably furnished but without a desk or other appurtenances of status. Instead, there is only a large coffee table with books and papers on it, couch and soft chairs around it. Three clean-cut, conventionally dressed young men start questioning him in a kindly, sympathetic manner. Within a few minutes, the addict feels that he is at long last in control of the situation. These are obviously social worker types whom he can con out of their back teeth. They let him continue without interruption for several minutes before one of them brings him up short.

"Hey, stop this garbage. Who do you think you're talking to!"

The two interviewers speak to each other: "Did you ever hear such s--t in your life!"

"This dope fiend thinks he's inside another joint."

"He didn't get enough affection and love from his mudder and fodder, I bet."

They continue to ridicule the now devastated addict before beginning a "cleanup" operation. They explain they are not social workers, as he had obviously thought, who can be fooled, bamboozled and conned. On the contrary, they are reformed addicts who only a short time before would have behaved exactly as he did. But now they are living in an environment where honesty, reliability and responsibility are the watchwords. Here one gets nothing for nothing. You have to earn everything. You can lie and cheat no more.

During the early orientation interviews, the addict will repeatedly be advised that, despite his physical stature and chronological age, he is a child in terms of maturity, responsibility and ability to think ahead. He will be regarded as a 3-year-old who must be told what to do with the expectation that if he disobeys he will be punished promptly. The whole design of the program is to help him grow from a child of 3 to an adult. We have only one year available for this progress, so he'll have to work hard if he wants to make it. On the other hand, if he wishes to return to chasing the bag, to be a childish addict, to die in some gutter from an o.d., that would be his decision.

Finally, the newcomer is advised that we have little confidence in the usual preoccupation of social workers, psychologists and psychiatrists with the finding of the essential *cause* of his addiction. The addict uses the professional to slough off responsibility for his behavior. The personnel at Daytop does not permit the addict to blame for his behavior his parents, the school, the neighborhood, associates or society. The only cause recognized at Daytop for being an addict is STUPIDITY.

In other words, the concept of the drug addict as an ill person and therefore automatically entitled to the recognized prerogatives of the role of the ill in our society in terms of sympathetic understanding, special concern, leniency and forgiveness is vehemently fought as an ideology.

"Did anybody force you to stick a dirty needle into your arm and inject yourself with milk sugar?" the addict is challenged. "Was it your father or mother who insisted you shoot up? Was it the tough cop on the beat? Was it your girl friend or school teacher?"

If the addict attempts to extricate himself from his tendency to throw blame in all directions, the resident and staff bring him to the reality of his behavior: that he alone is to blame and the only tenable explanation for his behavior is simple, unadulterated stupidity on his part.

The Resocialization Process Continues

After his initial interview, the defendant is introduced to some senior members of the house who shake him down from head to toenails with the thoroughness of experts. He is advised that from this point onward, so long as he wishes to remain in the Lodge, he may not make any phone calls, write any letters, receive mail or possess money without specific permission. All these steps are necessary to help him be reformed and become a man. On the other hand, he is not held in the Lodge by force. He can leave any time he wants to. There are no bars on the windows or locks on the doors. "We don't need you, you need us!" he is told over and over.

At the same time the newcomer receives this orientation, his family obtains some astonishing advice: For the time being, they are to become as cold, rejecting and hostile to the defendant as they possibly can. If he telephones, they are not to answer; if he sneaks out a letter, they should return it unopened to Daytop Lodge; if he appears at their home with the pitiful, woebegone, contrite attitude the addict knows so well how to assume and starts to make excuses for leaving the Lodge, they are to say: "Go back to Daytop. Get lost. We have nothing to say to you," and slam the door in his face.

Group Therapy by Authentic Encounters

The principal formal medium for effecting value and behavioral changes is a variety of group therapy sessions called group encounters. These are compulsory for all residents and are held three times a week in the evening from 8 to 9:30. The population of the house is divided in groups of three with an approximately even number of no more than 10 at each session. The composition of the group is changed for every session and any house member may request he be included in an encounter with any specific other residents. Or, if the member demands it, an emergency encounter may be scheduled on only a few minutes' notice.

How do these sessions materially differ from conventional group therapy? In the first place, there is no formal leader, but each group includes at least one member trained and experienced in this form of group interaction. Second, the search for elusive primary causes for addiction based on some alleged childhood trauma or deprivation is hooted down as a waste of time and a maneuver on the part of the participant to avoid facing his problems. Third, the resident's behavior in specific terms become the subject of discussion and criticism rather than events of decades ago. Finally, every member is expected to react spontaneously on a visceral level employing, if he feels the need for it, the crudest terminology and vehement verbal expression. The group concentrates on reaching a "gut level" with the intent of having participants react at a rock bottom emotional level rather than on the intellectual plane that is so frequently characteristic of conventional group therapy.

The vehemence of these interchanges is hard to believe. Four-letter epithets and gutter language bounce off the walls as the participants engage in the process of "ungluing" a man to make him open to the possibility of basic change. The members examine each other and are critical about the extent to which they are adhering to the basic precepts of the house for remaking themselves into honest, decent, conscientious human beings. They remind each other that they are trying to become worthwhile people free of the criminal code of the street and prepared to accept the square values about the primary goodness of hard work, decent relations with one's fellows, concern about the welfare of his brothers. The primary rules of the house are: 1. No drugs or alcohol of any type. 2. No physical violence. 3. No shirking of responsibility. These are repeated so that no newcomer has the excuse that he didn't know the law. If a dispute develops during the day, the contenders are expected to maintain their decorum until the opportunity to square off at a group encounter arrives. The group meeting is repeatedly presented to the residents as a "pressure cooker" for fast personality change, as well as the safety valve for house arguments.

The process of indoctrination started during the admission procedure continues throughout the residence of the addict. At least a dozen times a day the newcomer hears someone tell him that the group is antidrug, antialcohol and anticrime. He is reminded that, like a 3-year-old child, he may not be permitted outside the building alone because he could get killed. He must check in and out at the desk and leave only with the permission of a coordinator in the company of a senior resident. He is not to speak to newcomers and at the beginning he must realize that, as an addict, the only thing he really knows how to do is to shoot dope and to go to prison.

The newcomer is forbidden to engage in the type of conversation that constitutes 90% of the verbal intercourse that takes place in the usual institutional setting of drug addicts. He may not express any sympathy for the code of the street, which calls on a criminal to remain silent about the antisocial activities of his peers. He is expected to apply an honor code that is stricter in many respects than the one imposed at West Point. The law of the street, which forbids squealing, finking and bearing tales, the resident is advised, may be appropriate for dope-shooting addicts and criminals, but here at the Lodge we are involved in saving lives, and any member who fails to assume responsibility for straightening out a tottering brother is endangering that man's salvation as well as the fate of the entire enterprise. On this score, it is not sufficient for a resident to abstain from violating any of the tenets of the organization himself. On the contrary, he is expected to bring up at the thrice-weekly encounter meetings a critique of a fellow member who may be careless about such a triviality as washing his coffee cup in order to gain practice in informing the environment when a fellow resident is thinking of leaving to return to the use of drugs. A man may be censured for not calling an emergency fireplace meeting to discuss the waywardness of a buddy who seems to be "in a bag," involved in morbid self-analysis instead of working for the welfare of all.

The Seminar Meetings

Residents at Daytop Lodge are provided an opportunity to deal with abstract and sometimes highly philosophical material in the course of the daily seminar sessions, which take place after lunch. A passage from Ralph Waldo Emerson, for example, may be written on the blackboard and members in turn get up and react to the material on an extemporaneous level.

To continue the resocialization process, every Saturday night a party is held to which outsiders are invited. The residents mingle with the guests and practice their newly acquired skills in social relations. Students from colleges and universities within a radius of 50 miles are frequent visitors at these get-togethers.

The Status Ladder

The management of Daytop Lodge is involved in the operation of a carefully formulated status system in which ascendancy is gained by displaying the virtues of old-fashioned hard work, integrity, honesty and concern for the well-being of one's fellow men. The length of time in which a resident has remained "clean" is a primary factor in moving up the status ladder. The resident manager, with the help of his two assistants, is on a constant lookout for developing the potential of each member and the prospects for moving up are constantly discussed at the group encounters and even during casual conversations during the day.

SPECIAL MEETINGS AND PROCEDURES

Probe sessions are held from time to time to analyze some particular problem or difficulty that might have been developing. For example, since the composition of the house is almost equally divided between white, Negro and Puerto Ricans, meetings of the various ethnic groups may be held under the leadership of the resident manager to discuss any stresses that may be related to matters of bias and discrimination.

Formal role-training sessions, at which members are provided with a chance to try out various situations they may encounter in the community, constitute a favorite form of teaching.

Promotion to the procurement team, which has the duty of visiting community merchants in an effort to obtain donations of items not available under terms of the grant, is another form of therapeutic endeavor.

The house is now experimenting with the most intensive form of group therapy, a *Marathon Encounter*, which is planned to last for 24 hours, during which members will continue in constant interaction to reach, as Deitch expresses it, "the most fundamental of gut levels."

We have been approached by the city administration to assist in the establishment of a Daytop Lodge type of program involving a minimum of 300 addicts, with the possibility of reaching a maximum of 1,000, to be housed within a complex to be called Daytop Village. We are inclined to feel that the larger number of residents will provide a richer environment, including the presence of females, for the dynamics leading to personality change and speedier maturation to occur.

POSTSCRIPT 1969:

Daytop Lodge opened in September, 1963; by the middle of December, 1965, sixty-two probationers had been admitted. Some data are available about this group in an article entitled "Daytop Lodge—A Two Year Report" which can be found in a U.S. Department of Health, Education, and Welfare publication, *Rehabilitating the Narcotic Addict*, issued by the U.S. Government Printing Office in February, 1966. In the meantime, a final research report was submitted to the National Institute of Mental Health in February, 1969.

24. Action for Mental Health

The Joint Commission on Mental Illness and Health is a multidisciplinary, non-profit organization representing thirty-six national agencies concerned with mental health and welfare. By unanimous resolution of the United States Congress in 1955, the Commission was authorized to conduct a study of the mental health of the nation and to present to Congress, the United States Surgeon General and the fifty governors a report of its findings and its recommendations for possible federal and state mental health programs.

This article is a condensation of *Action for Mental Health* the 100,000 word final report of the Commission.

This digest deals primarily with major mental illness, or psychoses, or schizophrenia—in a broad sense somewhat synonymous labels.

The report *Action for Mental Health* is perhaps the most important document ever published as far as mental illness is concerned for it will more than likely serve as a major guide for years to come. Indeed, as you have already seen (Selection 13) it has already led to the creation of community mental health centers. As noted in previous selections, the report has been properly criticized by many, but such criticisms should not detract from some of the major recommendations.

The Mental Health Study Act of 1955 directed the Joint Commission on Mental Illness and Health, under grants administered by the National Institute of Mental Health, to analyze and evaluate the needs and resources of the mentally ill people of America and make recommendations for the national mental health program.

The purpose of this final report is to arrive at a program that would approach adequacy in meeting the needs of the mentally ill—to develop a plan of action, in other words, that would satisfy us that we are doing the best we can toward their recovery.

The latter is not at present the case. We have not been able to do our best for the mentally ill to date, nor have we been able to make it wholly clear what keeps us from doing so. Attempts to provide more humane care for the mentally ill and to transform "insane asylums" into hospitals and clinics true to the healing purpose of medicine have occurred periodically during the last two centuries. While each reform appears to have

Under no circumstance, does the Digest constitute an appropriate substitute for the thoughtful and extensive analysis to be found in ACTION FOR MENTAL HEALTH. For documentation of statements in this Digest, the interested reader is referred to the full work, published by Basic Books Incorporated, 59 Fourth Avenue, New York, N.Y. 10003.

gained sufficient ground to give its supporters some sense of progress, each has been rather quickly followed by backsliding, loss of professional momentum, and public indifference.

Even if we can find the road to a substantial reduction in the human and economic problems of mental illness, we are obliged to remain in full view of certain intervening observations that provide little cause for hope except as we can dispose of them. We must note, for instance, the curious blindness of the public as a whole and of psychiatry itself to what in reality would be required to fulfill the well publicized demand that millions of mentally ill shall have sufficient help in overcoming the disturbances that destroy their self-respect and social usefulness.

Further, we must rise above our self-preservative functions as members of different professions, social classes, and economic philosophies and illuminate the means of working together out of mutual respect for our fellow man. We each have a responsibility that is common to all—our responsibility as citizens of a democratic nation founded out of faith in the uniqueness, integrity and dignity of human life.

Why Has Care of the Mentally Ill Lagged?

The United States Congress, in the last ten years, has given the American public a working demonstration of a new willingness to accept leadership and responsibility in active efforts to help citizens who are threatened by mental illness. The federal government's chief exemplifications of this demonstration may be found in the programs of the National Institute of Mental Health and the Veterans Administration. The good example has been followed in the efforts of state legislatures, governors, and their public health, mental health, and public welfare agencies in many states.

It is tempting to congratulate ourselves on the gains scored—in increased amounts of money spent for mental health research, in the increases in mental health personnel, in the beneficial effects of the new drugs. But the demand for public mental health services is still largely unmet, despite the gains.

One of the most revealing findings of our mental health study is that comparatively few of 277 state hospitals—probably no more than 20 per cent—have participated in innovations designed to make them therapeutic, as contrasted to custodial, institutions. Our information leads us to believe that more than half of the patients in most state hospitals receive no active treatment of any kind designed to improve their mental condition. This is the core problem and unfinished business of mental health. Eight of every ten mental hospital patients are in state institutions. These hospitals carry a daily load of more than 540,000 patients, and look after nearly a million in a year's time.

Commonly, a clearly defined, well established public demand and need for a particular health program is sufficient to stimulate aggressive public action toward its support and progressive steps to organize whatever high-quality facilities may be needed. Quick responsiveness in meeting the demand is not characteristic in the mental illness field, however.

Mental illness, commonly regarded as America's No. 1 health problem, ranked fourth in the categorical interests of the National Institutes of Health in 1950, as measured by dollars spent; by 1960, it had risen to second, behind cancer (see Table 1). The gains of the voluntary cam-

TABLE 1   TOTAL APPROPRIATIONS OF CONGRESS FOR MAJOR ACTIVITIES
OF THE NATIONAL INSTITUTES OF HEALTH, 1950-1961*
(IN MILLIONS OF DOLLARS)

Fiscal Year	Cancer	Mental Health	Heart	General			
1950	$ 18.9	$ 8.7	$ 10.7	$ 12.0	(Arthritis, Allergy and Infectious		
1951	20.0	9.5	14.2	14.3	Diseases, Neurology and Blindness		
1952	19.6	10.5	10.0	15.7	became separate categories in 1954.)		
1953	17.9	10.9	12.0	16.6	*Arthritis*	*Allergy*	*Neurology*
1954	20.2	12.1	15.2	4.7	$ 7.0	$ 5.7	$ 4.5
1955	21.7	14.1	16.7	4.7	8.2	6.1	7.6
1956	25.0	18.0	18.9	5.9	10.8	7.8	9.9
1957	48.4	35.1	33.4	12.1	15.9	13.2	18.7
1958	56.4	39.2	35.9	14.0	20.3	17.4	21.3
1959	75.3	52.4	45.6	29.0	31.2	24.0	29.4
1960	91.2	68.1	62.2	46.0	46.9	34.0	41.4
1961	111.0	100.9	86.9	83.9	61.2	44.0	56.6
Totals	$555.6	$379.5	$361.7	$258.9	$201.5	$152.2	$189.4

* Source: D.H.E.W.-P.H.S.-National Institutes of Health Operating Appropriations by Activity, 1950 through 1961. From Office of the Director, N.I.M.H.

paign have not been commensurate, however. Voluntary mental health funds ranked eighth at the beginning and seventh at the end of the period, and were eighth in grand total, as shown in Table 2.

Over a ten-year period, poliomyelitis had the greatest public appeal, followed by tuberculosis, cancer, heart disease, crippled children, cerebral palsy, muscular dystrophy, and mental health, in that order.

Despite the repeated snakepit exposés and the great amount of attention given to mental illness by the press, surveys have shown that mental illness has had a lower reader impact than has heart disease, cancer, or polio.

Despite the "big push" in recent years to do something about major mental illness, the average proportion of general state expenditures and of state health expenditures going for the care of mental hospital patients actually declined.

TABLE 2   TOTAL FUNDS RAISED NATIONALLY IN TEN LEADING VOLUNTARY HEALTH CAMPAIGNS, 1950-1959*

(IN MILLIONS OF DOLLARS)

	Polio	TB	Cancer	Heart	Crippled Children	Cerebral Palsy	Muscular Dystrophy	Mental Health[b]	Arthritis	Multiple Sclerosis
1950	30.8	21.0	13.9	4.1	5.8	1.0	(a)	(c)	0.7	0.18
1951	33.5	21.7	14.6	5.5	6.1	2.1	(a)	0.7	1.0	0.19
1952	41.4	23.2	16.4	6.7	6.7	4.0	0.26	0.6	1.0	0.25
1953	51.4	23.8	19.8	8.5	7.7	6.4	0.6	0.7A	1.4	0.45
1954	65.0	24.0	21.7	11.3	8.1	8.2	4.0	1.7A	1.5	0.8
1955	52.5	24.6	24.4	13.6	8.5	7.5	3.9	2.4	1.8	1.3
1956	51.9	25.8	27.2	17.5	9.8	8.1	3.0	2.6	2.2	2.0
1957	44.0	26.3	29.6	20.5	10.3	8.4	3.7	3.8	2.4	2.3
1958	35.4	26.0	29.7	22.3	10.4	9.2	4.9	4.5	3.0	2.5
1959	31.3B	26.0	31.0B	24.0	10.3	9.5	4.6	5.5B	3.6	(d)
Total	437.2	242.4	228.3	134.0	83.7	64.4	24.96	22.5	18.6	9.97

* "Rough" figures supplied by National Information Bureau for
(1) National Foundation, (2) National Tuberculosis Association, (3) American Cancer Society, (4) American Heart Association, (5) National Association for Crippled Children and Adults, (6) United Cerebral Palsy Association, (7) Muscular Dystrophy Association of America, (8) National Association for Mental Health, (9) Arthritis and Rheumatism Foundation, (10) National Multiple Sclerosis Society.

(a) No campaign.
(b) Figures for 1951 and 1952 from National Information Bureau, for 1953-1959 from National Association for Mental Health.
(c) Not available.
(d) Not available.
E: Estimate.
A: Approximate.

TABLE 3 MOVEMENT OF PATIENT POPULATION IN PUBLIC MENTAL HOSPITALS, UNITED STATES, 1956-1959

Item	1956	1957	1958	1959	1956 -1957	% Change 1957 -1958	1958 -1959
All admissions	185,597	194,497	209,503	223,225	4.8	7.7	6.5
First admissions	125,539	129,278	137,061	142,881	3.0	6.0	4.2
Readmissions	60,058	65,219	72,442	80,344	8.6	11.1	10.9
Discharges	133,208	145,116	161,972	175,727	8.9	11.6	8.4
Deaths in hospital	48,236	46,848	51,294	49,640	−2.9	9.5	−3.2
Resident patients at end of year	551,390	548,626	544,863	542,721	−0.5	−0.7	−0.4
Personnel employed full time at end of year	153,715	162,753	169,438	174,218	5.9	4.1	2.8
Maintenance expenditures:							
Total	$663,280,934.00	$731,875,462.00	$805,861,786.00	$854,354,503.00	10.3	10.1	6.0
Per patient	$1,194.88	$1,332.31	$1,475.26	$1,577.54	11.5	10.7	6.9

The quality of care given these patients may be judged from the fact that state hospitals spend an average of $4.44 per patient per day compared to $31.16 for community general hospitals and $12 or more per patient day both for tuberculosis and Veterans Administration psychiatric hospitals. Likewise, state hospitals have the lowest ratio of hospital personnel to patients, 0.32 per patient as compared to 2.1 in community general hospitals.

For the last four years, there has been a net decrease in the number of patients living in state hospitals (see Table 3). This trend primarily reflected the benefits of tranquilizing drugs, the drugs making it possible to increase the number of patients who can be released from the hospital. However, since the number of patients admitted to these hospitals has continued to climb, the net decrease in the hospitals' population cannot be said to represent a reduction in the mental illness problem. What has occurred is an increase in the turnover and a shift in the whereabouts of mental patients. More are being maintained at home or treated elsewhere.

There are two ways to measure progress: from the standpoint of how far we have come, or from the standpoint of how far we yet have to go. By the first measure, we have made progress. By the second measure, we have little cause for self-congratulation and no cause for relaxation of efforts.

The first and pivotal question in appraising where we now stand and next should go is this: *Why have our efforts to provide effective treatment for the mentally ill lagged behind our objectives, behind public demand, and behind attacks on other major health problems?*

WITH PROPER TREATMENT, THE SCHIZOPHRENIC PATIENT HAS THREE-IN-FIVE CHANCE OF LEADING A USEFUL LIFE IN THE COMMUNITY

We began with the statement that we have not done as well as we know how for the major mentally ill, in terms of humane and healing care. This is to say that if all or most had the benefit of modern treatment, more patients would recover or show improvement. Palpably, if this assumption is untrue then we have no immediate incentive for greater efforts to reduce lag and accelerate progress.

Actually, the typical patient with schizophrenia or other functional psychosis (so called because no organic cause is known) has a much better outlook than do patients with some of the better known chronic degenerative diseases, such as cancer of the lung or stomach.

Treatment of mental illness stands on two rational pedestals, one social and one medical: humanitarianism and science.

Modern methods of treatment of major mental illness seek to systematize and capitalize on a historic trend away from punishment and toward "moral treatment," based on humane consideration for the patient as an individual and member of society. No longer does progressive psychiatry hold with the early dictum that "terror acts powerfully on the body through the medium of the mind, and should be employed in the cure of madness." We do still see residual manifestations of this latter approach in shock treatments.

To moral treatment has been added both psychotherapeutic and sociological insight into how patients may be treated either individually or in groups to bring about solutions of their problems of living with themselves and with others. To psychotherapy and social therapy (the "therapeutic community") have been added the tranquilizing drugs, which may be described as "moral treatment in pill form." These drugs quiet the patient and make him more agreeable and easier to work with. In summary of what we know about the treatment of the major mental illnesses which fill our public mental hospitals, we may say:

1. The persistent attitude that schizophrenia is a hopeless, incurable disease requiring the patient to be removed from human society for the rest of his life is baseless.

2. The idea that the patient is totally insane is likewise without foundation. Medical psychology has consistently observed and generally accepts the fact that functional psychosis involves only certain of the components of the personality. The patient is sick in some ways and healthy in others. Rational treatment directs itself toward salvaging the healthy and reducing the sick parts of the mind.

3. Human beings regard loss of liberty, forcible detention, removal from the community, and imprisonment as punishment for wrongdoing; the mentally ill are no exception. It is generally agreed that the typical locked-ward state hospital, centering its interest on the physical rather than the mental welfare of the patient, increases the patient's disability by reinforcing rather than counteracting public pressure to reject the patient from the community. As the pioneer reformer, Clifford Beers, said, "Madmen are too often man-made." The open hospital, with unlocked wards, is one antidote to this disabling process. Another is treatment in mental health clinics of patients not actually requiring hospitalization. Many of the patients in state hospitals do not need to be there.

4. The insistent professional preoccupation with "cures" presents a blind alley. The present state of our scientific knowledge does not permit psychiatry as yet to formulate exact tests of cure. The outlook for the schizophrenic, the main source of the long-term accumulation of pa-

tients in state hospitals, is not poor but good under optimum treatment conditions. He has a one-in-five chance of spontaneous recovery without systematic treatment. Through proper treatment, he has at least a three-in-five and perhaps as much as four-in-five chance of improving sufficiently to lead a useful life in his community.

Many People—Including Physicians—Find it Hard to Recognize Psychological Illness as Illness

The way society handles its mentally ill has been the subject of scandalized attack many times. But, as already implied, repeated exposure of the shameful, dehumanized condition of the mentally sick people who populate the back wards of state hospitals does not arouse the public to seek sweeping humanitarian reforms, let alone stimulate widespread application of modern methods of treatment. Presumably, if we can answer why there has not been a strong public response (as there has been, for example, in the campaigns against tuberculosis, cancer and heart disease) we then can determine why effective treatment for the mentally ill has lagged.

The answer, according to our analysis in the following pages, is that the mentally ill are singularly lacking in appeal. They tend to disturb or offend other people and, when they do, people generally treat them as disturbers and offenders and, of course, as if they were responsible for their behavior. In contrast, it has been the special view of the mental health professions that people should understand and accept the mentally ill and do something about their plight.

The public has not been greatly moved by this protest. People do feel sorry for the mentally ill, but, in the balance, they do not feel as sorry as they do relieved to have out of the way persons whose behavior disturbs and offends them. Patients with major mental illness come to be viewed as "impossible people" and mental institutions as places where they are sent when their families and communities "no longer can stand them."

The fact that society tends to reject the mentally ill is, of course, well known; little significance seems to have been attached to it, however. The full reach of the rejection mechanism is little recognized and even denied by some who have learned to overcome it in their own professional relations with persons suffering mental disturbances or disorders.

We can name a number of processes, all of which add up to, or reinforce, the fact that the mentally ill repel more than they appeal. One characteristic of a psychotic is that he becomes a stranger among his own people. Since antiquity mankind has been prone to feel hostility toward the stranger, and this applies equally to any persons who behave strangely. A social system depends on order, and order depends on predictability in the behavior of one's fellows.

Normal persons for the most part want to do what they have to do to "get along." The typical psychotic does not. In consequence, society conventionally closes ranks against him. Identified major mental illness carries a stigma that cuts the bonds of human fellowship.

Many other diseases—tuberculosis, syphilis, cancer, for example—have at times stigmatized their victims. But the stigma of a disease recognized to be physical and lethal tends to disappear, or be offset, as it becomes better understood and publicly attacked. The reason, as we analyze it, is not that science has found causes and cures—the causes and cures of cancer and the leading forms of heart disease are still the subject of an intensive search.

Rather, the physically sick person fits society's deep-seated conception of a sick person. Feeling helpless, he turns to others for help and, receiving help, is responsive to it. He evokes sympathy. Commonly, the acutely ill psychotic does not appear to want help or accept help but, quite the reverse, thinks he is not sick and may interpret "help" as "harm." He repels sympathy. He is mad.

This lack of appeal has many dimensions. The rise of state hospitals and their persistence, despite all efforts to reform them, is the most outstanding example. Mental health authorities are in general agreement that society uses these huge institutions as dumping grounds for social rejects, rather than as true hospitals.

A rejection effect may also be detected in the rise of the mental hygiene movement. Its founder, Clifford Beers, as his book "A Mind That Found Itself" clearly reveals, intended the movement to be primarily one of stopping brutal treatment of the mentally ill and converting mental hospitals into humane, healing institutions. It did not become so. Attention became focused on mentally healthy living rather than help for the sick.

The mentally ill's lack of appeal as a public cause has been reflected in a lack of strong leadership and strong organization in the voluntary mental health movement, some state organizations excepted. An organization can hardly develop and mature, as a matter of fact, if followers or members cannot be persuaded in sufficient numbers to identify with the cause at hand. It has been observed that the mentally ill are inherently handicapped in any effort to form a strong public pressure group. Lacking in a reasonable capacity to get along with other people, they find organization behind a leader to be difficult, if not impossible. The friends or relatives are equally immobilized through an aversion to identifying themselves with the mentally ill.

Several studies of public attitudes have shown a major lack of recognition of mental illness as illness, and a predominant tendency toward rejection of both the mental patient and those who treat him. There is a general agreement on these points in contrast to the lack of confirmation often characterizing parallel studies in the mental health field. (It is encouraging to note, however, that these negative attitudes are less among younger and better educated persons than the older and less educated groups.)

The circle of negligence and indifference becomes complete when we recognize that many members of learned professions are likewise prone to turn their back on the core problem of major mental illness.

General practictioners as well as other members of the medical profession have been found in a majority of instances to be both uninformed and unsympathetic when they are confronted with mental illness. The same observation applies, oddly enough, to many psychiatrists in private practice when we narrow discussion to the core problem of severe mental illness. The main concern of the popular psychoanalyst is with neurosis rather than psychosis; this is also true of other types of psychiatrists in private practice. Their major focus is on minor and more easily treatable forms of mental illness. Even mental hospital superintendents themselves, it has been noted, may share the public's stigmatizing attitudes toward mental patients.

In summary, we need to become conscious, at the action level, of two points if we are to overcome the lag in the care of the mentally ill: (1) People find it difficult to think about and recognize psychological illness as illness, or to see sickness as having psychological forms. (2) The major mentally ill as a class lack in appeal, which is to say that they are overburdened with liabilities as persons and as patients.

To explain the first point: Man is prima facie an outward-looking, tool-operating, thing-oriented creature, the man of science not excepted. We use our unique human intelligence principally to think about picturable, tangible, concrete, measurable, recordable things. Recent anthropological and neurological evidence indicates that tools were used by prehistoric apes in the absence of a human brain, and that continued use of tools may have conditioned the way in which the human brain evolved. Also, the interpretation is borne out by the more rapid advancement of the physical and mathematical than of the behavioral and social sciences, and by the fact that the most crucial questions facing mankind today involve psychological and social conduct. In any event, education of the average man appears to favor greater understanding of matter than of mind. Most of us are in this way psychologically handicapped persons, mentally blind to our physical bias.

To elaborate the second point: It is not so much his symptoms themselves that bring the psychotic patient into a mental hospital—many people in the general population have equally strange symptoms—but that his behavior reaches a point where people no longer can stand it. Violence is more the exception than the rule, popular misconceptions to the contrary. It is basically that normal people are disturbed by the patient's refusing to comply with expectations of time and place. Challenged by the problem, the psychiatrist in the hospital nonetheless may find the patient uncooperative—too wearing, too trying, too tiring. Thus the most conscientious and devoted doctor may be forced to turn his back on the patient, completing the circle of rejection.

It should now be clear that one way around the impasse of public and professional attitudes that we appear to have erected would be to emphasize that persons with major mental illness are in certain ways *different* from the ordinary sick. With such an understanding and agreement, it might then be possible to proceed in the light of fuller reason to adopt more helpful attitudes.

The Mentally Ill Usually Behave Irresponsibly; Society Usually Behaves toward Them the Same Way

It is commonly stated that one in ten is mentally ill or psychologically disturbed. When this estimate is limited to those with severe disorders that are socially disruptive or individually incapacitating, the ratio is perhaps one in 100. Society has organized itself and its handling of the one in 100 out of primary concern for the 99 who do not disturb their fellow men sufficiently to acquire the mental patient label. This does not mean, however, that we would long hesitate in modifying the system of exiling and thereafter dehumanizing patients whose illness makes them socially unacceptable if we could be shown that a more desirable alternative is available.

The current trend, among more progressive mental health professionals and interested laymen, is to recognize and to pursue alternatives—to demonstrate that negative public attitudes are not insurmountable roadblocks; to show that it is possible to develop and practice friendly and accepting attitudes toward the mentally ill, to show that it is possible to work with them, to treat them as human beings, and get good results. For example, during the last six years more than 1000 volunteer students from Harvard and Radcliffe colleges and Brandeis University have worked regularly with chronic psychotics at Metropolitan State Hospital in Waltham, Mass. They have been active in ward improvement projects and as case aides—without harm to themselves or the patients. On the contrary, there has been a mutual benefit, in the notable improvement of patients and higher motivation of students, some of whom have chosen mental health as their career work. Many other examples of lay volunteers who work with mental patients could be cited.

It is a characteristic of the mentally ill that they behave in an irresponsible manner; it is a characteristic of society that we behave toward them in the same manner. The findings of the various projects undertaken as part of the Joint Commission's mental health study bear out our belief that this circle of rejection can be broken. Indeed, there are many signs that the process is well under way.

In all categories of service—hospitals, clinics, community agencies, schools, for example—we found a tremendous demand for authoritative information about mental illnesses and for access to available services. Waiting lists are the rule. It is a demand that we have not begun to meet. Only in the meeting of it will we have the opportunity for large-scale demonstration that public attitudes can be improved and mentally troubled persons can be helped.

In our nationwide survey of the American people's views of their own mental health, one in four adults disclosed he at some time had had a psychological problem in which professional help would have been useful. One out of seven actually sought help—mainly for problems involving marriage, personal adjustment, or children. Forty-two per cent of those who sought help turned to their clergymen, 29 per cent to physicians in general, 18 per cent to psychiatrists and psychologists, and 10 per cent to social agencies and marriage clinics.

More than half of these troubled persons were sure that they had been helped—more in problems they saw as physical or external to them than as psychological or within themselves. But more were helped in making personal adjustments than in solving marital troubles.

The foregoing study together with our studies of community services, churches and schools indicated the following: While the younger generation and better educated persons have greater recognition of the psychological nature of many of their problems and therefore see the need to deal with them psychologically, the demand for such services is not being met. Indeed, mental health facilities and skills are inadequate wherever one looks, whether to mental or general hospitals, clinics, counseling services, clergymen, family doctors, special rehabilitation services, or elsewhere.

Much information has been disseminated. Many meetings have been held. But the shortage of trained mental health personnel works totally against the purposes of mental health education. Increased mental health education only serves to tax already inadequate mental health services.

The Joint Commission made an intensive study of the demand for and supply of mental health professional manpower—particularly psychiatrists, psychologists, psychiatric nurses, and psychiatric social workers.

This study made forcibly clear that the great shortages of manpower in these categories is inextricably related to the shortage of professional manpower in general—teachers, lawyers, physicians, scientists, technologists. And the professional manpower shortage is related to defects in our system of public school and college education. Most importantly, a large part of the nation's potential brainpower is being lost between high school and college. In fact, only about one-tenth of American youth become college graduates; only one-third of those of outstanding intelligence in high school go on to finish college.

It is of special interest to a national mental health study, we may say in passing, that our culture does not manifest a great respect for the mind. Our minds, the findings indicate, seem to be of small moment to us, whether normal or sick. The critical problem is one of intellectual motivation. What examples do we set? What new challenges do we offer? What spiritual rewards do we offer? What degree of economic security do we provide?

Our manpower study concluded, with frank pessimism, that sufficient professional personnel to eliminate the glaring deficiencies in our care of mental patients will never become available if the present population trend continues without a commensurate increase in the recruitment and training of mental health manpower. The only possibilities for changing this negative outlook for hundreds of thousands of mental hospital patients would require a great change in our social attitudes, and a consequent massive national effort in all areas of education, including large increases in the number of persons engaged in mental health work, or a sharp break-through in mental health research.

A Sound Research Attack on Mental Illness Must Be Mounted on a Long-Term Base

The demand for professional services for the custody and continuous care of patients with schizophrenia or cerebral arteriosclerosis could be greatly reduced by a major break-through in the prevention or treatment of either of these conditions with a biochemical or other technic that could be administered to large numbers by a single therapist. Together, these patients fill the great majority of mental hospital beds.

But even with maximum research support, we cannot count on increased purchasing power in the science market to produce the desired result within a given time. A characteristic of scientific research is that it ultimately produces results of potential benefit to us all, but we cannot predict when the result will come or even that it will be the one we are looking for. There was a lag of forty years between the time Karl Landsteiner discovered the cause of poliomyelitis and when John Enders' group accomplished the tissue-culture break-through that made production of a polio vaccine possible. Sir Alexander Fleming was not looking for a penicillin when he observed its effects, and yet the antibiotics have made more difference in the control of infectious diseases than any other drug in medical history. It was research in anesthesia and motion sickness rather than mental health that brought us the tranquilizing drugs.

Our purpose here is not to be defeatist; only realistic. The enormous task of taking care of mental patients is matched by the enormous research lag in the study of human behavior. Only by making the research possible can we hope to overcome the lag. What we mean is that our total national investment in mental health research—in time, money, men and research and training facilities—simply does not measure up to the need for useful and reliable knowledge that could form the foundation of future progress.

The mental health sciences address themselves to the alleviation of a complex of biological, psychological, and sociological problems that have plagued man through his history; mental health scientists face this task with an incredibly small fund of knowledge about causes and cures. It is a field where much-qualified guesses abound and general agreement is difficult to obtain.

A sound research attack on problems of mental illness and mental health can be mounted on no other base than a *long-term* one. The prospect of a crash program and a quick break-through is not realistic in the absence of a vast increase in basic knowledge. We have the examples in other fields, such as cancer and heart disease, where intensified research has been going on for some years in response to an earlier public focus of effort to solve these health problems. Hopes have been high and have remained so. Yet even in these areas the quick fulfillment of grand objectives is not yet at hand.

We can again illustrate our point via the major advance represented by introduction of the tranquilizing drugs, now used in the treatment of probably one-third of all mental hospital patients. Although these drugs quiet the patients, inspire hopefulness, and make mental hospital employment more interesting and attractive, they do not relieve but rather increase the need for professional experience and skills. The effects of the drugs must be closely watched and evaluated, for they are not without harm. At the same time, they make many more patients accessible to psychotherapy, rehabilitation and discharge from the hospital. Such drugs actually increase the need for trained therapists and helping personnel.

In making a statement of the aims and strategy for a more effective research effort in the mental health field, certain characteristics of the research enterprise must be taken into account.

One characteristic is the great *diversity* of persons, sciences, methods and goals involved in "mental health research."

Another characteristic is the sharp cleavage in attitudes about *basic* and applied research: Basic research is defined as any scientific inquiry for the purpose of discovering and generalizing truths about the essence of nature, including man; applied research here refers to studies directed primarily toward the practical problems of preventing mental illness or treating mental patients. This cleavage leads to a neglect of basic research as impractical or unpromising, and to the false assumption that basic research should be done in universities; applied research, in hospitals.

Efforts should be made to increase communication between researchers and practitioners. Their differing interests and training at present lead them in opposing directions. One result is poorly designed or "sloppy" clinical research. Actually, research is a service to practitioners as well as to the patients served.

Our study shows that the mental health research output is concentrated in a relatively small number of major universities and their medical centers. Smaller colleges and state mental hospitals account for an extremely small portion of the total research effort. There should be support for *flexible* and *experimental* programs of *stimulating* research in many different areas and settings.

The mental health sciences are preponderantly dependent on the federal government for their financial support, and becoming more so. The greatest single source is the National Institute of Mental Health. The federal percentage of total support for mental health research in 1958 was 57 per cent; the state percentage was 20 per cent The pharmaceutical foundations supplied 17 per cent; private foundations and other sources, less than 6 per cent. In 1959 and again in 1960, Congress sharply increased its N.I.M.H. appropriations.

The above figures adequately demonstrate that federal government policies determine the shape, size, direction and soundness of the over-all effort in mental health research. Current policy, emphasizing annual grants for specific projects by individual investigators favors short-term research and applied research, as opposed to the long-term, more fundamental approach needed.

The present effectiveness of our mental health services is seriously limited by large gaps in our scientific knowledge about the fundamentals of mental illness and mental health. Our research recommendations therefore will concern themselves with the particular kinds of support needed to fill the gaps as fast as possible.

SCIENCE AND EDUCATION ARE RESOURCES THAT MUST HAVE
ADEQUATE SUPPORT FROM HUMAN SOCIETY, WHETHER
PUBLIC OR PRIVATE

The philosophy the federal government needs to develop and crystallize is that science and education are resources—like natural resources. They can meet an ends test but not a means test or a time schedule. Science and education operate not for profit but profit everybody; hence, they must have adequate support from human society, whether public or private. The following recommendations are designed to help achieve this:

Recommendations

1. A much larger proportion of total funds for mental health research should be invested in basic research as contrasted with applied research. Only through a large investment in basic research can we hope ultimately to specify the causes and characteristics sufficiently so that we can predict and therefore prevent or cure various forms of mental illness or disordered behavior.

2. Congress and the state legislatures should increasingly favor long-term research in mental health and mental illness as contrasted with short-term projects.

3. Increased emphasis should be placed on, and greater allocations of money be made for, venture, or risk, capital both in the support of persons and of ideas in the mental health research area.

4. The National Institute of Mental Health should make new efforts to invest in, provide for, and hold the young scientist in his career choice. This recommendation would require that more full-time positions be supported for ten-year periods as well as some on the basis of lifetime appointments.

5. Support of program research in established scientific and educational institutions, as initiated by the National Institutes of Health, should be continued and considerably expanded in the field of mental health.

6. The federal government should support the establishment of mental health research centers, or research institutes operated in collaboration with educational institutions and training centers, or independently.

7. Some reasonable portion of total mental health research support should be designated as capital investment in building up facilities for research in states or regions where scientific institutions are lacking or less well developed.

8. Diversification should be recognized as the guiding principle in the distribution of federal research project, program, or institute grants from the standpoint of categories of interest, subject matter of research, and branches of science involved.

The Lag in Treating the Mentally Ill Is Reflected in the Continued Existence of Custodial Care Hospitals

The patient care portion of our study centers on new patterns in the treatment of the mentally ill in the community and in institutions. These patterns, which together comprise the current trend in care of the mentally ill, involve:

Providing immediate help for the emotionally disturbed.

Extending the care of mental patients into the community via clinics and other agencies.

A broader conception of what constitutes treatment.

Individualizing of patient care in mental hospitals.

The breaking down of barriers between the hospital and the community—in effect, the open-hospital movement.

The development of a therapeutic milieu in mental hospitals—social treatment.

Development of after-care programs concerned with adequately supporting the patient so he can remain in the community or return there.

The practitioners who are developing new treatment programs believe in them and hope that they will result in better care and more effective treatment. The one constant in each new method appears to be the enthusiasm of its proponents, and most probably such enthusiasm transmits itself to patients in beneficial ways.

The salient characteristic of the best available treatment of psychotics, as we now understand it, is that some kind of relationship—psychological or social—takes place between the patient and the helping person. This relationship can be formed by informed laymen working individually or in groups under the guidance of psychiatrists, clinical psychologists, or psychiatric social workers, as well as by these and other classes of mental health workers—for example, nurses, attendants and occupational and recreational therapists.

But programs reflecting newer concepts of treatment are relatively rare and unevenly distributed, with the large majority of state hospitals remaining custodial and punitive in their approach. The thesis of ACTION FOR MENTAL HEALTH, that the lag in the treatment of the mentally ill reflects a fundamental pattern of social rejection, is nowhere better evidenced than by the continued existence of these "hospitals" that seem to have no defenders but endure despite all attacks.

To achieve better care of patients, the mental hospital needs to be integrated into the community. This means keeping the hospital and its staff in closer touch with all the community's public and private service agencies. It means an end to the hospital's isolation from the community; in isolation, the backward, custodial system may thrive, whereas in the mainstream of community activity, a hospital's shortcomings may come to attention.

The state hospital must cease to be treated as a target for political exploitation. Patronage must end. These hospitals and their logical community extensions—clinics and after-care programs—must be manned in all cases by properly motivated career workers and not by hacks, professional or lay. These workers need to be well trained and well paid; they need the opportunity to do a good job and hence to demonstrate to the public what they can do.

The newer programs do nothing to solve the manpower problem, although they indicate the direction in which a solution may lie. This brings us to recommendations for improved care of the mentally ill.

A NATIONAL MENTAL HEALTH PROGRAM SHOULD AVOID THE RISK OF FALSE PROMISE IN PUBLIC EDUCATION

Recommendations

1. Policy. In the absence of more specific and definitive scientific evidence of the causes of mental illnesses, psychiatry and the allied mental health professions should adopt and practice a broad, liberal philosophy of what constitutes and who can do treatment within the framework of their hospitals, clinics and other professional service agencies, particularly in relation to persons with psychoses or severe personality or character disorders that incapacitate them for work, family life, and everyday activity. All mental health professions should recognize:

A. That certain kinds of medical, psychiatric and neurological examinations and treatments must be carried out by or under the immediate direction of psychiatrists, neurologists or other physicians specially trained for these procedures.

B. That psychoanalysis and allied forms of deeply searching and probing "depth psychotherapy" must be practiced only by those with special training, experience and competence in handling these technics without harm to the patient (namely, by physicians trained in psychoanalysis or intensive psychotherapy plus those psychologists or other professional persons who lack a medical education but have an aptitude for, adequate training in, and demonstrable competence in such technics of psychotherapy).

C. That nonmedical mental health workers with aptitude, sound training, practical experience, and demonstrable competence should be permitted to do general, short-term psychotherapy—namely, the treating of persons by objective, permissive, nondirective technics of listening to their troubles and helping them resolve these troubles in an individually insightful and socially useful way. Such therapy, combining some elements of psychiatric treatment, of client counseling, of "someone to tell one's troubles to," and of love for one's fellowman, obviously can be carried out in a variety of settings by institutions, groups and by individuals, but in all cases should be pursued under the auspices of recognized mental health agencies.

2. *Recruitment and training.* The mental health professions need to launch a national manpower recruitment and training program, expanding on and extending present efforts and seeking to stimulate the interest of American youth in mental health work as a career. This program should include all categories of mental health personnel. This program should emphasize not only professional training but also short courses and on-the-job training in the subprofessions and upgrading for partially trained persons.

3. *Services to mentally troubled people.* Persons who are emotionally disturbed—that is to say, under psychological stress that they cannot tolerate —should have skilled attention and helpful counseling available to them in their community if the development of more serious mental breakdowns is to be prevented. This is known as secondary prevention, and is concerned with the detection of beginning signs and symptoms of mental illness and their relief; in other words, the earliest possible treatment. In the absence of fully trained psychiatrists, clinical psychologists, psychiatric social workers, and psychiatric nurses, such counseling should be done by persons with some psychological orientation and mental health training and access to expert consultation as needed.

4. *Immediate care of acutely disturbed mental patients.* Immediate professional attention should be provided in the community for persons at the onset of acutely disturbed, socially disruptive, and sometimes personally catastrophic behavior—that is, for persons suffering a major breakdown. The few pilot programs for immediate, or emergency, psychiatric care now in existence should be expanded and extended as rapidly as personnel becomes available.

5. *Intensive treatment of acutely ill mental patients.* A national mental health program should recognize that major mental illness is the core

problem and unfinished business of the mental health movement, and that among those with severe mental illnesses the intensive treatment of those with critical and prolonged breakdowns should have first call on fully trained members of the mental health professions. There is a need for expanding treatment of the acutely ill mental patient in all directions, via community mental health clinics, general hospitals, and mental hospitals, as rapidly as psychiatrists, clinical psychologists, psychiatric nurses, psychiatric social workers, and occupational, physical and other non-medical therapists become available in the community.

A. Community Mental Health Clinics. Community mental health clinics serving both children and adults, operated as outpatient departments of general or mental hospitals, as part of state or regional systems for mental patient care, or as independent agencies, are a main line of defense in reducing the need of many persons with major mental illness for prolonged or repeated hospitalization. Therefore, a national mental health program should set as an objective one fully staffed full-time mental health clinic available to each 50,000 of population. Greater efforts should be made to induce more psychiatrists in private practice to devote a substantial part of their working hours to community clinic services, both as consultants and as therapists.

B. General Hospital Psychiatric Units. No community general hospital should be regarded as rendering a complete service unless it accepts mental patients for short-term hospitalization and therefore provides a psychiatric unit or psychiatric beds. Every community general hospital of 100 or more beds should make this provision. A hospital with such facilities should be regarded as an integral part of a total system of mental patient services in its region.

It is the consensus of the Mental Health Study that definitive care for patients with major mental illness should be given if possible, or for as long as possible, in a psychiatric unit of a general hospital and then, on a longer-term basis, in a specialized mental hospital organized as an intensive psychiatric treatment center.

C. Intensive Psychiatric Treatment Centers. Smaller state hospitals, of 1000 beds or less and suitably located for regional service, should be converted as rapidly as possible into intensive treatment centers for patients with major mental illness in the acute stages or with a good prospect for improvement or recovery if the illness is more prolonged. All new state hospital construction should be devoted to these smaller intensive treatment centers.

6. *Care of chronic mental patients.* No further state hospitals of more than 1000 beds should be built, and not one patient should be added to any existing mental hospital already housing 1000 or more patients. It is recommended that all existing state hospitals of more than 1000 beds be

gradually and progressively converted into centers for the long-term, combined care of persons with chronic diseases, including mental illness. This conversion should be completed in the next ten years.

Special technics are available for the care of the chronically ill and these technics of socialization, relearning, group living, and gradual rehabilitation or social improvement should be expanded and extended to more people, including the aged who are sick and in need of care, through conversion of state mental hospitals into combined chronic disease centers.

It would be necessary to provide the intensive treatment services for the acutely ill, outlined in the preceding section, before large state hospitals could be converted to chronic diseases. It also would be necessary to make certain changes in federal and state laws.

7. *After-care, intermediate care, and rehabilitation services.* The objective of modern treatment of persons with major mental illness is to enable the patient to maintain himself in the community in a normal manner. To do so, it is necessary (1) to save the patient from the debilitating effects of institutionalization as much as possible, (2) if the patient requires hospitalization, to return him to home and community life as soon as possible, and (3) thereafter maintain him in the community as long as possible. Therefore, after-care and rehabilitation are essential parts of all service to mental patients, and the various methods of achieving rehabilitation should be integrated in all forms of services, among them: day hospitals, night hospitals, after-care clinics, public health nursing services, foster family care, convalescent nursing homes, rehabilitation centers, work services, and ex-patient groups. We recommend that demonstration programs for day and night hospitals and the more flexible use of mental hospital facilities, both in the treatment of the acute and the chronic patient, be encouraged and augmented through institutional, program, and project grants.

Public Information on Mental Illness

A national mental health program should avoid the risk of false promise in "public education for better mental health" and focus on the more modest goal of disseminating such information about mental illness as the public needs and wants in order to recognize psychological forms of sickness and to arrive at an informed opinion in its responsibility toward the mentally ill.

It is possible to make certain general recommendations about dissemination of information concerning mental illness aimed at (1) greater public understanding of the mentally ill person and those who care for him, (2) the avoiding of misunderstanding in the relations of one professional group with another, and (3) the importance of making sure, in the relations of the mental health professions with the lay public, that others understand what we are driving at.

An important point has been missed in overinsistence that the public recognize that mentally ill persons are sick, the same as if they were physically sick, and should be treated no differently from other sick persons. Mental illness is different from physical illness in the one fundamental aspect that it tends to disturb and repel others rather than evoke their sympathy and desire to help.

A sharper focus in a national program against mental illness might be achieved if the information publicly disseminated capitalized on the aspect in which mental differs from physical illness. Such information should have at least four general objectives:

1. To overcome the general difficulty in thinking and recognizing mental illness as such—that is, a disorder with psychological as well as physiological, emotional as well as organic, social as well as individual causes and effects.

2. To overcome society's many-sided pattern of rejecting the mentally ill, by making it clear that the major mentally ill are singularly lacking in appeal, why this is so, and the need consciously to solve the rejection problem.

3. To make clear what mental illness is like as it occurs in its various forms and is seen in daily life and what the average person's reactions to it are like, as well as to elucidate means of coping with it in casual or in close contact. As an example, the popular stereotype of the "raving maniac" or "berserk madman" as the only kind of person who goes to mental hospitals needs to be dispelled. We have not made it clear to date that such persons (who are wild and out of control) exist, but in a somewhat similar proportion as airplanes that crash in relation to airplanes that land safely.

4. To overcome the pervasive defeatism that stands in the way of effective treatment. While no attempt should be made to gloss over gaps in knowledge of diagnosis and treatment, the fallacies of "total insanity," "hopelessness" and "incurability" should be attacked, and the prospects of recovery or improvement through modern concepts of treatment and rehabilitation emphasized. One aspect of the problem is that hospitalization taking the form of ostracization, incarceration or punishment increases rather than decreases disability.

Attention is also needed to the manner in which professional persons and groups approach the public, since winning friends and support for care of the mentally ill depends first and foremost on not giving cause for offense. We recommend that the American Psychiatric Association make special efforts to explore, understand and transmit to its members an accurate perception of the public's image of the psychiatrist. Such efforts could pay a great dividend in "education of the public" if the profession were to be educated, perhaps as a part of its formal training, against overvaluing, overreaching, and overselling itself.

The primary responsibility for preparation of mental health information for dissemination to laymen should rest with "laymen" who are experts in public education and mass communications and who will work in consultation with mental health experts. But the mental health expert and the educator or mass communications expert have the primary problem of fully communicating with one another before communicating with the public. Too often the basis for discussions among mental health professionals and laymen is the easy assumption on both sides that the other fellow doesn't "understand the problem" or "know what he is talking about."

As a matter of policy, the mental health professions can now assume that the public knows the magnitude if not the nature of the mental illness problem and psychiatry's primary responsibility for care of mental patients. Henceforth the psychiatrist and his teammates should seek ways of sharing this responsibility with others and correcting deficiencies and inadequacies without feeling the need to be overbearing, defensive, seclusive or evasive. A first principle of honest public relations bears repeating: To win public confidence, first confide in the public.

How Can We Make State Hospitals in Fact What They Now Are in Name Only—Hospitals for Mental Patients?

Federal, state and local expenditures for public mental patient services should be doubled in the next five years—and tripled in the next ten.

Only by this magnitude of expenditure can typical state hospitals be made in fact what they are now in name only—hospitals for mental patients. Only by this magnitude of expenditure can outpatient and former-patient programs be sufficiently extended outside the mental hospital, into the community. It is self-evident that the states for the most part have defaulted on adequate treatment for the mentally ill, and have consistently done so for a century. It is likewise evident that the states cannot afford the kind of money needed to catch up with modern standards of care without revolutionary changes in their tax structure.

Therefore, *we recommend that the states and the federal government work toward a time when a share of the cost of state and local mental patient services will be borne by the federal government, over and above the present and future program of federal grants-in-aid for research and training.* The simple and sufficient reason for this recommendation is that under present tax structure only the federal government has the financial resources needed to overcome the lag and to achieve a minimum standard of adequacy. The federal government should be prepared to assume a major part of the responsibility for the mentally ill insofar as the states are agreeable to surrendering it.

For convenience, the Veterans Administration mental hospitals can be taken as financial models of what can be done in the operation of public mental hospitals. *Congress and the National Institute of Mental Health, with the assistance of the intervening administrative branches of government, should develop a federal subsidy program that will encourage states and local governments to emulate the examples set by V. A. mental hospitals.*

Certain principles should be followed in a federal program of matching grants to states for the care of the mentally ill:

The *first principle* is that the federal government on the one side and state and local governments on the other should *share in the costs* of services to the mentally ill.

The *second principle* is that the total federal share should be arrived at in a series of graduated steps over a period of years, the share being determined each year on the basis of state funds spent in a previous year.

The *third principle* is that the grants should be awarded according to *criteria of merit and incentive* to be formulated by an expert advisory committee appointed by the National Institute of Mental Health.

In arriving at a formula, such an expert committee would establish conditions affecting various portions of the available grant, including the following:

1. Bring about any necessary changes in the laws of the state to make professionally acceptable treatment as well as custody a requirement in mental hospitalization, to differentiate between need of treatment and need of institutionalization, and to provide treatment without hospitalization.

2. Bring about any necessary changes in laws of the state to make voluntary admission the preferred method and court commitment the exceptional method of placing patients in a mental hospital or other treatment facilities.

3. Accept any and all persons requiring treatment and/or hospitalization on the same basis as persons holding legal residence within the state.

4. Revise laws of the state governing medical responsibility for the patient to distinguish between administrative responsibility for his welfare and safekeeping and responsibility for professional care of the patient.

5. Institute suitable differentiation between administrative structure and professional personnel requirements for (1) state mental institutions

intended primarily as intensive treatment centers (i.e., true hospitals) and (2) facilities for humane and progressive care of various classes of the chronically ill or disabled, among them the aged.

6. Establish state mental health agencies with well defined powers and sufficient authority to assume over-all responsibility for the state's services to the mentally ill, and to coordinate state and local community health services.

7. Make reasonable efforts to operate open mental hospitals as mental health centers, i.e., as a part of an integrated community service with emphasis on outpatient and after-care facilities as well as inpatient services.

8. Establish in selected state mental hospitals and community mental health programs training for mental health workers, ranging in scope, as appropriate, from professional training in psychiatry through all professional and sub-professional levels, including the on-the-job training of attendants and volunteers. Since each mental health center cannot undertake all forms of teaching activity, consideration here must be given to a variety of programs and total effort. States should be required ultimately to spend 2½ per cent of state mental patient service funds for training.

9. Establish in selected state mental hospitals and community mental health programs scientific research programs appropriate to the facility, the opportunities for well designed research, and the research talent and experience of staff members. States should be required ultimately to spend 2½ per cent of state mental patient service funds for research.

10. Encourage county, town and municipal tax participation in the public mental health services of the state as a means of obtaining federal funds matched against local mental health appropriations.

11. Agree that no money will be spent to build mental hospitals of more than 1000 beds, or to add a single patient to mental hospitals presently having 1000 or more patients.

Our proposal would encourage local responsibility of a degree that has not existed since the state hospital system was founded, while at the same time recognizing that the combined state-local responsibility cannot be fulfilled by the means at hand.

Table 4 provides a hypothetical example of how a federal-state-local matching program incorporating the suggested merit and incentive features might work. We have assumed for ease of illustration that the states will soon reach an expenditure of $1 billion a year for mental patient care (in 1959 the figure was $854 million). We also have assumed that such a program can induce local tax participation to the extent of $60 million after a five-year period and $250 million after a ten-year period.

Our proposal is the first one in American history that attempts to encompass the total problem of public support of mental health services

TABLE 4   HYPOTHETICAL COSTS TO FEDERAL, STATE AND LOCAL GOVERNMENTS
OF DOUBLING EXPENDITURES FOR PUBLIC MENTAL PATIENT CARE IN FIVE YEARS
AND TRIPLING COSTS IN TEN YEARS UNDER PROPOSED MATCHING PLAN
(IN BILLIONS OF DOLLARS)

Year	State Expenditure	Federal Grants Without Local Participation	Total	Local Participation to Extent of:	Federal Grants for Local Participation	Grand Total
1	1.0	0.1	1.1	—	—	1.1
2	1.0	0.2	1.2	0.03	0.17	1.4
3	1.0	0.3	1.3	0.04	0.26	1.6
4	1.0	0.4	1.4	0.05	0.35	1.8
5	1.0	0.5	1.5	0.06	0.44	2.0
6	1.0	0.6	1.6	0.08	0.52	2.2
7	1.0	0.7	1.7	0.10	0.60	2.4
8	1.0	0.8	1.8	0.15	0.65	2.6
9	1.0	0.9	1.9	0.20	0.70	2.8
10	1.0	1.0	2.0	0.25	0.75	3.0

and to make minimum standards of adequate care financially possible.

The outstanding characteristics of mental illness as a public health problem are its staggering size, the present limitations in our methods of treatment, and the peculiar nature of mental illness that differentiates its victims from those with other diseases or disabilities. It would follow that *any national program against mental illness adopted by Congress and the states must be scaled to the size of the problem, imaginative in the course it pursues, and energetic in overcoming both psychological and economic resistances to progress in this direction.* We have sought to acquit our assignment in full recognition of these facts and judgments.

NOTES ON IMPLEMENTATION

The function of the Joint Commission has been that of a study group. We have made a study and from it drawn recommendations for a national mental health program. This completes our job.

It is easy, however, to visualize the next two steps, and even a third. The first is the formation of public opinion for or against the program we propose. The second is the formation of legislative opinion pro or con. The third, and one which we urge the Congress to take immediately, is the formation of a Committee of Consultants who would concern themselves with standards and requirements for implementation of our program and with the kinds of enabling legislation that will be needed. Eventually, we can see that a comparable expert committee, forming an effective channel of communication between the legislature and the mental health professions, will be needed in every state.

In the matter of establishing priorities as they relate to the broad areas of patient care, recruitment, professional education, and research in mental health, we would sound a note of caution. Solution of the mental health problem can and already does pursue two courses. One course is to make better use of the knowledge and experience in the treatment of mental illness that we already have massed, the knowledge on which the broader concepts of treatment in this report are based. Another course is to intensify the search for new knowledge in the hope of mastering the terrain of unknowns to be traversed, and of finding by-passes or more direct routes resulting in preventive measures or treatment methods that are faster working and better adapted to mass application.

The question is not which course to pursue more intensively. In medicine, professional services, education and research move together insofar as they center on or relate to patients. Indeed, it is impossible to separate the patients who must be cared for from the persons who must be trained to care for them, and it is impossible to separate either patients or professional personnel from the search for new knowledge that is of vital concern to both.

Indeed, we can see only one matter that takes priority over all others in the program we propose and that is to obtain vastly increased sums of money for its support. Without adequate financial resources, we cannot take care of patients, we cannot educate professional personnel for public service, and we cannot pursue the basic knowledge needed for the prevention and cure of mental illness.

Name Index

Abrahams, J., 120
Ackerman, N., 200, 205-206, 208-209, 217
Adams, H., 44-45
Adams, J. K., 159, 170
Agras, W. S., 186, 190
Alanen, Y. O., 106, 120
Albee, G., 13, 15, 152
Alexander, F., 158-159, 170
Allport, G. W., 52, 55
Amsel, A., 157, 171
Anderson, C., 290
Arieti, S., 123, 130
Armitage, S. G., 161-162, 170, 172
Artiss, K. L., 130
Artiss, S., 123-124
Atkinson, R. C., 10, 16
Atkinson, R. L., 160, 170
Auld, F., 153, 171
Ayllon, T., 222, 244
Azrin, N. H., 161, 170, 222, 244

Bach, G. R., 197, 199
Bales, R. F., 205, 218
Bandura, A., 152, 160, 162-165, 167, 169, 171
Barends, J., 185, 191
Barzun, J., 47, 55
Basamania, B., 217
Bassin, A., 289
Bassing, E., 268
Bateman, J. F., 257
Bateson, G., 106, 120, 209-210, 217, 219, 274
Beaglehole, E., 208, 217
Bean, L. L., 13, 16
Beatman, F. L., 200
Becker, C. L., 85

Becker, E., 123, 130
Beers, C., 306
Bell, D., 84
Bell, N. W., 206, 219
Bellak, C., 123
Bernal, M. E., 11, 15
Berne, E., 198-199
Bettelheim, B., 13, 15
Bibace, R., 152
Bielinski,, B., 156, 174
Bindman, A. J., 152
Bintz, J., 89
Birdsall, T. G., 225, 245
Bleuler, E., 117, 120, 211, 217
Bleuler, M., 211
Block, H. A., 290
Bochoven, J. S., 45-48, 55
Bolden, L., 157, 171
Bolgar, H., 152
Bott, E., 120
Bowen, M., 120, 210, 217, 274
Bradey, W., 217
Brady, J. V., 230, 244
Braginsky, B., 122-124, 130
Braginsky, D., 122
Breuker, J., 185, 191
Brewer, J., 152
Brill, A. A., 178, 190
Brill, H., 40
Brody, E. B., 257
Brown, E. L., 31, 48, 55
Brown, G. W., 45, 48, 55, 205, 217-218
Brown, M., 152
Buell, B., 120
Burgum, M., 203, 218
Burns, B. J., 11
Bushard, B. L., 42, 270

325

Butcher, R., 177, 189, 191

Cairus, R. B., 160, 171
Calvin, A. D., 157, 171
Cambareri, J., 152
Cameron, N., 120
Carstairs, G. M., 218
Casriel, D., 290
Caudill, W., 257
Challman, R. C., 152
Clausen, J. A., 214, 218
Clifford, B., 157, 171
Clifford, L. T., 157, 171
Cohen, H. L., 222, 244
Cohen, L. H., 40
Cohen, R. A., 273
Collins, B. J., 161, 174
Commager, H. S., 80
Cooke, G., 188, 190
Cope, T. P., 46, 55
Cornelison, A., 105
Cottrell, L., 213, 218
Cowen, E. L., 152
Crisp, A. H., 177, 189, 191
Culver, D. M., 27
Cummings, E., 44
Cummings, J., 44

Dahlstrom, W. G., 53, 55
Davidson, J. R., 156, 171
Davis, K., 254, 255
Davison, G., 181-184, 190
Day, J., 274
Deitch, D., 291
Delay, J., 120
DeLucia, J., 152
DeMyer, M. K., 222, 244
Deniker, P., 120
Denny, R., 80
Deutsch, M., 152
Devereaux, G., 257
Dingman, P. R., 152
Distler, L. M., 172
Dittes, J. E., 158, 171
Dollard, J., 153, 157-159, 164, 166, 168, 171-172
Dörken, H., 152
Dostoievski, F., 268
Douglass, E., 156, 171
Dunham, H. W., 257
Dunlap, K., 157, 171
Dupont, H., 152
Duryee, J. S., 11
Dysinger, R. H., 217

Egerton, J. W., 152

Edmonson, B. W., 157, 171
Edwards, J. E., 183
Empey, L. T., 286, 287
Erikson, C. W., 159, 171
Erikson, E., 80, 82, 86, 110, 120, 258
Erikson, K. T., 42, 256
Estes, W. K., 162, 171
Eysenck, H. J., 42, 169, 171, 177, 179, 184, 188, 190

Federn, P., 205
Feld, S., 16
Fenichel, O., 159, 171, 225, 244
Ferster, C. B., 161, 171, 221-222, 230-235, 244
Fierman, L. B., 123, 130
Findley, J. D., 230, 244
Fingarette, H., 255
Finison, L., 124, 130
Fisher, S., 120
Fishman, H. C., 157, 171
Fleck, S., 104, 120-121
Flügel, J. C., 120, 203, 206, 218
Foa, U. G., 51, 55
Foote, N., 213, 218
Frank, J. D., 4, 15, 167, 171
Frazee, H. E., 120
Freedman, D. X., 105, 123, 130
Freeman, H., 40
French, M. T., 159, 170
Freud, S., 6, 15, 24, 75, 117, 120, 203-204, 207, 218
Friedman, D. A., 189-190
Fromm, E., 73
Fromm-Reichmann, F., 120, 159, 171
Frumkin, R. M., 57, 61

Gale, D. S., 183, 191
Gale, E., 183, 191
Gallagher, E. B., 123-124, 130
Garmezy, N., 10, 16
Geer, J. H., 178, 191
Gelder, M., 177, 184, 188-189, 191
Gerand, D. L., 120
Gibson, R. L., 53, 56
Gilmore, H. R., 257
Glass, A. J., 42
Glazer, N., 80
Glidewell, J. C., 152
Goffman, E., 31, 123, 130, 197, 199
Goldberg, E. M., 121
Goldiamond, I., 220, 222, 225, 244, 245
Goldhamer, H., 11, 16
Goldman-Eisler, F., 55
Goodstein, L. D., 152
Gordon, J. E., 42

Gottlieb, A. L., 53, 55
Green, A., 120
Greenblatt, M., 48, 55
Grosse, M., 123, 130
Grunzke, M. E., 222, 245
Gurel, L., 152
Gurin, G., 14, 16

Hain, J., 177, 189, 191
Haley, J., 120-121, 217, 274
Hallowell, A. I., 208, 218
Harms, E., 49, 56
Harper, R., 152
Harvey, J., 157, 171
Hastings, D. W., 40
Heine, R. W., 167, 171
Hendrich, I., 178, 191
Hilgard, E. R., 10, 16, 222, 245
Hill, L., 113, 121
Hill, R., 214, 218
Hinkle, L. E., 73
Hirsch, S. I., 274
Hobbs, N., 4, 16, 133
Hollingshead, A., 13, 16, 23, 27-28, 57,
    61-62, 121, 214, 218
Holzberg, J., 124, 130
Hooker, D., 121
Hornstra, R., 5, 7, 16
Huston, A. C., 164, 171

Iscoe, I., 152
Israel, P., 64

Jackson, D. D., 106-107, 120-121, 200,
    209, 217-219, 274
Jackson, D. N., 53, 56
Jackson, N. C., 152
Jacobson, E., 176-177, 191
Jahoda, M., 4, 16, 204, 218
James, W., 225, 226, 245
Jenkins, R. L., 160, 162, 173
Johnson, A. M., 274
Jones, E., 24, 27
Jones, E. L., 158, 171
Jones, H. G., 154, 167, 172
Jones, M. C., 154, 158, 166, 172
Jung, C., 117, 121

Kamin, L. J., 162, 174
Kanner, L., 211
Kardiner, A., 209, 218
Kasinin, J., 208, 218
Kay, E., 105
Kelly, J. G., 152
Kerner, O. J. B., 152
Kimble, G. A., 10, 16

King, G. F., 161-162, 170, 172
Kirk, B., 152
Kitsuese, J. I., 28
Klebanoff, L., 152
Klein, M., 154, 172
Kleiner, A., 59
Kleiner, R. J., 56
Kluckhohn, C., 107, 121
Kluckhohn, F. R., 209, 214, 218
Knight, E., 218
Kohn, M. L., 214, 218
Korchin, S. J., 152
Kott, M., 152
Kraeplin, E., 117, 121
Kraines, S., 209, 219
Kramer, M., 10, 16
Krasner, L., 5, 16, 161, 169, 172, 174
Kruseman, A., 185, 191
Kubly, D., 157, 172
Kutner, L., 32

Lacey, J. I., 159, 172
Lang, P. J., 177-181, 183-184, 191
Langer, S., 25, 27, 254, 256
Langworthy, O. R., 121
Lasswell, H. D., 216, 218
Lavell, M., 56
Lazarus, A. A., 154, 167, 172, 177, 184,
    186-187, 189, 191
Lazovik, A. D., 177-181, 183-184, 191
Leary, T., 52-54, 56
Lehner, G. F. J., 157-158, 172
Lemert, E. M., 28
Levinson, D. S., 123-124, 130
Levinson, H., 152
Levitt, E. B., 235, 244
Lidz, R. W., 108, 113, 274
Lidz, T., 105, 108, 113, 121, 210, 218,
    274
Lifton, R. J., 69
Lifton, R. L., 73
Lindsley, O. R., 161, 171-172
Lippitt, R., 284
Lippman, W., 80
Lipsher, D. H., 162, 171
Liversedge, L. A., 163, 167, 172
Lodge, G. T., 53, 56
Lamont, J. F., 183-184, 191
Lorr, M. A., 126, 130, 160, 173

McCord, J., 104
McCord, W., 104
McMillan, J. J., 152
McNeill, H. V., 152
Maltzberg, B., 40, 57
Mark, J. D., 121

Marks, I., 177, 184, 188-189, 191
Marshall, A., 11, 16
Martin, B., 157, 172
Mattick, H. W., 284
Mausner, B., 166, 172
Max, L. W., 156, 172
Meade, M., 80
Mechanic, D., 31
Meissner, J. H., 157
Mendell, D., 120
Menninger, K., 7, 16
Messick, S., 53, 56
Meyer, A., 117, 121, 211
Meyer, V., 154, 167, 172, 177, 189, 191
Midelport, C. F., 210, 218
Migler, B. M., 230, 244
Miller, J. G., 72
Miller, N. E., 153, 157-159, 164, 166, 168, 171-172
Miller, P. E., 162, 171
Milton, O., 3
Mishler, K. B., 222, 245
Moore, N., 187-188, 191
Moore, R., 222, 245
Moreno, J. L., 197, 200, 208, 218
Morgan, J. J. B., 156, 172
Morse, R. T., 274
Mowrer, O. H., 156, 164, 169, 172, 197, 200
Murphy, H. B. M., 218
Murray, E. J., 162, 167, 172
Mussen, P. H., 166, 172-173
Myers, J. K., 13, 16

Nelson, S. E., 152
Newbrough, J. R., 152
Noble, T. D., 274
Nurnberger, J. I., 235, 244

Orlinsky, N., 152

Packard, F. A., 46, 55
Parkel, D., 123, 130
Parker, B., 105
Parsons, O. A., 53, 55
Parsons, T., 107, 115, 121-122, 203, 205, 218, 258, 264
Paul, G. L., 177, 180-181, 183-184, 186, 189, 191
Payne, D. E., 166, 173
Penrose, L. S., 209, 218
Peters, H. N., 160, 162, 173
Peters, R. S., 22, 27
Plant, T. F. A., 152
Plunkett, R. J., 42
Pollak, H. M., 208, 219

Pollak, O., 214, 219
Pollio, H., 6, 16
Prout, C. T., 122
Pruett, H. L., 11

Rachman, S., 154, 167, 172-173, 175, 177, 179, 182-185, 188, 190-191
Rakusin, J. M., 123, 130
Ramsay, R., 185, 191
Ray, D. B., 152
Raymond, M. S., 155, 167, 173
Razran, G., 159, 173
Redl, F., 274
Redlich, F., 13, 16, 23, 27-28, 57, 61-62, 121, 123, 130, 214, 218, 257
Rees, T. P., 46, 48, 56
Reichard, S., 122, 209, 219
Reider, N., 87
Reyna, J., 184, 191
Reynolds, D. J., 179
Reynolds, H. H., 222, 245
Richardson, H. B., 209, 213, 219
Riesman, D., 80, 256
Rioch, D., 63
Ring, K., 123-124, 130
Roback, A. A., 49, 56
Robinson, N. M., 160, 173
Roen, S. R., 152
Rogers, C. R., 158-160, 173
Rogers, J. M., 162, 167, 173
Rohles, F. H., 222, 245
Rose, A. M., 57
Rosenthal, D., 166, 173
Ross, D., 165, 171
Ross, H. A., 30
Ross, S., 165, 171
Roter, J. B., 170, 173, 198, 200
Rowland, H., 257
Rubenstein, E. A., 160, 173
Rudin, E., 207, 219
Ruesch, J., 209, 219
Rutherford, B. R., 157, 173
Ryckoff, I. M., 274

Sage, P., 218
Salter, A., 184, 191
Salzinger, K., 161, 173
Samler, J., 152
Saper, B., 152
Sarason, B. R., 162, 173
Satir, V., 200
Schafer, S., 105
Scheff, T. J., 27
Schein, E. H., 14, 63-64, 66, 73
Schmidberg, M., 160, 173
Schneidman, S., 152

Schooler, C., 123, 130
Schwartz, M. S., 209, 219, 257, 274
Scott, G., 152
Searles, H. F., 123, 130
Sears, P. S., 165, 173
Sears, R. R., 164, 173
Shah, S., 152
Shannon, D. T., 181, 186, 189, 191
Sheehan, J., 157, 173
Shelly, J. A., 289
Sherman, I. C., 209, 219
Sherman, S., 200
Shoben, E. J., 153-154, 173, 245
Shontz, F. C., 152
Siegel, J., 120
Silver, G. A., 152
Sivadon, P., 275
Skinner, B. F., 161, 167-168, 173-174
Smith, M. B., 133
Smith, R. I., 159, 172
Snow, C. P., 224, 245
Sobel, R., 209
Sohler, D. T., 122
Solomon, P., 14, 16
Solomon, R. L., 162, 174
Sommer, R., 219
Spiegel, J. P., 122, 206, 209, 214, 218-
        219, 274
Stanton, A. H., 209, 219, 257, 274
Star, S. A., 265, 266
Steinbeck, J., 14
Stern, E., 8, 16
Stevenson, I., 177, 189, 191
Stoller, F. H., 192
Strassman, H., 64, 66, 73
Strupp, H., 152
Sturmfels, G., 183, 191
Sullivan, H. S., 23, 117, 122, 159, 174,
        205, 208, 211, 219, 253
Super, D. E., 152
Swets, J. A., 225, 245
Sylvester, J. D., 163, 167, 172
Szasz, T., 17, 19, 21, 23-24, 27, 45, 56,
        123, 130, 253, 256
Szurek, S. A., 274

Tanner, W. P., 225, 245
Taylor, H. C., 152
Tempereau, C., 64
Terrace, H. S., 222, 245

Terry, D., 105
Thaler, M., 66, 73
Thirmann, J., 156, 174
Thompson, G. N., 156, 174
Tietze, T., 107, 122
Tillman, C., 122, 209, 219
Tilton, J. R., 161, 174
Towbin, A. P., 123, 130
Tuckman, J., 28, 56
Tyler, F. B., 152

Ullman, L. P., 5, 16, 161-162, 174

Varon, E. J., 120
Verhave, T., 222, 245
Veroff, J., 16
Voas, R. B., 173
Voegtlen, W. L., 156, 174

Wahl, C. W., 122, 209, 219
Wahler, R. G., 3, 6, 16
Wallace, J. A., 156, 174
Walters, R. H., 160, 163, 169, 171
Weakland, J. H., 120, 217, 219, 274
Weide, T. N., 162, 174
Welsh, G. S., 53, 55-56
Wertham, B., 152
Westley, W. A., 214, 219
Wheelis, A., 80
White, A. M., 153, 171
White, M. A., 122
Whiting, J. W. M., 164, 174
Whyte, W. H., 256
Williams, C. D., 158, 174
Williams, H., 63
Williams, R. I., 161, 174
Wilson, R., 89
Witmer, F. J., 156, 172
Wolff, H. C., 73
Wolpe, J., 154-156, 167-168, 174-177,
        182-184, 191
Wynne, L. C., 122, 162, 174, 210, 219,
        274

Yates, A. J., 157, 167, 174
Yolles, S. F., 152
York, R. H., 48, 55

Zander, A., 152
Zilboorg, G., 48, 56, 256

Subject Index

"Action for Mental Health," 4, 298-324
Alcoholism, treatment of, 155-156
Anxiety, 175-191
  anxiety hierarchy, 179
Authority
  anonymous, 73
  irrational, 76-77
  objective, 75
  parental, 75
  rational, 76-77

Brainwashing
  collaboration as a result of, 70-71
  drugs and, 72
  techniques of, 64-69, 72-73

Case histories
  criminal psychopath, 90-104
  "open" psychiatric hospital, 259-264
  schizophrenic, 109, 111, 114, 116
  sexually promiscuous women, 54-55, 114
Causes of deviant behavior
  environmental, 12
  mentalistic, 6
Character disorder, 27, 90, 289
  case history of, 89-104
  median age by race and sex, 61
  and race, 59
  and sexual promiscuity, 54-55
  and treatment, 289-297
Commitment procedures, 29-44
  criteria for commitment, 36-37
  examinations for commitment, 37-40
  steps involved in commitment, 32-40
Community psychology, 133-152
  Act of 1963, 137

Community Mental Health Centers, 133-152
Comprehensive Community Mental Health Centers, 134-135
  emphasis on children, 143-144
  range of help offered, 141-142
  role of mental hospitals, 138
  training of clinicians, 148-149
Conformity and behavior technology, 240-244
  as collaboration during Korean War, 64-71
  an inhibition of individual spontaneity, 76-79
  as sense of self-identity, 81-87
Creativity, definition of, 233-234
Cybernetics and behavioral analysis, 231-234

Deviant behavior
  as related to social class, 13
  as related to therapy, 13
Diagnosis, 27-44
  criticisms of, 36-37
  of family, conjointly, 201-202, 213-214
  median age, 61
  by race and sex, 59
  reliability of, 127
Disease view of mental illness, 4-11
Drug addiction, 289-297
  group therapy, 294-296
  as "con artists," 292-293

Ethics in psychiatry, 22-25, 37-40
  role of in psychoanalysis (Freud), 24

Family dysfunctioning and schizophrenia
  diagnosis and therapy, 200-207
  an origin of schizophrenia, 104-122
  summarized, 119
Financial expenditures
  appropriatiins of National Institutes of
    Health, 300
  by federal government, 312
  recommendations for increases in, 320-
    323
  total funds raised by voluntary health
    campaigns, 301
Functional psychoses
  behavioral characteristics of, 54
  confusion about, 45
  diagnosis, 126-127
  family dynamics and origin of, 104-
    122
  median age by race and sex, 61
  see also psychosis
  and race, 59
  see schizophrenia
  and social class, 13-16, 56-62, 307
  techniques of family therapy for, 205

Gang society and treatment of mental
    illness, 282-288
Goals and values in psychotherapy, 24
  in science and psychotherapy, 254-255
Group therapy
  behavioral, 186-187
  patient controlled, 192
  with television, 192-198

Identity, defined, 82
  place of "will" in, 88-89
  and psychoanalysis, 82
  quest for, 80-89
Illness, concept of, 20
Individualism, defined, 82
  related to change in social character,
    81-82
Insight, 6
Interpersonal behavior, 11, 27, 51-55

Joint Commission on Mental Illness and
    Health, 45
  report of, 298-324

"Medical model" of mental illness, 4, 6,
    15, 269
Mental health programs, recommenda-
    tions for, 315-320
Mental hospitals, 122-130
  American compared to European, 273

case history of American "open" psy-
    chiatric hospital, 259-264
continued existence of custodial care
    in, 314-315
expenditure per patient, 303
movement of patient population in, 302
"open door," 276-282
Mental illness
  attitudes toward, 265-267
  as brain disease, 18
  as deviation from a norm, 20-21, 264-
    265
  disease view, 4-11
  environmental variables in, 282-288
  epistemological errors in, 19
  factor-analytic interpretation of, 51-54
  historical, 52
  "medical model," 4, 15, 269
  personal responsibility for, 245-255
  psychosocial nature of, 11, 19-22
  race and, 56-62
  sexual promiscuity and, 54-55
  societal confusion and uncertainty
    about, 264-267, 305-308
  treatment of as "moral therapy," 45-48
Mental patients
  attitudes toward, 304-305
  inventory of behavior themes, 259-260
  normal behavior, 129-130

Neurosis
  behavioral traits of, 175-191
  change in patterns of, 85-87
  defined, 175-176
  guilt, 77-78
  Oedipus Complex as basis for, 75-76
  see psychoneuroses
  phobias, 178-179
  social origins, 73-79
  as "socially patterned" defect, 78

"Open Door" mental hospitals, 273-282
Operant Conditioning, 153-157, 159-162,
    228-231
  as exemplified in "open door" hospitals,
    275-282
  as "self-control," 235-240

Perception, subliminal, 225-228
Predictions of deviance, 9-11
Problems in living, 11, 19-22
  research on, 53
Pseudoanalogues taken from non-psycho-
    logical fields, 49-50
Psychiatric diagnosis, 4-5
  see diagnosis

Psychiatrist
    impersonal approach, 49-50
    relation to patient, 21
    role of as "participant-observer," 23
Psychiatry
    role of ethics in, 22-24
Psychoanalyst, tasks of, 79
Psychoneuroses, 175-191
    change in patterns of, 85-87
    see neuroses
    Oedipus Complex as basis for, 75-76
    social origins of, 73-79
Psychopathic criminal, 89-104
┼Psychosis
    behavioral traits of, 122-130
    see functional psychosis
    median age by race and sex, 61
Psychosocial, 11-15, 21
    errors in regarding, 19-20
    as type of symptomatology, 50
Psychotherapy
    as behavioral control, 167, 220-245
    conjoint diagnosis for, 213-214
    for disturbed children, 143-144
    goal of, 79
    historical development of family ther-
        apy, 207-212
    as a learning process, 152-166; counter
        conditioning, 153-157; discrimina-
        tion learning, 158-159; extinction,
        157-158; punishment, 162-164;
        methods of reward, 159-162, 229-
        231
    moral issues in, 254-255
    new approaches, 175, 192
    outcome of, 177
    relation to social sciences, 213-217
    research, 152-170
    as social imitation, 164-166
    structured to lower social class boys,
        286-288
    use of television, 192-198
    values, 254-255

Race and marital status, 60
    by median age, 61
    and occupational category, 58
    psychiatric diagnosis, 59

Reciprocal inhibition, 177
Research, cybernetic and electronic
        models, 220-221
    MMPI, 53-54
    mental health, 149
    "moral therapy," 45-46
    projective techniques, 53
    behavior therapy, 177
Role of patient, defined, 257-258
    in mental hospital, 126-127, 256-272
    "role-commitment," 257-258
    "role-validation," 257

Schizophrenia
    behavior on open ward, 126-127
    characteristics of, 54
    new classification scheme for, 7
    family dynamics and origin of (upper
        class), 104-122
    family treatment, 207-212
    frequency of occurrence, 298-323
    see functional psychoses
    patient's ability to manipulate, 122-130
    psychiatric interview, 122-130
    psychiatrists' agreement, 127
    see psychosis
    and race, 59-61
    similarity to normals, 129-130
Self-control as operant conditioning, 235-
        240
Sexual promiscuity and mental illness,
        54-55
    psychopathic personality, 89-104
Social character, evolution of, 80-85
Social class, 13, 56-63
Stress, chronic in American Prisoners of
        War of the Chinese, 63-73
Symptoms
    "symptom-underlying cause formula-
        tion" of Mowrer, 169-170

Traits
    personality, 52-55

"Will"
    decline of, 88-89
    evolution of concept of, 88-89